I AM THAT I AM

Tracing the Footprints of God

Judy Azar LeBlanc

Dennis: May you be blessed doubly for all of your faithfulness to us & to the Kingdom –

Judy Azar LeBlanc

CrossLink Publishing

I AM THAT I AM
Tracing the Footprints of God

CrossLink Publishing
www.crosslink.org

ISBN 978-1-936746-10-1

Other books by Judy Azar LeBlanc:
Theology 101 in Bite-Size Pieces;
A Bird's Eye View of the Riches of Divine Grace
Many Faces to Many Places
Things My Father Never Taught Me
The Compromise
The Unveiling

Awards:
2011 International Book Award Christianity
2008 National Indie Excellence
2007 Reader Views Literary Choice
2006 USA Book News

"Thy words were found and I ate them, and thy words became for me a joy and the delight of my heart" (Jeremiah 15:16).

Contents

I AM THAT I AM

Tracing the footprints of God

Introduction

"In the beginning was the Word and the Word was with God. He was in the beginning with God" (John 1:1-2); *"And the Word became flesh and dwelt among us"* (v. 14).

There are hundreds of books written about different aspects of God's character – His attributes, His Spirit, His nature, His sovereignty, His omniscience, His disposition, and His omnipotence just to name a few. Thousands of Christians attend church every Sunday, attend Bible studies during the week, watch televangelists, listen to the radio, or surf the internet searching for more knowledge about who God is and what He promises His people. The purpose of this book is to paint a portrait illuminating God's essence as reflected in all of the covenants God has placed humanity under since creation, through all of Jesus' parabolic teachings on the kingdom of God, and in all of the written accounts of the miracles He accomplished through the visible manifestation of Himself in Jesus Christ. Further insight into the essence of God is provided by the written accounts of His divine names and titles revealing different facets of the divine nature of the unchanging God of the universe. Without a doubt, the apostle Paul knew just about all that was humanly possible to know about God when he made this poignant statement. *"For since the creation of the world His invisible attributes, His eternal power and divine nature, have been clearly seen, being understood through what has been made, so that they are without excuse"* (Romans 1:20).

However, having knowledge of God and having a personal relationship with Him are entirely two different matters. The Gnostics who had been given the knowledge of God believed the information was exclusively given to those who were privileged intellectuals or learned. However, Scripture reveals that God has never been exclusive about revealing Himself to anyone who is willing to *hear* what He has to say, and does reveal Himself generously to those whose heart hungers after Him. I love what Jesus said to Philip when he asked Him to show him the Father. Jesus said, *"Have I been with you so long, and you still do not know me, Philip? Whoever has seen Me has seen the Father. How can you say, 'Show us the Father'? "* (John 14:9). Scripture also reveals that God's desire is, has, and always will be to have a loving relationship with his Creation. He loves to spend time with us, and He loves to reveal Himself to us. Having a personal relationship with God can be likened to a marriage. Over the course of the relationship, there are times when we do not *feel* loved or feel very loving. Nevertheless, not *feeling* the love flow freely does not negate the existence of it. Likewise, the most important aspect of having a loving relationship with God is not to base His love on a *feeling* but rather on the certainty of the knowledge of His love for us. It is my contention that the more we know about God, His nature, His character, and His reputation, there will be no doubt left in our minds as to whether or not He deeply loves His creation and will do exactly all that He said He will do—and that we can take to the bank!

"Have I been with you so long, and you still do not know me, Philip? Whoever has seen Me has seen the Father. How can you say, 'Show us the Father'? " (John 14:9).

The Recreation

Studying Scripture is like panning for gold in an endless flowing river of love. An abundance of testimonials confirming God's earnest desire to communicate with humanity, to have a loving relationship with His creation, and of His demonstration of His deep love for humanity have been written. The testimony of God's magnificent creation of the universe begins with the singular verse, *"In the beginning, God created the heaven and the earth"* (Genesis 1:1). The Hebrew word for heaven is shâmayim (pronounced *shaw-mah'-yim*), and means "the visible heavens, sky as abode of the stars as the visible universe, the sky, atmosphere, and the invisible heaven (as the abode of God)" (NAS Old Testament Hebrew Lexicon, 2010, H8064, http://www.biblestudytools.com/lexicons/hebrew/nas/, 2012). By definition, this suggests that both the heavens and the heavenly hosts were created *before* the creation of the first man, Adam. Scientific evidence in a variety of fields concur that earth is well over 4 billion years old. Thus, at some dateless point in time, between the perfect creation of the heavens and the earth (Genesis 1:1), and that period when *"the earth became formless and void, and darkness was over the surface of the deep, and the Spirit of God was moving over the surface of the waters"* (Genesis 1:2; Isaiah 24:1; Jeremiah 4:23-26), the first angelic act of rebellion occurred in the heavenly sphere, Lucifer was judged, and one third of the heavenly hosts were cast down to earth (Revelation 12:4). The Prophet Isaiah describes Lucifer's deliberate plan for the hostile takeover. He writes:

> *"I will ascend to heaven; I will raise my throne above the stars of God; I will sit enthroned on the mount of assembly, on the utmost heights of the sacred mountain. I will ascend above the tops of the clouds; I will make myself like the Most High"* (Isaiah 14:12–14).

The great Prophet Ezekiel to whom God entrusted the foretelling of His plan of salvation centuries before the birth of Christ reveals the motives and the consequences of that fall:

> *"You were blameless in your ways from the day you were created, until righteousness was found in you. By the abundance of your trade you were internally filled with violence, and you sinned: Therefore I have cast you as profane from the mountain of God. And I have destroyed you, O covering cherub, from the midst of the stones of fire. Your heart was lifted up because of your beauty; you corrupted your wisdom by reason of your splendor. I cast you to the ground; I put you before kings, that they may see you. By the multitude of your iniquities, in the unrighteousness of your trade, you profaned your sanctuaries. Therefore I have brought fire from the midst of you; it has consumed you, and I have turned you to ashes on the earth in the eyes of all who see you"* (Ezekiel 28:15-18).

Through Ezekiel's revelation, Dr. Merrill F. Unger states, "we have a record of the origin of sin and a panoramic view of the career of the greatest of the fallen angels" (Unger's *Commentary On The Old Testament*, 2002, p. 1553). Thus, at some dateless point in time *after* God saw that every thing that He had made was "very good" (Genesis 1:30), the angelic rebellion occurred in the heavenly sphere, and one third of the stars of heaven were swept away and cast down to earth making the earth void and filled with darkness (v. 2). Consequently, the havoc that was produced in the heavens by this rebellion corrupted God's perfect system and not only gave birth to the diabolical system that we now live under, but also caused God to re-create earth and make it habitable for man. Dr. Merrill F. Unger writes:

> "The heaven that God created (remade) was evidently not the sphere of the planets and stars, but the immediate atmospheric heaven surrounding the earth, as the re-creative activity of the first four days suggests (1:4-19). Light on the first day was

solar. But light from the heavenly bodies, which God had made in eternity past (v. 16), could not penetrate the chaotic shroud that enveloped the earth. Verse 2 in Hebrew is apparently circumstantial to verse 3. It tells the earth's condition when God began to re-create it, and specifically to separate light from chaotic darkness. It "was" a chaos of wasteness, emptiness, and darkness. God did not create it in this state (Job 38:4-7; Isa. 45:18). It was reduced to this condition because it was the theater where sin began in God's originally sinless universe in connection with the revolt of Lucifer and his angels (Isaiah 14:12-14; Ezekiel 28-13, 15:17; Revelation 2:4)."

Dr. Merrill Unger concludes, "The chaos was the result of God's judgment upon the originally sinless earth" (Ibid., p.5).

What's in a Name

The sovereignty, power, nature, character, and faithfulness of God can all be traced back to the Old Testament name of God Almighty. The Hebrew translation for God is 'ĕlôhîym (*el-o-heem'),* the "*plural* form of the self-existent or eternal One", which reveals that the plurality in the Godhead is one essence as recorded in Genesis 1:26a. *"Then God said, "Let Us make man in Our image, according to Our likeness*" "; (NAS Old Testament Hebrew Lexicon, 2010, H430, http://www.biblestudytools.com/lexicons/hebrew/nas/, 2012). Dr. Allen P. Ross observes:

> "Human life was created in (literally "as," meaning "in essence as") the image of God (v. 27). This image was imparted only to humans (2:7). Image (*selem*) is used figuratively here, for God does not have a human form. Being in God's image means that humans share, though imperfectly and finitely, in God's nature, that is, in His communicable attributes (life, personality, truth, wisdom, love, holiness, justice), and so have the capacity for spiritual fellowship with Him" (The Bible Knowledge Commentary: Old Testament, 1983, p. 29, ed. John F. Walvoord, Roy B. Zuck).

God introducing Himself as LORD God (yehôvâh 'ĕlôhîym), a God of power and perfection for the first time is found in Genesis Chapter 2. "*Then the LORD God formed man of dust from the ground, and breathed into his nostrils the breath of life; and man became a living being"* (Genesis 2:7). Dr. C. I. Scofield translates both of the names Elohiym and Jehovah-Elohiym. He writes:

> "The English word for Elohim (sometimes El or Elah) is God, the first of the three primary names of Deity, is a uni-plural noun formed from El = strength, or the strong one, and Alah, to swear, to bind oneself by an oath so implying faithfulness. This

uni-plurity implied in the name is directly asserted in Genesis 1:26a (plurality) and in Genesis 1:27 (Unity)" (Genesis 1, p. 3).

(1) "The primary meaning of the name LORD Jehovah is "the self-existent One". Literally as in Ex. 3:14, "He that is who He is, therefore the eternal I AM." But *Havah* from which Jehovah, or *Yahwe*, is formed, signifies to become, that is to become known, thus pointing to self-revelation. Combining these meanings of *Havah*, we arrive at the meaning of the name Jehovah. He is the self-existent One who reveals Himself" (Ibid., p. 6).

(2) "It was God (Elohim) who said, "Let us make man in our image" (Genesis 1:26); but when man, as in the second chapter of Genesis, is to fill the scene and become dominant over creation, it is the LORD God (Jehovah Elohim) who acts." (Ibid., p. 6).

(3) "Jehovah is distinctly the redemptive name of Deity. When sin entered the world and redemption became necessary, it was Jehovah Elohim who sought the sinning ones (Genesis 3:9-13) and clothed them" (Ibid., p. 6).

The combined divine name of our majestic, omnipotent, omniscient, omnipresent, all-sufficient, self-existing Creator, and Master of the universe, *Jehovah-Elohiym*, is explained with staggering revelation by Dr. Herbert Lockyer. He states:

"The double title LORD God occurs for the first time in connection with God's creative work (Genesis 2:4). JAH—The Independent One is a shortened form of *Jehovah*, which, "though compelled to mention such a name, the transcribers dare not write it in full." Pronounced *ya*, this name signifies, *He is*, and can be made to correspond to I AM, just as *Jehovah* corresponds to the fuller expression I AM THAT I AM. The name *Jah* first occurs in the original, in the triumphal Song of Moses, Exodus 15:2. It is affirmed that as JAH is the *present* tense of the verb "to be," it suggests Jehovah as the PRESENT LIVING GOD—the Presence of God in daily life, or His present activity and oversight on behalf of His own.

JEHOVAH—The Eternal, Ever-Loving One: Among all the divine names none is so sublime and solemn as the one we are now to consider. It was also known as "The Name of Four Letters" because from the Hebrew it is spelled YHVH, in English. Such is Jewish reverence for this august name that even today they refrain as much from writing it, or pronouncing it. Scholars are not sure as to the exact pronunciation of the Hebrew for *Jehovah.* Leading Hebrew translators agree that probably it is *Yahveh*, or *Yahve*, or *Yahweh.* The name is generally printed in some capitals, LORD, and is thus distinguished from the other Hebrew words translated *Lord.* LORD, *Lord* and *lord* convey very different shades of thought both in Hebrew and Greek. LORD, however, is only applied to Him who is known as Jehovah—The Self-Existing One: but *Lord* is also applied to Jehovah" (Lockyer, All the Divine Names and Titles in the Bible, 1975, pp. 16-18).

Lastly, of the name Jehovah, Matthew Henry notes:

"Here is a name given to the Creator which we have not yet met with, and that is *Jehovah* – the LORD, in capital letters, which are constantly used in our English translation to intimate that in the original it is *Jehovah.* All along in the first chapter, he was called *Elohim* – a God of *power*, but now *Jehovah-Elohim* – a God of *power and perfection*, a finishing God" (Matthew Henry's *Commentary on the Whole Bible*, 1991, Volume 5, p. 11).

In his book, *The New Evidence That Demands A Verdict*, Josh D. McDowell quotes a paraphrase of the *Cosri* by R. Jehuda Halevi who in turn quotes from Dr. E. W. Hengstenberg's explanation of the significance of each of the divine names of the Deity.

> "Each divine name bore a special significance, and they were not necessarily synonymous. {Elohim} is the most general name of the Deity; it distinguishes him only in his fullness of power without reference to his personality or moral qualities—to any special relation in which he stands to men—either as to the benefits he bestows, or to the requirements he makes. On this account, where God has witnessed of himself and is truly known, another name is added to *Elohim*—this is the name *Jehovah*, peculiar to the people who received his revelation and his covenant .... The name Jehovah is unintelligible to all who are not acquainted with that development of the Divine essence which is represented by it; while Elohim distinguishing him as God in those respects which are known to all men, is universally intelligible .... The name *Jehovah* is the *nomen proprium* {proper name} of God, and being one that expresses the inmost nucleus of his essence, is only intelligible where God has come forth, laid open the recesses of his heart, and has permitted his creatures to behold them, so that, instead of an obscure undefined being, of whom thus much only is known and affirmed, that he is powerful, that he is immense—he here exhibits himself the most personal of all persons, the most characteristic of all characters (Hengstenberg, DGP, 216-217)" (Josh McDowell, *New Evidence that Demands A Verdict,* 1999, p. 480).

Hence, the *dominant* name over creation changes from God (Elohiym) who said, "let Us make man in Our image" in Chapter 1, to LORD God (*Jehovah*-Elohiym) in Chapter 2. Of great significance, however, as Dr. C. I. Scofield points out, *Jehovah*, the distinct redemptive name of Deity, is not introduced to us in Scripture until Chapter 2. This suggests that when *Jehovah*-Elohiym formed man out of the dust of the ground and breathed into his nostrils the breath of life (Genesis 2:7), a plan of redemption was already in place.

Moreover, when the LORD God (Jehovah-Elohiym) "caused every tree that is good for food and pleasant to the sight to grow", the tree of 'knowledge of good and evil', and the 'tree of life' were both present in the garden, which indicates that evil and life eternal were already present on earth when Adam and Eve were placed in the Garden of Eden (Genesis 2:9).

As we begin our journey of tracing the footprints of God, we will be introduced to many other compounded names and titles that reflect different facets of His Deity. Dr. Lewis Sperry Chafer offers a short list of the compounded names of Jehovah that are frequently used throughout the Old Testament. Of these, he writes:

> "The primary name Elohim is compounded with Shaddai, as El Shaddai, translated in the A.V. as 'Almighty God' (Gen. 17:1); with Elyon, as El Elyon, translated in the A.V. as 'Most High,' or 'most high God' (Gen. 14:18); and with Olam, as El Olam, translated in the A.V. as 'everlasting God' or God of Eternity (Gen. 21:33).
>
> The supreme name of J*ehovah* Elohim, compounded with Adonai, as Jehovah-Adonai, 'Lord GOD' is translated as Lord Master (Genesis 15:2), and Jehovah-Sabaoth translated as 'LORD of hosts' (1 Samuel 1:3). The supreme name of Jehovah is further compounded with Jehovah-Jireh, "the LORD will provide," (Genesis 22:14). Jehovah-Rapha, "The LORD that healeth," (Exodus 15:26). Jehovah-Nissi, "The LORD our banner", (Exodus 17:8-15). Jehovah-Shalom, "The LORD our peace", (Judges 6:23, 24). Jehovah-Ra-ah, "The LORD my shepherd", (Psalms 23:1). Jehovah-Tsidkenu, "The LORD our righteousness", (Jeremiah 23:6), and Jehovah-Shammah, "The LORD is there" (Ezekiel 48:35)" (Systematic Theology, 1978, Volume I, p. 269).

In conclusion, augmenting our appreciation of divine names reflecting different facets of God's nature, character, and personality, Dr. Hebert Lockyer adds the following: "Jehovah-*Hoseenu*—The Lord

Our Maker (Psalm 95:6); Jehovah-*M'Kaddesh*—The Lord who sanctifies (Exodus 31:13); Jehovah-*Makkeh*—Jehovah that smites (Ezekiel 7:9). Lastly, he adds Jehovah-*Gmolah*—The God of Recompense (Jeremiah 51:6)" (Lockyer, All the Divine Names and Titles in the Bible, 1975, pp. 20, 33, 56-57).

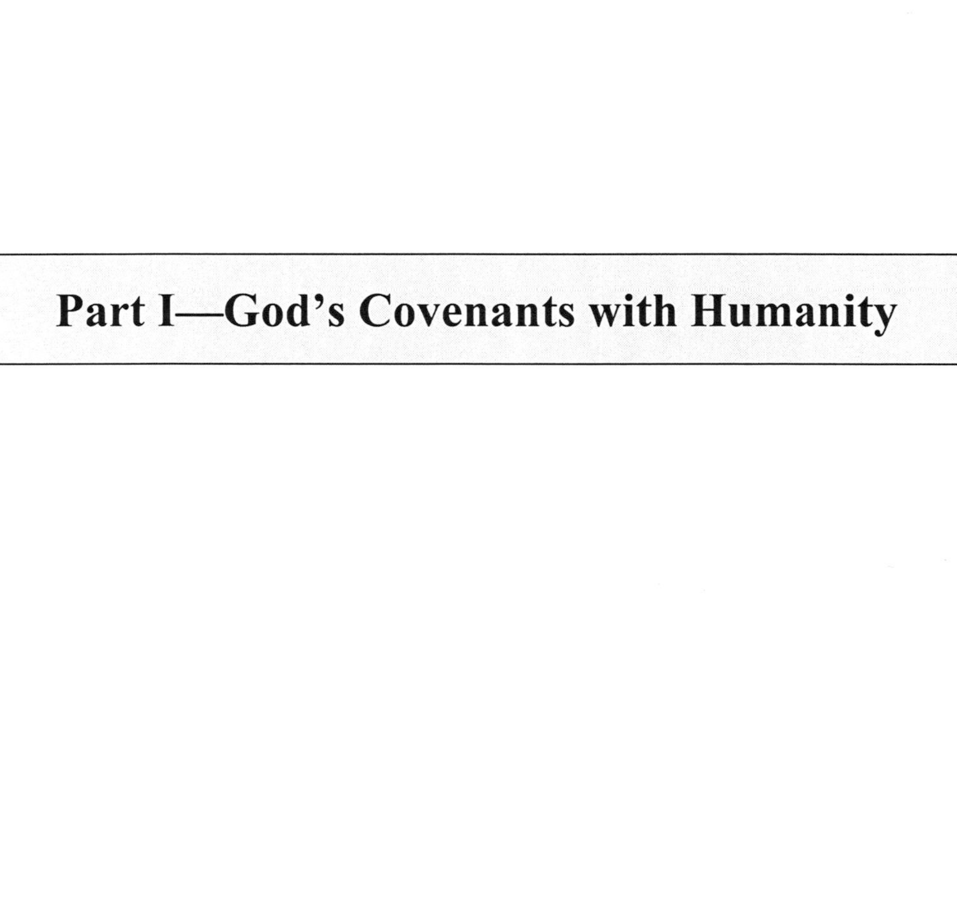

Part I—God's Covenants with Humanity

Introduction

Since the day that God created man to function as His representative, Scripture reveals that He has always placed man under a covenant. God's desire to communicate with man can be traced through the records of the covenants God has made with His creation since eternity past. Between the first Edenic Covenant and the last New Covenant of grace, God instituted the Adamic, the Noahic, the Abrahamic, the Mosaic, the Palestinian/Deuteronomic Land Covenant, and the Davidic Covenant. The key word "covenant" is not found in Scripture until God promises to preserve humanity and nature through Noah, *"But I will establish my covenant with you; and you shall come into the ark, you, your sons, your wife, and your sons' wives with you"* (Genesis 6:18). The first of these great eight recorded covenants God entered into with man was with Adam in the Garden of Eden, otherwise known as the Edenic Covenant. The definition of a covenant as we know it to be is a solemn agreement that is characteristically unalterable and permanently binding. It means to bind oneself by an oath, which of course implies faithfulness, and can be either conditional or unconditional. Whereas a conditional covenant guarantees that God will complete His promises *if* man obeys the stipulations of that covenant, an unconditional covenant guarantees the ultimate fulfillment immutably depends *solely* upon God for the fulfillment of His promises. With the exception of the Edenic and Mosaic Covenants, the remaining six, the Adamic Covenant, the Noahic Covenant, the Abrahamic Covenant, the Palestinian/Deuteronomic Land Covenant, the Davidic Covenant, and the New Covenant have all been unconditional. A point of interest is drawn to the relationship of each of God's covenants with its corresponding dispensation by Dr. Lewis Sperry Chafer. Dr. Chafer defines the term dispensation as "a period which is identified by its relation to some particular purpose of God – a purpose to be accomplished within that period" (*Systematic Theology,* 1978, Volume I, p. 40). Though the dispensation may end, the covenants themselves continue.

"The Edenic Covenant—*The Dispensation of Innocence*, which extended from the creation to the fall of Adam."

"The Adamic Covenant—*The Dispensation of Conscience*, which extended from Adam's fall to the flood, in which age conscience was, apparently, the dominating feature of human life on earth and the basis of man's relationship with God."

"The Noahic Covenant—*The Dispensation of Human Government*, which extended from the flood to the call of Abraham, is characterized by the committing of self-government to men, and is terminated by the introduction of a new divine purpose."

"The Abrahamic Covenant—*The Dispensation of Promise,* which continued from the call of Abraham to the giving and acceptance of the Mosaic Law at Sinai."

"The Mosaic Covenant—*The Dispensation of the Law*, which extended from the giving of the Law of Jehovah by Moses and its acceptance by Israel at Sinai (Ex. 19:3—31:18)."

"The New Covenant—*The Dispensation of Grace*, which extends from the death of Christ until His return to receive His Bride"

"*The Dispensation of the Kingdom Rule*, which continues from the second advent of Christ on for a thousand years and ends with the creation of a new heaven and a new earth" (*Systematic Theology,* 1978, Volume I, pp. 40-41).

The Edenic Covenant—Genesis 1:28-30; 2:15-17

One of the most fascinating Old Testament accounts in Scripture is that of the location of the Garden of Eden, termed the "Cradle of Civilization".

"Now a river flowed out of Eden to water the garden; and from there it divided and became four rivers. The name of the first is Pishon; it flows around the whole land of Havilah, where there is gold. And the name of the second river is Gihon; it flows around the whole land of Cush. And the name of the third river is Tigris; it flows east of Assyria. And the fourth river is the Euphrates" (Genesis 2:10-14).

Traditional and generally accepted belief based on Scripture is that the Garden of Eden was located near the mouth of the Euphrates River, currently situated in modern day Iraq, "where the Euphrates and Tigris rise in the Caucasus mountain region of southwest Asia, flow southeastward, and empty into the Persian Gulf. Thus man may be said to have been created at or about the center of the earth's surface; for this Caucasus-Euphrates region is the approximate center of Eastern Hemisphere, which is the largest of the two Hemispheres" (Halley's Bible Handbook, 1965, p. 64).

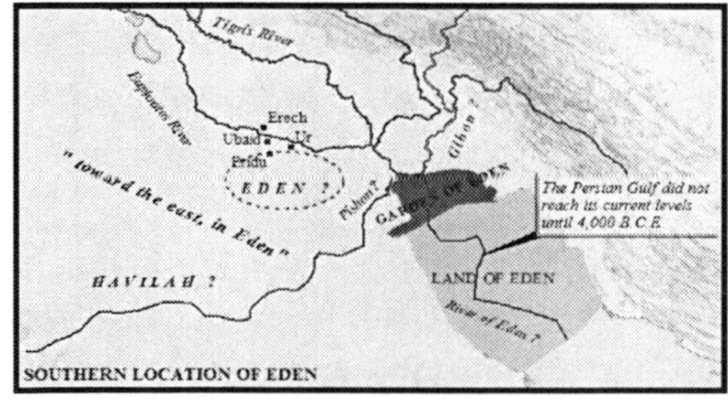

Ancient Location of Eden

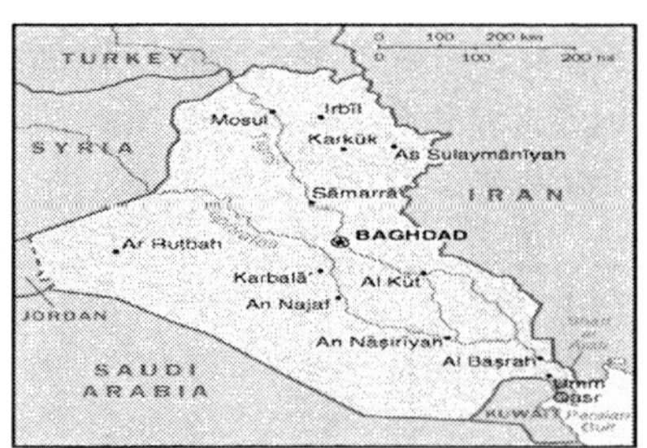

Modern Day Iraq

Images provided by Israel-a-history-of.com; http://geography.about.com/library/cia/blciraq.htm, 2012.

However, Dr. Roland K. Harrison seems to believe that a more realistic identification of Eden is with Armenia, where the Tigris and Euphrates have their origin. He states, "The Pishon and Gihon branches have been supposed to be the Choruk and the Aras, which empty into the Black Sea and the Caspian Sea respectively." On the other hand, he does conclude by writing, "No theory, ancient or modern, of the location of Eden and its celebrated garden is entirely free from difficulties. On the basis of currently available information, it would appear that the one that locates Eden near the head of the Persian Gulf combines the greatest number of probabilities of every kind" (Eerdman's *International Standard Bible Encyclopedia,* Volume E-J, 1982, p. 17, ed. Geoffrey W. Bromiley).

The Edenic Covenant – Genesis 1:28-30; 2:15-17: "*And God blessed them; and God said to them, "be fruitful and multiply, and fill the earth, and subdue it; and rule over the fish of the sea and over the birds of the sky, and over every living thing that moves on the earth." Then God said, "Behold, I have given you every plant yielding seed that is on the surface of all the earth, and every tree which has fruit yielding seed; it shall be food for you; and to every beast of the earth and to every bird of the sky and to every thing that moves on the earth which has life, I have given every green plant for food"; and it was so"* (Genesis 1:28-30). "T*hen the LORD God took the man and put him into the Garden of Eden to cultivate it and keep it. And the LORD God commanded the man, saying, "from any tree of the garden you may eat freely; but from the tree of the knowledge of good and evil you shall not eat, for in the day that you eat from it you shall surely die" "* (Genesis 2:15-17).

The first conditional covenant whereby God governs His new creation was between the Triune God (Elohiym) and newly created man, and was made with Adam in the Garden of Eden while he was in the state of innocence. The length of time during this period is not recorded. However, while Adam was under grace, God divinely blessed him with the sole *condition* that he could not eat from the tree of knowledge of good and evil. This divine blessing can be found in the first two chapters of Genesis.

> *"And God blessed them; and God said to them, be fruitful and multiply, and fill the earth, and subdue it; and rule over the fish of the sea and over the birds of the sky, and over every living thing that moves on the earth. Then God said, Behold, I have given you every plant yielding seed that is on the surface of all the earth, and every tree which has fruit yielding seed; it shall be food for you; and to every beast of the earth and to every bird of the sky and to every thing that moves on the earth which has life, I have given every green plant for food; and it was so"* (Genesis 1:28-30).

In addition to giving Adam (man) authority over earth and dominion over all living things, God placed Adam in the Garden of Eden and provided him with everything that he needed.

> *"Then the LORD God* (Jehovah-Elohiym) *took the man and put him into the Garden of Eden to cultivate it and keep it. And the LORD God commanded the man, saying, from any tree of the garden you may eat freely; but from the tree of the knowledge of good and evil you shall not eat, for in the day that you eat from it you shall surely die"* (Genesis 2:15-17).

Inasmuch as Adam was given freedom to eat from the *tree of life*, but forbidden to eat from the *tree of knowledge* of good and evil implies that his state of grace was conditional. Dr. Merrill F. Unger notes:

> "The dispensation of Innocence, based on the Edenic Covenant (Genesis 1:26-28) between the Triune God (first party) and newly created man (second party), governed man's life in the Edenic innocence and stipulated his dominion and subjugation of the earth. It presented a simple test of obedience, with death the penalty of disobedience (2:15-17), and it ended as a

specific time period when man fell. But man's disobedience and fall did not nullify the covenant's stipulations of be fruitful and multiply, fill the earth, and subdue it. These elements of the covenant remained in force. What changed is man's fall into sin would alter the divine blessing" (Unger's Commentary On The Old Testament, 2002, p. 8).

The moment Adam disobeyed God, he immediately became *conscious* of his disobedience and attempted to hide.

> "*Then the eyes of both of them were opened, and they* ***knew*** *that they were naked; and they sewed fig leaves together and made themselves loin coverings. And they heard the sound of the LORD God walking in the garden in the cool of the day, and the man and his wife hid themselves from the presence of the LORD God among the trees of the garden"* (Genesis 3:7-8).

This moment of transition is what I like to call the "birth of a conscious". Using a similar scenario, experience tells us that when we tell a child to stay away from the cookie jar, and he disobeys, the first thing the child will do is: 1) hide the evidence, 2) deny it, or 3) blame it on someone else. Watch what happens when Adam and Eve are called upon by God. *"Then the LORD God called to the man, and said to him, 'Where are you'?"* And Adam responds by saying, *"I heard the sound of Thee in the garden, and I was afraid because I was naked; so I hid myself"* (Genesis 3:9-10). Note that Adam's nakedness had not been an issue prior to his disobedience. *"And He said, who told you that you were naked? Have you eaten from the tree of which I commanded you not to eat?"* (v. 11) Watch what happens next – *"And the man said, the woman whom thou gavest to be with me, she gave me from the tree, and I ate"* (v. 12). Don't you just love it? After Adam blames Eve, she blames the serpent. *"Then the LORD God said to the woman, 'What is this you have done?' And the woman said, 'The serpent deceived me, and I ate'* " (v. 13). The moment Adam disobeyed God, the fellowship that he had freely enjoyed with Him was immediately broken. *"But like Adam they have transgressed the covenant"* (Hosea 6:7). Since then, Scripture reveals that God is the One who has made the concerted effort to restore the relationship between God and man. Moreover, after the fall, man's positional standing with God changed from being in a state of innocence to that of being in a state of consciousness, and the relationship between God and man changed from being in a state of grace to being in a state of a need for redemption.

Thus, though anticipated by God, the first rebellious act in the universe that corrupted all of which God *originally* created as perfect and good, created the diabolical system that we now live under; and as a consequence of man's first disobedient act, humanity inherited Adam's fallen nature which causes man to choose to be independent from God (Genesis 3:6). Therefore, between God's command to Adam to stay away from the tree of the knowledge of '*good and evil'*, and by the conversation that Eve had with the 'serpent' in Genesis 3:1-5, clearly indicates that Satan and evil were already present in the earth. As we well know, the war between good and evil has long since been an ongoing battle.

The Adamic Covenant—Genesis 3:14-19

After Adam broke the condition of the original covenant, he falls from grace, loses his fellowship with God, and judgment and expulsion from the Garden follows. However, it did not end there. The LORD God, *Jehovah-Elohiym,* places Adam under an unconditional covenant that now governs fallen humanity by *Jehovah-*Elohiym (the redemptive name of Deity). During this period, man goes from the state of innocence (grace) to the state of consciousness, or as Dr. Chafer defines it, the dawning of the new dispensational age of *conscience.*

The Adamic Covenant – Genesis 3:14-19: *"And the LORD God said to the serpent, "because you have done this, cursed are you more than all cattle, and more than every beast of the field; on your belly shall you go, and dust shall you eat all the days of your life; and I will put enmity between you and the woman, and between your seed and her seed; he shall bruise you on the head, and you shall bruise him on the heel." To the woman He said, "I will greatly multiply your pain in childbirth, in pain you shall bring forth children; yet your desire shall be for your husband, and he shall rule over you." Then to Adam He said, "because you have listened to the voice of your wife, and have eaten from the tree about which I commanded you saying, 'you shall not eat from it'; cursed is the ground because of you; in toil you shall eat of it all the days of your life Both thorns and thistles it shall grow for you; and you shall eat the plants of the field; by the sweat of your face you shall eat bread, till you return to the ground, because from it you were taken; for you are dust, and to dust you shall return" "*(Genesis 3:14-19).

This new unconditional covenant now covers fallen man, and with it came both judgment and expulsion from the garden. However, the fall did not nullify the previous covenant stipulations of be fruitful and multiply, fill the earth, and subdue it (Genesis 1:27). These elements of the covenant remained in force. *"Therefore the LORD God sent him out from the garden of Eden, to cultivate the ground from which he was taken. So, He drove the man out; and at the east of the garden of Eden He stationed the cherubim, and the flaming sword which turned every direction, to guard the way to the tree of life"* (Genesis 3:23-24). The act of placing the cherubim described by Ezekiel as having four faces and four wings with human-like hands underneath their wings (10:21) to guard the *way* to the tree of life, representing salvation and eternal life, and the flaming sword turning in every direction, representing the Word (Hebrews 4:12), is quite significant. Thousands of years later, Christ revealed to humanity that He is the *Word* (John 1:1), *"the way, the truth and the life: no one comes to the Father, but through Him"* (John 14:6), and that by faith in Him, we may once again enter into salvation and eat freely from the *tree of life* (Revelation 2:7). Additionally, during the early rise of the Church, the apostle Luke records that believers in Christ were called "the followers of the Way" (Acts 9:2; 24:14).

Of significance, immediately following the disobedient act committed by Adam and Eve, God first addresses Adam, then Eve, and then the serpent. However, when God passes judgment, He addresses the participants in reverse order and judges the serpent first, then Eve, and lastly Adam.

> *"And the LORD God said to the serpent, because you have done this, cursed are you more than all cattle, and more than every beast of the field; on your belly shall you go, and dust shall you eat all the days of your life; and I will put enmity between you and the woman, and between your seed and her seed; he shall bruise you on the head, and you shall bruise him on the heel"* (vv. 14-15).

> *"To the woman He said, I will greatly multiply your pain in childbirth, in pain you shall bring forth children; yet your desire shall be for your husband, and he shall rule over you"* (v. 16).

> *"Then to Adam He said, because you have listened to the voice of your wife, and have eaten from the tree about which I commanded you saying, 'you shall not eat from it'; cursed is the ground because of you; in toil you shall eat of it all the days of your life Both thorns and thistles it shall grow for you; and you shall eat the plants of the field; by the sweat of your face you shall eat bread, till you return to the ground, because from it you were taken; for you are dust, and to dust you shall return" "* (vv. 17-19).

Paul sheds light about this reversal by writing the following: *"For our struggle is not against flesh and blood, but against the rulers, against the powers, against the world forces of this darkness, against the spiritual forces of wickedness in the heavenly places"* (Ephesians 6:12). Inherent in the redemptive name of *Jehovah*, when the LORD God addresses the serpent in verse 15, we see God's first promise of a Messiah and victory over evil when He makes this solemn oath. *"and I will put enmity between you and the woman, and between your seed and her seed; he shall bruise you on the head, and you shall bruise him on the heel."* In his exposition of the Old Testament, Dr. John Gill gives a short explanation of this great promise. He states:

> "the heel of Christ is meant His human nature, and who was in it frequently exposed to insults, temptations, and persecutions of Satan, and was at last brought to a painful and accursed death; though by dying He got an entire victory over him and all of his enemies and obtained salvation for His people" (Gills Expositor, Exposition of The Old Testament, Volume I, 1976, p. 28).

Of this same solemn oath, Dr. Allen P. Ross writes:

> "God said there would be a perpetual struggle between satanic forces and mankind. It would be between Satan and the woman, and their respective offspring or the "seeds". The "offspring" of the woman was Cain, then all humanity at large, and then Christ and those collectively in Him. The

"offspring" of the serpent includes demons and anyone serving his kingdom of darkness, those whose "father" is the devil (John 8:44). Satan would cripple mankind (you will strike at his heel), but the Seed, Christ, would deliver the fatal blow (He will crush your head)" (The Bible Knowledge Commentary: Old Testament, 1983, p. 32, ed. John F. Walvoord, Roy B. Zuck).

And of this great prophecy, Dr. Merrill F. Unger observes:

"His redemptive work was initiated by the first announcement of the gospel (Lat., protevangelium, "original evangel"), which envisioned the tremendous opposition of Satan and his agents to the Good News of God's redeeming grace. The very first enunciation of the gospel of grace through faith was cradled in a warning of conflict. It foreshadows the incessant activity of satanic powers to oppose the salvation of lost mankind and to resist the Good News by which the fallen race is to be rescued from sin and the power of Satan and demons. The Savior would come through the woman's progeny (the Messianic line to Christ). But since the "the seed of the woman" focuses on an individual, whose miraculous birth gave Him a preeminent title to be called "the seed of the woman" (see Gal. 4:4), the designation constitutes the first great prophecy of the coming virgin-born, incarnate Son of God and Savior" (Unger's Commentary On The Old Testament, 2002, p. 19).

Finally, "The Highway of Seed", as termed by Dr. C. I. Scofield, traces the lineage of the seed of the 'first promise of a Redeemer' through Adam's descendants:

"Abel, Seth, Noah (Gen. 6. 8-10), Shem (Gen. 9. 26, 27), Abraham (Gen. 12. 1-4), Isaac (Gen. 17. 19-21), Jacob (Gen. 28. 10-14), Judah (Gen. 49. 10), David (2 Sam. 7. 5-17), Immanuel-Christ (Isa. 7. 9-14; Mt. I. 1. 20-23; 1 John 3. 8; John 12. 31)" (Genesis 3, p. 9).

Thus, the Adamic Covenant not only carries with it some elements from the Edenic and judgment, but also introduces the age of consciousness, hard toil, and physical death. The earth is cursed with thorns and thistles, and Satan's messenger, the serpent, is cursed above all land creatures. The woman is placed under the headship of man and her pain in childbirth is 'multiplied'. Of profound significance, verse 15 carries the great prophecy of a coming Messiah and of the victory over evil by the finished work of Christ on the cross.

The Postdiluvian Noahic Covenant —Genesis 9:1-17

Setting the Stage

Noah is historically known as the "Antediluvian Patriarch" who walked upright before God. He was Methuselah's grandson, the son of Lamech (Genesis 5:28), and the father of three sons, Shem, Ham, and Japheth (5:32) who were all born before the flood. A quick overview of Noah's lineage from Adam to the period of Noah is traced by Dr. C. I. Scofield's "Highway of Seed", as follows: The recorded names of three of Adam's sons were Cain, Abel, and Seth (4:1-2; 25). After Cain killed Abel, he, like Adam, was removed from the presence of the LORD and settled in the land of Nod, east of Eden (4:16). At the age of one hundred and thirty, Adam became the father of Seth (5:3), and through the direct line of Seth, six generations are counted to the birth of Methuselah, son of Enoch, who fathered Lamech, Noah's father (5:6-30). The recorded chronology of events leading up to the flood is short. During this period, the sons of the godless line of Cain had intermarried with the godly line of Seth, and wickedness had been on an endless violent rampage. The destructive malignancy grieves Elohiym and causes Him to pass judgment (6:1-11). However, before Elohiym executes His judgment, He chooses Noah to preserve a remnant of humanity, informs Noah of His plans, commissions him to build an ark (6:8-22), and more importantly, promises to establish a new covenant with him (6:18). The rain lasted for forty days (7:17), the whole earth was covered with water, with the exception of Noah and his family, all flesh was destroyed (7:17-23), and the first Postdiluvian Covenant is instituted.

The Noahic Covenant – Genesis 9:1-17: *"And God blessed Noah and his sons and said to them, "be fruitful and multiply, and fill the earth. The fear of you and the terror of you will be on every beast of the earth and on every bird of the sky; with everything that creeps on the ground, and all the fish of the sea, into your hand they are given. Every moving thing that is alive shall be food for you; I give all to you, as I gave the green plant. Only you shall not eat flesh with its life, that is, its blood. And surely I will require your lifeblood; from every beast I will require it. And from every man, from every man's brother I will require the life of man. Whoever sheds man's blood, by man his blood shall be shed, for in the image of God He made man. And as for you, be fruitful and multiply; populate the earth abundantly and multiply in it." Then God spoke to Noah and to his sons with him, saying, "Now behold, I Myself do establish My covenant with you, and with your descendants after you; and with every living creature that is with you, the birds, the cattle, and every beast of the earth with you; of all that comes out of the ark, even every beast of the earth. And I establish My covenant with you; and all flesh shall never again be cut off by the water of the flood, neither shall there again be a flood to destroy the earth." God said, "This is the sign of the covenant which I am making between Me and you and every living creature that is with you, for all successive generations; I set My bow in the cloud, and it shall be for a sign of a covenant between Me and the earth. And it shall come about, when I bring a cloud over the earth, that the bow will be seen in the cloud, and I will remember My covenant, which is between Me and you and every living creature of all flesh; and never again shall the water become a flood to destroy all flesh. When the bow is in the cloud, then I will look upon it, to remember the everlasting covenant between God and every living creature of all flesh that is on the earth." And God said to Noah, "This is the sign of the covenant which I have established between Me and all flesh that is on the earth" "* (Genesis 9:1-17).

In the everlasting covenant God made with the second father of humanity, the same elements of "be fruitful and multiply, and fill the earth" that were originally in the antediluvian covenants remain in force. *"And God Blessed Noah and his sons and said to them, be fruitful and multiply, and fill the earth"* (Genesis 9:1). What is notably different between the two covenants, however, is their diet. Under the antediluvian Edenic/Adamic Covenants, the diet God had given to man, bird, and animal life was food from every plant yielding *seed*, and every tree which has *fruit* yielding seed (Genesis 1:29-30). In the postdiluvian Noahic Covenant, in addition to God giving every green plant yielding seed and fruit, He adds *meat* from every living moving thing with the condition that the blood be drained out of the meat. *"Every moving thing that is alive shall be food for you; I give all to you, as I gave the green plant.; Only you shall not eat flesh with its life, that is, its blood"* (vv. 3-4). Moreover, of great significance, inherent in the prohibition of eating the blood is the provision of upholding the sacredness of life, and the institution of capital punishment. *"Whoever sheds man's blood, by man his blood shall be shed, for in the image of God He made man"* (v. 6). Dr. Merrill F. Unger points out the significance of this prohibition.

> "The blood, representing the life (Lev. 17:11-14), was to be held sacred in token of the sacredness of human life (v. 4), and by stipulating the responsibility of both man and beast in destroying human life – life was required for life (v. 5). His life would be required by the constituted government as a punishment and as a deterrent against the wholesale violence that had necessitated the Flood" (Unger's Commentary On The Old Testament, 2002, p. 44).

Thus, the Noahic Covenant not only carries with it the same elements of "be fruitful and multiply, and fill the earth" that were part of the antediluvian Edenic/Adamic Covenants, but it also makes changes to their diet by adding meat with the prohibition of eating the blood, which represented life. It introduces the responsibility of human government for God, and for maintaining respect for the sanctity of life, institutes the concept of capital punishment as a deterrent.

Finally, of great significance, God ratifies the covenant by making a solemn oath to Himself, to Noah, to every living creature with him, and to all of his descendents that a flood would never again destroy the earth. Moreover, after Noah leaves the ark, he builds an altar to the LORD (Jehovah), offers a sacrifice of worship to Him, and when the LORD (Jehovah) "smelled" the soothing aroma, He avowed to Himself that He would never again curse the ground because of man, or destroy every living thing. "*While the earth remains, seedtime and harvest, and cold and heat, and summer and winter, and day and night shall not cease*" (Genesis 8:21-22). Most notable is that it is not until after the account of the flood that we find the first mention of seasonal changes. (v. 22), which may suggest the institution of climatic change. On this important revelation, Dr. Merrill F. Unger writes:

> "While the earth remaineth. This verse almost certainly refers to the new climate and the changes it brought on the antediluvian earth. If the Flood caused new atmospheric conditions that prevail today and was partly the result of the condensation of a great celestial watery canopy, alteration in the earth's climate resulted. Greater extremes of heat and cold, distinct seasons of summer and winter, and more pronounced times of sowing and reaping were the result. It may well be that day and night became more pronounced as the atmosphere cleared and the solar rays were less diffused" (Ibid., p. 44).

Lastly, as a sign of His faithfulness and in accordance with Himself, Elohiym seals His oath by placing a rainbow over the earth as a reminder of this everlasting covenant. *"I set My bow in the cloud, and it shall be for a sign of a covenant between Me and the earth"* (v. 13), and then confirms it with Noah. *"And God said to Noah, this is the sign of the covenant which I have established between Me and all flesh that is on the earth"* (v. 17).

> *"This is the sign of the covenant which I have established between Me and all flesh that is on the earth"* (Genesis 9:17).

The Abrahamic Covenant—Genesis 12:1–22:18

A Fresh Start

Hence, a remnant of humanity is preserved through Noah, the second father of humanity. Although the elements of "be fruitful and multiply, and fill the earth" remain in force, the changes to the postdiluvian Noahic Covenant from the antediluvian Adamic Covenant were the institution of human government, a change of diet, respect for the sanctity of life, and the concept of capital punishment. The sons of Noah separated and became individual nations. The Japhethites, believed to have become the progenitors of the Caucasian races of Europe and Asia, went northward and settled in regions around the Black and Caspian Seas (Genesis 10:2-5). The Hamites went southward towards what we know today to be Central Arabia, Egypt, the Eastern Shore of the Mediterranean, and the East Coast of Africa. Canaan, the son of Ham and his descendants, settled in lands that they named after themselves (Genesis 10:6-20). Finally, the Shemites, the line from which Abraham is born, settled in the central region of the 'cradle' whose descendants are believed to include the Babylonians, Assyrians, Lydians Syrians, and Persians (Merrill F. Unger, Unger's Bible Dictionary, 1967, pp. 51-56).

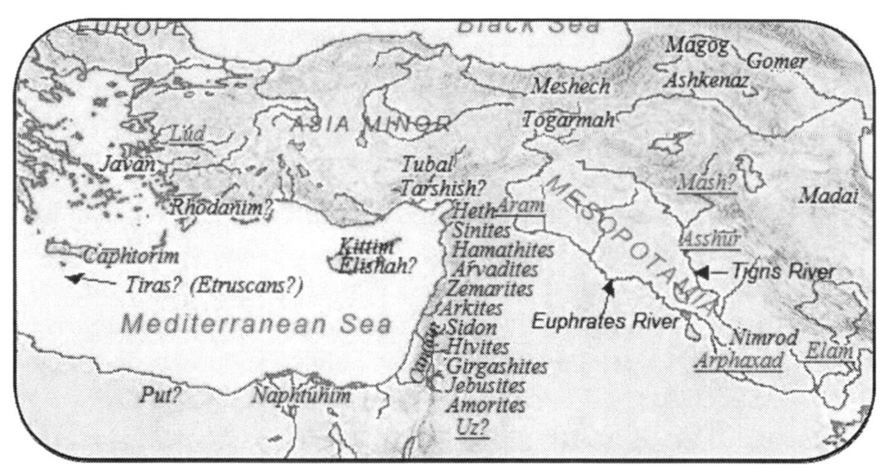

The Table of Nations
Image provided by Israel a History Online
http://www.israel-a-history-of.com/old-testament-map.html, 2012.

Abraham, who was then called Abram, was the ninth generation of the direct line of Shem, Noah's first-born (11:10-26). His father's name was Terah (tenth descendant of Noah), who was the son of Nahor from the land of Ur located in modern day Iraq. After Abram's brother Haran died, his father, Terah, intending to move his family to the land of Canaan (named after Noah's grandson's descendants), travelled as far as Haran and settled there (11:27-31). It is after the death of Abram's father that God calls him. The covenant made with Abraham ushered in the new age of 'the Dispensation of Promise', which continued from the call of Abraham to the giving and acceptance of the Mosaic Law at Sinai.

The Call of Abraham

Striking similarities between Noah and Abraham's disposition are notable. 1) They each found *grace* in the eyes of the LORD Jehovah, 2) both received a promise from God prior to the actual giving of the covenants, 3) by faith they both believed and were obedient, and 4) they both were counted as righteous before God. *"Noah was a righteous man, blameless in his time; Noah walked with God"* (Genesis 6:9); And of Abraham: *"Then he believed in the LORD; and He reckoned it to him as righteousness"* (Genesis 15:6). Although the account of the covenant between God and Abraham is not given until Genesis Chapter 17, the calling, the journey, the promise, and reaffirmations of the promise begin in Genesis Chapters 12 through 15, and ratified in Chapter 22 when the LORD Jehovah *swears* by it to Himself.

> *"Now the LORD (Jehovah) said to Abram, "go forth from your country, and from your relatives, and from your father's house, to the land which I will show you; and I will make you a great nation, and I will bless you, and make your name great; and so you shall be a blessing; and I will bless those who bless you, and the one who curses you I will curse. And in you all of the families of the earth shall be blessed" "* (12:1-3).

And Abram believed God, packed up his belongings, took his wife and his household, and left the comfort of his home to go to a foreign country. Can you imagine doing something like this at the age of 75? What faith.

> *"So Abram went, as the LORD had spoken to him; and Lot went with him. Now Abram was seventy-five years old when he departed from Haran. And Abram took his wife Sarai and Lot his nephew; and all their possessions which they had accumulated, and the persons which they had acquired in Haran; and they set out for the land of Canaan; thus they came to the land of Canaan. And Abram passed through the land as*

far as the site of Shechem, to the oak of Moreh. Now the Canaanites were in the land. And the LORD appeared to Abram, and said, 'to your descendants I will give this land.' So he built an altar there to the LORD, who had appeared to him." (Genesis 12:4-7).

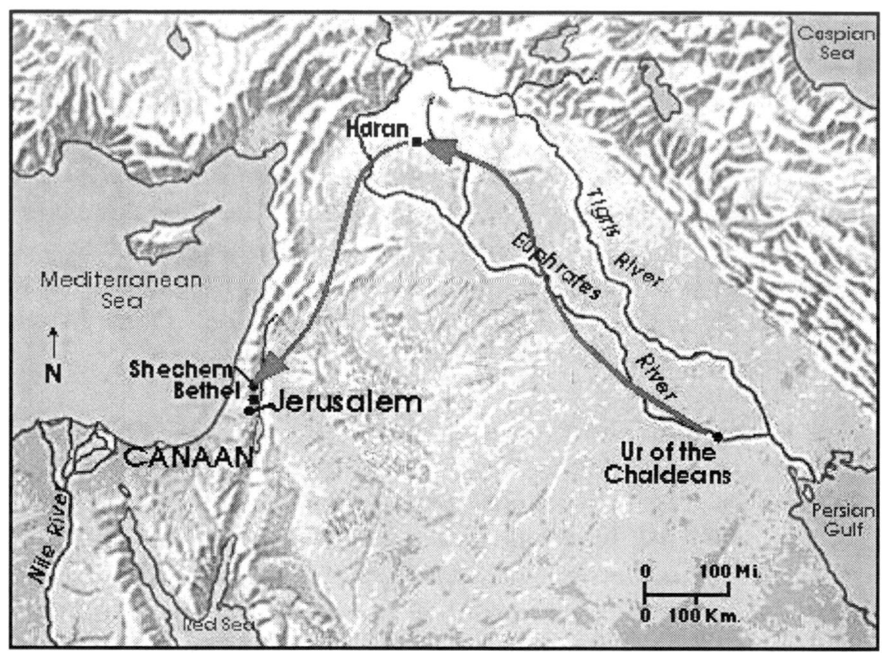

The probable route taken by Abraham and his clan as they traveled from their native land 'Ur of the Chaldeans' to the land of Canaan.

Map provided by Bible Archeology http://www.bible-archaeology.info/abraham.htm, 2012.

The Promise Confirmed

After Elohiym appears to Abram at his first stopover in Shechem (modern day Neblus located in the West Bank), he builds an altar to God and worships Him (12:7). From Shechem, Abram continues his journey southward until he comes to a place called Bethel where he makes his second stopover on a mountain. Overlooking Bethel on the west and Ai on the east (later destroyed under the leadership of Joshua 7-8), Abram builds a second altar to God and worships Him there (v. 8).

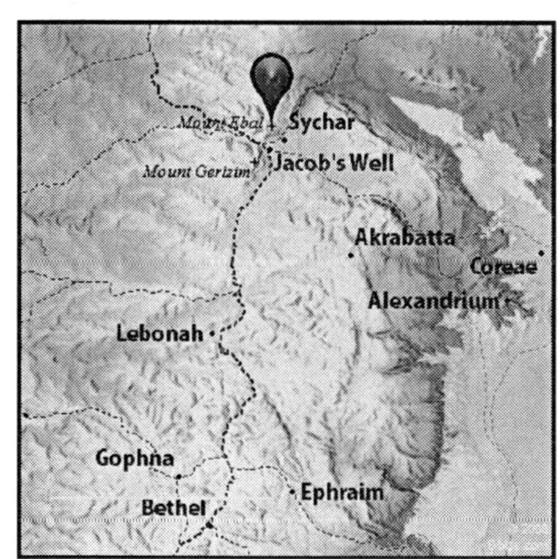

Shechem

Bethel

Map provided by Bible Atlas
http://bibleatlas.org/mount_ebal.htm, http://bibleatlas.org/bethel.htm, 2012.

The narrative between the chapters of Genesis 12 and 13 tells of Abram's migration further south to Egypt, where to survive a famine, he takes his household to a place called Negev. Because of her beauty, his wife Sarai is taken by the Pharaoh who eventually finds out that she is Abram's wife, releases her, and expels them from the land. Abraham then takes his household back to Bethel and settles there. Shortly thereafter, his nephew Lot separates his household from Abram's family and migrates eastward to the valley of the Jordon

(12:9—13:12). After the separation, God appears to Abram a third time to confirm the promises He had made to him earlier.

> *"And the LORD said to Abram, after Lot had separated from him, "Now lift up your eyes and look from the place where you are, northward and southward and eastward and westward; for all the land which you see, I will give it to you and to your descendants forever. And I will make your descendants as the dust of the earth; so that if anyone can number the dust of the earth, then your descendants an also be numbered. Arise, walk about the land through its length and breadth; for I will give it to you." Then Abram moved his tent and came and dwelt by the oaks of Mamre, which are in Hebron, and there he built an altar to the LORD"* (Genesis 13:18).

A Conversation with God

Wouldn't you love to sit down and have a conversation with God? Abraham did. After Abram settles his household in Bethel, Genesis 14 tells of a long war occurring between the kings of the land where Lot, Abram's nephew, had settled, and of the rescue of him by Abram. On his way back to Bethel, Abram stops at a place called Mambre (north of modern day Hebron), where on this occasion God appears to him in a vision to confirm His promise to make an everlasting covenant with him. When Abram recognizes the LORD (Jehovah), and addresses Him personally as 'Lord God' – Jehovah-*Adonai*, 'Master Jehovah', we are introduced to a new name of the Deity.

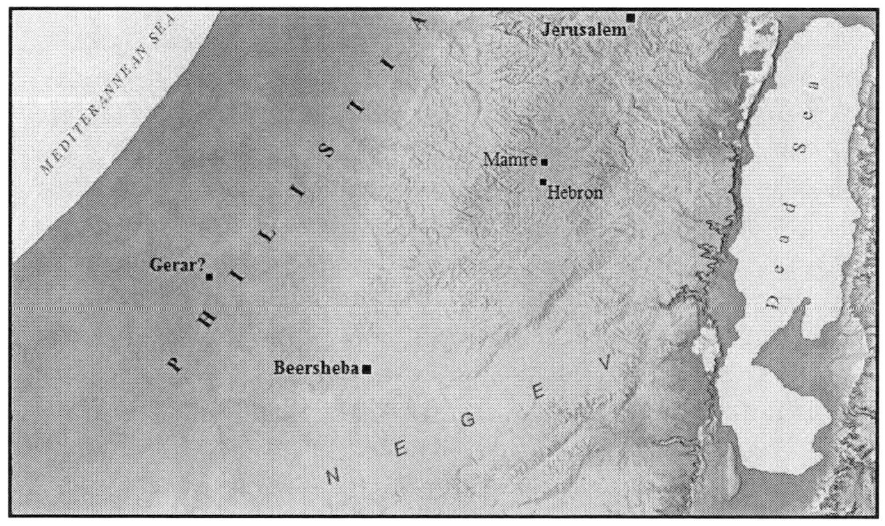

Ancient Mambre
Image provided by Israel History Online
http://www.israel-a-history-of.com/old-testament-map.html#The%20Negev%20-%20Home%20of%20Abraham, 2012.

"After these things the word of the LORD came to Abram in a vision, saying, "Do not fear, Abram, I am a shield to you; your reward shall be very great." And Abram said, "O Lord GOD, what wilt Thou give me, since I am childless, and the heir of my house is Eliezer of Damascus?" And Abram said, "Since Thou hast given no offspring to me, one born in my house is my heir." Then behold, the word of the LORD came to him, saying, "This man will not be your heir; but one who shall come forth from your own body, he shall be heir." And he took him outside and said, "Now look toward the heaven, and count the stars, if you are able to count them." And He said to him, "So shall your descendants be." Then he believed in the LORD; and He reckoned it to him as righteousness. And he said to him, "I am the LORD who brought you out of Ur of the Chaldeans, to give you this land to possess it." And he said, "O Lord GOD, how may I know that I shall possess it?" So He said to him, "Bring me a three year old heifer, and a three year old female goat, and a three year old ram three years old, and a turtledove, and a young pigeon." Then he brought all these to Him and cut them in two, and laid each half opposite the other; but he did not cut the birds. And the birds of prey came down upon the carcasses, Abram drove them away. Now when the sun was going down, a deep sleep fell upon Abram; and behold, terror and great darkness fell upon him. And God said to Abram, "Know for certain that your descendants will be strangers in a land that is not theirs, where they will be enslaved and oppressed four hundred years. But I will judge the nation whom they will serve; and afterward they will come out with many possessions. And as for you, you shall go to your fathers in peace; you shall be buried at a good old age. Then in the fourth generation they shall return here, for the iniquity of the Amorite is not yet complete." And it came about when the sun had set, that it was very dark, and behold, there appeared a smoking oven and a flaming torch which passed between these pieces. On that day the LORD made a covenant with Abram, saying, "To your descendants I have given this land,

from the river of Egypt as far as the great river, the river Euphrates: the Kenite and the Kenizzite and the Kadmonite and the Hittite and the Perizzite and the Rephaim and the Amorite and the Canaanite and the Girgashite and the Jebusite." " (Genesis 15:1-21).

In this powerful confirmation to Abram, the prophecy of the enslavement and oppression of the Hebrew nation at the hand of the Egyptians is foretold. "*And God said to Abram, "Know for certain that your descendants will be strangers in a land that is not theirs, where they will be enslaved and oppressed four hundred years" "* (v. 13); Abram is promised an heir to His promises, and the Land Covenant is reconfirmed.

The Covenant Ratified

Scripture is silent on the exact number of years that pass between the time that God confirms His covenant with Abram and the time He ratifies it. However, ten years after Abram had been living in the land of Canaan, Chapter 16 does give a short narrative of the intercession on his behalf by his wife, Sarai, who promises Abram an heir through her Egyptian bond slave Hager. It also records Abram's age as being eighty-six when Ishmael was born, and ninety-nine years of age when God ratified the covenant between them.

> *"Now when Abram was ninety-nine years old, the LORD (Jehovah) appeared to Abram and said to him, "I am God Almighty; Walk before Me, and be blameless. And I will establish My covenant between Me and you, And I will multiply you exceedingly." And Abram fell on his face, and God talked with him, saying, "As for Me, behold My covenant is with you, and you shall be the father of a multitude of nations. No longer shall your name be called Abram, But your name shall be Abraham; For I will make you the father of a multitude of nations. And I will make you exceedingly fruitful, and I will make nations of you, and kings shall come forth from you. And I will establish My covenant between Me and you and your descendants after you throughout their generations for an everlasting covenant, to be God to you and to your descendants after you. And I will give to you and to your descendants after you, the land of your sojourning, all the land of Canaan, for an everlasting possession; and I will be their God." God said further to Abraham, "Now as for you, you shall keep My covenant you and your descendants after you throughout their generations. This is My covenant, which you shall keep, between Me and you and your descendants after you: every male among you shall be circumcised. And you shall be circumcised in the flesh of your foreskin; and it shall be the sign of the covenant between me and you. And every male*

among you who is eight days old shall be circumcised throughout your generations, a servant who is born in the house or who is bought with money from any foreigner, who is not of your descendants. A servant who is born in your house or who is bought with your money shall surely be circumcised; thus shall My covenant be in your flesh for an everlasting covenant. But an uncircumcised male who is not circumcised in the flesh of his foreskin, that person shall be cut off from his people; he has broken My covenant" " (Genesis 17:1-14).

When God ratifies His everlasting covenant with Abraham, we are introduced to a new name of the Deity that is part of God's character known as El Shaddai, translated 'Almighty God' (Gen. 17:1). The significance of the name change is explained by Dr. C. I. Scofield. He writes:

"The etymological signification of Almighty God (*El Shaddai*) is both interesting and touching. God (El) signifies the "Strong One" (Gen. 1, 1, note). The qualifying word *Shaddai* is formed from the Hebrew word "shad," the breast, invariably used in Scripture for a woman's breast; e.g. Gen. 49. 25; Job 3. 12; Psa. 22.9; Song 1. 13; 4. 5; 7. 3, 7, 8; 8. 1, 8, 10; Isa. 28; 9; Ezk. 16. 7. *Shaddai* therefore means primarily "the breasted." God is "*Shaddai*," because He is the Nourisher, the Strength-giver, and so, in a secondary sense, the Satisfier, who pours Himself into believing lives. As a fretful, unsatisfied babe is not only strengthened and nourished from the mother's breast, but also is quieted, rested, satisfied, so *El Shaddai* is that name of God which sets Him forth as the Strength-giver and Satisfier of His people" (Genesis 16, p. 26).

Moreover, El Shaddai changes Abram's name to Abraham, 'father of a multitude of nations' (v. 5), his wife Sarai changes to Sarah, 'mother of nations' (v. 15), and the great prophecy of a promised Messiah found in the antediluvian Adamic Covenant is also found to be inherent in the oath of El Shaddai. *"And in you all of the families of the earth shall be blessed."* Of this great prophecy, Dr. C. I. Scofield notes:

> "This is the great evangelic promise fulfilled in Abraham's Seed, Christ (Gal. 3. 16; John 8. 56-58). It brings into greater definiteness the promise of the Adamic Covenant concerning the Seed of the woman (Gen. 3. 15)" (Genesis 15, p. 25).

Finally, in Chapter 22 of this journey, after God (Elohiym) asked Abraham to offer his son Isaac as a burnt offering to Him (vv. 2-10), when the angel of the LORD (Jehovah) intercedes to provide him with the sacrificial ram, we are introduced to the name Jehovah-*Jireh*, "the LORD will provide". God then seals His covenant with Abraham by swearing an oath to Himself.

> *"Then the* angel *of the LORD called to Abraham a second time from heaven, and said, "By myself I have sworn," declares says the LORD, "because you have done this thing, and have not withheld your son, your only son, indeed I will greatly bless you, and I will greatly multiply your seed as the stars of heavens, and as the sand which is on the seashore; and your seed shall possess the gate of their enemies. And in your seed all the nations of the earth shall be blessed, because you have obeyed my voice" "* (Genesis 22:15-18).

The word "sworn" in Hebrew is shâbaʻ (pronounced *shaw-bah'),* meaning "properly to *be complete or to seven oneself* as if by repeating a declaration seven times". Added to "seven" is shebaʻ-shibʻâh (pronounced *sheh'-bah, shib-aw'*), which means "the sacred full one" (Strong's H7650, H7651). Thus, by making this powerful declaration, the LORD Jehovah seals this everlasting covenant with an immutable oath made between Himself (in the full essence of the Godhead) and Abraham. Of this extraordinary act of obedience on Abraham's part, Dr. Merrill F. Unger writes:

> "Abraham's passing the severest test of faith with flying colors called forth the most solemn ratification of the covenant, indicated by six points: (1) There were the appearance and voice of the preincarnate Christ (the eternal Word with God, who was God, John 1:1-2; cf. Gen. 22:11). (2) This constituted a second appearance, Deity doubly honoring the occasion. (3) The covenant was sealed with a most solemn declaration – swearing by Himself, there being none greater (Psalm 105:9). (4) It clearly intimated that Abraham *had done* what God asked him, namely, to offer his only son as a burnt offering. (5) It expanded the scope of covenant blessing. In the earliest annunciation of the promises, Abraham was assured that he individually would be a source of world blessing (12:3; 18:18); now it is in "thy seed" (v. 17), repeated to Isaac (26:3) and Jacob (28:14). But even this expanded blessing centered in Christ, the coming seed (Gal. 3:16; cf. John 8:56) and could only be realized in Him. (6) It promised victory over enemies; "Thy seed" shall possess (take over) the gate of his enemies (v. 17; cf. 24:60; Num. 24:17-19), comprehending more deeply spiritual foes (Matt. 16:18; Eph. 6:10-20; Col. 1:13; 2:15). The 'gate' meant access to a walled city, and 'possessing' it meant control of the town (cf. 24:10)" (Unger's Commentary On The Old Testament, 2002, p. 71).

In conclusion, the everlasting covenants God made with Noah and Abraham, He sealed them by swearing an oath to Himself. Moreover, in the all important and historic everlasting covenant God made with Abraham, two great prophecies are foretold. The prophecy of Israel going into bondage by the hands of the Egyptians for four hundred years, their redemption, the judgment that would befall their oppressors (15:13-14), and the prophecy of a Messiah as foretold in Genesis 3:15, "in your seed *all* nations of the earth will be blessed" (22:18). Additionally, God solemnly promises to: 1) make make Abraham a great nation, 2) to personally bless him spiritually and temporally, 3) to make his name great, 4) Abraham was to become a great blessing, 5) to bless those who bless Abraham, 6) to curse those who curse him (Genesis 12:1-3), and 7) to give him and his descendants all of the land of Canaan for an everlasting possession (12:4-7; 13:18; 15:18-21). As a sign of the ratification of the covenant between them, the act of circumcision of the flesh was instituted. When God Almighty (El Shaddai) ratified His everlasting covenant with Abraham, He gave him five more promises. (1) To multiply him exceedingly, (2) Abraham would be the father of a multitude of nations, (3) kings would come forth from him, (4) the everlasting covenant would be established between God and Abraham's descendants throughout their generations, and (5) at the age of ninety-nine, Abraham was promised that an heir to the covenantal promises would be born to him from Sarah, and through him *all families of the earth* would be blessed. God then permanently changed their names from Abram to Abraham, "the father of a multitude of nations", the great patriarch of faith, and his wife from Sarai to Sarah, "a mother of nations" (17:15-17).

Lastly, in addition to the names of God, *Elohiym,* LORD God, *Jehovah-Elohiym,* we have now been introduced to the names of Jehovah-*Adonai*, 'Master Jehovah', Jehovah-*Jireh*, 'The LORD will provide', and El *Shaddai*, 'God Almighty'.

The Abrahamic Covenant Confirmed to Isaac —Genesis 26:1-5

Compared to the life of Abraham, a short biography is given about Isaac, his marriage to Rebekah, the birth of the twins, Esau and Jacob, and as Divine Providence would have it, Esau sacrifices his first-born birthrights to Jacob for a bowl of lentil stew and some bread (Genesis 25:34). The significance of this turning point is history is what sets the stage for the fulfillment of God's promises to Abraham through Jacob. In Dr. Roland K. Harrison's study on the custom of first-born rights in the patriarchal period, he connects the spiritual significance to the time of the Exodus, as well as to the family custom. He writes:

> "Already in the patriarchal period a ram was deemed an acceptable sacrificial substitute for the first-born (Gen. 22:13), but at the time of the EXODUS God renewed His claim to the first-born of humans and animals (Ex. 13:1-16). Since heathen practices involving child sacrifice were abhorrent to God, the first-born child was *redeemed* while corresponding animals were offered as a sacrificial offering. But even the firstling of an ass could be redeemed through the sacrifice of a kid. A special degree of sanctity was accorded to first-born male animals, and certain prohibitions were attached to them (Dt. 15:19)"
>
> "The first-born possessed definite privileges which were denied to other members of the family. The Law forbade the disinheriting of the first-born (t. 21:15-17). Such legislation, in polygamous times, was necessary to prevent a favorite wife from exercising undue influence over her husband in distributing his property, as in the case of Jacob (Gen. 25:23). The oldest son's share was twice as large as that of any other son. When Elisha prayed for a double portion of Elijah's spirit, he simply wished to be considered the first-born, i.e., the successor, of the dying prophet. Israel was Yahweh's first-form (Ex. 4:22); cf. Jer. 31:9) [Ephraim]). Israel, as compared with

> other nations, was entitled to special privileges. She occupied a unique position in virtue of the special relationship between Yahweh and the nation. In three passages (Rom. 8:29; Col. 1:15; He. 1:6), Jesus Christ is the first-born — among many brethren (Rom. 8:29) — of every creature (Col. 1:16)" (Eerdman's *International Standard Bible Encyclopedia,* Volume E-J, 1979, p. 308, ed. Geoffrey W. Bromiley).

An additional comment on the custom of first-born rights in patriarchal period is noted by Dr. Merrill F. Unger.

> "The firstborn was the head of the whole family. Originally the priesthood belonged to the tribe of Rueben, as the firstborn, but was transferred to the tribe of Levi (Num. 3:12-16; 8:18). The firstborn enjoyed an authority over those who were younger similar to that possessed by a father (Gen. 35:23; 2 Chron. 21:3). As head of the family he had also, according to patriarchal custom, to provide food, clothing, and other necessities in his house for his mother till death, and his unmarried sisters till their marriages" (The New Unger's Bible Dictionary, 1988, p. 429, ed. R. K. Harrison).

Meanwhile, Isaac and his household are living in the south country near the place where Ishmael was born (Genesis 24:62), a severe famine strikes the land, and Isaac moves his household to Gerar, the land of the Philistines (26:1). Though it is not explicitly recorded that Isaac was on his way to Egypt, the following conversation between the LORD (Jehovah) and Isaac suggests that Isaac was planning to take his household to the land of Egypt when Jehovah interceded.

The Covenant Confirmed – Genesis 26:1-5: *"And the LORD appeared to him, and said, "Do not go down to Egypt; stay in the land of which I shall tell you. Sojourn in this land, and I will be with you, and bless you; for to you and to your descendants I will give all these lands, and I will establish the oath which I swore to your father*

Abraham. And I will multiply your descendants as the stars of heaven, and will give your descendants all these lands; and by your descendants all the nations of the earth shall be blessed; because Abraham obeyed Me and kept my charge, My commandments, My statutes, and My laws." "

Thus, Isaac settles in Gerar and God blesses him beyond measure. *"And the man became rich, and continued to grow richer until he became very wealthy"* (v. 13), which created so much jealously among the Philistines that king Abimelech finally had to kick Isaac and his household out of the land (v. 14). Subsequently, Isaac returns to Beersheba where the LORD appears to him a second time to confirm the Abrahamic everlasting Covenant to him. *"And the LORD appeared to him the same night and said, 'I am the God of your father Abraham; Do not fear, For I am with you. I will bless you, and multiply your descendants, for the sake of My* servant *Abraham' "* (Genesis 26:24). Although it is implied that Isaac knew God as the LORD Jehovah, it is hard to imagine what he must have thought when God makes the staggering announcement of "*I AM Elohiym*", the God of your father.

In conclusion, the LORD now introduces Himself to Isaac as "*Elohiym*", the God of his father, to reassure him that He will keep the covenant that He made with his father. Isaac receives the confirmation that he and his descendants will receive the personal blessings, possession of the Promised Land, his descendants will be multiplied as the stars, and finally, the hidden prophecy of "in your seed" all the nations of the earth will be blessed.

The Abrahamic Covenant Confirmed to Jacob —Genesis 28:10–35:12

Setting the Stage

Compared to the life of Isaac, the biography given about Jacob is quite a saga. As second born, Jacob purchases the first-born birthright from his twin brother Esau with a bowl of lentil stew and some bread (Genesis 25:34). In order to receive the promises given in the blessing to the first-born, Jacob deceives his father into believing he was Esau. The lengthy narrative given in Chapter 27 tells the story of Isaac who is now old, bedridden, blind, and ready to pass the first-born blessing on to Esau. He calls for Esau to bring him his favorite dish so that he could bless him. *"Now then, please take your gear, your quiver and your bow, and go out to the field and hunt game for me; and prepare a savory dish for me such as I love, and bring it to me that I may eat, so that my soul may bless you before I die"* (Genesis 27:3-4). Meanwhile, Isaac's wife, Rebekah, overhears the conversation and quickly prepares Isaac's favorite dish. Then she takes Esau's hunting garments, fits them onto Jacob, and sends him to Isaac's bedside. Jacob then tricks his father into thinking that he is Esau and asks him for the blessing. After Isaac touches and smells the hairy garments Jacob is wearing, he believes that Jacob is indeed his twin brother Esau, asks Jacob to kiss him, and then passes the first-born blessing on to him (vv. 5-29).

> *"So he came close and kissed him; and when he smelled the smell of his garments, he blessed him and said, 'See, the smell of my son is like the smell of the field which the LORD has blessed; Now may God give you of the dew of heaven, And of the fatness of the earth, And an abundance of grain and new wine; May peoples serve you, And nations bow down to you; Be master of your brothers, and may your mother's sons bow down to you. Cursed be those who curse you, and blessed be those who bless you' "* (Genesis 27:27-29).

Subsequently, Esau prepares his father's favorite dish and takes it to him at his bedside. Unaware that Jacob has already received the first-born blessing from his father, he asks his father to give him the blessing. When Esau finds out that the blessing was already given to Jacob, he becomes enraged and devises a plan to kill Jacob (27:30-41). Meanwhile, Rebekah finds out, tells Jacob about Esau's plan, and talks Isaac into sending Jacob away. In response, Isaac charges Jacob to go to Paddan-aram (Haran) and choose a wife from his Uncle Laban's household, and then passes on the blessing of the promises that were made to Abraham by *El Shaddai* (27:42—28:1-2).

> *"And may God Almighty bless you and make you fruitful and multiply you that you may become a company of peoples. May He also give you the blessing of Abraham, to you and to your descendants with you; that you may possess the land of your sojourning, which God gave to Abraham"* (28:3-4).

The Confirmation

Armed with only the blessings given to him by his father, Jacob flees Beersheba. While Jacob is on the road to Haran, the LORD comes to him in a dream, identifies Himself as *Jehovah*, (the self-existent One who reveals Himself), the God of his father, and confirms all of the promises given to him under the Abrahamic everlasting Covenant.

> *"Then Jacob departed Beersheba and went toward Haran. And he came to a certain place, and spent there that night, because the sun had set; and he took one of the stones of the place and he put it under his head, and lay down in that place. And he had a dream, and behold, a ladder set on the earth with its top reaching heaven; and behold, the angels of God were ascending and descending on it. And behold, the LORD stood above it and said, "I am the LORD, the God of your father Abraham and the God of Isaac; the land on which you lie I will give it to you and to your descendants; Your descendants shall also be like the dust of the earth, and you shall spread out to the west and to the east and to the north and to the south; and by you and in your descendants shall all the families of the earth be blessed. Behold, I am with you, and will keep you wherever you go, and will bring you back to this land; for I will not leave you until I have done what I have promised you" "* (Genesis. 28:10-15).

Meanwhile, the narrative in Chapters 29—30 tell of Jacob's twenty year stay in Haran, of his marriages to Rachael and to her sister Leah, and of his flight from Haran. While Jacob and his family are migrating back to the land of Canaan, Chapter 32 tells of the twenty year grudge that Esau bitterly held against Jacob, and of Jacob's fear of Esau's revenge. After Jacob crosses the Jordan River, he hears that Esau is coming with a company of four hundred men to attack him and fears for his life. It is here that Jacob stops to pray for deliverance from the hand of his brother. During the course of night, Jacob wrestles with an angel of God until daybreak, the angel touches the socket of his thigh and dislocates it, and still Jacob refuses to let go until the angel blesses him. After the angel of God asks Jacob for his name and he replies, the angel then changes his name from Jacob to Israel. "*And he said, "Your name shall no longer be Jacob, but Israel; for you have striven with God and with men and have prevailed" "* (vv. 24-32). But it doesn't end there—Chapter 34 goes on to tell the story of the hideous crime that is committed against Dinah, Jacob's daughter, while they are living in Succoth near Shechem, the outworking of a tragic plot committed by the sons of Jacob against the Shechemites, and of the taking of all of the Shechemite's wealth, including their idols.

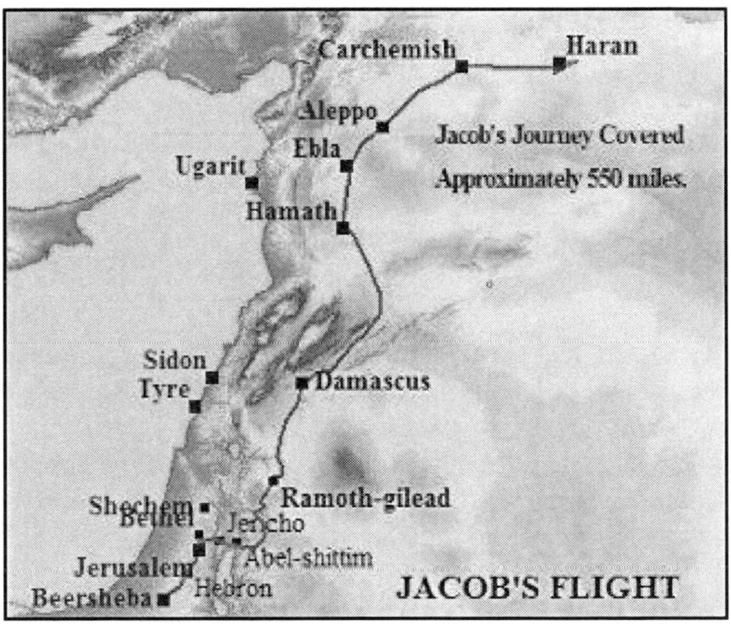

Jacob's Journey
Image provided a History of Israel Online
http://www.israel-a-history-of.com/old-testament-map.html#ground, 2012.

Chapter 35 continues with God's command to Jacob to return to Bethel. However, before departing, as an act of purification, Jacob instructs his household to destroy all of their false idols, bathe, and change their clothes (v. 2). Upon arriving at Bethel, Jacob builds an altar to God as he was instructed, and it is here that God (*El Shaddai*) appears to him to confirm the name change and to re-confirm the covenant blessings and promises that He made to his grandfather, Abraham. This is the turning point in Jacob's life—the advent of the birthing of the nation of Israel through which a company of nations are born.

> *"Then God appeared to Jacob again when he came from Paddan-aram, and He blessed him. And God said to him, "Your name is Jacob; You shall no longer be called Jacob, But* ***Israel*** *shall be your name." Thus He called him Israel. God also said to him, "I am God Almighty; Be fruitful and multiply; a nation and a company of nations shall come from you, And kings shall come forth from you. And the land which I gave to Abraham and Isaac, I will give it to you, And I will give the land to your descendants after you" "* (35:9-12).

In conclusion, the great promises of the covenant *El Shaddai* made with Abraham are now confirmed to Jacob. God permanently changes his name from Jacob to Israel, confirms the inheritance of the Promised Land, and confirms the promise of the royalty that would be coming from his bloodline. Lastly, we find the hidden prophecy of "in your seed" all the families of the earth will be blessed.

The Mosaic Covenant—Exodus 19:3–31:18

The Abrahamic everlasting Covenant confirmed to both Isaac and to Jacob extends from the dispensation of 'the age of promise' to the 'age of the Dispensation of the Law', which covers the time period of the giving of the Law of Jehovah to Moses, and its acceptance by Israel at Sinai.

Setting the Stage

The postdiluvian Abrahamic everlasting Covenant confirmed to Isaac and Jacob, included elements of the original antediluvian Edenic/Adamic Covenants of "be fruitful and multiply", God's sworn oath that Abraham's name would be great, from him kings and nations would come forth, and the land of Canaan was given as an inheritance to the new nation of Israel. As the father of the new nation, Jacob's twelve sons, who later become the tribes of Israel, are Ruben, Simeon, Levi, Judah, Dan, Naphtali, Gad, Asher, Issacher, Zebulun, Joseph, and Ben. However, Ruben and Levi are not counted in the inheritance or enrolled in the official records of genealogy of birthright. First, because Ruben forfeited his first-born birthrights when he defiled his father's bed (Genesis 35:22), Jacob transferred them to his grandsons, Manasseh and Ephraim (Genesis 48:1-20), the sons of Joseph. "*Now the sons of Reuben the first-born of Israel (for he was the first-born, but because he defiled his father's bed, his birthright was given to the sons of Joseph the son of Israel; so that he is not enrolled in the genealogy according to the birthright*" (1 Chronicles 5:1). Secondly, Jacob's third son, Levi, whose direct descendants were Aaron, Moses, and Miriam (Jacob's great-great grandchildren, 1 Chronicles 6:1-3), later became the Levites who were set aside for the priestly service of God (Numbers 26:57-62), thus bringing the count back up to the 'twelve tribes of Israel' (Children of Jacob by Wayne Blank, http://www.keyway.ca/htm2002/jacobch.htm, 2012).

The Calling of Moses by the Great 'I AM'

Set apart from the Israelites, Moses was raised and educated in the inner-courts of the Pharaoh. His great grandfather was Levi, and his father, Amram, was Jacob's great grandson (Exodus 6:16-20). As Divine Providence would have it, a famine struck the land of Canaan, and Jacob moved his household to Egypt where his son Joseph was then governor of the land. As prophesied to Abraham, by permission given by the Pharaoh, Jacob's household settles in the land of Goshen (Genesis 46:1-33).

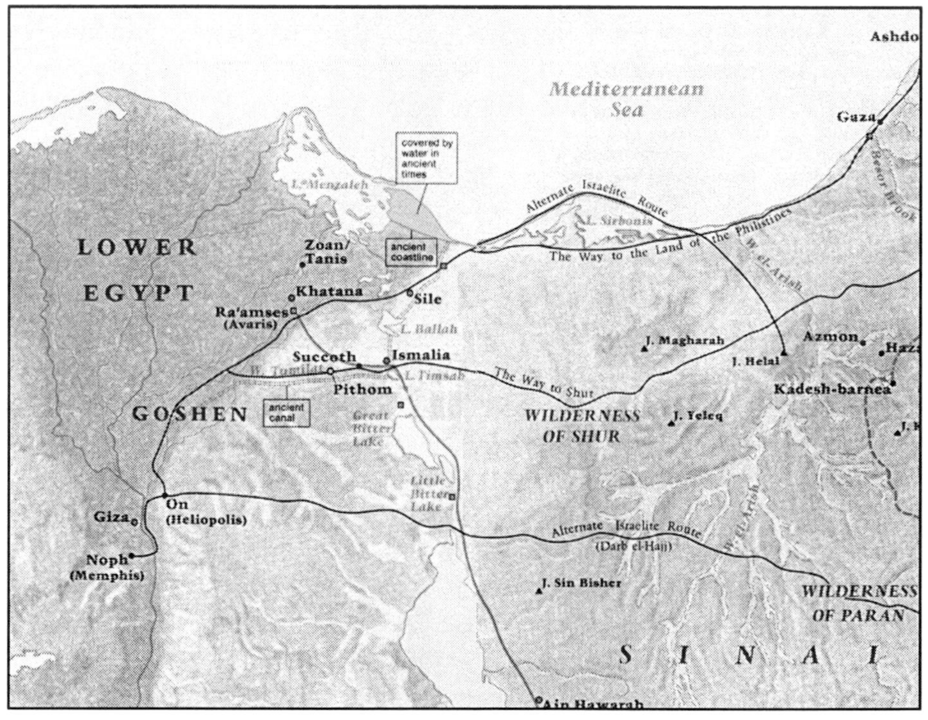

Land of Goshen
Image provided a History of Israel Online
http://www.israel-a-history-of.com/twelve-tribes-of-israel.html#Israelites%20Leave%20Egypt%20Under%20Moses, 2012.

Centuries pass (Exodus 12:40) and both Joseph and the benevolent Pharaoh who had given Jacob's family permission to settle in Egypt have passed away, and the Israelites are now under the brutal control of a Pharaoh who has no knowledge of the history of Joseph or of the permissive settlement of the Israelites in their land. One day the Pharaoh takes note that the Hebrew population was increasing at an alarming rate and orders the midwives to kill all newly born male Hebrew children (Exodus 1:1-22). In order to spare the life of Moses, his mother, Jochebed, hides him in a basket and places it in the Nile River. Meanwhile, Moses' sister, Miriam, follows the basket down river. When Miriam sees the Pharaoh's daughter discover Moses, she offers to find someone for the young daughter who could nurse Moses in her place. The young Pharaoh's daughter agrees, and Miriam brings her Moses' birth mother, Jochebed, to act as his nursemaid (Exodus 2:1-10). Now fully grown, Moses witnesses one of his countrymen being beaten by an Egyptian and kills him. Fearing for his life, Moses flees Egypt (vv. 12-15), settles in the land of Midian, and marries the daughter of a Midianite priest (vv. 16-21). Thus by the time Moses receives his calling from God, he is nearly eighty years old, and the Israelites had already been in oppression by the hands of the Egyptians for 400 years, exactly as God had prophesied to Abraham (Genesis 15:13).

A Conversation with God

One day, while Moses is pasturing a flock in the mountain of Horeb (Mt. Sinai), he becomes fascinated by the sight of a blazing fire coming from within a bush. While Moses is fixated on the wonder of the bush burning yet not being consumed, the LORD *Jehovah* calls out his name and says, *"I am the God* (Elohiym) *of your father, the God Abraham, the God of Isaac, and the God of Jacob"* (v. 6). As Jehovah-*Elohiym* is tasking Moses to return to Egypt and free the sons of Israel, a lengthy and interesting conversation takes place between them that begins in Exodus 3:12 and continues through Exodus 4:17. However, during the course of the conversation, Moses receives a stunning revelation when he asks God for His name. "*Behold, I am going to the sons of Israel, and I shall say to them, 'The God of your fathers has sent me to you.' Now they may say to me, 'What is His name?' What shall I say to them?"* And God declares to Moses, *"**I AM** WHO **I AM**"; Thus you shall say to the sons of Israel, '**I AM** has sent me to you.' "* (Exodus 3:13-14). Dr. C. I. Scofield adds further clarification to the significance attached to the name *I AM* as Jehovah-*Yahweh*, the redemptive name given to the sons of Israel. He notes:

> "The primary meaning of the name LORD Jehovah is "the self-existent One". Literally as in Ex. 3:14, "He that is who He is, therefore the eternal I AM." But *Havah* from which Jehovah, or *Yahwe*, is formed, signifies to become, that is to become known" (Genesis 1, p. 6).

In this stunning revelation of the name, I AM as the eternal Creator and Consummator of redemption, Dr. Unger states:

> *"The name I AM is derived from the Hebrew* hâyâh ("to be"); thus, "He who was, is, and shall be." He is "I was who I was," "I am who I am," and "I shall be who I shall be." The human deliverer was to go in the name of Jehovah (Yahweh). the divine Deliverer, the eternal One, who had come to fulfill His covenant with and keep His promise to the afflicted descendants of Abraham, Isaac, an Jacob" (Unger's Commentary On The Old Testament, 2002, p. 107).

Later, when God is about to show His redemptive power to the Egyptians, Moses is given the revelation of God's personal name when He declares, *"I appeared to Abraham, Isaac and Jacob as God Almighty* (El Shaddai), *but by My name, LORD* (Jehovah-*Yahweh*), *I did not make myself known to them"* (Exodus 6:3). Of this new revelation, Dr. Merrill F. Unger continues:

> "The LORD reminded Moses of His covenant with the patriarchs under the name El-Shaddai (God Almighty, Gen. 17:1). Now that He was about to deliver them from Egyptian bondage (sin), Pharaoh (Satan), and Egypt (the world), He was about to reveal the meaning of His personal redemptive name,

> Jehovah (Yahweh). What is meant is that its meaning had not yet been revealed. The reason is simply because redemption from Egypt, typical of redemption in Christ, was not wrought in Canaan but was to be wrought in Egypt. The people, through the revelation of the name Yahweh, were to see the mighty manifestation of God's *grace* and *power* in redeeming His people from Egypt" (Ibid., p. 110).

The record of the deliverance of the sons of Israel that was orchestrated by the great *I AM* and executed through Moses is recorded in the Book of Exodus. This interesting and lengthy narrative can be found in Exodus Chapters 3—14. The purpose of previous short narrative is to lay the groundwork for the giving of the Mosaic Covenant *after* the sons of Israel become an independent nation under the leadership of Moses. However, the devastating plagues that were inflicted upon the Egyptian people have often been questioned to which several answers can be found. (1) To fulfill His covenantal promise as foretold to Abraham, "*But I will also judge the nation whom they will serve, and afterward they will come out with many possessions*" (Genesis 15:14). (2) To show them that HE is who HE is, the only self-existent, omnipotent, omniscient and omnipresent God of the universe, *"I am the LORD and there is no other; Besides Me, there is no god"* (Isaiah 45:5), and (3) to impose judgment upon their gods, "*Upon their gods also the Lord executed judgments*" (Numbers 33:4). Below is a biblical summary of the ten judgments God executed upon the Pharaoh, Egypt, and their gods through the hands of Moses and Aaron.

Egypt and the Plagues

"*For our struggle is not against flesh and blood, but against the rulers, against the powers, against the world forces of this darkness, against the spiritual forces of wickedness in the heavenly places*" (Ephesians 6:12).

Plagues	Egyptian gods Affected
Plague #1 – Exodus 7:14-25 The waters of the Nile turned to blood which included rivers, streams, pools and reservoirs. All of the fish died and the water became foul and undrinkable Blood ran throughout all of the land.	Osiris – The god of underground Hapi – The spirit of the Nile
Plague #2 – Exodus 8:1-15: Frogs covered the land and entered into houses, climbed into beds, into kitchen utensils and into ovens.	Heket –The goddess of birth/fertility
Plague #3 – Exodus 8:16-19 All of the dust became swarms of lice that attacked both man and beast.	Geb – The god of the earth
Plague #4 – Exodus 8:20-32 Swarms of flies covered the land. God set apart the land of Goshen from the rest of the land so that neither the land nor the children of Israel were affected.	Amon-Ra – The creator and king of gods
Plague #5 – Exodus 9:1-7 A severe and deadly pestilence attacked the animals of Egypt. God set apart the cattle belonging to the children of Israel so they were not affected.	Apis – Represented as a bull (Apis the bull) Bast (Bastet) – The cat goddess of love Hathor – The cow headed goddess of the desert.
Plague #6 – Exodus 9:8-12 Ashes were taken from a furnace and thrown into the air so that the resulting dust became boils which attacked both and man beast.	Imhotep – He was a deified person who was worshipped as the god of medicine. Serapis – god of healing

Plague #7 – Exodus 9:13-35
Severe hail and lightening rained down upon Egypt unlike they had ever seen. It struck down both man and beast and destroyed their vegetation. God set apart the land of Goshen from the rest of the land so that neither the children of Israel, their land, or their cattle were affected.

Horus – The falcon headed god had the sky.
Nut – The goddess of the sky
Shu – The god of the wind/air

Plague #8 – Exodus 10:1-20
Locusts had never been known in Egypt, but were known in other lands. The surface of the land was covered so thick with them that it darkened the land, and any vegetation whatsoever that had escaped the hail was now completely consumed by the locusts.

Ernutet – The goddess of childbirth and of harvest.
Nepri – The god of the grain
Osiris – The god of agriculture and ruler of the dead

Plague #9 – Exodus 10:21-29
A heavy darkness covered all of the land of Egypt for three days, but all of the children of Israel had light in. their dwellings.

Ra – The god of the sun
Horus – The god of the sky
Shu – The god of the air
Tem – The god of sunset

Plague #10 – Exodus 11:1—12:50
Death was imposed upon every first born in the land for both man and beast. The children of Israel were spared by of applying the blood of a lamb around the 'doors' of their houses so that when death came, they would be passed over.

God's final judgment upon the Pharaoh and upon Egypt as foretold in Genesis 15:14-15. All of the Egyptian gods were showcased as being false, therefore were completely following the newly given instructions

Passover Instituted – Exodus 12:14-24

(Fredrick Bush, Eerdman's *International Standard Bible Encyclopedia*, Volume K-P, 1986, p. 878, ed. Geoffrey W. Bromiley; Against All the Gods of Egypt by David Padfield, http://padfield.com/downloads/otbooks.html, 2012; The Book of Exodus by Kevin Saunders, Logos Bible Teaching Ministry, Chandler, Arizona, 2006).

"The LORD had also executed judgments on their gods" (Numbers 33:4).

The Giving of the Covenant

"And Moses went up to God, and the LORD called to him from the mountain, saying, "Thus you shall say to the house of Jacob and tell the sons of Israel: 'You yourselves have seen what I did to the Egyptians, and how I bore you on eagles' wings, and brought you to Myself. 'Now then if you will indeed obey My voice and keep My covenant, then you shall be My own possession among all the peoples, for all the earth is Mine; and you shall be to Me a kingdom of priests and a holy nation.' These are the words that you shall speak to the sons of Israel" (Exodus 19:3-6).

Now that the children of Israel have been delivered from bondage, God sets them aside as a holy nation. As promised to Abraham, Isaac, and Jacob, from their seed would come forth nations and kings, and a kingdom of priests. The children of Israel are now entering into a new age – the *Dispensation of the Law,* which extended from the giving of the Law by Jehovah through Moses, and its acceptance of the Law by Israel at Mount Sinai (Exodus 19:3—31:18). Dr. Unger stresses that the covenant is 'particular' to the children of Israel, and does not nullify any of the elements in previous covenants. However, two distinguishing factors between the giving of the previous covenants and the Mosaic Covenant stand out. 1) Whereas the previous covenants were given to individuals and to their descendants, the Mosaic Covenant was given to the nation of Israel. 2) The covenant blessings that were given by God in the previous covenants were everlasting, whereas the covenant blessings given in the national covenant are conditionally based on obedience. Thus, though disobedience did not nullify the covenant, it did make those who willfully practiced it ineligible to receive the covenant blessings under the Law, but did not nullify the promises made in the unconditional Abrahamic everlasting Covenant.

> "Through Moses, God gave the covenant to Israel as a theocratic nation. Note that this covenant was in operation during the legal age; it was given only to Israel. The rest of humanity was under the Age of Conscience (Gen. 3:23), Human Government (Gen. 8:20) and Promise (Gen. 12:1) that the Abrahamic Covenant would bring blessing to the entire race."
>
> "The Mosaic Covenant is in three divisions: (1) the commandments, expressing the righteous will of God (20:1-26); (2) the judgments, governing the social life of Israel (21:1—24:11; and (3) the ordinances, governing the religious life of Israel (24:12 —31:18)" (Unger's Commentary On The Old Testament, 2002, p. 124).

While the Mosaic Covenant is a lengthy and intricate one, a brief summary of a the particulars of the covenant God made with Israel including the receiving of a new identity as a nation, moral codes by which to live by, civil laws, and ceremonial laws. A brief summary of those laws are listed below.

The Moral Law – The Ten Commandments

"Then God spoke all these words, saying:

(1) I am the LORD your God, who brought you out of the land of Egypt, out of the house of slavery. You shall have no other gods before Me.

(2) You shall not make for yourself an idol, or any likeness of what is in heaven above or on the earth beneath or in the water under the earth. You shall not worship them, or serve them; for I, the LORD your God, am a jealous God, visiting the iniquity of the fathers on the children, on the third and fourth generations of those who hate Me. But showing lovingkindness to thousands, to those who love Me and keep My commandments.

(3) *You shall not take the name of the LORD your God in vain, for the LORD will not leave him unpunished who takes His name in vain.*
(4) *Remember the Sabbath day, to keep it holy. Six days you shall labor and do all your work, in it you shall not do any work, you or your son or your daughter, your male or your female servant or your cattle or your sojourner who stays with you. For in six days the LORD made the heavens ad the earth, the sea and all that is in them, and rested on the seventh day; therefore the LORD blessed the Sabbath day and made it holy.*
(5) *Honor your father and your mother, that your days may be prolonged in the land which the LORD your God gives you.*
(6) *You shall not murder.*
(7) *You shall not commit adultery.*
(8) *You shall not steal.*
(9) *You shall not bear false witness against your neighbor.*
(10) *You shall not covet your neighbor's house; you shall not covet your neighbor's wife or his male servant or his female servant or his ox or his donkey or anything that belongs to your neighbor"* (Exodus 20:1-17).

Special attention is drawn to the fourth commandment regarding the keeping of the Sabbath. After God ratified His covenant with Abraham, the act of circumcision was instituted as a sign of remembrance. However, after the ratification of the Mosaic Covenant, the sign of remembrance given to the nation of Israel was the execution of keeping the Sabbath holy.

> *"But as for you, speak to the sons of Israel, saying, 'You shall surely observe My Sabbaths; for this is a sign between Me and you throughout your generations that you may know that I am the LORD who sanctifies you' "* (Exodus 31:13). 'So *the sons of Israel shall observe the Sabbath, to celebrate the Sabbath throughout their generations as a perpetual covenant. It is a sign between Me and the sons of Israel forever' "* (Exodus 31:16-17a);

Dr. Unger notes a significant difference between the symbolic meanings of the two signs. He states:

> "Even as circumcision had been given as a token of the Abrahamic Covenant (Gen. 17:9-13), the keeping of the Sabbath was instituted as a *symbol* of the Mosaic Covenant to Israel (31:13). It was the distinguishing mark of the LORD's elect nation, chosen to be an example to all the other nations of the earth, showing the blessing of salvation and dedication" (Unger's Commentary On The Old Testament, 2002, p. 128).

Civil Laws

A detailed description of the civil statutes are recorded in Exodus 20:22—23:1-33. Below is a brief topical listing of those statutes.

- Concerning worshiping the LORD (20:22-26).
- Concerning slaves (21:1-11).
- Capital offences such as murder (21:12-17; 22:18-20).
- Non-capital offences (21:18-32).
- Property rights (21:33—22:15).
- Civil regulations concerning oppression and affliction against widows, virgins, orphans, idolatry, and strangers (22:16-24).
- Lending and borrowing (22:25-27).
- First-fruit offerings (22:29-30).
- Diet (22:31).
- Administration of legal justice (23:1-9).
- Annual agricultural Festivals: The Feast of Unleavened Bread, Feast of Harvest, and the Feast of Ingathering (23:14-22).

Ratification of the 'Book' of the Covenant

Before God gives the ceremonial instructions to the new nation, He summons Moses, Aaron, Nadab, Abihu (Aaron's two sons, Numbers 3:2), and 70 of the elders to Mount Sinai.

> "*Then He said to Moses, "Come up to the LORD, you and Aaron, Nadab and Abihu and seventy of the elders of Israel, and you shall worship at a distance. Moses alone, however, shall come near to the LORD, but they shall not come near, nor shall the people come up with him." Then Moses came and recounted to the people all the words of the LORD and all the ordinances; and all the people answered with one voice, and said "All the words which the LORD has spoken we will do!"* " (Exodus 24:1-3).

The ratification process is as intricate as the giving of the covenant and is fully covered in Exodus 24. Of great prophetic significance, however, is the ratification process was completed by sprinkling the blood of the sacrificial ram on *both* the altar and on the people, and termed "the blood of the covenant".

> *"And Moses wrote down all the words of the LORD. Then he arose early in the morning, and built an altar at the foot of the mountain with twelve pillars for the twelve tribes of Israel. And he sent young men of the sons of Israel, and they offered burnt offerings and sacrificed young bulls as peace offerings to the LORD. And Moses took half of the blood and put it in basins, and the other half of the blood he sprinkled on the altar. Then he took the book of the covenant and read it in the hearing of the people; and they said "All that the LORD has spoken we will do, and we will be obedient!" So Moses took the blood and sprinkled it on the people, and said, "Behold, the blood of the covenant, which the LORD has made with you in accordance with all these words"* " (Exodus 24:4-8).

Dr. John D. Hannah provides insight into this unique and historical ratification process recorded in verses 1-8.

> "Then Moses prepared the people for the ratifying of the Law. First Moses made an altar at the foot of Mount Sinai and erected 12 stone pillars to represent Israel's 12 tribes. Since the Levitical priesthood had not yet been organized, young Israelite men (perhaps the dedicated firstborn, 13:1-16), and Moses served as priests and offered burnt offerings and fellowship offerings to the LORD. In the ratification ceremony Moses sprinkled blood on the altar (24:6) and on the people (v. 8) who had heard Moses read the Book of the Covenant and had promised once again to obey it (v. 7; cf. v. 3). This is the only time in the Old Testament when *people* were sprinkled with blood. The sprinkled blood, then, symbolized the legal transaction between God represented by the altar, Ex. 24:6) and the people (represented by the stones). Israel was thus ceremonially set apart through blood (the blood of the covenant) as the people of the true God. Later the New Covenant, established by Jesus, was also ratified by blood" (The Bible Knowledge Commentary: Old Testament, 1983, pp. 145-146, ed. John F. Walvoord, Roy B. Zuck).

Finally, as a sign of remembrance of the ratification of the Mosaic Covenant between God and the children of Israel, the observance of the Sabbath was instituted. *"But as for you, speak to the sons of Israel, saying, 'You shall surely observe My Sabbaths; for this is a sign between Me and you throughout your generations, that you may know that I am the LORD who sanctifies you' "* (31:13).

Ceremonial Regulations

Soon after the Mosaic Covenant was ratified, God summons Moses back up to Mount Sinai where he communes with God for forty days and nights (Exodus 24:18). During his communion with God, Moses is given a set of elaborate instructions on how the nation was to conduct her ceremonial worship, and an intricate set of architectural plans for building the sacred sanctuary. The architectural plans for building the Ark of the Covenant and specific ceremonial statutes are recorded in Exodus Chapters 25—31. The Hebrew word for tabernacle, mishkân, literally means 'a dwelling place' (NAS Old Testament Hebrew Lexicon, 2010, H4908, http://www.biblestudytools.com/lexicons/hebrew/nas/, 2012).

> *"And let them construct a sanctuary for Me, that I may dwell among them. According to all that I am going to show you, as the pattern of the tabernacle and the pattern of all its furniture, just so you shall construct it"* (Exodus 25:8–9).

Below is a condensed listing of those specifications and ceremonial statutes given to Moses as part of the ceremonial law.

- Offcrings for thc sanctuary (25:1-7).
- Directions for the building of the Ark (25:8-15).
- Mercy Seat. (25:17-22).
- Table of Showbread and Dishes (25:23-30).
- The Lampstand (25:31-40).
- Curtains for the Tabernacle (26:1-13).
- Boards and Bars of the Tabernacle (26:14-30).
- The Veil and Screen (26:31-37).
- The altar of – Burnt offering (27:1-8).
- The Court (27:9-19).
- The lamp oil (27:20-21).
- The Priest's Garments include the breastplate, tunic, robe, turban, and sash (28:1-43).
- The sacrifices for the consecration of the priests and the holy garments and (29:1-35).
- The daily offerings (29:36-46).
- The altar of incense (30:1-10).
- Atonement money (30:11-16).

- The anointing oil and incense (30:17-38).
- Observance of the Sabbath (31:13-17).

In his closing comments on the Mosaic Covenant, Dr. William D. Barrick states:

> "It is true that the Mosaic Covenant was the most conditional of all the biblical covenants. Of all the covenants, it dealt specifically with how the people of God should live. The fulfillment of the promises and blessings of any of the covenants for any particular individual or generation was dependent upon their obedience to God's revelation. Disobedience annulled the blessings of God for that individual or generation in his/her/its own time, but disobedience did not invalidate the unconditional terms of the covenant" (The Mosaic Covenant by Dr. William D. Barrick, http://www.tms.edu/tmsj/tmsj10o.pdf, 1999, p. 225).

Lastly, in addition to the names of God, *Elohiym,* LORD God, *Jehovah-Elohiym* , Jehovah-*Adonai*, 'Master Jehovah', Jehovah-*Jireh*, 'The LORD will provide', and El *Shaddai*, 'God Almighty', we have now been introduced to Jehovah's redemptive name of *Yahweh*, the God of Israel, and the all-powerful, all-sufficient, self-existent One – The great *I AM* who *I AM.*

The Land Covenant—Deuteronomy 1:5–30:20

The Land Covenant is also known as the Palestinian or the Deuteronomic Covenant. However, as we follow the footprints of God, we find that it is an integral part of the unconditional covenant blessings and promises that God made with Abraham, Isaac, and Jacob.

"And I will give to you and to your descendants after you, the land of your sojourning, all the land of Canaan, for an everlasting possession; and I will be their God" (Genesis 17:8).

Setting the Stage

Though the new nation of Israel inherited the land from their forefathers, they have been set apart as a kingdom of priests and a holy nation, and placed under the new Mosaic Covenant with God that *conditioned* the blessings for obedience, and ineligibility of those blessings for disobedience. Whereas the Book of Leviticus is dedicated to a detailed exposition of the Law, the Book of Deuteronomy contains an intricate and lengthy exposition of the statutes and ordinances contained in the Mosaic Covenant that are reiterated to the nation of Israel ***before*** they take possession of the Promised Land, and a detailed set of regulations and statutes of their obligations to God on how the nation is to conduct herself ***while*** they are in possession of the Promised Land. A brief summarization of these conditions is presented in the famous four discourses of Moses.

First Discourse—Deuteronomy 1:5–4:43

Moses' first discourse contains a lengthy reminder to Israel of her forty year experiences in the wilderness, a review of their successes and failures, and of God's faithfulness to them. *"Across the Jordan in the land of Moab, Moses undertook to expound this law"* (Deuteronomy 1:5). Below is a brief outline of the topics covered by Moses in his discourse

- A complete review of God's mighty acts performed on behalf of the children of Israel between Horeb and Beth Peor (Deuteronomy 1:5—3:29).
- An exhortation to obey the Law and to resist idolatry (4:1-43).

Second Discourse—Deuteronomy 4:44–26:19

The second discourse contains the conditions under which Israel enters into the Promised Land and the details of their obligations to God ***while*** they are in possession of the Promised Land. Moses begins his lengthy discourse by recapitulating the Law given to them at Mount Horeb followed by an exhortation of obedience, commands and warnings, a lengthy and elaborate set of laws pertaining to the conduct of the new nation while they are in the Promised Land, and concludes with a firm declaration of their commitment to God (Deuteronomy 4:44—26:19).

- **Recapitulation of the Law at Horeb: 4:44—5:33**
  A call to obedience (5:1-5).
  The Ten Commandments restated (5:6-21).
  The mediatorial role of Moses restated (5:22-33).
- **The Great Commands and Warnings: 6:1—11:32**
  The command to love the LORD (6:5-19).
  The transmission of the covenant (6:20-25).
  The command to be separate (7:1-5).
  The basis for the command (7:6-11).
  The reward for obedience (7:12-16).
  An encouragement for victory (7:17-26).
  A warning against a spirit of independence (8:1-6).
  An exhortation to remember God's gracious dealings (8:7-20).
  A warning against a spirit of self-righteousness (9:1-6).
  An exhortation to total commitment to the LORD (9:7–11:32).
- **The code of specific laws: 12:1—26:15**
  The command to destroy Canaanite worship centers (12:2-4).
  Instructions about where to worship the LORD (12:5-7).
  Instructions about what to offer in worship (12:15-28).
  Avoidance of pagan cultic practices (12:29-32).
  The solicitation to idolatry by a false prophet (13:1-5).

- **The code of specific laws: 12:1—26:15 – Continued**

  The solicitation of idolatry by family members or friends (13:6-11).
  The destruction of an apostate town (13:12-18).
  Prohibition of pagan mourning rites (14:1-2).
  Clean and unclean food (14:3-21).
  The law of the tithe (14:22-29).
  The cancellation of debts (15:1-11).
  The freeing of servants (15:12-18).
  The law of first-born animals (15:19-23).
  The pilgrim festivals (16:1-17).
  - Passover (16:1-8).
  - The Feast of Weeks (16:9-12).
  - The Feast of Tabernacles (16:13-17)

  The instruments of theocracy (16:18–18:22).
  - Judges and officials (16:18–17:13).
  - The king (17:14-20).
  - The priests and Levites (18:1-8).
  - The prophets (18:9-22).

  The cities of refuge and criminal law (19:1-21).
  - Cities of refuge for manslaughter (19:1-13).
  - Displacing a boundary market (19:14).
  - The law of witnesses (19:15-21).

  Regulations for warfare (20:1-20).
  - The command not to fear a superior enemy (20:1-4).
  - Those exempted from military service (20:5-9).
  - Israel's foreign policy (20:10-18).
  - Prohibition against destroying fruit trees (20:19-20).

  Other laws (21:1-23).
  - Unsolved murders (21:1-9).
  - Family laws (21:10-14).
  - Rights of the first-born (21:15-17).
  - The rebellious son (21:18-21).
  - Disposition of a criminal corpse (21:22-23).

  Laws governing conduct (22:1-30).
  - Duty of brotherly love (22:1-8).

Prohibition against mixtures (22:9-12).
Marriage violations (22:13-30).

- **Laws of Sanctity for the Congregation: 23:1—25:19**

  Exclusions from the assembly (23:1-8).
  Cleanliness of the camp (23:9-14).
  Concerning runaway slaves (23:15-16).
  Against prostitution (23:17-18).
  Lending and borrowing (23:19-20).
  Vows (23:21-23).
  Eating from a neighbor's field (23:24-25).
  Divorce/remarriage (24:1-5).
  Pledges (24:6).
  Kidnapping (24:7).
  Skin diseases (24:8-9).
  Collecting pledges (24:10-13).
  Paying workers (24:14-16).
  Treatment of strangers, orphans, and widows (24:17-22).
  Prosecuting criminals (25:1-3).
  Working oxen (25:4).
  Levirate marriage (25:5-10).
  Stopping a fight (25:11-12).
  Differing weights/measures (25:13-16).
  Destruction of the Amalekites (25:17-19).

- **Laws on Liturgical Ceremonies: 26:1-15**

  Presentation of firstfruits (26:1-11).
  Presentation of three year tithe (26:12-15).

- **Declaration of commitment: 26:16-19**

  Israel's responsibility to the LORD and the LORD's responsibility to Israel (26:16-17).

Third Discourse—Deuteronomy 27:1–30:20

The third discourse contains the details of their covenant renewal commitment, and the 'declaration of blessings and curses'.

- **A Covenant Renewal Commanded: 27:1-11**
  The writing of the Law (27:1-4).
  Sacrificial offerings (27:5-8).
  A call to obedience (27:9-10).
- **Blessings and Curses: 27:11-26—28:15-68**
  The arrangement of the Tribes (27:11-14).
  The twelve curses (27:15-26).
  Blessings contingent on *obedience* (28:1-14).
  As it relates to the nation (28:1-7).
  As it relates to agriculture (28:9-12).
  As it relates to her reputation (28:13-14).
  Curses/judgments against *disobedience* (28:15-68).
  As it relates to prosperity (28:16-19).
  Destruction (28:20).
  Disease (28:21-22).
  Drought (28:23-24).
  Defeat in battle (28:25-26).
  Physical disease (28:27-29).
  Oppression (28:30-35).
  Exile (28:36-37).
  Crop and economic ruin (28:38-44).
  Explanation for the curses (28:45-48).
  The nation would be besieged (28:49-57).
  Destruction of the nation (28:58-68).

Fourth Discourse—Deuteronomy 29:1–30:20

"These are the words of the covenant which the LORD commanded Moses to make with the sons of Israel in the land of Moab, besides the covenant which He had made with them at Horeb" (Deuteronomy 29:1).

The Covenant Oath Renewal

The Book of Numbers contains a record of the history of the wilderness experiences of the nation of Israel for their unbelief. Therefore, in his last discourse, Moses makes one last summons to the covenant oath, and one final appeal to obedience.

- A review of God's faithfulness (29:2-8).
- The essence of covenant renewal (29:9-15).
- A reminder of the curses/judgments for disobedience (29:16-29).
- Terms and challenges of the covenant (30:1-20).
- Blessings promised after repentance (30:1-10).
- Final appeal to obedience (30:11-20).

(The Bible Knowledge Commentary: Old Testament, 1983, pp. 262-316, ed. John F. Walvoord, Roy B. Zuck).

Summary

Concluding his analysis of the Land Covenant, Dr. C. I. Scofield summarizes:

> "The Palestinian Covenant gives the conditions under which Israel entered the land of promise. It is important to see that the nation has never as yet taken the land under the unconditional Abrahamic Covenant, nor has it ever possessed the whole land (cf. Gen. 15. 18, with Num. 34. 1-12). The Palestinian Covenant is in seven parts:
>
> 1. Dispersion for disobedience, v. 1 (Deut. 28. 63-68. See Gen. 15. 18, note).
> 2. The future repentance of Israel while in the dispersion, v. 2.
> 3. The return of the Lord, v. 3 (Amos 9. 9-14; Acts 15. 14-17).
> 4. Restoration to the land, v. 5 (Isa. 11. 11, 12; Jer. 23. 3-8; Ezk. 37. 21-25).
> 5. National conversion, v. 6 (Rom. 11. 26, 27; Hos. 2. 14-16).
> 6. The judgment of Israel's oppressors, v. 7 (Isa. 14. 1, 2; Joel 3. 1-8; Mt. 25. 31-46).
> 7. National prosperity, v. 9 (Amos 9. 11-14)" (Deuteronomy 30, p. 250).

To compliment Dr. Scofield's brief summary, Dr. Renald E. Showers adds a comprehensive explanation of the seven covenantal promises.

> "Two significant things should be observed concerning the Deuteronomic Covenant. The first is the background of the covenant. This covenant was established by God with the nation of Israel after the establishment of the Mosaic Covenant (the Law), and it was separate from the Mosaic Covenant. Deuteronomy 29:1 states, "These are the words of the covenant, which the LORD commanded Moses to make with the children of Israel in the land of Moab, beside the covenant

which he made with them in Horeb." (A comparison of Exodus 19 and 20 with Deuteronomy 5 indicates that Horeb and Sinai are two different names for the same mountain, the mountain where God established the Mosaic Covenant with Israel.).

In preparation for the establishment of the Deuteronomic Covenant, God made promises of blessing and cursing to the nation of Israel. In Deuteronomy 28:1-14 God promised that if Israel obeyed the Mosaic Law, He would bless the nation abundantly and make it the head nation of the world. But then God warned that if Israel disobeyed the Mosaic Law, He would curse the nation abundantly with such things as drought, famine, pestilence, foreign oppression, captivity, and worldwide dispersion (Deuteronomy 28:15-68). Having given these preparatory promises, God entered into the Deuteronomic Covenant relationship with Israel. In Deuteronomy 29:10-13 Moses said to Israel, "Ye stand this day, all of you, before the LORD your God: your captains of your tribes, your elders, and your officers, with all the men of Israel, your little ones, your wives, and thy sojourner who is in thy camp, from the hewer of thy wood unto the drawer of thy water; that thou shouldest enter into covenant with the LORD thy God, and into his oath, which the LORD thy God maketh with thee this day; that He may establish thee today for a people unto himself, and that he may be unto thee a God, as he hath said unto thee, and as he hath sworn unto thy fathers, to Abraham, to Isaac, and to Jacob."

God established the Deuteronomic Covenant at the end of Israel's 40 years of wilderness wondering, just a short time before the nation was to invade Canaan (Deuteronomy 29:5-8). The place of its establishment was the land of Moab (Deuteronomy 29:1), east of the Dead Sea across from the land of Canaan. The parties of the covenant were God, the new generation of the people of Israel that was to invade Canaan, and succeeding generations of the nation. In Deuteronomy 29:14-15 Moses said to Israel, "Neither with you only do I make this covenant and this oath, but with him who stands here with us this day before the LORD our God, and also with him who is not here with us this day." As a new generation was about to begin a new chapter in Israel's history, it had to be reminded in a solemn way of Israel's special covenant relationship with Jehovah. This reminder appears to have been the purpose of the Deuteronomic Covenant.

The Promises of the Covenant

The second significant thing to be observed concerning the Deuteronomic Covenant is the fact that God made very significant promises to Israel in conjunction with the establishment of the covenant (Deuteronomy 30:1-10). Moses indicated that these promises will be fulfilled when all the blessings and curses promised in Deuteronomy 28 have been fulfilled and when Israel genuinely returns to God and obeys Him: "And it shall come to pass, when all these things are come upon thee, the blessing and the curse, which I have set before thee, and thou shalt call them to mind among all the nations, to which the LORD thy God hath driven thee, and shalt return unto the Lord thy God, and shalt obey his voice according to all that I command thee this day, thou and thy children, with all thine heart, and with all thy soul" (Deuteronomy 30:1-2).

First, God promised to gather the scattered Israelites from all over the world: "That then the LORD thy God will turn thy captivity, and have compassion upon thee, and will return and gather thee from all the nations where the LORD thy God hath scattered thee. If any of thine be driven out unto the outmost parts of heaven, from there will the LORD thy God gather thee, and from there will he fetch thee" (Deuteronomy 30:3-4).

Second, God promised to restore the Israelites to the land of their ancestors: "And the LORD thy God will bring thee into the land which thy fathers possessed, and thou shalt possess it; and he will do thee good, and multiply thee above thy fathers" (Deuteronomy 30:5).

Third, God promised to regenerate the Israelites of that future time and their descendants, thereby causing them to love Him totally: "And the LORD thy God will circumcise thine heart, and the heart of thy seed, to love the LORD thy God with all thine heart, and with all thy soul, that thou mayest live" (Deuteronomy 30:6). Circumcision of the heart is the Old Testament designation for regeneration (compare Romans 2:29).

Fourth, God promised to judge Israel's enemies: "And the LORD thy God will put all these curses upon thine enemies, and on them who hate thee, who persecuted thee" (Deuteronomy 30:7).

Fifth, God promised that the Israelites of that future time will obey Him: "And thou shalt return and obey the voice of the LORD, and do all his commandments which I command thee this day" (Deuteronomy 30:8).

Sixth, God promised to prosper those future Israelites greatly: "And the LORD thy God will make thee plenteous in every work of thine hand, in the fruit of thy body, and in the fruit of thy cattle, and in the fruit of thy land, for good; for the LORD will again rejoice over thee for good, as he rejoiced over thy fathers" (Deuteronomy 30:9). Centuries after God made these promises of the Deuteronomic Covenant to Israel, He repeated a number of them to later generations of Israelites through the Prophets Jeremiah (Jeremiah 32:36-44) and Ezekiel (36:22-38)" (The Deuteronomic Covenant by Dr. Renald E. Showers, http://www.ankerberg.com/Articles/_PDFArchives/biblical-prophecy/BP1W0502.pdf, 2012).

The Covenant Confirmed to Joshua

The Torch Passed

Prior to his death, Moses assembles the nation of Israel to advise them that God had chosen Joshua, the son of Nun, and descendant of the tribe of Ephraim (1 Chronicles 7:22-27) to be their new leader (Deuteronomy 31:3). According to the instructions given to Moses by the LORD, Moses calls Joshua and passes the 'torch' on to him.

> *"So the LORD said to Moses, "Take Joshua the son of Nun, a man in whom is the Spirit, and lay your hand on him; and have him stand before Eleazar the priest and before the entire congregation; and commission him in their sight. And you shall put some of your authority on him, in order that all the congregation of the sons of Israel may obey him. Moreover, he shall stand before Eleazar the priest, who shall inquire for him by the judgment of the Urim before the LORD. At this command they shall go out and at his command they shall come in, both he and the sons of Israel with him, even all the congregation" "* (Numbers 27:18-21).

The land promise that bore its roots from God's sworn oath to Abraham was executed by giving the holy nation of Israel the deed to the land under the Deuteronomic Covenant. *"And I will give to you and to your descendants after you, the land of your sojourning, all the land of Canaan, for an everlasting possession; and I will be their God"* (Genesis 17:8). When Moses passes the torch to Joshua, God reconfirms His promise to him.

The Covenant Confirmed – Joshua 1:1-4: *"Now it came about after the death of Moses, the servant of the LORD that the LORD spoke to Joshua the son of Nun, Moses' servant, saying, "Moses My servant is dead; now therefore arise, cross the Jordan, you and all this people, to the land which I am going to them, to the sons of Israel. Every place on which the sole of your foot treads, I have given it to you, just as I spoke to Moses. From the wilderness and this Lebanon, even as far as the great river, the river Euphrates, all the land of the Hittites, and as far as the Great Sea towards the setting of the sun, will be your territory." "*

Immediately following the confirmation, God strengthens and encourages Joshua by making this powerful statement:

> *"No man will be able to stand before you all the days of your life. Just as I have been with Moses, I will be with you; I will not fail you or forsake you. Be strong and courageous, for you shall give this people possession of the land which I swore to their fathers to give them. Only be strong and very courageous; be careful to do according to all the law which Moses My servant commanded you; do not turn from it to the right or to the left, so that you may have success wherever you go"* (1:5-7).

The Covenant Oath Renewal – Joshua 24:1-28

Like Moses, prior to his death, Joshua summoned the nation of Israel to Shechem, calls for the elders of Israel, their leaders, judges, and officers to present themselves before God, and begins his farewell discourse by reviewing the history of God's mighty acts and of His faithfulness to them (24:1-13). Equally, Joshua reminds the nation of their responsibilities under the covenant, makes one last summons to the covenant oath, and one final appeal to obedience. Certain stipulations of the covenant were restated, particularly the exhortation to revere and to serve God, obey the Law, and resist idolatry (vv. 14). Joshua further reminds the nation of the consequences of forsaking God's ways (v. 20). Finally, Joshua writes the testimony of the oath taken before God in the Book of the Law, and sets up a large stone under the oak that was by the sanctuary of the LORD (v. 26).

> "*You are witnesses against yourselves that you have chosen for yourselves the LORD, to serve Him." And they said "We are witnesses." "Now therefore, put away the foreign gods which are in your midst, and incline your hearts to the LORD, the God of Israel." "And the people said to Joshua, "We will serve the LORD our God and we will obey His voice" "* (vv. 22-24).

In conclusion, the Book of Joshua details the failures and conquests that were made in the process of conquering the land of Canaan under the commanding leadership of Joshua, and a record of the division of the land of Canaan among the tribes of Israel (Joshua 13:1–22:9). In particular, two interesting facts about the choice made of Joshua as the new military leader are noted. (1) Prior to his death, Moses, like his forefathers, passed on the blessing to each of the tribes, and among the many choice blessings given to Ephraim and Manasseh under the preeminence of Joseph (Deuteronomy 33:13-16) is the blessing of *military might* and *success*. "*As the first-born of his ox, majesty is his, and his horns are the horns of the wild-ox; with them he shall push the peoples, all at once, to the ends of the earth. And those are the ten thousands of Ephraim, and those are the thousands of Manasseh*" (v. 17). Secondly, as a descendant of the tribe of Ephraim, Dr. Bruce K. Waltke observes that "the original Hebrew name of Joshua is Hoshea (Numbers 13:16), which means 'deliverer', but Moses changed his name from Hoshea to Joshua, meaning 'Yahweh saves' " (Eerdman's *International Standard Bible Encyclopedia,* Volume E-J, 1979, p. 1133, ed. Geoffrey W. Bromiley).

The Davidic Covenant

"I have made a covenant with My chosen; I have sworn to David My servant, I will establish your seed forever, And build up your throne to all generations. Selah" (Psalms 89:3-4).

It All Fits Together

Tracing the footprints of God's relationship to man and His eternal divine plan of redemption through the dispensational covenants noted by Dr. Chafer continues with connecting David's lineage directly to Adam through "The Highway of Seed" with each of the corresponding dispensations.

	(The Edenic Covenant) "*The Dispensation of Innocence*, which extended from the creation to the fall of Adam."
Adam to Seth (Genesis 4:25).	(The Adamic Covenant) "*The Dispensation of Conscience*, which extended from Adam's fall to the flood, in which age conscience was, apparently, the dominating feature of human life on earth and the basis of man's relationship with God."

Six generations of direct descendants from Seth to Methuselah, Noah's great grandfather (5:6-21).

From Methuselah came Lamech, and from Lamech came Noah (5:25-29).

(The Noahic everlasting Covenant) "*The Dispensation of Human Government*, which extended from the flood to the call of Abraham, is characterized by the committing of self government to men, and is terminated by the introduction of a new divine purpose."

From Noah came Shem, Methuselah's great-great grandson (5:32).

From Shem, nine generations of direct descendants to Abraham are recorded (11:10-26).

The direct line continues from Abraham to Isaac, (21:3).

(The Abrahamic everlasting Covenant) "*The Dispensation of Promise*, which is continued from the call of Abraham to the giving and acceptance of the Mosaic Law at Sinai."

From Isaac to Jacob (25:23-26).

From Jacob's son, Judah, who was Abraham's great grandson (29:35).

From Judah to his son Perez, and from Perez are six generations of direct descendants to Boaz (Matthew 1:2-5).

From Boaz came his son Obed, and to Obed was born Jesse, and to Jesse was born David, the great grandson of Boaz (vv. 5-6), and the thirtieth generation from the direct line of Adam.

Though the Mosaic Covenant was given to the newly created holy nation of Israel through Jacob's great-great grandson Moses, descendant of Levi (1 Chronicles 6:1-3), it was still in effect at the time God made His covenant with David.

(The Mosaic Covenant)
"The Dispensation of the Law, which extended from the giving of the Law of Jehovah by Moses, and its acceptance by Israel at Sinai (Ex. 19:3—31:18)." Made (*Systematic Theology,* 1978, Volume I, pp. 40-41).

Thus, by manner of His covenants, God progressively revealed His plan for redemption as promised to Adam (Genesis 3:15), initiated through Abraham (Genesis 12; 15; 17; 22), followed by the redemption of the children of Israel, and by the birth of a new nation that was orchestrated through Moses in Exodus and Deuteronomy. Lastly, through King David's progeny, God establishes the everlasting throne of His kingdom.

The Covenant—2 Samuel 7:8-16

"Now therefore, thus you shall say to My servant David, 'Thus says the LORD of hosts, "I took you from the pasture, from following the sheep, that you should be ruler over My people Israel. And I have been with you wherever you have gone and have cut off all your enemies from before you; and I will make you a great name, like the names of the great men who are on the earth. I will also appoint a place for My people Israel and will plant them, that they may live in their own place and not be disturbed again, nor will the wicked afflict them any more as formerly, even from the day that I commanded judges to be over My people Israel; and I will give you rest from all your enemies. The LORD also declares to you that the LORD will make a house for you. When your days are complete and you lie down with your fathers, I will raise up your descendants after you, who will come forth from you, and I will establish his kingdom. He shall build a house for My name, and I will establish the throne of his kingdom forever. I will be a father to him and he will be a son to Me; when he commits iniquity, I will correct him with the rod of men and the strokes of the sons of men, but My lovingkindness shall not depart from him, as I took it away from Saul, whom I removed from before you. And your house and your kingdom shall endure before Me forever; your throne shall be established forever." ' "

Aside from the Abrahamic everlasting Covenant, the Davidic Covenant, sometimes referred to as the Royal Covenant, is one of the most significant covenants recorded in the Old Testament, and one of the most important covenants to understand. It not only provides a perspective on the nature of the political environment of Israel in today's world, but also provides insight into the prophetic future of the kingdom of God in the millennium, the fulfillment of His first promise of a coming Messiah and of the victory over evil as promised under the Adamic Covenant (Genesis 3:15). As we follow God's footprints through the covenant, we find David fully receives the spiritual and personal blessings given to Abraham, Isaac, and Jacob. *"And I will make you exceedingly fruitful, and I will make nations of you, and kings shall come forth from you"* (Genesis 17:6). *"And I will give to you and to your descendants after you, the land of your sojourning, all the land of Canaan, for an everlasting possession; and I will be their God"* (v. 8). However, though the covenant is unconditional, the element of chastisement for disobedience is pronounced by God through the Psalmist.

> *"If his sons forsake My law, and do not walk in My judgments, if they violate My statutes, and do not keep My commandments, then I will visit their transgression with the rod, and their iniquity with stripes. But I will not break off My lovingkindness from him, nor deal falsely in My faithfulness. My covenant I will not violate, nor will I alter the utterance of My lips. I will not lie to David, his descendants shall endure forever, and his throne as the sun before Me. It shall be established forever like the moon, and the witness in the sky is faithful"* (Psalms 89:30-37).

Dr. John F. Walvoord provides an important analysis of the interpretation of the Davidic Covenant, a glimpse of the historical background, and a summary of the provisions on understanding how it affects Israel in the future. He maintains that the Davidic Covenant deserves an important place in determining the purposes of God, and confirms the doctrine of a future reign of Christ on earth.

> "David had the godly ambition to build a temple to Jehovah. The incongruity of allowing thc ark of God to remain in a temporary tent-like tabernacle while he himself lived in the luxury of a house of cedar seemed to call for the erection of a suitable permanent building to be the center of worship. To Nathan, the prophet, was revealed that God intended David to build something more enduring than any material edifice. David's "house" was to be his posterity and through them his

throne and his kingdom were to continue forever. The main features of the covenant are included in the following passage: "When thy days are fulfilled, and thou shalt sleep with thy fathers, I will set up thy seed after thee, which shall proceed out of thy bowels, and I will establish his kingdom. He shall build a house for my name, and I will establish the throne of his kingdom forever. I will be his father, and he shall be my son: if he commits iniquity, I will chasten him with the rod of men and with the stripes of the children of men; but my loving kindness shall not depart from him, as I took it from Saul, whom I put away before thee. And thy house and thy kingdom shall be made sure for ever before thee: thy throne shall be established forever" (2 Sam 7:12-16).

The provisions of the Davidic covenant include, then, the following items: (1) David is to have a child, yet to be born, who shall succeed him and establish his kingdom. (2) This son (Solomon) shall build the temple instead of David. (3) The throne of his kingdom shall be established forever. (4) The throne will not be taken away from him (Solomon) even though his sins justify chastisement. (5) David's house, throne, and kingdom shall be established forever.

To Solomon, then, was promised a throne which would be established forever. To David was promised posterity, a throne, and a kingdom established forever. The promise is clear that the throne passed on through Solomon to David's posterity was never to be abolished. It is not clear whether the posterity of David should be through the line of Solomon. It will be shown later that this fine point in the prophecy was occasioned by the cutting off of the posterity of Solomon as far as the throne is concerned.

What do the major terms of the covenant mean? By David's "house" it can hardly be doubted that reference is made to David's posterity, his physical descendants. It is assured that they will never be slain *in toto*, nor displaced by another family entirely. The line of David will always be the royal line. By the term "throne" it is clear that no reference is made to a material throne, but rather to the dignity and power which was sovereign and supreme in David as king. The right to rule always belonged to David's seed. By the term "kingdom" there is reference to David's political kingdom over Israel. This kingdom was spiritual only in the sense that it was given to David by the anointing of God's prophet. The kingdom was by its nature earthly, political, and limited to Israel. By the expression "forever," it is signified that the Davidic authority and Davidic kingdom or rule over Israel shall never be taken from David's posterity. The right to rule will never be transferred to another family, and its arrangement is designed for eternal perpetuity. Whatever its changing form, temporary interruptions, or chastisements, the line of David will always have the right to rule over Israel and will, in fact, exercise this privilege. This then, in brief, is the covenant of God with David.

The covenant has many confirmations in the Old Testament. Specifically, Psalm 89 speaks repeatedly on this theme. "I have made a covenant with my chosen, I have sworn unto David my servant: Thy seed will I establish forever, and build up thy throne to all generations.... My loving-kindness will I keep for him for evermore; and my covenant shall stand fast with him. His seed also will I make to endure forever, and his throne as the days of heaven. If his children forsake my law, And walk not in mine ordinances; If they break my statutes, And keep not my commandments; Then will I visit their transgression with the rod, And their iniquity with stripes. But my lovingkindness will I not utterly take from him, nor suffer my faithfulness to fail. My covenant will I not break, nor alter the thing that is gone out of my lips. Once have I sworn by my holiness: I will not lie unto David: His seed shall endure forever, and his throne as the sun before me. It shall be established for ever as the moon and as the faithful witness in the sky (Ps 89:3, 4, 28-37)" " (Eschatological Problems VII: The Fulfillment of the Davidic Covenant, 2009, John F. Walvoord, http://bible.org/seriespage/eschatological-problems-vii-fulfillment-davidic-covenant, 2012).

This critical analysis presented by Dr. Walvoord is beautifully summarized by Dr. Andy Woods. In excerpts taken from his analysis, Dr. Woods states where the covenant stands today and agrees with Dr. Walvoord's position on the doctrine of a future reign of Christ on earth.

"This seed aspect of the Abrahamic Covenant's promises is later amplified in what is known as the Davidic Covenant. After God rejected Saul, who was the nation's first king, God selected David from among Jesse's sons (1 Sam. 16:1) leading to David's anointing as the nation's second king (1 Sam. 16:13) In time, God entered into a covenant with David, which promised that through David's lineage would come an eternal house, throne, and kingdom (2 Sam 7:13-16). In other words, God through David's lineage would usher in an eternal dynasty and throne. Several reasons make it apparent that these promises should be construed literally. The promises are terrestrial or earthly in nature. They concern David's physical line. They are made exclusively with national Israel rather than the church, which was not yet in existence (Matt 16:18). There is nothing in the context of 2 Sam 7 which would lead the reader to the conclusion that these promises are to be either allegorized or spiritualized. Since these promises are an amplification of the seed component of the Abrahamic Covenant, they share the Abrahamic Covenant's literalness, terrestrial nature, unconditionality, and eternality (Gen 17:8; Ps 89:34-36).

The Old Testament continually reaffirms that there would eventually arise a Davidic descendant who would usher in all that was unconditionally promised to both Abraham and David

(Ps 89; Amos 9:11; Hosea 3:5; Isa 7:13-14; 9:6-7; Ezek 34:23; 37:24). The Gospel accounts affirm Jesus Christ as the long awaited Davidic descendant prophesied in both the Abrahamic and Davidic Covenants. For example, Matthew's Gospel connects Christ genealogically to both Abraham and David (Matt 1:17). Matthew also routinely associates Christ with the title "Son of David" (Matt 9:27). Luke similarly shows Jesus to be the rightful heir to God's promises to David (Luke 1:32-33, 68-69) and notes in Acts 2:30 that Jesus is the unique Davidic descendant who will one day rule the world from David's Throne (Ps 132:11).

While the Abrahamic and Davidic Covenants are unconditional, the Mosaic Covenant (Exod 19–24) **is conditional** (Exod 19:5-6, 8). Thus, any given generation within Israel must meet the conditions of the Mosaic Covenant in order to experience the blessings promised in the Abrahamic and Davidic Covenants. They must enthrone the king of God's own choosing (Deut 17:15) thereby satisfying the condition of obedience found in the "Mosaic Covenant".

Thus, it was incumbent upon first-century Israel to enthrone Christ in order to enter into all of the covenantal blessings. While the opportunity to enthrone Christ as the Davidic king and consequently enter into the Davidic kingdom was presented to the nation through the preaching of John the Baptist (Matt 3:2), Christ (Matt 4:17), the Twelve (Matt 10:5-7), and the Seventy (Luke 10:9), Israel tragically rejected this kingdom offer (Matt 12). Such a rejection not only led to first-century Israel's failure to experience the kingdom blessings (Matt 21:43) but also to a long interim age when the Davidic kingdom would be in a state of abeyance or postponement (Luke 19:11).

During this time of postponement, Peter carefully notes how the ascended Christ has been elevated to the Father's right hand (Acts

2:33-34; Ps 110:1). In this position of glory (John 17:5), Christ pursues His ministry known as His "Present Session" in which He functions as priest (Heb 7:3b). Even in His present ministry, Christ retains His identity as the unique Davidic heir (Rev 3:7; 5:5; 22:16) who will one day occupy the earthly Davidic Throne in fulfillment of God's promise to David in 2 Sam 7:13-16.

The fact that the Davidic Covenant is not being fulfilled in the present in no wise negates its future fulfillment. When the disciples inquired as to when the kingdom would be restored to Israel, Christ never challenged the idea of an eventual fulfillment. Rather, He simply challenged the disciples' presupposition of its immediate fulfillment (Acts 1:6-7). In the future Tribulation period, the offer of the kingdom will once again be extended to Israel as well as globally (Matt 24:14). Unlike at the First Advent, this time the offer will be accepted leading to Christ's return (Matt 23:37-39) and subsequent earthly kingdom (Matt 25:34; Rev 20:1-10). During this glorious one-thousand year era, everything that was promised in the Abrahamic and Davidic Covenants will find a literal fulfillment when Christ will rule the world from David's Throne (Matt 25:31) in Jerusalem (Zech 14:16-18). This earthly kingdom will then merge into the Eternal State (1 Cor 15:24-28; Rev 22:1-5) thereby fulfilling the Davidic Covenant's eternal requirement (2 Sam 7:16)"
(The Prophetic Significance of the Davidic Line and Covenant by Dr. Andy Woods,
http://www.bibleprophecyblog.com/2011/06/prophetic-significance-of-davidic-line.html, 2011).

Dr. C. I. Scofield succinctly concludes:

"This covenant, upon which the glorious kingdom of Christ "of the seed of David according to the flesh" is to be founded, secures:

1. A Davidic "house"; i.e. posterity, family.
2. A "throne"; i.e. royal authority.

3. A kingdom; i.e. sphere of rule.
4. In perpetuity; "for ever."
5. And this fourfold covenant has but one condition; disobedience in the Davidic family is to be visited with chastisement, but not to the abrogation of the covenant (2 Sam. 7. 15; Psa. 89. 20-37; Isa. 24. 5; 54. 3). The chastisement fell; first in the division of the kingdom under Rehoboam, and, finally, in the captivities (2 ki. 25. 1-7). Since that time but one King of the Davidic family has been crowned at Jerusalem and He was crowned with thorns. But the Davidic Covenant confirmed to David by the oath of Jehovah, and renewed to Mary by the angel Gabriel, is immutable (Psa. 89. 30-37), and the Lord God will yet give to that thorn-crowned One "the throne of his father David" (Lk. 1. 31-33; Acts 2. 29-32; 15. 14-17)" (II Samuel 7, p. 362).

In summary, the Davidic Covenant is God's everlasting promise to David that He would make his name great, appoints a place for His people Israel, and declares that He will raise up descendants from him through which He will establish His kingdom. God also promised David that his son would build a house for His name, and promised to establish the throne of His kingdom forever. Though unconditional, should willful disobedience be practiced among David's progeny, chastisement would follow, but would not alter one single promise of the covenant (Psalms 89:30-37). Lastly, the fulfillment of the Davidic Covenant is currently believed to be held in abeyance until the literal fulfillment when Christ rules the world from David's Throne. Finally, in addition to the names of God, *Elohiym;* LORD God, *Jehovah-Elohiym* ; Jehovah-*Adonai*, 'Master Jehovah'; Jehovah-*Jireh*, 'The LORD will provide'; El *Shaddai*, 'God Almighty'; Jehovah's redemptive name of *Yahweh*, the God of Israel; the all-powerful, all-sufficient, self-existent One – The great *I AM* who *I AM,* we are introduced to Jehovah-*Sabaoth*, the LORD of hosts.

At a Glance

The Edenic Covenant was the first conditional covenant whereby God governed His new creation, and was made between the Triune God, *Jehovah-Elohiym,* and newly created *man*, Adam, while he was in the state of innocence. God blessed Adam, gave him authority over earth, dominion over all living things, and placed him in the Garden of Eden under the condition that *if* he ate from the tree of knowledge of good and evil, *then* he would experience immediate spiritual death (Genesis 1:28-30; 2:15-17).

After Adam broke the condition of the covenant, he fell from grace, lost his fellowship with God, and judgment and expulsion from the Garden followed. God then placed fallen *humanity* under a second covenant commonly known as the antediluvian Adamic Covenant. This unconditional unilateral covenant governed all of fallen humanity by Jehovah-Elohiym (the redemptive name of Deity), and not only carried with it some of the elements from the Edenic and judgment, but also introduced the age of consciousness, hard toil, and physical death. The earth was cursed with thorns and thistles, and Satan's messenger, the serpent, was cursed above all land creatures. The woman was placed under the headship of man and her pain in childbirth was 'multiplied'. Of profound significance, Genesis 3:15 carried the great prophecy of a coming Messiah and of the victory over evil by the finished work of Christ on the cross (Genesis 3:14-19).

Following God's execution of judgment on the wickedness that prevailed on the earth, God made an everlasting covenant with Noah, every living creature, and with all successive generations, that earth would never again be destroyed by water. The signature of His solemn oath is the permanent placement of the rainbow over the earth that is usually visible during or immediately following rain. Additionally, the postdiluvian Noahic Covenant ushered in the *Dispensation of Human Government* and carried the same elements of "be fruitful and multiply, and fill the earth" that were part of the antediluvian Adamic Covenant. It also changed their diet by adding meat with the prohibition of eating flesh with its blood, which represented life, and for maintaining respect for the sanctity of life, instituted the concept of capital punishment as a deterrent. (Genesis 9:1-17).

The Abrahamic everlasting Covenant ushered in the *Dispensation of Promise*. In this historic and all important everlasting covenant, two great prophecies are given to Abraham. The prophecy of Israel going into bondage by the hands of the Egyptians for four hundred years, their redemption, the judgment that would befall their oppressors (15:13-14), and the prophecy of a Messiah as foretold in Genesis 3:15, "in your seed *all* nations of the earth will be blessed" (22:15-18). The covenant also carried seven promises sworn to Abraham. 1) To make Abraham a great nation, 2) personal spiritual and temporal blessings, 3) to make his name great, 4) Abraham would become a great blessing, 5) to bless those who bless Abraham, 6) curse those who curse him (Genesis 12:1-3), and 7) God gave all of the land of Canaan to Abraham and to his descendants for an everlasting possession (12:4-7; 13:18; 15:18-21). As a sign of the ratification of the covenant between them, the act of circumcision of the flesh was instituted. When God Almighty (El Shaddai) ratifies His everlasting covenant with Abraham, He gave him five more promises. 1) To multiply him exceedingly, 2) Abraham would be the father of a multitude of nations, 3) kings would come forth from him, 4) the everlasting covenant would be established between God and Abraham's descendants throughout their generations, and 5) at the age of ninety-nine, Abraham was promised that an heir to the covenantal promises would be born to him from Sarah, and through him, *all families of the earth* would be blessed. God then permanently changed their names from Abram to Abraham, "the father of a multitude of nations", the great patriarch of faith, and his wife from Sarai to Sarah, "a mother of nations" (17:15-17). Of great significance, in accordance with Himself, both the Noahic and Abrahamic everlasting Covenants were sealed by Almighty God's immutable oath, and lastly, the Abrahamic Covenant was confirmed to Abraham's son Isaac, and to his grandson Jacob (Genesis 28:10–35:12).

After the children of Israel were delivered from Egyptian bondage, God set them apart from all other peoples as a new nation. As promised to Abraham, Isaac, and Jacob, from their seed would come forth nations and kings, and a kingdom of priests. The children of Israel enter into a new age – the *Dispensation of the Law,* which extended from the giving of the Law by Jehovah-*Yahweh* through Moses, and its acceptance of the Law by Israel at Mount Sinai. It is considered one of the most conditional covenants in Scripture in that *if* the children of Israel obeyed the laws of the covenant, then they would receive the blessings of the covenant, and *if* they did not, then judgment and punishment would follow. Though disobedience did not invalidate the covenant, it did make those who willfully practiced it ineligible for the covenant blessings. The particulars of the covenant that God made with the new nation of Israel included the receiving of a new identity as a holy nation, commandments, judgments, moral codes, civil laws, ceremonial laws and regulations by which the holy nation was to live by while in possession of the Promised Land. Finally, as a sign of the ratification of the covenant, strict observance of the Sabbath was instituted (Exodus 19:3–31:18).

After the Mosaic Covenant was established with Israel, God gives her the deed to the Promised Land under the Deuteronomic Covenant through Moses. In his four discourses, Moses begins with the reiteration of the statutes and ordinances contained in the Mosaic Covenant, followed by a more detailed exposition of the regulations and statutes of their obligations to God on how the nation is to conduct herself *while* they are in possession of the Promised Land. The promise was unconditional, but the possession was conditionally based on obedience to the Mosaic Law. In his third discourse, Moses spoke to the nation on the blessings she would enjoy for obedience, and the curses that would befall her for willful disobedience. Simply stated, God would bless the nation abundantly and make her the head nation of the world *if* they were obedient; but, *if* they willfully disobeyed the Mosaic Law, the consequential curses would be destruction, disease, drought, famine, oppression, exile, economic ruin, and destruction of the nation (Deuteronomy 1:1–30:20). On a final note, though disobedience did carry heavy consequences, it did not nullify the covenant; Israel still holds the deed to the Land of Promise that God promised to Abraham (Genesis 17:7-8), which was confirmed to Isaac (Genesis 26:1-5), and to Jacob (Genesis 28:13).

The Davidic Covenant is the last and most crucial covenant of the Old Testament. It contains God's everlasting promise to David that his house, his kingdom, and his throne will be established forever. C. I. Scofield writes, "It is the covenant, upon which the glorious kingdom of Christ "of the seed of David according to the flesh" is to be founded" (II Samuel 7, p. 362). Though the covenant is unconditional, "*if*" willful disobedience is practiced by anyone in the 'royal dynasty', chastisement would follow, but would not alter one single promise of the covenant. (Psalms 89:30-37). Finally, the fulfillment of the Davidic Covenant is currently believed to be held in abeyance until a literal fulfillment when Christ will rule the world from David's Throne (Luke 1:32-33). Dr. C. I. Scofield provides a succinct summary of the key elements in the Old Testament covenants.

> "(1) The Edenic Covenant (Gen. 1. 26-28, note) conditioned the life of man in innocency. (2) The Adamic Covenant (Gen. 3. 1-19, note) conditions the life of fallen man and gives promise of a Redeemer. (3) The Noahic Covenant (Gen. 9. 1, note) establishes the principle of human government. (4) The Abrahamic Covenant (Gen. 15, 18, note) founds the nation of Israel, and confirms, with specific additions, the Adamic promise of redemption. (5) The Mosaic Covenant (Ex. 19. 25, note) condemns all men. "for that all have sinned." (6) The Palestinian Covenant (Deut. 28.-30. 3, note) secures the final restoration and conversion of Israel. (7) The Davidic Covenant (2 Sam. 7. 8-17, note) establishes the perpetuity of the Davidic family (fulfilled in Christ, Mt. 1.1; Lk. 1. 31-33; Rom. 1.3), and of the Davidic kingdom, over Israel and over the whole earth; to be fulfilled in and by Christ (2 Sam. 7. 8-17; Zech. 12. 8; Lk. 1. 31-33; Acts 15. 14-17; 1 Cor. 15. 24)" (Hebrews 8, pp. 1297-1298).

Finally, to Noah, God gave His solemn oath that the earth would never again be destroyed by water, and as a sign of His faithfulness in accordance with Himself, Elohiym seals His oath by placing a rainbow over the earth as a reminder of this everlasting covenant (Genesis

9:17). In ratifying the Abrahamic everlasting Covenant, God also pledged His solemn oath to Abraham, and as a sign of remembrance, the act of circumcision of the flesh was instituted (Genesis 17:11). Lastly, in the ratification ceremony of the Mosaic Covenant between God and Israel, Moses offered burnt offerings to God, sprinkled the blood on both the altar and on the people (Exodus 24:8), and as a sign of remembrance, keeping the Sabbath holy was instituted (Exodus 31:17).

The New Covenant

"Behold, I will do a new thing; now it shall spring forth; shall ye not know it?" (Isaiah 43:19).

It All Fits Together

The Adamic Covenant between God and Adam conditioned the life of fallen man, and gave the promise of a redeemer. The Abrahamic Covenant was between God, Abraham, and Abraham's seed. It founded the new nation of Israel, confirmed the promise of a redeemer, and is the foundation of the Deuteronomic Land and Davidic Covenants. The Mosaic Covenant was between God and the new nation of Israel given through Moses, and conditioned the life under which the new nation was to live by as a holy nation. The Deuteronomic Land Covenant is the deed to the land promised to Abraham and to his descendents. It conditioned the holy nation of Israel on how they were to live *after* they enter the Promised Land. The Davidic Covenant was between God and David, and established the Davidic kingdom as promised to Abraham.

The New Covenant, as testified to in the New Testament, is one of the most unique, efficacious, divinely instigated, unconditional covenants that the great I AM THAT I AM has ever made with humanity since creation. It recuperates that which Adam lost under the Edenic Covenant, fulfills the promise that God made to Adam in Genesis 3:15 of, "in your seed all the nations of the earth shall be blessed" (Genesis 22:15) that was promised under the Adamic and Abrahamic Covenants, establishes the everlasting throne, and everlasting King and kingdom covenanted to David, and above all, fulfills the Law of the Mosaic Covenant as revealed by Christ Himself in the Sermon on the Mount. "*Do not think that I came to abolish the Law or the Prophets; I did not come to abolish but to fulfill. For truly I say to you, until heaven and earth pass away, not the smallest letter or stroke shall pass away from the Law, until all is accomplished"* (Matthew 5:17-18). Christ is the seed of David from the line of Judah, and King and heir to the throne of the kingdom under the Davidic Covenant.

Dr. C. I. Scofield traces the relationship of Christ in the New Covenant to each of the preceding covenants in his beautifully written summary.

> "The relation of Christ to the eight covenants is as follows: (1) To the Edenic Covenant, Christ, as the "second man" and the "last Adam" (1 Cor 15:45 - 47), takes the place over all things which the first Adam lost (Col 2:10; Heb 2:7 - 9). (2) He is the Seed of the woman of the Adamic Covenant (Gen 3:15; John 12:31; Gal 4:4; 1 John 3:8; Rev 20:10), and fulfilled its conditions of toil (Mark 6:3) and obedience (Phil 2:8; Heb 5:8). (3) As the greatest Son of Shem, in Him was fulfilled supremely the promise to Shem in the Noahic Covenant (Gen 9:16, note; Col 2:9). (4) He is the Seed to whom the promises were made in the Abrahamic Covenant, the Son of Abraham obedient unto death (Gen 22:18; Gal 3:16; Phil 2:8). (5) He lived sinlessly under the Mosaic Covenant and bore for us its curse (Gal 3:10 - 13). (6) He lived obediently as a Jew in the land under the Palestinian Covenant, and will yet perform its gracious promises (Deu. 28:1 - 30:9). (7) He is the Seed, Heir, and King under the Davidic Covenant (Mat 1:1; Luke 1:31 - 33). And (8) His sacrifice is the foundation of the New Covenant (Mat 26:28; 1 Cor 11:25)" (Hebrews 8, p. 1298).

The "Highway of Seed" by Dr. C I. Scofield is also worth repeating. It traces the lineage of Christ and the 'first promise of a Redeemer' back to the seed of Adam's descendants.

> "Abel, Seth, Noah (Gen. 6. 8-10), Shem (Gen. 9. 26, 27), Abraham (Gen. 12. 1-4), Isaac (Gen. 17. 19-21), Jacob (Gen. 28. 10-14), Judah (Gen. 49. 10), David (2 Sam. 7. 5-17),

Immanuel-Christ (Isa. 7. 9-14; Mt. I. 1. 20-23; 1 John 3. 8; John 12. 31)" (Genesis 3, p. 9).

Additionally, Matthew lights up the 'highway of seed' by tracing the ancestry of Christ from the Davidic line. With few words, Matthew begins by stating, *"The genealogy of Jesus Christ, the son of David, the son of Abraham"* (Matthew 1:1). Matthew continues tracing the seed from the line of Judah, Jacob's son, to whom was born Perez, and from Perez follow six generations of direct descendants to Boaz. From Boaz came his son Obed, and to Obed was born Jesse, and to Jesse was born King David, the great grandson of Boaz (vv. 5-6). Matthew then continues with the lineage of David whose son was Solomon, and from King Solomon fourteen generations of direct descendants are listed *before* the Babylonian deportation occurred, followed by fourteen more generations before the birth of Joseph, the husband of Mary. Matthew finishes his record by summing up the generations that passed from the time of Abraham to the time of Christ, which came to a grand total of forty-two generations (Matthew 1:3-17). Luke also traces the forty-two generations of the 'highway of seed' of Christ from Joseph's lineage to King David, and also includes the names of seventy-two generations from the direct line of Seth, the son of Adam (Luke 3:23-38). Thus confirming what Paul wrote, "Christ being *born of the seed of David according to the flesh*" (Romans 1:3), and of the great prophecy given in Genesis 3:15.

The New Covenant Foretold

By definition, to declare something new implies that it has never existed before. Following the footprints of God through the records of the covenants in the Old Testament now leads us into the New Testament. However, it should not come as a surprise that it pleased God to give His people a hope by the foretelling of this encouraging news through His Prophets Jeremiah, Ezekiel, and Joel.

> *"Behold, days are coming", declares the LORD, "when I will make a new covenant with the house of Israel and with the house of Judah. Not like the covenant which I made with their fathers in the day I took them by the hand to bring them out of the land of Egypt, My covenant which they broke, although I was a husband to them," declares the LORD. "But this is the covenant which I will make with the house of Israel after those days," declares the LORD, "I will put My law within them, and on their heart I will write it; and I will be their God, and they shall be My people. And they shall not each again, each man his neighbor and each man his brother, saying 'Know the LORD,' for they shall all know Me, from the least of them to the greatest of them," declares the LORD, "for I will forgive their iniquity, and their sin I will remember no more" "* (Jeremiah 31:31-34; Hebrews 8:7-12).

And to Israel, His 'first-born' the prophecy came through Ezekiel.

> *"For I will take you from the nations, gather you from all the lands, and bring you into your own land. Then I will sprinkle clean water on you, and you will be clean; I will cleanse you from all your filthiness and from all your idols. Moreover, I will give you a new heart and put a new spirit within you; and I will remove the heart of stone from your flesh and give you a heart of flesh. And I will put My Spirit within you and cause you to walk in My statutes, and you will be careful to observe My ordinances. And you will live in the land that I gave to your*

forefathers; so you will be My people, and I will be your God" (Ezekiel 36:24-28).

And through the Prophet Joel.

"And it will come about after this that I will pour out My Spirit on all mankind; and your sons and daughters will prophesy, your old men will dream dreams, your young men will see visions. And even on the male and female servants I will pour out My Spirit in those days. And I will display wonders in the sky and on the earth, the sun will be turned into darkness, and the moon into blood, before the great and awesome day of the LORD comes. And it will come about that whoever calls on the name of the LORD will be delivered" (Joel 2:28-32);

In anticipation of the fulfillment of this promise, announcements of the coming Messiah through the 'seed of a woman' are made to the house of David through Isaiah. *"Therefore the LORD Himself will give you a sign: Behold, a virgin will be with child and bear a son, and she will call His name Immanuel"* (7:14). Zechariah, the father of John the Baptist, was given a similar prophecy at the birth of his son, telling him that John would be the one who would 'prepare the way' for the Messiah by giving God's people the *knowledge* of salvation by the forgiveness of their sins (Luke 1:13-17).

"Blessed be the Lord God of Israel, For He has visited us and accomplished redemption for His people, And has raised up a horn of salvation for us In the house of David His servant; As He spoke by the mouth of His holy prophets from of old – Salvation FROM OUR ENEMIES, and FROM THE HAND OF ALL WHO HATE US; to show mercy toward our fathers, And to remember His holy covenant, The oath which He swore to Abraham our father, To grant us that we, being delivered from the hand of our enemies, Might serve Him without fear, In holiness and righteousness before Him all our days. And you, child, will be called the prophet of the Most High; For you will go on BEFORE THE LORD to PREPARE HIS WAYS; To give

> *to His people the knowledge of salvation by the forgiveness of their sins"* (Luke 1:68-77).

To confirm the prophecy of the coming of Christ, God sent His angel Gabriel to Mary to make the final announcement.

> *"And behold, you will conceive in your womb, and bear a son, and you shall name Him Jesus. He will be great, and will be called the Son of the Most High; and the Lord God will give Him the throne of His father David; and He will reign over the house of Jacob forever; and His kingdom will have no end"* (Luke 1:31-33).

Finally, in anticipation of this historical event, an angel was sent to Joseph to confirm that it was indeed Mary through whom the Messiah would come, and instructed Joseph to name his son Jesus. "*And she will bear a Son; and you shall call His name Jesus, for it is He who shall save His people from their sins"* (Matthew 1:21).

Offer of the New Covenant

"For God so loved the world that He gave His only begotten Son, that whoever believes in Him should not perish, but have eternal life. For God did not send the Son into the world to judge the world; but that the world should be saved through Him" (John 3:16-17).

The New Covenant is an unconditional, spiritual covenant made between God, Israel, and humanity. It contains one of the richest treasuries of covenant promises ever recorded, and is probably one of the easiest to understand, which by nature makes it hard to accept. It *was inaugurated and ratified solely by the sacrificial blood of Christ* (John 19:30; Hebrews 9:12), by *the resurrection* (Luke 24:13-40; John 20:24-29; 21:1-23; Acts 1:3), and *the ascension* (Luke 24:46-51; John 20:17) *of God's only begotten Son, Jesus Christ.* Moreover, the establishment of the New Covenant ushered in the *Dispensation of Grace*, which extends from the death and resurrection of Christ until His return to receive His Bride, the Church (*Systematic Theology,* 1978, Volume I, pp. 40-41).

The New unconditional Covenant of grace pledges forgiveness of sin (inherited from Adam), "*I will forgive their iniquity, and their sin I will remember no more*" (Jeremiah 31:31-34), and offers the free gift of salvation by faith in Jesus Christ, or an immediate transference from spiritual death to eternal life to those who believe. "*Whoever believes in Him should not perish, but have eternal life*" (John 3:16). The New Covenant of grace restores the intimate love relationship between God and humanity that was lost by the fall of Adam, and restores the privilege to 'eat freely from the tree of life' that was originally afforded to him in the Garden of Eden. "*Even as Thou gavest Him authority over all mankind, that to all whom Thou hast given Him, He may give eternal life. This is eternal life, that they may know Thee, the only true God, and Jesus Christ whom Thou hast sent*" (John 17:2-3).

Additionally, as newly adopted sons and daughters of God, the New Covenant of grace promises an inheritance of all spiritual blessings of the kingdom of God—it is no wonder that it is called "The Good News". The New Covenant was first offered to and rejected by God's "first-born" nation of Israel, "*Then you shall say to the Pharaoh, 'Thus says the LORD, Israel is My son, My first-born'* " (Exodus 4:22), and is currently being offered to all of humanity with the only prerequisite "*if you confess with your mouth Jesus as Lord, and believe in your heart that God raised Him from the dead, you shall be saved*" (Romans 10:9-10).

The Greatest Commandment

It is all about love isn't it. The innate need for love is universal. It is the greatest gift ever given to humanity. It has no boundaries and knows no prejudices; and above all, it has no fear. The two greatest commandments ever given by God are about love. During His ministry on earth, the Pharisees asked Jesus which commandment in the Law was the greatest, and Jesus answered,

> "*And you shall love the LORD your God with all your heart and with all your soul, and with all your mind* (Deuteronomy 6:5). *This is the great and foremost commandment.* And *a second is like it, You shall love your neighbor as yourself* (Leviticus 19:18). *On these two commandments depend the whole Law and the Prophets*" (Matthew 22:37-40).

The greatest demonstration of God's unconditional love for humanity was accomplished when He sent His only Beloved Son as the sacrificial lamb to be the atonement of the sin of the world so that by reconciliation, humanity may once again enjoy the close and loving relationship with Him that was intended since eternity past.

The Ratification

When the LORD Jehovah ratified the everlasting covenant He made with Abraham, He made a solemn oath between Himself in the full essence of the Godhead (sheba' shib'aĥ, a declaration made seven times), and as a sign of the ratification, the act of circumcision of the flesh was instituted. Of greater significance, when God executed His final judgment of death upon every first born in the land of Egypt, the children of Israel were spared by applying the blood of a lamb around the doors of their houses so that when death came, they would be passed over (Exodus 12:14-24). Likewise, for the Mosaic Covenant, the ratification of the covenant was made with a burnt offering by which the *blood* was sprinkled on both the altar and on the people, and the sign of remembrance was strict observance of the Sabbath. However, the ratification of the New Covenant of grace is based *solely* on the shed blood of Jesus Christ, the sacrificial Lamb of God who came to take away the sin of the world (John 1:29). Moreover, because of the blood He shed for us, when death comes, whoever believes in Him will be passed over and spared the final judgment of eternal death. Finally, in anticipation of His death, as a sign of remembrance of the ratification of the New Covenant, Jesus (*Jehoshua-Elohiym*) instituted the observance of communion at the Last Supper.

> *"And while they were eating, Jesus took bread, and after a blessing, He broke it and gave it to the disciples and said, "Take, eat; this is My body." And He took a cup and gave thanks, and gave it to them, saying, "Drink from it, all of you; for this is My blood of the covenant, which is to be shed on behalf of many for forgiveness of sins" "* (Matthew 26:26-28; Mark 14:22-24, Luke 22:19-20).

Today, the Body of Christ (His Bride, the Church) around the world practices this observance in remembrance of the price that Christ paid on our behalf for the atonement of sin. In his letter to the Corinthians, Paul succinctly states, *"you are not your own: For you have been bought with a price"* (1 Corinthians 6:19c-20a).

> *"Drink from it, all of you; for this is My blood of the covenant, which is to be shed on behalf of many for forgiveness of sins"* (Matthew 26:26-28; Mark 14:22-24, Luke 22:19-20).

The Inauguration

"And I will ask the Father, and He will give you another Helper, that He may be with you forever; that is the Spirit of truth, whom the world cannot receive, because it does not behold Him or know Him, but you know Him because He abides with you, and will be in you. I will not leave you as orphans; I will come to you" (John 16-18).

The promise of redemption and deliverance from spiritual death to a new life that was promised by Jehovah-Elohiym since creation was fulfilled by the sacrificial death, resurrection, and ascension of Christ. *"For He delivered us from the domain of darkness, and transferred us to the kingdom of His beloved Son, in whom we have redemption, the forgiveness of sins. And He is the image of the invisible God, the first-born of all creation"* (Colossians 1:13-15). However, the inauguration of the New Covenant of grace did not take place until after the resurrected Christ ascended to be seated at the right hand of the throne of God (Acts 1:9-11; Mark 16:19; Hebrews 1:3; 1 Peter 3:22), and poured forth His Holy Spirit at Pentecost (Acts 2:1-21), thus ushering in the Dispensation of Grace, and fulfilling prophesies foretold by the prophets of old. In his New Covenant studies, Dr. Larry D. Pettegrew gives a succinct explanation of the inauguration including a short note on the provisions, and offers a short conclusion.

> "*The Provisions*. The specific terms "New Covenant" and "everlasting covenant" do not exhaust NT references to the New Covenant. Clearly the provisions of the New Covenant are also operative, beginning with the inauguration of the New

Covenant on the day of Pentecost. Peter insists, that in initial fulfillment of the promised Holy Spirit, Christ, "having been exalted to the right hand of God, and having received from the Father the promise of the Holy Spirit, poured forth this which you both see and hear" (Acts 2:33). Actually, all the teaching about the Holy Spirit in the New Testament (especially about the "promise of the Spirit" [Eph 1:13; Gal. 3:14]) is evidence that the New Covenant has been inaugurated.

The new level of forgiveness of sins promised in OT prophecies of the New Covenant also pervades the NT. "Above all things," writes Leon Morris, "the new system that Jesus had established meant the forgiveness of men's sins. . . . His blood avails to put them in right relationship to God." Morris notes that the remedy for sins, in the Book of Hebrews alone, is prevalent: 1:3; 2:17; 8:12; 9:15, 26, 28; 10:12, 17, 18, 26. Morris concludes, "The effect of all this is to stress the completeness with which Christ has dealt with sin. Whatever needed to be done He has done, fully, finally. Sin no longer exists as a force. . . . Christ has made it null and void. He has broken its power." The "entire New Testament teaching on forgiveness" in fact, is "an extended exposition of the blessing of the new covenant". . . ." (The New Covenant by Larry D. Pettegrew, *The Master's Seminary Journal*, Fall 1999, pp. 267-268, http://www.tms.edu/tmsj/tmsj10q.pdf).

CONCLUSION

"This essay has emphasized that the relationship of Christ to the New Covenant and the church to Christ does not in any way negate the future fulfillment of the New Covenant with Israel. The Lord made the New Covenant with Israel and presented it to Israel as a foundation of the messianic kingdom program. But the nation rejected the Messiah and His kingdom. Thus the New Covenant will not be fulfilled with Israel until the Day of the Lord events when the nation in repentance afflicted (Isa 53:4; cf. Zech 12:10-14). Before that happens, Gentiles outside God's

> covenant program and Jews under the shadow of a curse are blessed to be able to participate in the New Covenant. This they can do through Spirit baptism into Christ at the time of conversion. Though the Servant/Messiah came to His own people, 'His own did not receive Him. But as many as received Him, to them He gave the right to become the children of God, even to those who believe in His name . . .' (John 1:11-12)" (Ibid., pp. 270-271).

Dr. Pettegrew regards the New Testament as being the 'New Covenant document' that should be viewed as 'an instruction manual' on how to live out the New Covenant in the present age of grace.

> "Christ inaugurated the New Covenant by pouring out the Holy Spirit on the day of Pentecost. The New Testament thus becomes a New Covenant document" (Ibid., pp. 266-267).

More importantly, the *Jehovah-Elohiym* of the Old Covenant of redemption revealed Himself in the flesh in the New Covenant of redemption as the person of Jesus Christ (*Jehoshua-Elohiym*), the Son of God, which is the most highly exalted name of the Deity under which God has sworn that every knee of those who are in heaven, on earth and under the earth will bow, and every tongue will confess that the great I AM THAT I AM, *Jesus Christ* is Lord (Isaiah 45:23; Philippians 2:9-11).

Spiritual Blessings under the New Covenant of Grace

"Remember Him before the silver cord is broken and the golden bowl is crushed, the pitcher by the well is shattered and the wheel at the cistern is crushed" (Ecclesiastes 12:6).

Salvation

Beginning with the seven days of creation and ending with the seven last plagues mentioned in Revelation 21:9, Scripture is saturated with the number seven. Recalling the Hebrew word for *sworn* (shâba') is translated to mean "to take an oath; to be complete or to seven oneself as if by repeating a declaration seven times", the fact that Jesus (*Jehoshua-Elohiym*) commits the believer to the Father for safe-keeping seven times in His farewell prayer to the Father (John 17:2-24), He is taking an immutable oath between Himself (in the full essence of the Godhead) and the believer under this everlasting covenant.

(1) *"Father, the hour has come; glorify Thy Son, that the Son may glorify Thee, even as Thou gavest Him authority over all mankind that to all whom Thou has given Him, He may give eternal life" (*17:1-2).

(2) *"I manifested Thy name to the men whom Thou gavest Me out of the world"* (17:6b).

(3) *"Thine they were and Thou gavest them to Me, and they have kept Thy word"* (17:6c).

(4) *"I ask on their behalf; I do not ask on behalf of the world, but of those whom Thou hast given Me; for they are Thine"* (17:9).

(5) *"Holy Father, keep them in Thy name, the name which Thou hast given Me; that they may be one, even as We are"* (17:11c).

(6) *"While I was with them, I was keeping them in Thy name which Thou hast given Me; and I guarded them, and not one of them perished but the son of perdition, that the Scripture might be fulfilled"* (17:12).

(7) *"Father, I desire that they also, whom Thou has given Me, be with Me where I am, in order that they may behold My glory, which Thou hast given Me; for Thou didn't love Me before the foundation of the world"* (17:24).

Of this exalted position, Dr. Scofield writes:

"Seven times Jesus speaks of believers as given to Him by the Father (vs. 2, 6 twice, 9, 11, 12, 24). Jesus Christ is God's love-gift to the world (John 3:16), and believers are the Father's love-gift to Jesus Christ. It is Christ who commits the believer to the Father for safe-keeping, so that the believer's security rests upon the Father's faithfulness to His Son Jesus Christ" (John 17, p. 1139).

Moreover, because of the oath taken between God and Christ, all that He asked for on our behalf has already been done. It can be thought of in terms of being a done deal—signed with His blood, sealed with His Spirit, and delivered by the God Most High as a sacred oath to His Son.

Forgiveness

"In Him we have redemption through His blood, the forgiveness of our trespasses, according to the riches of His grace, which He lavished upon us" (Ephesians 1:7–8).

Under the New Covenant of grace, the forgiveness of sin is unconditional and includes the forgiveness of sins past, present, and future as it relates to salvation. The word *forgiveness* in Greek carries numerous definitions that convey different meanings. In his writings to both the Ephesians (1:7) and to the Colossians (1:14), lexiconists point out that Paul uses the Greek word *aphesis*, which means "to release from bondage or imprisonment; a pardon of sins (letting them go as if they had never been committed), and a remission of the penalty." If in fact this means that we are already forgiven for whatever transgressions we are currently committing and includes those we have yet to commit, then what did John mean when he wrote the following? "*If we confess our sins, He is faithful and righteous to forgive us our sins and to cleanse us from all unrighteousness*" (1 John 1:9). The seeming paradox that we are forgiven yet must be forgiven can be easily cleared up by understanding the differences between the definitions of the different words used by the apostles. As opposed to the word *aphesis* that Paul uses, John uses *aphiemi,* which means, "to disregard" (Thayer's Greek Lexicon, 2009, G859, G863, pp. 88-89). Paul's use of *aphesis* relates to man's permanent standing in Christ while John's use of *aphiemi* relates to man's standing within the body of Christ. One relates to the kind of forgiveness that a believer receives the moment salvation occurs, while the other relates to personal forgiveness *after* salvation. The first relies completely on God to forgive the believer, while the second relies on man to *ask* for forgiveness from God for personal offences committed after salvation. In either case, the act of forgiveness relies wholly upon God's character in accordance with His divine nature (Ephesians 2:7). This great spiritual truth is revealed by Jesus in John's historical Upper Room Discourse.

> *"He poured water into a basin and began to wash the disciple's feet, and to wipe them with the towel with which He was girded"* (John 13:5). *"Simon Peter said to Him, "Lord, not my feet only, but also my hands and my head." Jesus said to him, "He who has bathed needs only to wash his feet, but is completely clean; and you are clean" "* (13:9-10).

John MacArthur comments on the need for daily forgiveness *after* salvation.

> "The cleansing that Christ does at salvation never needs to be repeated—Atonement is complete at that point. But all who have been cleansed by God's gracious justification need constant washing in the experiential sense as they battle sin in the flesh. Believers are justified and granted imputed righteousness (Phil. 3:8-9), but they still need sanctification and personal righteousness (Phil. 3:12-14)" (The MacArthur Bible Commentary, 2005, p. 1402).

Redemption

"I have wiped out your transgressions like a thick cloud, and your sins like a heavy mist. Return to Me, for I have redeemed you" (Isaiah 44:22b).

There are two different Hebrew words used in the Old Testament that define the term redemption. The first word, pâdâh, is translated to mean "to ransom, redeem, rescue, and deliver". The greatest act of pâdâh in the Old Testament was the divine manifestation of God's

Almighty power in redeeming His people from the hands of the Egyptians. The second term, gâ'al, is translated to mean "to redeem, or to act as kinsman-redeemer" (NAS Old Testament Hebrew Lexicon, 2010, H6299, H1350, http://www.biblestudytools.com/lexicons/hebrew/nas/, 2012). Corresponding to ga'al, an illustrative narrative of the foreshadowing of Christ as our kinsman-redeemer can be found in the beautifully written story of Boaz and Ruth that sketches out the *legal* responsibilities of a kinsman-redeemer for those who were under the Law. In order to continue the family line, the custom required a close relative to marry the widow of the deceased kinsman (Deuteronomy 25:5–10). Although not explicitly stated on the pages of this story, some striking similarities parallel Boaz's act of ga'al on behalf of Ruth, and Christ's act of redemption on behalf of His church. As the story is written, Ruth was a widowed Moabite who after marrying a Judaite became a convert; therefore she was under the Mosaic Law. Because Boaz was not Ruth's nearest relative, he had no legal responsibility to act on her behalf as kinsman-redeemer. Nevertheless, by a show of His love and grace, Boaz found a way to fulfill the law and ultimately became Ruth's kinsman-redeemer.

In the New Testament, however, the definition of the Greek term of redemption carries a much deeper meaning. The terms *redeem* and *redeemed* are translated as (1) *Lutroo,̄* "to liberate by payment of ransom; to deliver from evils of every kind, both internal and external". (2) *Lutrōsis,* "a deliverance from the penalty of sin", and (3) exagorazō, "of Christ freeing the elect from the dominion of the Mosaic Law at the price of his death" (Thayer's Greek Lexicon, 2009, G1805, G3084, G3085, pp. 220, 384). Since Christ did not come to abolish the Law but to fulfill it (Matthew 5:17), these particular qualities are peculiar to the term *redemption* in the New Testament. Therefore, the moment our souls are redeemed by our kinsman-redeemer, we are delivered from the power of the prince of darkness (the diabolical system that is hostile toward God) and transported into God's kingdom (*lutroo*̄), delivered from the penalty of sin (*lutrōsis*), and freed from the Law (*exagorazo*̄). More importantly, because the price that was paid to buy back what rightfully belongs to God was the full actualization of the crucifixion, resurrection, and ascension of Christ, the power of redemption is in the hands of the redeemer and not of the redeemed.

"You are not your own: For you have been bought with a price" (1 Corinthians 6:19c-20a).

Justification

"So then as through one transgression there resulted condemnation to all men, even so through one act of righteousness there resulted justification of life to all men" (Romans 5:18).

Imputation Must Have a Direction

The supernatural act of divine imputation of the righteousness of Christ occurs at the time of salvation (Romans 4:22-25). Though the terms 'to be justified' and 'to be made righteous' are used interchangeably throughout the New Testament, Paul, when writing to the Romans, particularly uses the term 'justification' in a legal sense. The term justification is translated from the Greek word dikaiōsis to mean 'a judicial decree' made by God by which He acquits man and declares them free from guilt through the imputed righteousness of Christ, "*who was delivered up because of our transgressions and was raised because of our justification*" (Romans 4:25; 5:18). The second word that Paul uses is dikaiōma, translated to mean "the act of God declaring men free from guilt and acceptable to Him" (Thayer's Greek Lexicon, 2009, G1347, G1345, p. 151). Paul summarizes by saying, "*So then as through one transgression there resulted condemnation to all men, even so through one act of righteousness there resulted justification of life to all men*" (Romans 5:16). Both declare that the judicial decree that acquits man, declares him free from condemnation and judgment, and presents him righteous before God was done *solely* by an act of God. *"being justified as a gift by His grace through the redemption which is in Christ Jesus; whom God displayed publicly as a propitiation in His Blood through faith"* (Romans 3:24). Thus, we are pronounced innocent on all counts of the charges against us, and as in all legal cases, because of the existence of the clause of double jeopardy, we can never be charged for any of these crimes again. Moreover, because of the acquittal, these crimes will never appear on our record.

Reconciliation

"For while we were enemies, we were reconciled to God through the death of His Son; much more, having been reconciled, we shall be saved by his life" (Romans 5:10).

To say that we were reconciled to God connotes that there once was harmony in the relationship between God and man. Lexiconists translate this Greek term as katallassō and define it to mean "to receive one into favor or to return to favor with" (Thayer's Greek Lexicon, 2009, G2644, p. 333). In Paul's message to the Corinthians, he states that God's love for His creation ran so deep that when the relationship between Himself and His creation was broken, He took it upon Himself (in the full essence of the Godhead) to reconcile the world by manifesting Himself in the flesh, bound it with the death and resurrection of Christ, and sealed it with His spirit through His ascension (2 Corinthians 5:18–21). The term world that Paul uses is kosmos, meaning 'the universe', is significant inasmuch as it is defined to mean His perfect creation in its entirety as He originally created it to be prior to the angelic rebellion that resulted in the corruption of His perfect system. This includes the relationship that man had with God, His constitution, His government, and the angelic sphere (Ibid., G2889, pp. 356-357). However, reconciliation of an estranged relationship requires a willingness of both parties to want to be reconciled. In his careful analysis, Dr. Chafer clarifies the differences between the reconciliation of the world and the reconciliation of the believer to God that Paul presented to the Corinthians. He notes:

> "A difference will be recognized between the reconciliation of the world as declared in 5:19–and the reconciliation of the individual–as declared in 5:20–21. The reconciliation of the world does not obviate the reconciliation of the individual. The latter is that form of reconciliation which is applied to the believer's heart and results in a perfect and unending peace between God and the reconciled believer. To be perfectly reconciled to God on the ground of the merit of Christ, as it is true of every child of God, is a position of blessedness indeed and is one of the riches of God's Divine Grace" (*Systematic Theology,* Volume III, p. 236).

As in the case of all estranged relationships, to be reconciled to God now wholly depends upon the willingness of the individual to be reconciled to Him—God did His part, now individuals must do theirs.

Delivered from the Power of Darkness

"For He delivered us from the domain of darkness, and transferred us to the kingdom of His beloved Son" (Colossians 1:13).

The concept of deliverance from the domain of darkness and transference into God's kingdom of light (*lutroo)* may be illustrated by visualizing a type of Star *Wars* scenario where an evil force similar to a Darth Vader, a prince in the galaxy of light, plots to overthrow the empire. When his plan is uncovered, he is cast out of the empire and sentenced to darkness forevermore. Vader promises to overtake the forces of light by turning them over to the dark side. In attempt of doing so, Vader kidnaps children from the empire and holds them as prisoners in his dungeon. While the galactic war between the forces of darkness and the forces of light is being fought outside the prison gates, Skywalker comes to the rescue, and in a blink of an eye, the gates are opened and the prisoners are spirited away from the galactic sphere of darkness and taken to a magnificent kingdom in the sphere of light. However much of a fantasy this picture paints, it is not far from the truth. In his exposition of Colossians 1:13, Dr. Norman L. Geisler notes:

> "This light is the spiritual sphere to which believers have been transferred from the dominion of darkness (Luke 22:53; Acts 26:18; Eph. 6:12). From this dominion (*exousias*, "power, authority") of darkness (John 3:19–20) believers have been rescued, delivered. Through Christ they were brought from a rebel kingdom and placed under the sovereignty of their rightful King" (The Bible Knowledge Commentary: New Testament, 1983, p. 672, ed. John F. Walvoord, Roy B. Zuck).

In his careful analysis of the great exchange, Dr. Chafer observes:

> "In Colossians 1:13, the term "translated" evidently refers to the removal from the sphere of Satan's dominion to that of Christ. The kingdom is that of God, which may be considered also the kingdom of the Son of His love. Entrance into the kingdom of God is by the new birth (John 3:5). Such a position is far more than merely to be delivered from darkness, however much the advantage of that may be; it is to be inducted into an established in the kingdom of God's dear Son" *(Systematic Theology,* Volume III, 248).

Thus, at the moment of salvation, a believer is supernaturally transferred from the domain of darkness into the spiritual sphere of light in the kingdom of God.

Heavenly Citizenship

"For our citizenship is in heaven, from which also we eagerly wait for a Savior, the Lord Jesus Christ" (Philippians 3:20).

In addition to the supernatural acts that simultaneously occur at the time of salvation—forgiveness of all transgressions, past, present, and future, redemption, justification, reconciliation, and immediate transference from the domain of darkness into the kingdom of God—a further provision in the New Covenant of grace granted to the believer is the divine position of heavenly citizenship. In the natural realm, one ordinarily becomes a legal citizen of their country by natural birth. Likewise, in the spiritual realm a believer becomes a legal citizen of the kingdom by *spiritual* birth. The supernatural act of a spiritual birth was explained to a Pharisee called Nichodemus when he stated that it was not possible for a man to enter into his mother's womb a second time to be born again. Jesus replied, "*Truly, truly, I say to you, unless one is born of water and the Spirit, he cannot enter into the kingdom of God. That which is born of the flesh is flesh; and that which is born of the Spirit is spirit"* (John 3:5–6). With few words, Dr. Edwin A. Blum explains the difference. He writes:

> "There are two distinct realms: one is of fallen man (the flesh) and the other is of God (the Spirit). A fallen person cannot regenerate himself; he needs a divine operation. Only God's Holy Spirit can regenerate a human spirit" (The Bible Knowledge Commentary: New Testament, 1983, p. 281, ed. John F. Walvoord, Roy B. Zuck).

Paul was keenly aware of the new spiritual position. In writing to the Philippians, Paul encourages them to remember that while they are being enculturated by earthly social norms and mores, they are to set their minds on the spiritual reality of their new heavenly position (Philippians 3:19–20). Of this same provision, Dr. Chafer comments:

"Citizenship itself—whether realized at the present moment or not—is an abiding position accorded to all who believe. In truth, the occupation of that citizenship by instant removal from this sphere would be the normal experience for each Christian when he is saved" *(Systematic Theology,* Volume III, p. 252).

Direct Access to God the Father

"Let us therefore draw near with confidence to the throne of grace, that we may receive mercy and may find grace in time of need" (Hebrews 4:16).

In the Old Testament, high priests ordained by God were the only ones who were allowed direct access into the inner sanctuary of the tabernacle (mishkān̂) to act as mediators on behalf of God's people; otherwise, this amazingly high privilege was only given to a handful of notable men of great faith such as Abraham, and Moses. The painstaking instructions given to Moses for the construction of the tabernacle include precise dimensions for the construction of the Ark of the Covenant, the mercy seat, the veil that separated the holy place from the inner holy of holies where the Ark was kept, and the door that separated the inner portion from the outer portion of the sanctuary are given in detail in Exodus 25–27. *"And let them construct a sanctuary for Me, that I may dwell among them. According to all that I am going to show you, as the pattern of the tabernacle and the pattern of all its furniture, just so you shall construct it"* (Exodus 25:8–9).

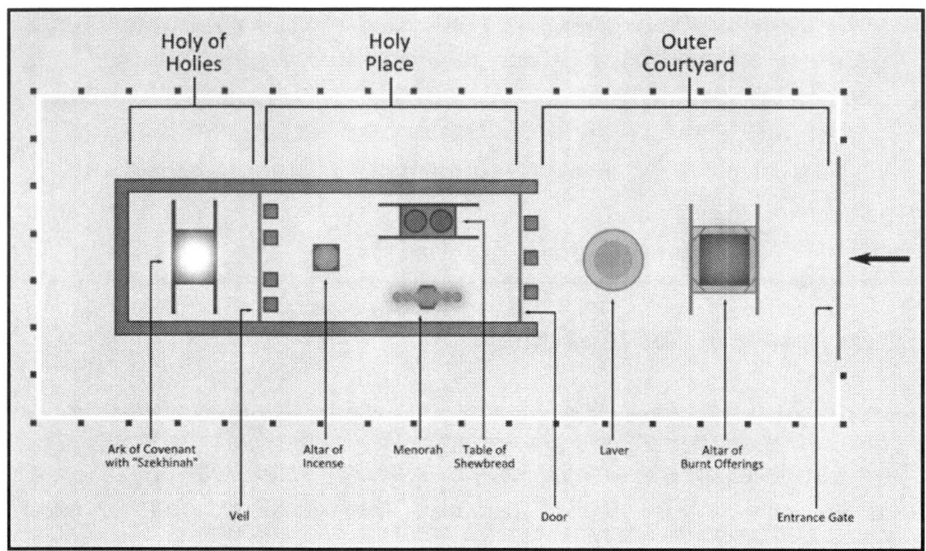

Moses' Tabernacle
Source: http://commons.wikimedia.org/wiki/File:Tabernacle.png, 2009

Precisely as instructed, the mercy seat and the cherubim that were stationed on top of the Ark of the Covenant were made of pure gold, and the cherubim facing one another were placed as guardians (Genesis 3:24). "*The cherubim shall have their wings spread upward, covering the mercy seat with their wings and facing one another; the faces of the cherubim are to be turned toward the mercy seat" and a gold cherub at each end that overshadowed the mercy seat"* (Exodus 25:20).

The Mercy Seat, illustration from the 1890 Holman Bible http://commons.wikimedia.org/wiki/File:Holman_The_Mercy_Seat.jpg, 2010

The moment Christ released his last breath, the veil that separated the inner holy of holies from the holy place was supernaturally torn down, thus restoring to the believer the same high privilege that was once afforded to Adam before his fall from grace. Dr. Westerholm expresses the importance of understanding the symbolic need for the tabernacle, the role that the high priest played as mediator between the people and God, the blood sacrifices made for the atonement of sin on behalf of the nation, and the supernatural change that occurred the moment Christ died on the cross. He writes:

> "It is in the Epistle to the Hebrews that most clearly develops the relation between the tabernacle of the old dispensation and the 'great salvation' of the new. The author emphasizes the divinely ordained but imperfect role that the tabernacle and its

services played. The tabernacle was but a copy of the heavenly sanctuary (Heb. 8:5; 9:24; Acts 7:44; Rev: 15:5) and was designed to foreshadow things to come (10:1). Its regulations were temporary (9:10), its sacrifices imperfect (9:9; 10:1–4), and the access it afforded to the divine presence very limited (9:7). But Christ has offered Himself as a perfect, once-for-all sacrifice (9:12–14, 26). He has entered the heavenly sanctuary not made with human hands (8:2; 9:11), thereby opening a 'new and living way' into God's presence for all believers (10:19–22; 6:19). Believers can therefore approach the 'throne of grace' (i.e., the heavenly counterpart of the tabernacle 'mercy seat' with the confidence that they will obtain the mercy and grace that they need (4:16)" (Eerdman's *International Standard Bible Encyclopedia*, Volume Q-Z, 1988, p. 705, ed. Geoffrey W. Bromiley).

This historic event is recorded by Matthew, Mark, and Luke.

"And behold, the veil of the temple was torn in two from top to bottom, and the earth shook; and the rocks were split" (Matthew 27:51).

"And Jesus uttered a loud cry, and breathed His last, And the veil of the temple was torn in two from top to bottom" (Mark 15:38).

"And it was now about the sixth hour, and darkness fell over the whole land until the ninth hour, the sun being obscured; and the veil of the temple was torn in two" (Luke 23:45).

Under the New Covenant, the veil symbolizing the separation between God and man no longer prohibits a believer from entering into the inner most holy of holies. By the fully efficacious blood sacrifice of Jesus Christ, and acting as the new High Priest on behalf of humanity, through the supernatural power of the Holy Spirit, a believer in Christ is now granted direct access to His throne of grace. The apostle John simply states, "*What we have seen and heard we proclaim to you also, that you also may have fellowship with us; and indeed our fellowship is with the Father, and with His Son Jesus Christ"* (1 John 1:3).

Adoption

"He predestined us to adoption as sons through Jesus Christ to Himself, according to the kind intention of His will, to the praise of the glory of His grace, which He freely bestowed upon us in the Beloved" (Ephesians 1:5–6).

Another provision afforded the believer under the New Covenant of grace is the supernatural act of divine adoption. In natural adoption, an outsider may become a legitimate member of a family through the legal system. Likewise, in spiritual adoption, because Christ signed the adoption papers with His own blood, a spiritual child of God goes from being an outsider to a fully legitimate child of God. Moreover, this divine act of adoption places believers in a new position that makes them eligible to receive all of the benefits and privileges that are afforded to all other legitimate family members in the body of Christ, including an inheritance. The Greek word that Paul uses for adoption is uihothesia (pronounced *hwee-oth-es-ee'-ah*), which means "the nature and condition of the true disciples in Christ, who by receiving the Spirit of God into their souls become sons and daughters of God" (Thayer's Greek Lexicon, 2009, G5206, p. 634). Christ calls the spiritual birth "born-again" (John 3:3-6). Once the adoption has been completed, God "*seals it with the Holy Spirit of promise who is given as a pledge of our inheritance, with a view to the redemption of God's own possession, to the praise of His glory*" (Ephesians 1:13-14), and then showers His children with personal gifts from the full Godhead.

"If you then, being evil, know how to give good gifts to your children, how much more shall your heavenly Father give the Holy Spirit to those who ask Him?" (Luke 11:13).

Gifts from God the Father – Romans 12:3-8: *"For through the grace given to me I say to every man among you not to think more highly of himself than he ought to think; but to think so as to have sound judgment, as God has allotted to each a measure of faith"* (v. 3).

(1) Faith (v. 3).
(2) Prophecy (v. 6).
(3) Service (v. 7).
(4) Teaching (v. 7).
(5) Exhortation (v. 4).
(6) Giving (v. 8).
(7) Leadership (v. 8).
(8) Mercy (v. 8).

Ministry Gifts from God the Son – Ephesians 4:7-12: *"But to each one of us grace was given according to the measure of Christ's gift"* (v. 7).

(1) Apostles (v. 11).
(2) Prophets (v. 11).
(3) Evangelists (v. 11).
(4) Pastors (v. 11).
(5) Teachers (v. 11).

Spiritual Gifts from God the Holy Spirit – 1 Corinthians 12:1-11: *"Now there are varieties of gifts, but the same Spirit, And there are varieties of ministries, and the same Lord. And there are varieties of effects, but the same God who works all things in all persons. But to each one is given the manifestation of the Spirit for the common good"* (vv. 4–7).

(1) Word of wisdom through the Spirit (v. 8).
(2) Word of knowledge according to the same Spirit (v. 8).
(3) Faith by the same Spirit (v. 9).
(4) Healing by the one Spirit (v. 9).
(5) The effecting of miracles (v. 10).
(6) Prophecy (v. 10).
(7) The distinguishing of spirits (v. 10).
(8) Various kinds of tongues (v. 10).
(9) Interpretation of tongues. "But one and the same Spirit works all these things, distributing to each one individually just as He wills" (vv. 10–11).

Thus, by the divine act of spiritual adoption, as sons and daughters through the blood of Christ, believers instantly become members of the household of God, and then are showered with personal gifts from the full Godhead.

> *"For the gifts and the calling of God are irrevocable"* (Romans 11:19).

The Inheritance

"I pray that the eyes of your heart may be enlightened, so that you may know what is the hope of His calling, what are the riches of the glory of His inheritance in the saints" (Ephesians 1:18).

The term inheritance is translated from the Greek word klēronomia to mean "the eternal blessedness in the consummated kingdom of God which is to be expected after the visible return of Christ" (Thayer's Greek Lexicon, 2009, G2817, p. 349). An inheritance is usually thought of in terms of an earthly estate that is legally left to a loved one *after* the person passes away. However, if the phrase *earthly estate* is replaced with *heavenly estate*, then as "legal" citizens of heaven by spiritual birth, and sons and daughters of the family of God, it stands to follow that as heirs of God and joint-heirs with Christ (Romans 8:17), after Christ's earthly death believers legally inherited the riches of the kingdom. Dr. Donald K. McKim and Dr. Frank E. Hirsh shed light on the fullness of this divine provision afforded to the believer.

> "In the New Testament inheritance as the ordinary transmission of property from father to son is found in the parables of Jesus (Mat. 21:38; Mk. 12:1–8; Lk. 15:11–13; 20:14). In these instances sonship is firmly linked with inheritance, reflecting the common Greek and Oriental view. But the New Testament also uses the verb *Kleronomeo* and noun *Kleronomia* in a theological sense as an eschatological concept. In such cases these terms refer to the kingdom of God (see Lk. 10:25; 18:18) as the inheritance now to be claimed by the heirs, the sons of God (Mt. 19:29; 25:34; Mk. 10:17; 1 Cor. 6:9ff.). This sonship is based "not … on physical descent … but on the divine call and appointment" " (Eerdman's *International Standard Bible Encyclopedia,* Volume E-J, 1982, p. 824, ed. Geoffrey W. Bromiley).

Dr. Lewis Sperry Chafer explains the significance of what being a joint-heir with Christ means to the believer. He writes:

> "Each Christian is a gift of the Father to the Son; however, beyond the treasure which he is to Christ as a gift from the Father, Ephesians 1:18 asserts that the believer is also the *inheritance of the Father*. Much is promised the believer respecting his future place in glory. It is written: 'And the glory which thou gavest me I have given them; that they may be one, even as we are one' " (John 17:22); (*Systematic Theology,* Volume III, p. 261).

The apostle Peter shares his knowledge on our future inheritance. He states, "*Blessed be the God and Father of our Lord Jesus Christ, who according to His great mercy has caused us to be born again to a living hope through the resurrection of Jesus Christ from the dead, to obtain an inheritance which is imperishable and undefiled and will not fade away, reserved in heaven for you"* (1 Peter 1:3-4). In his letter to the Ephesians, Paul describes who, how, and why the guarantee is given to the believer. He explains, "*In Him, you also, after listening to the message of the truth, the gospel of your salvation—having also believed, you were sealed in Him with the Holy Spirit of promise, who is given as a pledge of our inheritance, with a view to the redemption of God's own possession, to the praise of His glory"* (1:13–14). A short excerpt from Discovering the Believer's Inheritance in Ephesians by Ray C. Stedman explains the concept of the supernatural seal and how it preserves the believer.

> "Just as the seal on a letter preserved it from tampering, the Spirit's presence speaks of God's preserving seal upon our lives. The *New International* Version brings out this concept with clarity in rendering Paul's concept of the Holy Spirit as "a deposit guaranteeing our inheritance." In Greek, the word *deposit* is *arrhabon*, which means "a down payment." If you've ever bought a car, you know what *arrhabon* is all about. You sign a paper and pay a down payment, a deposit, and that is the *arrhabon*, the guarantee that there is more to come. The presence of the Spirit in your life—the joy and the peace He gives—is the guarantee that there is more yet to come from God. The Spirit is the down payment on a much greater, fuller, richer experience of God than you have ever known before. The Holy Spirit is just the beginning of the blessings you will receive in Christ" (Our Riches in Christ: Discovering the Believer's Inheritance in Ephesians by Ray C. Stedman, http://www.raystedman.org/ephesians/richesinchrist.html#anchor18617, 2010).
>
> Dr. Harold W. Hoehner concurs:
>
> "The Holy Spirit who seals is a deposit guaranteeing our inheritance. The 'deposit' is more than a pledge which could be returned; it is a down payment with a guarantee of more to come (cf. "the firstfruits of the Spirit," Rom. 8.23). 'A deposit

> guaranteeing' translates the Greek *arrhabon* (used elsewhere in the New Testament only in 2 Cor. 1:22; 5:5). It guarantees believers' 'inheritance' of salvation and heaven (cf. 1 Peter 1:4). In essence, the 'deposit' of the Holy Spirit is a little bit of heaven in believers' lives with a guarantee of much more yet to come" (The Bible Knowledge Commentary: New Testament, 1983, p. 619, ed. John F. Walvoord, Roy B. Zuck).

To compliment the words of Dr. Hoehner, Dr. Chafer lists the 'firstfruits' of the spirit as follows:

> "These present ministries of the Spirit are said to be an 'earnest' (2 Cor. 1:22; Eph. 1:14) and 'firstfruits' (Rom. 8:23) of the Spirit. There are five of these present riches: (1) The believer is *born* of the Spirit (John 3:6), by which operation Christ is begotten in the one who exercises saving faith. (2) The believer is *baptized* by the Spirit (1 Cor. 12:13), which is a work of the Holy Spirit by which the believer is joined to Christ's Body and comes to be in Christ, and therefore a partaker of all that Christ is. (3) The believer is *indwelt* or *anointed* by the Spirit (John 7:39; Rom. 5:5; 8:9; 2 Cor. 1:21; Gal. 4:6; 1 John 2:27; 3:24) by which Presence the believer is equipped for every conflict and service. (4) The believer is *sealed* by the Spirit (2) Cor. 1:22; Eph. 4:30), which is the work of God the Holy Spirit by which the children of God are made secure unto the day of redemption. (5) The believer may be *filled* with the Spirit (Eph. 5:18), which ministry of the Spirit releases His power and effectiveness in the heart in which He dwells" *(Systematic Theology,* Volume III, p. 264).

Freed from the Law

"*Do not think that I came to abolish the Law or the Prophets; I did not come to abolish, but to fulfill"* (Matthew 5:17).

The Old Testament believers were bound by the covenantal Law (tôrâh) that was given to Moses. The covenantal Law was a judicial system based on a complex set of legal directives wherein condemnation and blessings were based on strict obedience to the Law. However, under the New Covenant of grace, based on the *sole merit* of the stupendous work of the crucifixion, death, and resurrection of Christ, the penalty that the judicial Law demanded was paid in full, and believers are now free from the Law. Below is a handy 'at a glance' list of distinguishing differences between the old merit system of the old covenantal Law and the new unmerited system of the New Covenant of grace.

> "*But this is the covenant which I will make with the people of Israel after those days,*" *declares the LORD,* "*I will put My law within them, and on their heart I will write it; and I will be their God, and they shall be My people*" " (Jeremiah 31:33).

Old Covenant (Law)	Versus	New Covenant (Grace)
A merited system—blessings based strictly on human efforts.		An unmerited system—blessings based on the sole works of Christ.
A position or standing under the requirements of the Law.		A position of standing under God's grace.
Conditional (based on works).		Unconditional (based on faith).
Merited righteousness based on obedience to the Law.		Unmerited righteousness in Christ based on Christ's fulfillment of the Law.
Yoked to the merit system.		Freed from the merit system.

Unforgiven until the penalty was paid.	Forgiven (past, present, and future). Christ paid the penalty.
A circumcision of the flesh. (Ephesians 2:11).	A spiritual circumcision of the heart. (Colossians 2:11).
Affects outer behavior—Law did not change the inner heart.	Affects inner behavior—new law changes the inner the heart.

Dr. Lewis Sperry Chafer soberly summarizes:

> "The solution of the problem is to be found in the fact that the law is a system demanding human merit, while the injunctions addressed to the Christian under grace are unrelated to human merit. Since the child of God is already accepted in the Beloved and stands forever in the merit of Christ, application of the merit system to him is both unreasonable and unscriptural" (*Systematic Theology,* Volume III, p. 240).

In conclusion, the unconditional New Covenant of grace made between God and man contains one of the richest treasuries of covenant promises ever recorded in the history of humanity. The New Covenant of grace restores the intimate love relationship between God and humanity that was lost by the fall of Adam, and gives believers the same privilege to 'eat freely from the tree of life' that was originally afforded to him in the Garden of Eden. The New Covenant was ratified *solely* by the sacrificial blood of Christ (John 19:30; Hebrews 9:12), His resurrection (Luke 24:13-40; John 20:24-29; 21:1-23; Acts 1:3); and was inaugurated after His ascension (Luke 24:46-51; John 20:17) by pouring forth His Spirit on the day of Pentecost. Moreover, the New Covenant of grace fulfills the Old Covenantal Law given to Moses, and ushers in the *Dispensation of Grace*, which extends from the death of Christ until His return to receive His Bride, the Church. Through Christ's extraordinary faithfulness and obedience, the New Covenant of grace offers the free gift of salvation by faith, or an immediate transference from spiritual death to eternal life to those who believe, pledges forgiveness of sin (inherited from Adam), and offers redemption and deliverance from spiritual death to a new life. At the time of salvation, it supernaturally seals the believer with His Spirit, and imputes the righteousness of Christ into him thereby justifying him as righteous before God. Through the process of divine adoption, it allows the believer direct access to God the Father through Jesus Christ, guarantees permanent citizenship in heaven, and pledges an inheritance of all divine blessings of the kingdom of God that were once lost to us. Finally, in anticipation of His death, the sign Jesus instituted in remembrance of His sacrifice for the giving of the New Covenant the act of communion was established. More importantly, the great I AM THAT I AM, *Jehovah-Elohiym* of the Old Covenant of redemption now introduces humanity to the most highly exalted name of the Deity as *Jesus Christ* (*Jehoshua-Elohiym*), the Son of God.

> *"Truly, truly, I say unto you, before Abraham was, I AM"* (John 8:58),

At a Glance

In closing, God's desire to communicate with man can be traced through the records of the covenants God has made with His creation since eternity past. The first conditional covenant whereby God governed His new creation was made between the Triune God, *Jehovah-Elohiym,* and newly created *man* (Adam) while he was in the state of innocence. God blessed him, gave him authority over earth, dominion over all living things, and placed him in the Garden of Eden under the condition that *if* he ate from the tree of knowledge of good and evil, *then* he would experience immediate spiritual death (Genesis 1:28-30; 2:15-17).

After Adam broke the condition of the covenant, he fell from grace, lost his fellowship with God, and judgment and expulsion from the Garden followed. God then placed fallen *humanity* under a second covenant commonly known as the antediluvian Adamic Covenant. This unilateral unconditional covenant governed all of fallen humanity by Jehovah-Elohiym (the redemptive name of Deity) ushered in the *Dispensation of Conscience*, and carried elements from the Edenic Covenant, judgment, introduced the age of consciousness, hard toil, and physical death. The earth was cursed with thorns and thistles, and Satan's messenger, the serpent, was cursed above all land creatures. The woman was placed under the headship of man and her pain in childbirth was 'multiplied'. Moreover, Genesis 3:15 carried the great prophecy of a coming Messiah and of the victory over evil by the finished work of Christ on the cross (Genesis 3:14-19).

Following the execution of judgment upon the wickedness that prevailed on the earth, God made an everlasting covenant with Noah, every living creature, and with all successive generations, that earth would never again be destroyed by water. The signature of this solemn oath He swore to is the permanent placement of the rainbow over the earth that is usually visible during or immediately following rain. Additionally, the postdiluvian Noahic Covenant ushered in the *Dispensation of Human Government* and carried the same elements of "be fruitful and multiply, and fill the earth" that were part of the antediluvian Adamic Covenant. It also changed their diet by adding meat with the prohibition of eating flesh with its blood, which represented life, and for maintaining respect for the sanctity of life, instituted the concept of capital punishment as a deterrent. (Genesis 9:1-17).

The Abrahamic everlasting Covenant ushered in the *Dispensation of Promise.* In this historic and all important everlasting covenant, two great prophecies were given to Abraham. The prophecy of Israel going into bondage by the hands of the Egyptians for four hundred years, their redemption, the judgment that would befall their oppressors (15:13-14), and the prophecy of a Messiah as foretold in Genesis 3:15, "in your seed *all* nations of the earth will be blessed" (22:18). God solemnly solemnly promised to: 1) make Abraham a great nation, 2) to personally bless him spiritually and temporally, 3) to make his name great, 4) Abraham was to become a great blessing, 5) to bless those who bless Abraham, 6) to curse those who curse him (Genesis 12:1-3), and 7) to give him and his descendants all of the land of Canaan for an everlasting possession (12:4-7; 13:18; 15:18-21). As a sign of the ratification of the covenant between them, the act of circumcision of the flesh was instituted. When God Almighty (El Shaddai) ratified His everlasting covenant with Abraham, He solemnly promised to: 1) multiply him exceedingly, 2) Abraham would be the father of a multitude of nations, 3) kings would come forth from him, 4) the everlasting covenant would be established between God and Abraham's descendants throughout their generations, and 5) at the age of ninety-nine, Abraham was promised that an heir to the covenantal promises would be born to him from Sarah, and through him, *all families of the earth* would be blessed. God then permanently changed their names from Abram to Abraham, "the father of a multitude of nations", and great patriarch of faith, and his wife's name from Sarai to Sarah, "a mother of nations" (Genesis 12:1–22:18), and sealed it by swearing an oath to Himself. The Abrahamic covenant was confirmed to Abraham's son Isaac, and to his grandson Jacob (Genesis 28:10–35:12). Lastly, in addition to the names of God, *Elohiym,* LORD God, *Jehovah-Elohiym,* we were introduced to the names of Jehovah-

Adonai, 'Master Jehovah', Jehovah-*Jireh*, 'The LORD will provide', and El *Shaddai*, 'God Almighty'.

After the children of Israel were delivered from Egyptian bondage, God set them apart from all other peoples as a new nation. As was promised to Abraham, Isaac, and Jacob, from their seed would come forth nations and kings, and a kingdom of priests. The children of Israel then entered into a new age – the *Dispensation of the Law,* which extended from the giving of the Law by Jehovah-*Yahweh* through Moses, and its acceptance of the Law by Israel at Mount Sinai. It is considered one of the most conditional covenants in Scripture in that *if* the children obeyed the laws of the covenant, then they would receive the blessings of the covenant, and *if* they did not, then judgment and punishment would follow. Though disobedience did not invalidate the covenant, it did make those who willfully practiced it ineligible for the covenant blessings. The particulars of the covenant that God made with the new nation of Israel included the receiving of a new identity as a holy nation, commandments, judgments, moral codes, civil laws, and ceremonial laws and regulations by which the holy nation was to live by. Lastly, in the ratification ceremony of the Mosaic Covenant between God and Israel, Moses offered burnt offerings to God, sprinkled the blood on both the altar and on the people (Exodus 24:8), and as a sign of remembrance, strict observance of the Sabbath was instituted (Exodus 19:3–31:18).

After the Mosaic Covenant was established with Israel, God gave her the deed to the land under the Deuteronomic Covenant, which was established at the end of Israel's 40 years of wilderness wondering, *before* they took possession of the Promised Land. It contains the conditions under which Israel entered the land of promise and was given to them through Moses. In his four discourses, Moses begins with the reiteration of the statutes and ordinances contained in the Mosaic Covenant, and then follows it by giving a more detailed exposition of regulations and statutes of their obligations to God on how the nation is to conduct herself *while* they are in possession of the Promised Land. The promise was unconditional; the possession was conditional based on obedience to the Mosaic Law. In his third discourse, Moses spoke to the nation on the blessings she would enjoy for obedience, and the curses that would befall her for willful disobedience. Simply stated, God would bless the nation abundantly and make her the head nation of the world *if* they were obedient; but, *if* they willfully disobeyed the Mosaic Law, the consequential curses would be destruction, disease, drought, famine, oppression, exile, economic ruin, and destruction of the nation (Deuteronomy 1:1–30:20). Though disobedience did carry heavy consequences, it did not nullify the covenant; Israel still holds the deed to the Land of Promise which God promised to Abraham in the everlasting covenant that He made with him (Genesis 17:7-8), which was reaffirmed to his son, Isaac (Genesis 26:1-5), and to his grandson, Jacob (Genesis 28:13).

The Davidic Covenant is the last and most crucial covenant of the Old Testament. It contains God's everlasting promise to David that his house, his kingdom, and his throne will be established forever. As Dr. Scofield pointed out, "it is the covenant, upon which the glorious kingdom of Christ "of the seed of David according to the flesh" was founded." As recorded by the Psalmist, this covenant contained the sole condition that "*if*" disobedience was practiced by anyone in the 'royal dynasty', chastisement would follow, but would not alter one single promise of the covenant. (Psalms 89:30-37). Dr. Scofield notes that the chastisement was later seen in the division of the kingdom under King Solomon's son, King Rehoboam (1 Kings 14:21), and in the captivities (2 Kings 25) (Psalms 89, p. 643). Finally, the fulfillment of the Davidic Covenant is currently believed to be held in abeyance until a literal fulfillment when Christ will rule the world from David's Throne (Luke 1:32-33).

Lastly, the historic and unparalleled unconditional New Covenant of grace was ratified *solely* by the sacrificial blood of Christ (John 19:30; Hebrews 9:12), His resurrection (Luke 24:13-40; John 20:24-29; 21:1-23; Acts 1:3), and inaugurated after His ascension (Luke 24:46-51; John 20:17) by pouring forth His Spirit on the day of Pentecost. Moreover, as Dr. C. I. Scofield pointed out, the New Covenant of grace fulfills the old covenantal Law given to Moses, and ushered in the *Dispensation of Grace*, which extends from the death of Christ until His return to receive His Bride, the Church. It restores the intimate love relationship between God and humanity that was lost by the fall of Adam, and gives believers the same privilege to 'eat freely from the tree of life' that was originally afforded to him in the Garden of Eden. The New Covenant of grace offers the free gift of salvation by faith, or an immediate transference from spiritual death to eternal life to those who believe, pledges forgiveness of sin (inherited from Adam), and offers redemption and deliverance from spiritual death to a new life. At the time of salvation, it supernaturally seals the believer with His Spirit, and justifies him before God through the imputation of the righteousness of Christ. Through the process of divine adoption, it allows the believer direct access to God the Father through Christ, guarantees permanent citizenship in heaven, and pledges an inheritance of all of the divine blessings of the kingdom of God that were once lost to us. Finally, in anticipation of His death, the sign that Jesus instituted in remembrance of His sacrifice for the giving of the New Covenant, the act of communion was established. More importantly, in addition to the names of God, *Elohiym;* LORD God, *Jehovah-Elohiym;* Jehovah-*Adonai*, 'Master Jehovah'; Jehovah-*Jireh*, 'The LORD will provide'; El *Shaddai*, 'God Almighty'; Jehovah's redemptive name of *Yahweh*, the God of Israel; and Jehovah-*Sabaoth*, the LORD of hosts; the all-powerful, all-sufficient eternal self-existent One – The great I AM THAT I AM, *Jehovah-Elohiym* of the Old Covenant of redemption now introduces humanity to the most highly exalted name of the Deity as *Jesus Christ* (*Jehoshua-Elohiym*), the Son of God.

"Therefore God highly exalted Him, and bestowed on Him the name which is above every name; that at the name of Jesus every knee should bow, of those who are in heaven, and on earth, and under the earth, and that every tongue should confess that Jesus Christ is Lord, to the glory of God the Father" (Philippians 2:9-11).

Part II—The Parabolic Ministry of Christ

The Parables

His Style

The art of teaching spiritual truth that Jesus used to reveal and protect the truth about the mysteries of the kingdom of heaven were parables, metaphors, allegories, similitudes, and proverbs. While the majority of Jesus' spiritual teachings were illustrated by parables, it is worthwhile to note the distinguishing characteristic of a parable as compared to the characteristics of other figures of speech that He used in His teachings. In his book entitled "All the Parables of the Bible", Dr. Herbert Lockyer points out the following distinguishing factors:

> "The parables display a pre-ordained harmony between things spiritual and things material. Material objects are used to express spiritual truths and reveal that nature is more than it seems. In a parable, an image borrowed from the visible world and is accompanied by a truth from the invisible or spiritual world."
>
> "A Metaphor distinctly affirms that one thing *is* another thing. The word itself comes from two Greek words meaning to carry over. One object is equated with another object. Example: "The Lord God is a sun and a shield" (Psalm 84:11)."
>
> "Allegories differ from metaphors in that no transference of qualities and properties takes place. Both parables and metaphors cover phrases and sentences, and serve to open and explain some hidden truth which cannot be as easily understood if not so draped" (Lockyer, All the Parables of the Bible, 1963, pp. 13-17).

Simply stated, a *parable* is a discourse whereby an image borrowed from the visible world is accompanied by a spiritual truth, whereas a *metaphor* simply transfers a spiritual truth to a physical object. *Allegories* have no hidden truth—the attribute of the concept being conveyed is identified with the actual object and compares by implication. A *similitude* differs from all other figures of speech in that it simply compares one thing with another by using the word 'like'. Two examples Jesus used to convey His message about the nature of the kingdom are, "*The kingdom of heaven is like a mustard seed; and the kingdom of heaven is like leaven*" (Matthew 13:31, 33).

The Parabolic Ministry of Jesus Recorded by Matthew

The Nature of the Kingdom

Have you ever wondered why Jesus spoke to the crowd in parables? The disciples wondered the same so they asked Jesus, "*Why do You speak to them in parables?*" (Matthew 13:10). And Jesus replied, "*To you it has been granted to know the mysteries of the kingdom of heaven, but to them it has not been granted*" (v. 11). Quoting from Isaiah 6, Jesus further explains to His disciples that the Jews had already been given the truth, and because they did not believe, it was taken away from them.

> *"Therefore I speak to them in parables; because while seeing they do not see, and while hearing they do not hear, nor do they understand. And in their case the prophecy of Isaiah is being fulfilled, which says, 'YOU WILL KEEP ON HEARING, BUT WILL NOT UNDERSTAND; AND YOU WILL KEEP ON SEEING, BUT WILL NOT PERCEIVE; FOR THE HEART OF THIS PEOPLE HAS BECOME DULL, AND THEY HAVE CLOSED THEIR EYES LEST THEY SHOULD SEE WITH THEIR EYES, AND HEAR WITH THEIR EARS, AND UNDERSTAND WITH THEIR HEART AND TURN AGAIN, AND I SHOULD HEAL THEM' "* (vv. 13-15).

To this, Dr. Louis A. Barbieri, Jr. further comments on the reasons for using these particular figures of speech:

> "Significantly Jesus did not speak of any 'mysteries' concerning the kingdom of heaven until the nation had made its decision concerning Him. That decision was made by the leaders when they attributed His divine power to Satan (9:34;

12:22-37). Now Jesus unveiled certain additional facts not given in the Old Testament about His reign on earth. Many Old Testament prophets had predicted that the Messiah would deliver the nation Israel and establish His kingdom on the earth. Jesus came and offered the kingdom (4:17), but the nation rejected Him (12:24). In view of that rejection what would happen to God's kingdom? The "secrets" of the kingdom now reveal that an entire Age would intervene between Israel's rejection of the King and her later acceptance of Him.

Second, Jesus spoke in parables to hide the truth from unbelievers. The secrets of the kingdom would be given to the disciples, but would be hidden from the religious leaders who rejected Him (13:11b), **but not to them**). In fact, even what they had previously known would no longer be clear to them (v. 12). Jesus' parabolic instruction thus carried with it a judgmental aspect. By using parables in public, Jesus could preach to as many individuals as before, but He could then draw the disciples aside and explain to them fully the meaning of His words.

Third, Jesus spoke in parables in fulfillment of **Isaiah** 6:9-10. When Isaiah began his ministry, God told him that people would not comprehend his message. Likewise, when Jesus began His ministry, many people saw His miraculous works but did not perceive; and they heard His Word but did **not … understand** (Matt.13:13-15)" (The Bible Knowledge Commentary: New Testament, 1983, p. 49, ed. John F. Walvoord, Roy B. Zuck).

The Third Great Discourse
The Seven Mystery Parables of the Kingdom of Heaven —Matthew 13

Dr. C. I Scofield defines a Scriptural mystery as "a previously hidden truth divinely revealed continues to maintain the supernatural element despite the revelation". Furthermore, Dr. Scofield sheds light on the divine timing of the unveiling of the mysteries of the kingdom. It is a new beginning—the dawning of the new Dispensation of Grace, the New Covenant, and the end of the Mosaic Law and the Old Covenant. He states:

> "The seven parables of Matthew 13 are called by our Lord "mysteries of the kingdom of heaven" (v. 11), taken together, describe the result of the presence of the Gospel in the world during the present age, that is, the time of seed-sowing which began with our Lord's personal ministry, and ends with the harvest" (Matthew 13, p. 1014).

The revelation of the seven mysteries of the kingdom that begin on the first pages of Chapter 13 in the Gospel of Matthew is considered Jesus' third great discourse. His first great discourse, the Sermon on the Mount, begins in Chapter 5 of Matthew and ends with Chapter 7. Chapter 10 contains the record of His second great discourse known as the Commissioning of His Disciples, or as Dr. Donald A. Hagner so aptly phrased it, "the Missionary Discourse" (Word Biblical Commentary, Volume 33A, 2000, p. 262, ed. Ralph P. Martin). While Jesus' fourth great discourse, the principles of life in the community of the kingdom is found in Chapter 18, His fifth great discourse, known as the Great Olivet Discourse, or the prophecy parables of the 'end of the world', is found in Chapters 24-25. Finally, Jesus' last Farewell Discourse known as the Upper Room Discourse is recorded exclusively in Chapters 13-14 of the Gospel of John

The First Mystery of the Nature of the Kingdom of Heaven—Matthew 13:3-23

"All these things Jesus spoke to the multitudes in parables, and He was not talking to them without a parable, so that what was spoken trough the prophet might be fulfilled, saying, "I WILL OPEN MY MOUTH IN PARABLES; I WILL UTTER THINGS HIDDEN SINCE THE FOUNDATION OF THE WORLD" " (Matthew 13:34-35; Psalms 78:2).

The Parable of the Sower – Matthew 13:3-9: *"Behold, the sower went out to sow; and as he sowed, some seeds fell beside the road, and the birds came and devoured them. And others fell upon the rocky places, where they did not have much soil; and immediately they sprang up, because they had no depth of soil. But when the sun had risen, they were scorched; and because they had no root, they withered away. And others fell among the thorns, and the thorns came up and choked them out. And others fell on the good soil, and yielded a crop, some a hundredfold, some sixty, and some thirty"* (Matthew 13:3-9; Mark 4:1-9; 13:18-23; Luke 8:4-8).

The first mystery of the nature of the kingdom is unveiled in the parable of the Sower in which Jesus illustrates the way in which the Gospel is sown in the world, and the different conditions that affect the growth of the Word. The revelation that He is the Sower, the Seed is the Word of God, and the field is the world is unmistakable since it is interpreted directly by Him.

> *"Hear then the parable of the sower. When any one hears the word of the kingdom, and does not understand it, the evil one comes and snatches away what has been sown in his heart. This is the one on whom the seed was sown beside the road. And the one on whom seed was sown on the rocky places, this*

> *is the man who hears the word, and immediately receives it with joy; yet he has no firm root in himself, but is only temporary, and when affliction or persecution arises because of the word, immediately he falls away. And the one on whom seed was sown among the thorns, this is the man who hears the word, and the worry of the world, and the deceitfulness of riches choke the word, and it becomes unfruitful. And the one on whom seed was sown. And the one on whom seed was sown on the good ground, this is the man who hears the word and understands it; who indeed bears fruit, and brings forth, some a hundredfold, some sixty, and some thirty"* (Matthew 13:18-23; Mark 4:13-20, Luke 8:11-15).

Dr. Donald A. Hagner insightfully reveals that the focus of the parable is not upon the sower or the seed, but upon the outcome of the seed, which is directly dependent upon the kind of environment in which it is sown within the hearts of man.

> "These circumstances are not the result of accident, but involve the grace of God and the responsiveness of human beings. The growth of the kingdom is the work of God" (Word Biblical Commentary, Volume 33A, 2000, p. 369, ed. Ralph P. Martin).

Moreover, and of great import, Dr. Hagner suggests that the spiritual messages taught in the parables impact the readers at their own spiritual level of growth.

> "Involvement of the reader in the interpretation of the parables is especially desirable since they are meant to be performative (or a "language event") as well as informative. That is they are intended to have an impact on the reader at the level of his or her existence and not simply to convey information: the parables interpret us as much as we interpret the parables" (Ibid., p. 365).

The Second Mystery of the Nature of the Kingdom of Heaven—Matthew 13:24-30

Following the explanation given on the conditions that contribute to the success or failure of the seed in the parable of the Sower, Jesus immediately presents an illustration on the fate of the seed by comparing the wheat with the sons of the kingdom, and the tares with the sons of the evil one.

The Parable of the Wheat and the Tares – Matthew 13:24-30: *"He presented another parable to them, saying, "The kingdom of heaven may be compared to a man who sowed good seed in his field. But while men were sleeping, his enemy came and sowed tares also among the wheat, and went away. But when the wheat sprang up and bore grain, then the tares became evident also. And the slaves of the landowner came and said to him, 'Sir, did you not sow good seed in your field? How then does it have tares?' And he said to them, 'An enemy has done this!' And the slaves said to him, 'Do you want us, then, to go and gather them up?' But he said, 'No; lest while you are gathering up the tares, you may root up the wheat with them. Allow both to grow together until the harvest; and in the time of the harvest I will say to the reapers, First gather up the tares and bind them in bundles to burn them up; but gather the wheat into my barn." ' "*

The Greek word for tare is *zizanion* (pronounced dziz-an'-ee-on), which means "a false grain or a weed", and was credited among the Jews to being degenerate wheat. The rabbis called it a 'bastard'. The seeds are poisonous to man and plant eating animals, producing sleepiness, nausea, convulsions, and death. The plants can be separated out, but the custom (as in the parable) is to leave the cleaning out till near the time of the harvest. "Our Lord describes the tares as 'the sons of the evil one'; false teachings" (Vines Expository Dictionary of Old and New Testament Words, 1996, p. 618).

Wheat and tares growing together
Image provided by dominicdemattos.blogspot.com/2011/07/sunday-reflection-wheat-and-tares.html, 2011.

After Jesus and His disciples left the multitudes, the disciples ask Jesus to explain the parable to them (v. 36), and Jesus answered saying,

> *"The one who sows the good seed is the Son of Man, and the field is the world; and as for the good seed, these are the sons of the kingdom; and the tares are the sons of the evil one; and the enemy who sowed them is the devil, and the harvest is the end of the age; and the reapers are angels. Therefore just as the tares are gathered up and burned with fire, so shall it be at the end of the age. The Son of Man will send forth His angels, and they will gather out of His kingdom all STUMBLING BLOCKS, AND THOSE WHO COMMIT LAWLESSNESS, and will cast them into the furnace of fire; in that place there shall be weeping and gnashing of teeth. Then THE RIGHTEOUS WILL SHINE FORTH, AS THE SUN in the kingdom of their Father. He who has ears, let him hear"* (Matthew 13:37-43).

In His explanation, Jesus makes it clear that He is the sower of the good seed, the field is the world, the good seed are the sons of the kingdom; the tares are the sons of the evil one; and the enemy who sowed them is the devil. The reapers are His angels, and the harvest at the end of the age, refers to our destiny at the end of the age of grace, which is also recorded by Paul and John (1 Thessalonians 4:16-17; John 14:3).

The Third Mystery of the Nature of the Kingdom of Heaven—Matthew 13:31-32

The Parable of the Mustard Seed – Matthew 13:31-32: *"He presented another parable to them, saying, "The kingdom of heaven is like a mustard seed, which a man took and sowed in his field; and this is smaller than all other seeds; but when it is full grown, it is larger than the garden plants, and becomes a tree; so that THE BIRDS OF THE AIR COME AND NEST IN ITS BRANCHES" "* (Matthew 13:31-32; Mark 4:30-32; Luke 13:18-19).

The Greek word for mustard seed is sinapi (pronounced sin'-ap-ee), and originates from the Egyptian word mustard. Usually about 1 mm in diameter, the mustard seed is well known for its tiny size. The mustards are annuals, and when they are planted in good soil, they reproduce with extraordinary rapidity often attaining a height of 10-12 feet (Vines Expository Dictionary of Old and New Testament Words, 1996, p. 423).

Center
Single Mustard Seed

Mature Mustard Tree

Images provided by faithfulthoughtspot.wordpress.com

In the parable of the Mustard Seed, Jesus continues to use the 'sowing of a seed' to illustrate the spiritual nature of the kingdom of heaven. Although He did not interpret this parable, the message is clear that His focus is on the single seed sown, and the extraordinary 'size' it becomes when it reaches full maturity.

The Fourth Mystery of the Nature of the Kingdom of Heaven—Matthew 13:33

In the parable of the Leaven, Jesus uses a similitude to convey His message on the nature of the dynamics of the kingdom of heaven by comparing it to leaven, commonly known as yeast.

The Parable of the Leaven – Matthew 13:33: *"He spoke another parable to them, "The kingdom of heaven is like leaven, which a woman took, and hid in three pecks of meal, until it was all leavened" "* (Matthew 13:33; Luke 13:20-21).

The Greek word for leaven (yeast) is zumē, pronounced *dzoo'-may*, is an ingredient that acts as a rising agent for dough through the process of fermentation. If you have ever made any baked goods from scratch, then you can relate to this concept. By adding a small amount of yeast to a lump of dough, it continues to permeate within the mix causing an astonishing effect over time (Vines Expository Dictionary of Old and New Testament Words, 1996, p. 362).

A varicty of interpretative views on this parable is offered to us by a variety of expert expositors, and all are valid. Viewed in context of the dynamics of the kingdom of heaven, William Barclay states:

> "Almost all scholars would agree that it speaks of the transforming power of Christ and of His kingdom in the life of the individual and of the world; but there is a difference of opinion as to how that transforming power works. (1) It is sometimes said that the lesson of this parable is that the kingdom works unseen. We cannot see the leaven working in the dough any more than we can see a flower growing; but the work of the leaven is always going on. Just so, it is said, we cannot see the work of the kingdom, but always the kingdom is working and drawing

individuals and the world nearer and nearer to God" (William Barclay, The Gospel of Matthew, Volume II, 2001, p. 95).

On the other hand, based on how leaven was perceived by the Jewish culture, Warren Wiersbe suggests that the leaven represents false doctrine. He writes:

"The mustard seed illustrates the false outward expansion of the kingdom, while the leaven illustrates the inward development of false doctrine and false living. Throughout the Bible, leaven is a symbol of evil. It had to be removed from Jewish homes during Passover (Ex. 12:15-19; 13:7). It was excluded from sacrifices (Ex. 34:35), with the exception of the loaves used at the Feast of Pentecost (Lev. 23:14-21). But there the loaves symbolized Jews and Gentiles in the church and there is sin in the church. Jesus used the leave to picture hypocrisy (Luke 12:1), false teaching (Matt. 16:6-12), and worldly compromise (Matt. 22:16-21). Paul used leaven to picture carnality in the church (1 Cor. 5:6-8) as well as false doctrine (Gal. 5:9). Sin is like leaven (yeast): It quietly grows, it corrupts, and it "puffs up" (1 Cor. 4:18-19; 5:2; 8:1)" (The Bible Exposition Commentary: New Testament, Volume I, 1989, pp. 46-47).

While William Barclay and Warren Wiersbe perceive the dynamics of the leaven working from within, William Hendriksen bases his perspective on the dynamics of the outward working of the leaven. He states:

"The point of the parable is that the yeast once inserted continues its process of fermentation until the whole batch has risen. So also the citizen of the kingdom demands that every sphere of life shall contribute its full share of service, honor, and glorify to him who is "King of kings and Lord of lords" (Rec. 19:16). Not as if on a sinful earth, before the return of Christ, this state of perfection will ever become a reality. Scripture clearly reveals that this will not be the case (Luke

17:25-30; 18:8; II Thess. 1:7-10; 2-8). But nothing less than the ultimate realization of this goal can ever be the aim of the believer. He is comforted by the prophecy of Isa. 11:0; "They shall not hurt nor destroy in all my holy mountain; for the earth shall be full of the knowledge of Jehovah, as the waters cover (the bottom of) the sea" " (New Testament Commentary: Exposition of the Gospel according to Matthew, 2007, p. 567).

Finally, Dr. Donald A. Hagner concludes:

"Although leaven symbolized the corrupting influence of evil in the OT (though not consistently; cf. Lev 23:17) and was thus to be purged entirely from Israelite households at Passover (Exod 12:15, 19), there is no indication that Matthew here thinks of the leaven as something evil. What he portrays, rather, is the dynamic power of leave whereby a small amount, which is imperceptible when first mixed in a lump of dough, has an eventual, inevitable, and astonishing effect upon the whole. In this sense, the parable is parallel to the immediately preceding parable of the mustard seed. Both speak of that which appears initially to be insignificant and of no consequence but which in time produces an astonishing and dramatic effect. The kingdom of God is like leaven in this way. Although at the beginning it looks unimpressive, it will have an effect that is out of all proportion with that beginning" (Word Biblical Commentary, Volume 33A, 2000, p. 389, ed. Ralph P. Martin).

Thus, what can be consistently seen in the similitudes of the Mustard Seed and the Leaven is that they both carry the same theme of 'a very small beginning produces astonishing results' over time.

The Fifth Mystery of the Nature of the Kingdom of Heaven—Matthew 13:44

After Jesus left the multitudes, he went into the house and continued to teach the disciples (Matthew 13:36). It was probably Peter's house since he came from Galilee and his home was in Capernaum on the northern shore of Galilee (Ralph Martin, Eerdman's *International Standard Bible Encyclopedia,* Volume K-P, 1986, p. 803, ed. Geoffrey W. Bromiley).

The Parable of the Hidden Treasure – Matthew 13:44: "*The kingdom of heaven is like a treasure hidden in the field, which a man found and hid; and from joy over it he goes and sells all that he has, and buys that field.*"

Though there is no record of Jesus interpreting this parable for the disciples, since Jesus had already established that the field is the world and sower is the Son of Man (vv. 37-38), they probably understood the analogy drawn between the kingdom, the field, and the hidden treasure. William Barclay notes that in the ancient world, ordinary people did not use banks; they hid their treasures in the ground. He further states that this was a common practice among the people.

> "Palestine was probably the most fought-over country in the world; and, when war threatened to flow over them, it was common practice for people to hide their valuables in the ground before they took to flight, in the hope that the day would come when they could return and regain them. Josephus speaks of 'the gold and the silver and the rest of the most precious furniture which the Jews had, and which the owners treasured up underground against the uncertain fortunes of war' " (William Barclay, The Gospel of Matthew, Volume II, 2001, p. 98).

Dr. C. I. Scofield concludes:

"The Church is the hidden treasure and the man who sold everything to buy the field is Christ who at the cost of His personal blood sacrificed his own life for us" (Matthew 13, p. 1017).

The Sixth Mystery of the Nature of the Kingdom of Heaven—Matthew 13:45-46

The Parable of the Pearl of Great Price – Matthew 13:45-46: *"Again, the kingdom of heaven is like a merchant seeking fine pearls, and upon finding one pearl of great value, he went and sold all that he had, and bought it."*

It was not by chance that Jesus chose pearls to use as an illustration of the nature of the kingdom. In ancient times, Middle Eastern cultures were the first to value pearls and pearl shells. The gems were said to be 'worth their weight in gold', and by 100 B.C., the Mediterranean enthusiasm for pearls had become a craze. Archaeological evidence indicates that almost 6,000 years ago people in the Persian Gulf region were sometimes buried with a pierced pearl resting in the right hand (American Museum of Natural History, Pearls, http://www.amnh.org/exhibitions/pearls/history/index.html, 2012). The process of the formation of a pearl is also quite fascinating. As products of living animals, pearls are unique among gems and exist in an impressive diversity of sizes, shapes, and colors. Finding two identical perfect pearls would be considered a rarity and would be prohibitive in cost. A pearl is not produced in the deep cores of earth, but is rather considered an abnormal growth that is produced by a living organism in living water. They are formed when a tiny object, typically a parasite, or some other tiny piece of organic matter becomes embedded in the tissue of the mollusk which then becomes an irritant in the tissue. In response, the combined substance of calcium carbonate (nacre) is secreted, and as the inner layer of nacre builds around the tiny piece of inorganic matter, it eventually forms a pearl (http://www.yvel.com/Assets/PearlGuide.pdf).

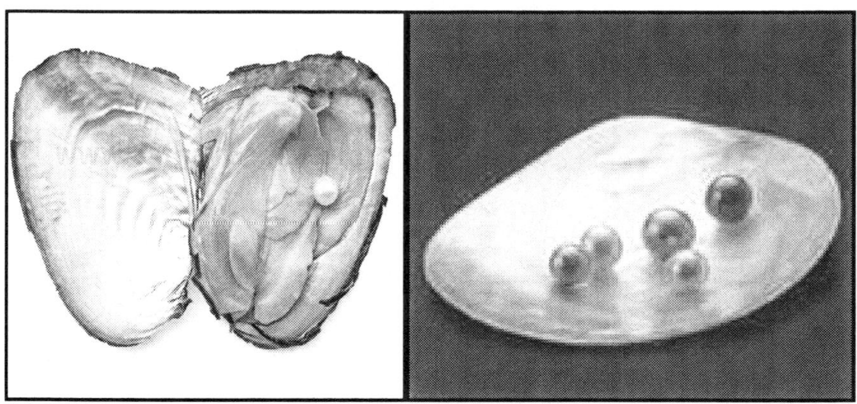

Images provided by cathaygems.com, and
Pearl Guide: http://www.yvel.com/Assets/PearlGuide.pdf, 2012.

Consistent with Jesus' teaching of the parables of the Mustard Seed and the Leaven, the parable of the Pearl of Great Price carries the same theme of 'a very small beginning produces astonishing results'. Likewise, in both parables of the Hidden Treasure and the Pearl of Great Price, the theme of 'great value' can be found. Dr. Hagner offers his own analogy of the similarities that can be seen in both of these parables.

> "Like a hidden treasure or a pearl that can be held in one's hand, the kingdom is known only to its joyful possessors" (Word Biblical Commentary, Volume 33A, 2000, p. 397, ed. Ralph P. Martin).

Moreover, in both the Hidden Treasure and the Pearl of Great Price parables, Jesus established that the man and the merchant who sacrifice everything to purchase the treasure and the pearl is the Son of Man. It is worth noting that the astonishing results all occur *within* the objects that Jesus analogizes in his parables. Along these lines, Dr. Lockyer offers his insightful comments:

> "It must not be forgotten that the formation of the pearl is a secret one. None but the eye of God watches the oyster transforming an intrusion into a pearl of intrinsic beauty and

great worth. Is it not so with the Church which Christ is now forming? Unknown and unseen His pearl is being fashioned. Last of all, the Church, an object of value and beauty, presently hid from the eyes of men, has the prospect of an honorable and exalted future. As pearls adorn the crowns of monarchs, so in the ages to come Christ will display His own and in them "show the exceeding riches of His grace; (Ephesians 2:7)" " (Lockyer, All the Parables of the Bible, 1963, p. 204).

"For you are not your own, you have been bought with a price"
(2 Corinthians 6:20)

The Seventh Mystery of the Nature of the Kingdom of Heaven—Matthew 13:47-50

The Parable of the Dragnet – Matthew 13:47-50: *"Again, the kingdom of heaven is like a dragnet cast into the sea, and gathering fish of every kind; and when it was filled, they drew it upon the beach; and they sat down, and gathered the good fish into containers, but the bad they threw away. So it will be at the end of the age; the angels shall come forth, and take out the wicked from among the righteous and will cast them into the furnace of fire; there shall be weeping and gnashing of teeth."*

The parable concluding His third great discourse on the nature of the kingdom apparently had no need for an interpretation. Jesus asked His disciples if they understood 'all these things', to which they replied, 'yes' (v. 51). Moreover, in the second half of His parable, Jesus clearly states what is meant by saying: *"So it will be at the end of the age; the angels shall come forth, and take out the wicked from among the righteous and will cast them into the furnace of fire; there shall be weeping and gnashing of teeth"* (vv. 49-50). Based on Jesus' explanation of the wheat and the tares, we can also safely conclude that the analogy drawn between good fish and the bad fish mean that the good fish are the righteous ones and bad fish are the wicked ones. That the parable of the Dragnet also carries the same theme of 'our destiny at the end of the age of grace' found in the parable of the Wheat and the Tares is noteworthy. In both instances, the wheat and tares are allowed to grow together before harvesting, and the good fish and bad fish remain together until the 'fisherman' casts His dragnet into the sea to gather them all up for the angels to separate. If you have ever watched a shrimp-boat out at sea, you will see fishermen casting out huge nets that drag the bottom of the sea. When the net is full, they pull it up, separate the shrimp from all of the other fish that were caught in the net, and then will typically throw the fish back into the sea. However, in the parable of the Dragnet, the bad fish are not thrown back into the sea but are thrown into a furnace of fire.

Finally, consistently found in both parables are the parallels drawn to the objects Jesus chooses to compare the spiritual world to the material world leads to understanding the nature of the kingdom in its present and future form. In the parable of the Wheat and the Tares, Jesus' clear explanation that the field is the world, the good seed are the sons of the kingdom, the tares are the sons of the evil one, the reapers are His angels, and the harvest is the end of the age, may likewise be found here. The sea parallels the world, the good fish parallels the good seed, the bad fish parallels the tares, and in both instances, the angels separate the good from the bad at the end of the age.

A clarification of the Greek translation of the term '*world*' specifically used in Matthew 13 is of value. The term world, translated from the Greek word kosmos, is defined as "an apt and harmonious arrangement or constitution, order, government. An ornament, decoration, adornment, the arrangement of the 'heavenly hosts' being an adornment of the heavens; the world, the universe; the earth, the inhabitants of the earth, men, the human family; the ungodly multitude; the whole mass of men alienated from God and hostile to the cause of Christ"(Thayer's Greek Lexicon, 2009, G2889, p. 356). Thus, by simple definition, the *world* as used in the parables of the Nature of the Kingdom of Heaven refers to a '*world system'* ruled by the prince of darkness.

In conclusion, for the first time in the history of humanity, through Jesus' parabolic teaching of the Seven Mysteries of the Kingdom of Heaven, the revolutionary spiritual concept of the nature of the *kingdom of heaven* was unveiled to the world. In His parabolic teaching, Jesus metaphorically uses physical objects to reveal spiritual truths. By comparing the kingdom of heaven to a field, a seed, to leaven, to hidden treasure, to a merchant who sold everything to buy the pearl of great value, and to a dragnet, makes it possible to understand the spiritual concept of the *nature* of the kingdom of heaven in its entirety. For easy reference, following is an adapted table listing the seven mysteries of the kingdom. It is also worth noting that with the exception of the unique parable of 'the growth of the seed' found in the Gospel of Mark 4:26-29, the seven mysteries of the kingdom are recorded successively in the Gospel of Matthew.

"For behold, the kingdom of God is in your midst" (Luke 17:21b).

Table I
Third Discourse
The Seven Mysteries of the Kingdom

From Early Summer A.D. 28 to Passover A.D. 29

PARABLE	PLACE	MATTHEW	MARK	LUKE
1. The Sower	Galilee	13:3-9; 18-23	4:1-9; 13-29	8:5-8; 11-15
2. The Wheat and the Tares	Galilee	13:24-30; 36-43		
**The Seed Growing	Galilee		4:26-29	
3. The Mustard Seed	Galilee	13:31-32	4:30-32	13:18-19
4. The Leaven	Galilee	13:33		13:20-21
5. The Hidden Treasure	Capernaum	13:44		
6. The Pearl of Great Price	Capernaum	13:45-46		
7. The Fishing Net	Capernaum	13:47-50		

**The only unique parable found in Mark

(Adapted from Dr. Herbert Lockyer, "Table of Parables", *All the Teachings of Jesus*, 1991, p. 305; John MacArthur, "The Parables of Jesus", *The MacArthur Bible Commentary*, 2005, p. 1209; Louis A. Barbieri, Jr., "The Parables of Jesus", *The Bible Knowledge Commentary: New Testament*, 1983, p. 35, ed. John F. Walvoord, Roy B. Zuck).

Spiritual Principles of the Kingdom of Heaven

The parable of the Unmerciful Servant is part of Jesus' fourth great discourse on 'life in the community of the kingdom' that is found in Chapter 18 of the Gospel of Matthew. It is commonly known as the discourse devoted to the spiritual principles of the church (Matthew 18:1-35, Word Biblical Commentary, Volume 33B, 2000, p. 514, ed. Ralph P. Martin).

The Parable of the Unmerciful Servant – Matthew 18:23-35: *"For this reason the kingdom of heaven may be compared to a certain king who wished to settle accounts with his slaves. And when he had begun to settle them, there was brought to him one who owed him ten thousand talents. But since he did not have the means to repay, his lord commanded him to be sold, along with his wife and children and all that he had, and repayment to be made. The save therefore falling down, prostrated himself before him saying, 'Have patience with me, and I will repay you everything.' And the lord of that slave felt compassion and released him and forgave him the debt. But that slave went out and found one of his fellow-slaves who owed him a hundred denarii; and he seized him and began to choke him, saying, 'Pay back what you owe' So his fellow-slave fell down and began to entreat him, saying, 'Have patience with me and I will repay you.' He was unwilling however, but went and threw him in prison until he should pay back what was owed. So when his fellow-slaves saw what had happened, they were deeply grieved and came and reported to their lord all that had happened. Then summoning him, his lord said to him, 'You wicked slave, I forgave you all that debt because you entreated me. Should you not also have had mercy on your fellow-slave, even as I had mercy on you?' And his lord, moved with anger, handed him over to the torturers until he should repay all that was owed him. So shall My heavenly Father also do to you, if each of you does not forgive his brother from your heart."*

There is no question that this discourse is a parable in its truest form of the definition of the word; and there is no question that the principle Jesus is teaching is on ‘forgiveness’ based on the new standards of spiritual principles of the kingdom. Prior to Jesus’ discourse, Peter asked our Lord, “*Lord, how often shall my brother sin against me, and I forgive him? Up to seven times?*” (v. 21) Jesus answered, *“I do not say to you, up to seven times, but up to seventy times seven”* (v. 22). This dramatic new kingdom standard on forgiveness that is being introduced can be seen in the comparison between the amounts of money that the king was owed by the servant as opposed to the amount of money that was owed the servant by his fellow-servant, and the difference between their willingness to forgive the debt.

In ancient times, a talent was understood to refer to silver. Thus “if a Roman calculation was used to calculate one single talent, then ten thousand talents” would be estimated to be worth approximately over one million pounds, or to some, three million dollars. However, if a Jewish calculation was used, then it would be estimated to be equivalent to approximately over three million pounds, or about ten million dollars (Herbert Lockyer, All the Parables of the Bible, 1963, p. 204). By comparison, 84 dinarii was only estimated to be equivalent to approximately one single pound, or a little over one dollar (The New Unger’s Bible Dictionary, 1988, p. 846, ed. R. K. Harrison). Hence, by using such a drastic comparison of the amounts of debt the servants owed to compare with the reactions of each, Jesus illustrates the new kingdom principle of forgiveness by simply saying, “*So shall My heavenly Father also do to you, if each of you does not forgive his brother from your heart”* (v. 35). The servant who asked the king for forgiveness received a full pardon for the extraordinary amount that he owed, whereas when the second servant asked for forgiveness, the first servant refused to pardon him at all. If the king forgave all, then the servant in turn should have forgiven all as well.

> *“I do not say to you, up to seven times, but up to seventy times seven”* (Matthew 18:22).

The Laborers in the Vineyard—Matthew 20:1-16

"For the kingdom of heaven is like a landowner who went out early in the morning to hire laborers for his vineyard. And when he had agreed with the laborers for a denarius for the day, he sent them into his vineyard. And he went out about the third hour and saw others standing idle in the market place; and to those he said, 'You too go into the vineyard, and whatever is right I will give you.' And so they went. Again he went out about the sixth and the ninth hour, and did the same thing. And about the eleventh hour he went out, and found others standing; and he said to them, 'Why have you been standing here idle all day long?' And when evening had come, the owner of the vineyard said to his foreman, 'Call the laborers and pay them their wages, beginning with the last group to the first.' And when those hired about the eleventh hour came, each one received a denarius. And when those hired first came, they thought that they would receive more; and they also received each one a denarius. And when they received it, they grumbled at the landowner, saying 'These last men have worked only one hour, and you have made them equal to us who have borne the burden and the scorching heat of the day.' But he answered and said to one of them, 'Friend, I am doing you no wrong; did you not agree with me for a denarius? Take what is yours and go your way, but I wish to give to this last man the same as to you. Is it not lawful for me to do what I wish with what is my own? Or is your eye envious because I am generous?' Thus the last shall be first and the first last."

In ancient times, a denarius was the daily wage of a laborer. The Greek word dēnarion (pronounced *day-nar'-ee-on)* is translated from Latin origin by James Strong "as being worth one penny". However, the value of the coin in this instance is not the focus. Preceding the telling of the parable, Jesus is having a discussion with a rich young man who wants to know what he can do to obtain eternal life

(Matthew:19:16-22). After listening to the conversation and hearing the answer that Jesus gave to the rich young man, the disciples asked Jesus "*Then who can be saved*?" (v. 25), and Jesus answers their question by telling them this parable. The parallel drawn of both workers receiving the same amount of wages at the end of the day might seem unfair, and probably would be very discouraging to any of us who worked all day and received the same amount of pay as the one who only worked part time. However, in this particular case, Jesus is answering the question pertaining to salvation, and though the New Covenant had not yet been ratified, the new spiritual kingdom concept of redeeming grace is clearly being introduced to His disciples. The focus is on the answer to the direct questions of 'who can be saved' that the disciples asked, and to "what good thing shall I do that I may obtain eternal life?" that the rich young man asked in the last verses of the previous chapter (Matthew 19:16). The analogy Jesus draws upon to illustrate the answer to these questions is seen in the comparison He makes between the kingdom of heaven, and the landowner and his vineyard. The generosity of grace that the landowner showed the last group of vineyard workers was equal to the generosity shown to the first. This principle is in effect even more so today. Those who believe at the eleventh hour receive the same generous amount of grace as those who believed at the first hour; both are saved by grace, and both receive the full amount of the riches of divine grace that our Lord lavishes upon us the moment we believe. Although it might seem unfair to some who have labored in the vineyard their whole lives as opposed to those who have not, Jesus addresses this concern in the parable by saying, *"Take what is yours and go your way, but I wish to give to this last man the same as to you"* (v. 14). Dr. Donald A. Hagner insightfully points to the 'real' focus of the message contained in the parable.

> "In the realm of grace upon which the kingdom proclaimed by Jesus is based, it is wrong to set one's mind on the rewards that will set one on a higher level than others. Indeed, even where such differences in future reward may be real, in comparison with the common reward that will be shared by all in the kingdom, they amount to nothing. The parable focuses on those who come last, not those who came first. In the kingdom where

> grace reigns supreme, the equality of saints is significantly conditioned on by the priority of the last. The sovereignty of grace relegates the doctrine of rewards to a position of lesser importance. Although nothing in the context suggests this, Matthew's church possibly identified those who worked the whole day with Israel and those who came last with the Gentiles, thus understanding the parable to signify the equality of gentile Christians with Jewish Christians" (Word Biblical Commentary, Volume 33B, 2000, p. 573, ed. Ralph P. Martin).

The fact that Jesus makes the point of saying that "the last shall be first and the first last" is also significant. In ancient times, wages were generally paid to the day laborers on rule of 'first come–first served'. Generally, the first to come would have received 'more' pay than that of the latecomer. William Hendriksen points out that had the day workers been paid according to the traditional rule, they would have immediately left and would not have seen what happened to the others (New Testament Commentary: Exposition of the Gospel according to Matthew, 2007, p. 738). Thus, the unusual request by the landowner of the vineyard to pay the workers in the reverse order beginning with the last group to the first is consistent with redeeming grace, and the idea that the first group complained about the latecomers being given equal pay illustrates it even more so. The first workers grumbled because they thought they 'would receive more' than the latecomers, whereas the latecomers, though not explicitly stated, were probably very grateful for the landowner's generosity because they knew that they 'didn't deserve it'.

In the material world the rule of 'first come—first served' is generally applied; but in the kingdom world, as illustrated by the parable, at whatever hour of the day we believe, the last is always given the same amount of saving grace as the first. In the final analysis, all spiritual teachings on kingdom principles are usually contrary to the principles of the world.

"and whoever wishes to be first among you shall be your slave"
(Matthew 20:27);

The Two Sons—Matthew 21:28-32

Jesus had already made His triumphal entry into Jerusalem, had already cleansed the temple, and had already healed the blind and the lame that had gone to him. When the people saw all of Jesus' wonderful acts, they praised Him, which outraged the religious leaders. Following this incident, Jesus leaves the city with His disciples, goes to Bethany, then returns to Jerusalem and goes back to the temple where he is confronted by the Jewish religious leaders who wanted to know from Him where and from whom had He received the authority to do the things that He was doing. In response to their question, Jesus poses them with the question, "*The baptism of John was from what source, from heaven or from men?*" Because the religious leaders were afraid to give the wrong answer, they agreed with each other to simply say, "*We do not know*" (vv. 1-27). Jesus then presents the first of the three successive parables to them.

The Parable of the Two Sons – Matthew 21:28-32: *"But what do you think? A man had two sons, and he came to the first and said, 'Son, go work today in the vineyard.' And he answered and said, 'I will, sir'; and he did not go. And he came to the second and said the same thing. But he answered and said, 'I will not'; yet he afterward regretted it and went. Which of the two did the will of his father?" They said, 'The latter.' Jesus said to them, 'Truly I say to you that the tax-gatherers and harlots will get into the kingdom of God before you.' "*

Consistent with God's Word, His spiritual teachings are timeless and universal. They have no boundaries—they just are; the lessons apply equally now as they did then. The same themes of 'the first shall be last and the last first' as well as the opportunity to receive the free gift of salvation found in the parable of the Laborers in the Vineyard can also be found in the parable of the Two Sons. Alongside these consistencies, Jesus' new kingdom teaching on 'outward actions stem from the heart' is also brought to light when the actions of first son are paralleled with the actions of the second son. Within these same comparisons, lessons on obedience and repentance can also be seen. The first son said, 'I will go' but did not, and the second son said, 'I will not go' but 'changed his mind' (repented) and did, proved him to be more obedient than the first.

Moreover, because the house of Israel rejected the free gift of salvation before it was offered to the gentile nations, Jesus makes the provocative statement that "*the tax-gathers and harlots will get into the kingdom of God before they do*" (v. 32). Historically, the tax-collectors and the prostitutes were despised and rejected by the religious leaders. Thus, the very idea that the 'sinners' were going to enter the kingdom of God before they did must have incensed the religious leaders all the more. Hence, by Jesus posing the question, "*which of the two did the will of his father?*", and the religious leaders giving the correct answer of "*the latter*", illustrates that the actions of the second son who had a change of heart and did go to the vineyard parallels the gentiles who believed the word of John the Baptist and Jesus. Likewise, the actions of the first son who said 'I will go' but did not go, parallels the house of Israel who ignored and rejected the messages of John the Baptist and of Jesus'. Warren W. Wiersbe makes the following observation:

> "The religious leaders committed two sins: They would not believe John's message and they would not repent of their sins. Of course, the leaders felt that they had no need to repent (Luke 18:9-14). But when they saw what repentance did for the publicans and sinners, they should have been convinced that John's message was true and salvation was real. Their rejection of John was actually a rejection of the Father who had sent him" (The Bible Exposition Commentary: New Testament, Volume I, 1989, p. 78).

By immediately following up with the parable of the Wicked Tenants, and its sequel, Jesus drives this point home.

"Thus says the LORD, Israel is My son, My first-born" (Exodus 4:22),

The Wicked Tenant Farmers—Matthew 21:28-32

"Listen to another parable. There was a landowner who PLANTED A VINEYARD AND PUT A WELL AROUND IT AND DUG A WINE PRESS IN IT, AND BUILT A TOWER, and rented it out to vine-growers, and went on a journey. And when the harvest time approached, he sent his slaves to the vine-growers to receive his produce. And the vine-growers took his slaves and beat one, and killed another, and stoned a third. Again he sent another group of slaves larger than the first; and they did the same thing to them. But afterward he sent his son to them, saying, 'They will respect my son.' But when the vine-growers saw the son, they said among themselves, 'This is the heir; come, let us kill him, and seize his inheritance.' And they took him, and cast him out of the vineyard, and killed him. Therefore when the owner of the vineyard comes, what will he do to those vine-growers?" (Matthew 21:28-32; Mark 12:1-11; Luke 20:9-18).

The religious leaders knew the Scriptures well. No doubt that the illustration of the slaves who were sent by the vineyard landowner to receive his produce are analogous to the prophets of old who were sent by God to the house of Israel to prophesy about the coming Messiah. Old Testament Scripture testifies to each of their deaths suffered by the hands of the nation. Dr. Donald A. Hagner observes:

> "The servants sent by the master of the vineyard were not only resisted, as were the OT prophets sent by God, but were severely treated and even put to death (the persecution of the prophets is a familiar theme in the OT; cf. Jeremiah, who was beaten, according to Jer 20:2, and Uriah the prophet, killed in Jer 26:21-23; Zechariah is stoned in 2 Chr 24:21; cf. the general reference to the killing of prophets in Neh 9:26). Repeatedly the lord of

the vineyard sent servants and repeatedly they were beaten or killed. Finally, the master decides to send 'his son'. The allusion here to the Father sending of His Son, Jesus (cf.10:40; 15:24) is unmistakable. The master of the vineyard thus sends the one closest to him, his son—his own flesh and blood—in the confidence that such an emissary will not receive the same treatment but will be received as the master himself would be" (Word Biblical Commentary, Volume 33B, 2000, pp. 620-621, ed. Ralph P. Martin).

Another factor to consider is the vineyard. The Prophet Isaiah had already disclosed that the "vineyard of the Lord of hosts *is* the house of Israel" (Isaiah 5:7). William Barclay provides a historical understanding on how this connection is made.

"The hedge around the vineyard was a thickset thorn hedge, designed to keep out both the wild boars which might ravage the vineyard, and the thieves who might steal the grapes. Every vineyard had its wine press. The wine press consisted of two troughs either hollowed out of the rock, or built of bricks; the one was a little higher than the other, and was connected with the lower one by a channel. The grapes were pressed in the higher trough, and the juice ran off into the lower trough. The tower served a double purpose. It served as a watch-tower, from which to watch for the thieves when the grapes were ripening; and it served as lodging for those who were working in the vineyard. The actions of the owner of the vineyard were all quite normal. In the time of Jesus, Palestine was a troubled place with little luxury; it was, therefore, very familiar with absentee landlords, who let out their estates and were interested only in collecting the rental at the right time. The rent might be paid in any of three ways. It might be a money rent; it might be a fixed amount of the fruit, no matter what the crop might be; and it might be an agreed percentage of the crop. Even the action of the cultivators was not unusual. The country was seething with economic unrest; the working people were discontented and

> rebellious; and the action of the cultivators in seeking to eliminate the son was not by any means impossible. Therefore it would have been easy for those who heard this parable to make the necessary identifications" (William Barclay, The Gospel of Matthew, Volume II, 2001, pp. 305-306).

The parable then concludes with a question Jesus poses to the religious leaders. "W*hen the owner of the vineyard comes, what will he do to those vine-growers*?" Not realizing that their answer would be the basis for their own judgment, the religious leaders replied, "*He will bring those wretches to a wretched end, and will rent the vineyard to other vine-growers, who will pay him at the proper season."* In turn, Jesus immediately pronounces the following judgment:

> *"Did you never read in the Scriptures, THE STONE WHICH THE BUILDERS REJECTED, THIS BECAME THE CHIEF CORNER stone; THIS CAME ABOUT FROM THE LORD, AND IT IS MARVELOUS IN OUR EYES?"* (Psalms 118:2-23). *"Therefore I say to you, the kingdom of God will be taken away from you, and be given to a nation producing the fruit of it. And he who falls on this stone will be broken to pieces; but on whomever it falls, it will scatter him like dust"* (vv. 42-44).

The fact that Jesus quotes from the Psalms was not coincidental. The religious leaders understood quite well that Jesus was speaking about them (v. 45), and Jesus had already made the statement that He did not come to abolish the Law or the Prophets, but to fulfill them (Matthew 5:17). Another factor to consider is the statement, '*The Stone which the builders rejected*'. The Prophets Isaiah and Daniel had already written about it and the religious leaders were quite familiar with these Scriptures as well (Isaiah 8:13-15; 28:16; Daniel 2:34, 44-45).

Finally, the concluding pronouncement of judgment made by Jesus makes it perfectly clear that the first son in the parable of the Two Sons, and the vine-growers in the parable of the Wicked Tenant Farmers both refer to the house of Israel. Dr. Louis A. Barbieri, Jr. sheds light on the harsh pronouncement of judgment. He writes:

"Because of their rejection, that generation of Israel would never be able to experience the kingdom of God (cf. comments on 21:18-22). But a future generation in Israel will respond in saving faith to this same Messiah (Rom. 11:26-27), and to that generation the kingdom will be given. By rejecting Jesus **the Stone**, these **builders** (Matt: 21:42) suffered judgment (**he on whom it** [the Stone] **falls will be crushed**). The religious leaders (then **the chief priests and the Pharisees**, v. 45; cf. v. 23) realized Jesus' remarks were directed toward **them**, and they tried their best to **arrest Him. But they were afraid of ... people** (cf. v. 26), who thought Jesus was a **Prophet** (cf. v. 11), so they were unable to act" (The Bible Knowledge Commentary: New Testament, 1983, p. 71, ed. John F. Walvoord, Roy B. Zuck).

Though this parable was addressed directly to the Jewish religious leaders, the messages are timeless and are therefore applicable today. William Barclay explains in detail how the symbology used in the parable reveals more about God's character.

"(1) It has much to tell us about God

(a) It tells of God's *trust* in human beings: The owner of the vineyard entrusted it to the cultivators. He did not stand over them to exercise supervision. He went away and left them with their task. God pays us the compliment of entrusting us with his work. Every task we receive is a task given us to do by God.

(b) It tells of God's *patience*: The master sent messenger after messenger. He did not come with sudden vengeance when one messenger had been abused and ill-treated. He gave the cultivators chance after chance to respond to his appeal.

(c) It tells of God's *judgment*: In the end, the master of the vineyard took the vineyard from the cultivators and gave it to others. God's sternest judgment is when he takes out of our hands the task which he meant us to do. To become useless to God is to sink to the lowest level.

(2) It has much to tell us about human nature

(a) It tells of human *privilege.* The vineyard was equipped with everything – the hedge, the wine press, the tower – which would make the task of the cultivators easy and enable them to discharge it well. God does not only give us a task to do; he also gives us the means whereby to do it.

(b) It tells of human *freedom.* The master left the cultivators to do the task as they liked. God is no tyrannical task-master; he is like a wise leader who allocates tasks and then trusts people to do them.

(c) It tells of human *answerability.* To everybody comes a day of reckoning. We are answerable for the way in which we have carried out the task God gave us to do.

(d) It tells of the *deliberateness of human sin.* The cultivators carry out a deliberate policy of rebellion and disobedience towards the master. Sin is deliberate opposition to God; it is the taking of our own way when we know quite well what the way of God is.

(3) It has much to tell us about Jesus.

(a) It tells of the *claim of Jesus*. It shows us quite clearly Jesus lifting himself out of the succession of the prophets. Those who came before him were the messengers of God; no one could deny them that honour; but they were servants; he was the Son. This parable contains one of the clearest claims Jesus ever made to be unique, to be different from even the greatest of those who went before.

(b) It tells of the *sacrifice of Jesus*. It makes it clear that Jesus knew what lay ahead. In the parable, the hands of the wicked men killed the son. Jesus was never in any doubt of what lay ahead. He did not die because he was compelled to die; he went willingly and with open eyes to death" (William Barclay, The Gospel of Matthew, Volume II, 2001, pp. 306-308).

"I am the true vine, and my Father is the vinedresser. Every branch in Me that does not bear fruit, He takes away; and every branch that bears fruit, He prunes it, that it may bear more fruit" (John 15:1-2).

The Wedding Feast—Matthew 22:1-14

The parable of the Wedding Feast is the last in the sequence of the three parables that Jesus spoke on *after* He had been confronted by the Jewish leaders. Perceiving that the messages in the parables were directed at them, the religious leaders desired to seize Him but were afraid of what the multitudes might do because they believed Jesus was a Prophet sent by God (Matthew 21:46).

The Parable of the Wedding Feast – Matthew 22:1-14: *"And Jesus spoke to them again in parables, saying, The kingdom of heaven may be compared to a king, who gave a wedding feast for his son. And he sent out his slaves to call those who had been invited to the wedding feast, and they were unwilling to come. Again he sent out other slaves saying, 'Tell those who have been invited, "Behold, I have prepared my dinner; my oxen and my fattened livestock are all butchered and everything is ready; come to the wedding feast." ' But they paid no attention and went their way, one to his own farm, another to his business, and the rest seized his slaves and mistreated them and killed them. But the king was enraged and sent his armies, and destroyed those murderers, and set their city on fire. Then he said to his slaves, 'The wedding is ready, but those who were invited were not worthy. Go therefore to the main highways, and as many as you find there, invite to the wedding feast.' And those slaves went out into the streets, and gathered together all they found, both evil and good; and the wedding hall was filled with dinner guests. But when the king came in to look over the dinner guests, he saw there a man not dressed in wedding clothes, and he said to him, 'Friend, how did you come in here without wedding clothes?' And he was speechless. Then the king said to the servants, 'Bind him hand and foot, and cast him into the outer darkness; in that place there shall be weeping and gnashing of teeth.' For many are called but few are chosen."*

The parable of the Wedding Feast carries the same theme of 'the first shall be last and the last first' that is found in first parables of the Two Sons and the Laborers in the Vineyard. The illustration of the king sending out his slaves to call the guests who had been invited to attend his son's wedding feast is analogous to the special invitation of the free gift of salvation that was initially offered to house of Israel. Likewise, the broadening of the invitation to include 'as many as you can find' reflects the inclusion of the gentile nations (vv. 9-10). On this point, William Barclay comments:

> "The events of the first two were completely in accordance with normal Jewish customs. When the invitations to a great feast, like a wedding feast, were sent out, the time was not stated; and when everything was ready, the servants were sent out with a final summons to tell the guests to come. So, the king in this parable had long ago sent out his invitations; but it was not until everything was prepared that the final summons was issued – and insultingly refused. This has a purely local meaning, driving home what had already been said in the parable of the wicked husbandmen; once again it was an accusation directed at the Jews. The invited guests, who when the time can refused to come; ages ago, they had been invited by God to be his chosen people; yet when God's Son came into the world, and they were invited to follow him, they contemptuously refused. The result was the invitation of God went out directly to the people in the highways and byways who never expected an invitation into the kingdom" (William Barclay, The Gospel of Matthew, Volume II, 2001, p. 310).

Additionally, the illustration of the slaves who had been sent out on behalf of the king to call those who had been invited and were seized, is paralleled with the prophets of old who had been sent forth to prepare the way for Jesus and were seized and put to death. Jesus concludes the parable with a pronouncement of judgment on the man who was not wearing proper wedding clothes, which coincides with the pronouncement of judgment concluding the parable of the Wheat and Tares and the Dragnet found in the parables of the Seven Mysteries of the Kingdom of Heaven. Though the parable was addressed directly to the Jewish religious leaders, the messages apply today. Unique to William Barclay's perspective, he states:

> "The invitation of God is to a feast as joyous as a wedding feast. His invitation is to joy. To think of Christianity as a gloomy giving up of everything which brings laughter and sunshine and happy fellowship is to mistake its whole nature. It is to joy that Christians are invited; and it is joy they miss, if they refuse the invitation.
>
> (b) It reminds us that the things which make people deaf to the invitation of Christ are not necessarily bad in themselves. In the parable, one man went to his estate; the other to his business. It is very easy to be so busy with the things of the present that the things of eternity are forgotten.
>
> (c) It reminds us that the appeal of Christ is not so much to consider how we will be punished as it is to see what we will miss.
>
> (d) It reminds us that in the last analysis God's invitation is the invitation of grace. Those who were gathered in from the highways and the byways had no claim on the king at all; they could never have expected an invitation to the wedding feast. It came from nothing other than the wide-armed, open-hearted, generous hospitality of the king. It was grace which offered the invitation, and it was grace which gathered them" (Ibid., pp. 312-313).

Finally, the introduction of the armies being sent to 'set their city on fire' is unique to the parable. Biblical history teaches that the temple in Jerusalem was indeed plundered and burned, and the city destroyed by the Roman armies in AD 70.

"O Jerusalem, Jerusalem, who kills the prophets and stones those who are sent to her! How often I wanted to gather your children together, the way a hen gathers her chicks under her wings, and you were unwilling. Behold, your house is being left to you desolate! For I say to you, from now on you shall not see Me until you say, 'BLESSED IS HE WHO COMES IN THE NAME OF THE LORD!' "
(Matthew 23:37-39).

Fifth Discourse
The Prophecy Parables

The next four parables, commonly known as the prophecy parables, are recorded successively in the Gospel of Matthew are associated with Jesus' fifth discourse otherwise known as The Olivet Discourse. The impetus for telling these parables, which were given privately to the disciples, is directly connected to a question that pertained to Jesus' prophecy about the destruction of the temple that the disciples asked Him as they were leaving the city of Jerusalem (Matthew 24:1-2). The disciples wanted to know: 1) when the temple would be destroyed, 2) what the signs of His coming would be, and 3) what the sign of the end of the age would be. *"Tell us, when will these things be, and what will be the sign of Your coming, and of the end of the age?"* (Matthew 24:3). Curiously, the answers to their questions are recorded in reverse order: Jesus first addresses the sign of the end of the age (Matthew 24:4-28), then addresses the sign of His second coming (Matthew 24:29-31). However, His answer to the third part of their question is not recorded by Matthew, but can be found in the Gospel of Luke. *"But when you see Jerusalem surrounded by armies, then recognize that her desolation is at hand"* (Luke 21:20).

Immediately following Jesus' lengthy reply (vv. 4-31) to the last part of the disciple's question, *"what will be the sign of the end of the age,"* Jesus replies, *"now learn the parable from the fig tree"* (v. 32), which is then followed by the additional two prophecy parables that are recorded consecutively.

The Parable of the Fig Tree – Matthew 24:32-44: *"Now learn the parable from the fig tree: when its branch has already become tender, and puts forth its leaves, you know that summer is near; even so you too, when you see all these things, recognize that He is near, right at the door. Truly I say to you, this generation will not pass away until all these things take place. Heaven and earth will pass away, but My words shall not pass away. But of that day and hour no one knows, not* *even the angels of heaven, nor the Son, but the Father alone. For the coming of the Son of Man will be just like the days of Noah. For as in those days which were before the flood they were eating and drinking, they were marrying and giving in marriage, until the day that NOAH ENTERED THE ARK, and they did not understand until the flood came and took them all away, so shall the coming of the Son of Man be. Then there shall be two men in the field; one will be taken, and one will be left. Two women will be grinding at the mill; one will be taken, and one will be left. Therefore be on the alert, for you do not know which day your Lord is coming. But be sure of this, that if the head of the house had known at what time of the night the thief was coming, he would have been on the alert and would not have allowed his house to be broken into. For this reason you be ready too; for the Son of Man is coming at an hour when you do not think He will"* (Matthew 24:32-44; Mark 13:28-37; Luke 21:29-36).

In this first parable in the sequence of four, Jesus illustrates 'the signs of the end of the age' by comparing them with the 'seasons' in which figs ripen, and with the 'conditions' that existed on earth before the flood. In the parable of the Fig Tree, Jesus likens the end of the age to the budding of the fig tree, which indicates that spring is at hand, and the fact that figs do not ripen until the summer, holds the expectation of a promise of what is to come. The disciples would have understood the comparison quite well. Figs were a common food staple and the fig tree was well known in Judea. The putting forth of its branches, leaves, and fruit were under constant observation by everyone. The comparison between the tender fig tree branches and soft leaves was the usual sign that winter was over, spring had come, and summer was on its way and the figs would be ready to pick, is compared to his exhortation to recognize that He is near, right at the door (v. 33). Moreover, when Jesus tells His disciples that the generation would not pass away until these things take place, He prefaces His statement with the word "verily (truly)". The Greek translation for the term verily is amēn, and when prefaced at the beginning of a discourse, it means, "I solemnly declare unto you"

(Thayer's Greek Lexicon, 2009, G281, p. 32), thus affirming that His word will come to pass.

Barren Fig Tree Tender Fig Branch
Images provided by Mitra Encyclopedia
http://encyclopedia.mitrasites.com/imgs/parable-of-the-budding-fig-tree.html
http://www.publicdomainpictures.net/view-image.php?image=5443&picture=fig, 2012.

A mature fig tree usually grows up to a height of about fifteen feet. There are several varieties of Palestinian fig trees. Its foliage is dense, and the fruit of the fig tree usually ripens during the summer months between June and August. By December, all of the trees have shed their leaves, and new leaf buds appear only in March when the tiny figs appear simultaneously in the leaf axils (R. K. Harrison, Eerdman's *International Standard Bible Encyclopedia,* Volume E-J, 1982, pp. 301-302, ed. Geoffrey W. Bromiley).

Similarly, Jesus draws a direct parallel between the signs of the condition of earth at the 'end of the age' with the conditions that existed in the days of Noah before judgment was executed on the wickedness on earth (Genesis 6:5-7). In preparation, God instructed Noah to build the ark, all the while the people carried on with their lives until the day came when God instructed Noah to enter the ark and shut the door tight. There is no record of the length of time that it took Noah to prepare the ark. However, Scripture does record that Noah was five hundred years old when he became the father of Shem, Ham, and Japheth, and was six hundred years old when the flood came (Genesis 7:6). He lived three hundred and fifty years after the flood, died at the age of nine hundred and fifty (Genesis 9:28-29), and in all his years, Noah did all that God commanded (Genesis 6:22).

Finally, Jesus' exhortation to 'be prepared' can be seen in the contrast He makes with the illustration of the unpreparedness of the people in the days of Noah. "*and they did not understand until the flood came and took them all away, so shall the coming of the Son of Man be*" (v. 39), and with the analogy of the head of the household and the thief who, "*had he known at what time of the night the thief was coming, he would have been on the alert and would not have allowed his house to be broken into*" (v. 43).

> "*Therefore be on the alert, for you do not know which day your Lord is coming*" (Matthew 24:42).

The Second Prophecy Parable—Matthew 24:45-51

The preceding parable of the Fig Tree is associated with the third part of the disciples' question of "what will be the sign of the end of the age?" This question is answered by Jesus: "*the Son of man is coming at an hour when you do not think He will*" (v. 44). The parable then concludes with an exhortation 'to be prepared.' Although this second parable is a continuation of Jesus' exhortation for us to be ready that concludes the preceding parable, it is in response to the second part of the disciples' question of "what will be the sign of Your coming?"

The Parable of the Faithful and Wicked Servants – Matthew 24:45-51: "*Who then is the faithful and sensible slave whom his master put in charge of his household to give them their food at the proper time: Blessed is that slave whom his master finds so doing when he comes. Truly I say to you, that he will put him in charge of all his possessions. But if that evil slave says in his heart, 'My master is not coming for a long time,' and shall begin to beat his fellow-slaves and eat and drink with drunkards; the master of that slave will come on a day when he does not expect him and at an hour which he does not know, and shall cut him in pieces and assign him a place with the hypocrites; weeping shall be there and the gnashing of teeth*" (Matthew 24:45-51; Luke 12:42-48).

The same theme of 'no one knows the hour of His coming' found in the preceding parable is seen in the surprise arrival of the great flood and in the surprise arrival of the wicked servant's master. In both instances, the people illustrated in the parables were caught unprepared. A comparison between the conditions of the heart can also be seen in the parallels drawn between the behavior of the faithful servant and Noah, and the behavior of the wicked servant and the 'wickedness that prevailed on earth in the days of Noah.' Whereas the first servant's faithfulness is reflected in his actions by doing what his master asked him to do while he was away, the actions of the wicked servant were like those of the people in the days of Noah.

Finally, the illustration of judgment that is passed upon the wicked servant, "*the master of that slave will come on a day when he does not expect him and at an hour which he does not know, and shall cut him in pieces and assign him a place with the hypocrites; weeping shall be there and the gnashing of teeth*" (v. 51), is similar to the judgment passed upon the man who was not wearing proper wedding clothes in the parable of the Wedding Feast (Matthew 22:1-14). *"Then the king said to the servants, Bind him hand and foot, and cast him into the outer darkness; in that place there shall be weeping and gnashing of teeth"* (Matthew 22:13). On this point, William Barclay offers his insightful comments:

> "To live without watchfulness invites disaster; thieves do not send a letter saying when they are going to burgle a house; the principal weapon in their wicked undertakings is surprise; therefore a householder who has valuables in the house must maintain a constant guard. But to get this picture right, we must remember that the watching of the Christian for the coming of Christ is not that of terror-stricken fear and shivering apprehension; it is the watching of eager expectation for the coming of glory and joy" (William Barclay, The Gospel of Matthew, Volume II, 2001, p. 370).

> *"For this reason you be ready too; for the Son of Man is coming at an hour when you do not think He will"* (Matthew 24:44).

The Third Prophecy Parable—Matthew 25:1-13

The third prophecy parable is in connection to the question 'what is the sign of Your coming' that Jesus already answered. Thus, the parable of the Ten Virgins drives home the urgent message on the importance of readiness. I like to call it 'the left behind' parable in the series.

The Parable of the Ten Virgins – Matthew 15:1-13: "*Then the kingdom of heaven will be comparable to ten virgins, who took their lamps, and went out to meet the bridegroom. And five of them were foolish, and five were prudent. For when the foolish took their lamps, they took no oil with them, but the prudent took oil in flasks along with their lamps. Now while the bridegroom was delaying, they all got drowsy and began to sleep. But at midnight there was a shout, 'Behold, the bridegroom! Come out to meet him.' Then all those virgins arose, and trimmed their lamps. And the foolish said to the prudent, 'Give us some of your oil, for our lamps are going out.' But the prudent answered, saying, 'No, there will not be enough for us and you too; go instead to the dealers and buy some for yourselves.' And while they were going away to make the purchase, the bridegroom came, and those who were ready went in with him to the wedding feast; and the door was shut. And later the other virgins also came, saying, 'Lord, lord, open up for us.' But he answered and said, 'Truly I say to you, I do not know you.' Be on the alert then, for you do not know the day nor the hour.*"

One of the greatest attributes of Jesus' parables is the timeless application of their messages. Of significance, in the opening statement of the parable of the Ten Virgins, Jesus begins by saying, "the kingdom of heaven '*will be*' comparable to the ten virgins", which reveals that He is speaking about the future. This future event may be likened to the illustration Jesus made in the parable of the budding Fig Tree in that by observing the tender branches, tells that summer is near and the fruit will ripen. Moreover, the parable was a reflection of the Jewish wedding custom of the day; thus the disciples would have easily understood the meaning of the comparison drawn between the wise and foolish virgins. William Barclay gives us a glimpse into the historical way in which Jewish weddings were practiced in Palestine.

> "The point of the story lies in Jewish custom which is very different from anything we know. When a couple married, they did not go away for a honeymoon. They stayed at home for a week; for a week they kept open house; they were treated, and even addressed, as prince and princess; it was the happiest week in all their lives. To the festivities of that week their chosen friends were admitted; and it was not only the marriage ceremony, it was also that joyous week that the foolish virgins missed, because they were unprepared.
>
> The story of how they missed it all is perfectly true to life. Dr. J. Alexander Findlay tells of what he himself saw in Palestine. 'When we were approaching the gates of a Galilean town,' he writes, 'I caught a sight of ten maidens gaily clad and playing some kind of musical instrument, as they danced along the road in front of our car; when I asked what they were doing, the interpreter told me that they were going to keep the bride company till her bridegroom arrived. I asked him if there was any chance of seeing the wedding, but he shook his head, saying in effect: "It might be tonight, or tomorrow night, or in a fortnight's time, nobody ever knows for certain." Then he went on to explain that one of the great things to do, if you could, at a middle-class wedding in Palestine was to catch the bridal party napping. So the bridegroom comes unexpectedly, and sometimes in the middle of the night; it is true that he is required by public opinion to send a man along the street to shout: "Behold! The bridegroom is coming!" but that may happen at any time; so the bridal party have to be ready to go out into the street at any time to meet him, whenever he

> chooses to come … Other important points are that no one is allowed on the streets after dark without a lighted lamp, and also that, when the bridegroom has once arrived, and the door has been shut, late-comers to the ceremony are not admitted.' There, the whole drama of Jesus' parable is re-enacted in the twentieth century" (William Barclay, The Gospel of Matthew, Volume II, 2001, pp. 372-373).

The attribute of the timelessness in the urgent message of the exhortation 'to be ready' continues to apply to the present as well as to the future. On this point, Warren W. Wiersbe offers his insights.

> "A wedding in that day had two parts. First, the bridegroom and his friends would go from his house to claim the bride from her parents. Then the bride and groom would return to the groom's house for the marriage feast. The suggestion here is that the groom has already claimed his bride and is now on his way back home.
>
> The church has known for two thousand years that Jesus is coming again, and yet many believers have become lethargic and drowsy. They are no longer excited about the soon-coming of the Lord. As a result, there is little effective witness given that the Lord is returning.
>
> The oil for burning reminds us of the special oil used in the tabernacle services (Ex. 27:20-21). Oil is usually a symbol of the Spirit of God, but I wonder if this particular oil is not also a symbol of the Word of God. The church should be "holding forth the word of life" in this dark and wicked world (Phil. 2:12-16). We need to keep the word of His patience (Rev. 3:10) and keep witnessing of the return of Jesus Christ.
>
> When the bridegroom and bride appeared, half of the bridesmaids were unable to light their lamps because they had no oil. "Our lamps are going out!" they cried. The bridesmaids who had oil were able to light their lamps and keep them shining bright. It was they who entered into the wedding feast and not the foolish girls who had no oil. This suggests that not

every professing Christian will enter heaven, for some really have not trusted Jesus Christ sincerely. Without the Spirit of God and the Word of God, there can be no true salvation.

Jesus ended this parable with the warning He had uttered before: "Watch" (Matt. 24:42; 25:13). This does not mean standing on a mountaintop gazing at the heavens (Acts 1:9-11). It means 'stay awake and be alert' " (The Bible Exposition Commentary: New Testament, Volume I, 1989, pp. 91-92).

Dr. C. I. Scofield concludes:

"The kingdom of heaven here is the sphere of profession, as in Mt. 13. All alike have lamps, but two facts fix the real status of the foolish virgins: They "took no oil," and the Lord said, "I know you not." Oil is the symbol of the Holy Spirit, and "If any man have not the spirit of Christ, he is none of his" (Rom. 9.9). Nor could the Lord say to any believer, however unspiritual, 'I know you not' " (Matthew 25, p. 1035).

"Be on the alert then, for you do not know the day nor the hour" (Matthew 25:13);
"Those who were ready went in with him to the wedding feast; and the door was shut" (v. 10).

The Fourth Prophecy Parable —Matthew 25:14-30

Though the fourth prophecy parable of the Ten Talents is a continuation of the Ten Virgins, it introduces the new themes of faithful stewardship, and the principle of the settling of accounts upon the master's return. Traces of the exhortation 'to be ready', and of judgment, may still be found within it. In the preceding parable of the Ten Virgins, Jesus began by saying, "*the kingdom of heaven will be comparable to*" **...** However, by Jesus continuing the parable of the Ten Talents by saying, "*for it is just like a man*", indicates that '*it'* refers to "the kingdom of heaven". Thus, it may be read, the kingdom of heaven is just like a man about to go on a journey.

The Parable of the Ten Talents – Matthew 25:14-30: *"For it is just like a man about to go on a journey, who called his own slaves, and entrusted his possessions to them. And to one he gave five talents, to another, two, and to another, one, each according to his own ability; and he went on his journey. Immediately the one who had received the five talents went and traded with them, and gained five more talents. In the same manner the one who had received the two talents gained two more. But he who received the one talent went away and dug in the ground, and hid his master's money. Now after a long time the master of those slaves came and settled accounts with them. And the one who had received the five talents came up and brought five more talents, saying, 'Master, you entrusted five talents to me; see, I have gained five more talents.' His master said to him, 'Well done, good and faithful slave; you were faithful with a few things, I will put you in charge of many things, enter into the joy of your master.' The one also who had received the two talents came up and said, 'Master, you entrusted to me two talents; see, I have gained two more talents.' His master said to him, 'Well done, good and faithful slave; you were faithful with a few things, I will put you in charge of many things; enter into the joy of your master.' And the one also who had received* *the one talent came up and said, 'Master, I knew you to be a hard man, reaping where you did not sow, and gathering where you scattered no seed. And I was afraid, and went away and hid your talent in the ground; see, you have what is yours.' But his master answered and said to him, 'You wicked, lazy slave, if you knew that I reap where I did not sow, and gather where I scattered no seed. Then you ought to have put my money in the bank, and on my arrival I would have received my money back with interest. 'Therefore take away the talent from him, and give it to the one who has the ten talents.' For to everyone who has shall more be given, and he shall have an abundance; but from the one who does not have, even what he does have shall be taken away. And cast out the worthless slave into the outer darkness; in that place there shall be weeping and gnashing of teeth."*

The urgent messages of 'be ready, for no one knows the day nor the hour your Lord is coming, and of judgment' that is illustrated in the preceding prophecy parables are once again illustrated. The story does not provide any specifics on the duration of the master's journey, it tells only that the master entrusted his servants with his possessions, went on a journey, and upon his return settled the accounts, then passed judgment. Adopting Dr. Donald A. Hagner's view of "spiritual messages taught in the parables impact the readers at their own personal level of spiritual growth" validates the diversity of interpretative views offered by a variety of expert expositors, which are noted in two parts. While Part I of the first set of diversified views pertain to the master and the talents, the concluding set pertains to the concluding paragraph on judgment. Among the more notable is Matthew Henry who offers a variety of insights into the complexity of the messages in the parable.

> "In this parable, 1. The *Master* is Christ, who is the absolute Owner and Proprietor of all persons and things, and in a special manner of his church; into his hands all things are delivered. [2.] The *servants* are Christians, his own servants, so they are

called; born in his house, bought with his money, devoted to his praise, and employed in his work. We have three things, in general, in this parable. [1.] The trust committed to these servants; Their master *delivered to them his goods*: having appointed them to work (for Christ keeps no servants to be idle), he left them something to work upon. [2]. Our receiving from Christ is in order to our working for him. Our privileges are intended to find us with business. The *manifestation of the Spirit* is given to every man to *profit withal*. [3.] Whatever we receive to be made use of for Christ, still the property is vested in him; we are but tenants upon his land, *stewards of his manifold grace*, 1 Pet. 4:10.

(1.) On what occasion this trust was committed to these servants: The *master was travelling into a far country*. This is explained, Eph. 4:8. *When he ascended on high, he gave gifts to men.*

(2.) In what proportion this trust was committed. [1.] He gave *talents*; a talent of silver is computed to be in our money three hundred and fifty three pounds. Note, Christ's gifts are rich and valuable, the purchases of his blood inestimable, and none of them mean. [2.] He gave to some more, to others less; to one *five* talents, to another *two*, to another *one*; to every one according to his several ability.

II. The different management and improvement of this trust, which we have an account of, v. 16-18.

(1.) They were diligent and faithful; *They went, and traded*; they put the money they were entrusted with, to the use for which it was intended – laid it out in goods, and made returns of it; as soon as ever their master was gone, they immediately applied themselves to their business.

(2.) They were successful; they doubled their stock, and in a little time made *cent per cent* of it: he that had *five talents*, soon made them *other five.* Trading with our talents is not always successful with others, but, however, it shall be so to ourselves, Isa. 49:4. Observe, the returns were in proportion to the receiving. The third did ill (v. 18); He that had received one talent, went, and hid his lord's money. Though the parable represents but one in three unfaithful, yet in history that answers this parable, we find the disproportion quite the other way, when ten lepers were cleansed, nine of ten hid the talent, and only one returned to give thanks, Luke 17:17, 18. The unfaithful servant was he that had but *one* talent; doubtless there are many that have five talents, and bury them all; great abilities, great advantages, and yet do no good with them.

III. The account of the improvement, v. 19.

(1.) The servants *giving up the account* (v. 20, 22); "*Lord, thou deliveredst to me five talents, and to me two;* behold, *I have gained five talents*, and *I have two talents more.*" *First* Christ's faithful servants acknowledge with thankfulness his vouchsafements to them; *Lord, thou deliveredst to me* such and such… Note, It is good to keep a particular account of our receivings from God, to remember what we have received, that we may know what is expected from us, and may render according to the benefit. *Secondly*, They produce, as an evidence o their faithfulness, what they have gained. Note, God's good stewards have something to show for their diligence; *Show me thy faith by thy works*. He that is a good man, *let him show it.* Jam. 3:13.

(2.) The master's acceptance and approbation of their account, v. 21, 23. First, He commended them: *Well done, good and faithful servant.* Note, The diligence and integrity of those who approve themselves the good and faithful servants of Jesus Christ, will certainly be *found to praise, and honour, and glory, at his appearing,* 1 Pet. 1:7. *Secondly*, He rewards them. The faithful servants of Christ shall not be put off with bare commendation; no all their work and labour of love shall be rewarded. [1.] In one expression agreeable to the parable; *Thou has been faithful over a few things, I will make thee ruler over many things*. It is usual in the courts of princes, and families of great men, to advance those to higher offices, that have been faithful in lower. Note, Christ is a master that will prefer his servants who acquit themselves well. Christ has honour in store for those that honour him—*a crown* (2 Tim. 4:8), *a throne* (Rev. 3:21), *a kingdom*, *ch.* 25:34. Here they are beggars; in heaven they shall be rulers. [2.] In another expression, which slips out of the parable into the thing signified by it; *Enter thou into the joy of thy Lord,* Note, The state of the blessed is a state of joy, not only because all tears shall then be wiped away, but all the springs of comfort shall be opened to them, and the fountains of joy broken up" (Matthew Henry's Commentary on the Whole Bible, 1991, Volume 5, pp. 301-304).

Dr. Herbert Lockyer adds:

"The main lines of interpretation are not difficult to follow. The wealthy master referred to as "Lord" by his servants is "the Son of Man," the Lord Jesus Christ. The journey into the far country refers to His departure into heaven after His Ascension. The servants, or bond-servants, or slaves were, in the first instance, the twelve disciples to whom Jesus addressed the parable, and then in a broader sense all born-again believers. By the talents we are to understand the spiritual gifts Jesus received for His servants and which he dispenses to them. The lord, absent from his home, suggests the withdrawal of Christ's visible presence form the earth; while his return is equivalent to the Master's promised return. The trading of the servants during their master's absence indicates the faithful use the Lord's people should make of spiritual gifts, and opportunities for service. The commendation of the servants by their master on his return sets forth what can be expected at the Judgment Seat of Christ, when our service is to be reviewed.

(1.) The Nature and number of talents. What are we to understand by talent? Today, we use the word in a different sense and speak of a person as being "talented" meaning, he has some outstanding natural ability in one direction or another. But here, the word means something different. The original word "talantos" is a noun rather of quantity, not a revelation of quality. "Talent," as used by Jesus, does not mean something we possess, but which He possesses and loans to His servants. All the talents in the parable belonged to the lord and were handed over by him to his servants to be used in trade. As to the distribution of the talents, the master gave one servant "five," another "two" and the third "one." Does this not teach that God's gifts accomplish much more through some than through others? The whole truth of God is of equal value, and every servant of Christ owns the whole revelation, but the fact remains that different servants receive from the Lord differing measures of spiritual understanding. We do not receive more from him than we can understand and use. The qualifying clause in the use of the talents is, "to every man according to his several ability."

(2.) The use and abuse of the Talents. When the servant received the five talents, and the second servant his two talents, we read that both of them went "straightway" (Mathew 25:16, 17 R.V.) and traded with same. What great force there is in this word, "straightway," meaning immediately! There was no delay. They knew not how long their master would be absent, so as soon as he left they started to trade. "What thy hand findeth to do, do it with thy might." They traded, or bartered until they doubled what they had. The one with five talents made other five —100%. In each case, original capital was doubled. Had the man with only one talent traded with it, his gain would have been the same. Are grace and power ours to double our original, spiritual capital? Having received grace, has growth been ours in grace? Has desire for prayer been intensified? Is our hope more firm and real? Have earlier aspirations ripened? Have our spiritual influence and results in service multiplied?

(3.) The Return and Reward of the Talents. The phrase, "after a long time the Lord of those servants cometh," does not imply that Jesus meant to teach that His second advent was not to be expected for centuries. He never set a time for His coming, seeing He may come at any time. This we know, there is always time enough before He comes for "diligent servants to double the capital entrusted to them." What a reckoning there was when the servants appeared before their lord! The first and second servants proudly related their success in trading, and gave their master back his own with double interest. Both were rewarded in exactly the same way. Both received the praise: "Well done!"

> Both received the promise: "I will make you ruler." Both received glory: "Enter thou into the joy of thy lord." "The joy of the Lord" is full a full joy: the joy, faithful service brings Him, the joy of His approval, the joy of seeing others in heaven because of our faithfulness" (Lockyer, All the Parables of the Bible, 1963, pp. 243-246).

William Barclay writes:

"There can be no doubt that originally in this parable the whole attention is riveted on the useless servant. There can be little doubt that he stands for the scribes and the Pharisees and for their attitude to the law and the truth of God. The useless servant buried his talent in the ground, in order that he might hand it back to his master exactly as it was. The whole aim of the scribes and Pharisees was to keep the law exactly as it was. In their own phrase, they sought 'to build a fence around the law'. Any change, any development, any alteration, anything new was to them anathema. Their method involved the paralysis of religious truth. Like the man with the talent, they desired to keep things exactly as they were – and it is for that they are condemned. In this parable, Jesus tells us that there can be no religion without adventure, and that God can find no use for the shut mind. But there is much more in this parable than that:

(1) It tells us that God gives us differing gifts. One man received five talents, another two, and another one. It is not our talent which matters; what matters is how we use it. God never demands from us abilities which we have not got; but he does demand that we should use to the full the abilities which we do possess. Human beings are not equal in talent; but they can be equal in effort. The parable tells us that

whatever talent we have, little or great, we must lay it at the service of God.

(2) It tells us that the reward of work well done is still more work to do. The two servants who had done well are not told to lean back and rest on their oars because they have done well. They are given greater tasks and greater responsibilities in the work of the master.

(3) It tells us that those who are punished are the people who will not try. The man with the one talent did not lose his talent; he simply did nothing with it. Even if he had adventured with it and lost it, it would have been better than to do nothing at all.

(4) It lays down a rule of life which is universally true. It tells us that to those who have, more will be given, and those who have not will lose even what they have. The meaning is this. If we have a talent and exercise it, we are progressively able to do more with it. But, if we have a talent and fail to exercise it, we will inevitably lose it" (William Barclay, The Gospel of Matthew, Volume II, 2001, pp. 377-378).

Dr. John Gill states:

"By these talents, special grace is not meant; for the parable speaks not of what was wrought in these servants, but of what was committed to their trust, and of what might lie useless by them, and be taken away from them; whereas special grace is internal, something implanted in man, and is an incorruptible seed, that can never be lost, or will be taken away; and it is certain, that one of these servants had not special and saving grace, but was wicked, slothful, and unprofitable, and was cast into utter darkness: but outward gifts are designed by the talents; and these not merely the gifts of natural knowledge and riches, the gifts of nature and providence; nor the external ministry of the word, Gospel ordinances, and opportunities of enjoying them; but ministerial gifts, such as fit and qualify men to be preachers of the Gospel, as appears from their name *talents*: they being the greatest gifts for usefulness and service in the church, as talents were the greatest of weights and coins among the Jews; from the nature of them, being what may be improved or lost, and for which men are accountable; from the persons to whom they were delivered, the servants of Christ; from the time of their delivery, when Christ went into a far country, to heaven, when he ascended on high, and received gifts for men, and gave them to them; and from the unequal distribution of them, being given to some more, and others less; all which perfectly agree with ministerial gifts: for it follows, *to another two, and to another one;* and these were given *to every man, according to his several ability,* or *according to his own power*; his proper power that belonged to him, as the Lord of these servants: for the sense is, not that he gave these talents, or gifts, according to the different capacities, abilities, stations, and employments of these men; but according to that power and authority which he, as Mediator, had, to dispense these gifts severally as he would; to some more, others less, as he know would best serve his interest and kingdom: *and straightway took his journey*: after he had signified, that all power in heaven and earth was given to him, by virtue of which he ordered them to go into all the world, and preach his Gospel, and administer his ordinances; for which he had, and would abundantly qualify them; with a promise of his presence with them to the end of the world; he took his leave of them, blessed them, and was parted from them, and went up into heaven" (Gills Expositor, Exposition of The New Testament, Volume VII, 1976, pp. 309-310).

William Hendriksen concludes:

"The point of the parable, then, is this, *Let everyone be faithful in using the opportunities for service which the Lord has given him.* These opportunities, bestowed upon each according to his (God-given) ability, should, out of gratitude to God, be improved in such a manner that the glory of God Triune is advanced, his kingdom extended, and his "little ones" benefited. A few subsidiary points may be noted:

a. Whatever we have, whether opportunities or ability to use them to advantage, belongs to God. We *possess*. God *owns*. What we have is still "his property" We are stewards. See Matt. 25:14; also Luke 16:2; 1 Cor. 4:1, 2; 6:19, 20; I Peter 4:10.
b. The Lord grants us opportunities for service in accordance with our ability to make use of them. Accordingly, since not all men have the same ability, therefore not all have the same, or an equal number of, opportunities. In the Day of Judgment the number (of opportunities for service, "talents") will not matter. The question is only, "Have we been faithful in their use?" See Matt. 25:15, 16, 19-23; also 7:24-27.
c. Not only *committing* murder, adultery, theft, etc. is wrong, but so is also *omitting* good deeds to the glory of God. See. Matt. 25:18, 26; also 25:41-45; James 4:17.
d. Jesus did not expect to return immediately. He knew that a relatively long time would elapse before his return. See Matt. 25:19; also 24:9, 14; 25:5; II Thess. 2:2; II Peter 3:4-9; Rev. 20:1-3; 7-11.
e. Everything should be done with a view to the day of reckoning that is coming. "How will this wish, thought, word, or deed, look on the day of final judgment?" is the question that should constantly be asked. See Matt. 25:19; also 25:35-45; Eccles. 12:14; Luke 12:47, 48; Rom. 2:16; II Cor. 5:10; Rev. 20:13.
f. Though, in the light of their meaning for eternity, our responsibilities here and now are very important, they

will be surpassed by those in the life hereafter. See Matt. 25:21, 23.

g. To share the Master's own joy and the joy of all the saved is the glory of the life hereafter. See Matt. 25:21, 23; also II Tim. 4:8; and N.T.C. on Eph. 3:15.
h. Instead of being true to his trust, a wicked and lazy person will offer excuses. See Matt. 25:24-30; also 7:22, 23; 25:44; Luke 13:26, 27. None will avail" (New Testament Commentary: Exposition of the Gospel according to Matthew, 2007, pp. 884-885).

The concluding paragraph of the parable tells of the wicked servant who tells his master the reason he didn't do anything with his talent is because '*he knew him to be a hard man, reaping where he did not sow, and gathering where he scattered no seed*' (v. 24). After a few strong words of disapproval, the master passes judgment by saying, "*You wicked, lazy slave, if you knew that I reap where I did not sow, and gather where I scattered no seed. Then you ought to have put my money in the bank, and on my arrival I would have received my money back with interest. 'Therefore take away the talent from him, and give it to the one who has the ten talents.' For to everyone who has shall more be given, and he shall have an abundance; but from the one who does not have, even what he does have shall be taken away. And cast out the worthless slave into the outer darkness; in that place there shall be weeping and gnashing of teeth*" (vv. 26-30).

On the surface, the harsh judgment passed upon the wicked servant may communicate that believers will be given a harsh judgment "if" we do not properly handle the talents that we have been given. However, there are other factors to be considered. 1) Jesus was speaking privately to His disciples who were soon to be given *full charge* of spreading the Gospel and building His Church. 2) Throughout Jesus' parabolic teachings, He compares or contrasts the *spiritual* nature of the kingdom with or against the principles of the world. 3) Because of the attribute of timelessness found in the parables, different interpretations apply to differing levels of individual spiritual growth. 4) At the time the parable was spoken to the disciples, the New Covenant of grace had not yet been instituted, thus it was a message on the urgency of the need for salvation that is now entrusted to all believers everywhere. Finally, because the only "if" clause contained in the New Covenant of grace is, *"if you confess with your mouth Jesus as Lord, and believe in your heart that God raised Him from the dead, you shall be saved"* (10:9-10), the commonly held view is that the harsh judgment pertains to those who have not yet been saved. Accordingly, different perspectives held by various expert expositors that have commented on this concluding paragraph are as follows. In his book entitled, *What on Earth is Happening*, Ray Stedman writes:

> "This may seem to be unduly strict treatment for the servant with one talent. He at least had the sense to bury the talent so he wouldn't lose it! The master got all of his money back. Why is he being so harsh? When the master returned, the unprofitable servant had a well rehearsed speech ready. The gist of his defense was this: 'Master, I know you are an unreasonable man. You expect other people to do all the work while you take all the benefits. If people fail to meet your unreasonable expectations, you punish them without mercy. I was afraid of you. I was afraid to risk what you gave me, because if I lost it, you would really be angry with me when you returned. So I played it smart. I kept the talent in a safe place to make sure it wouldn't get lost—see? Here it is, safe and sound! You didn't lose a penny!' The master does not debate the servant's characterization of him as a hard and unreasonable man. He accepts that appraisal and says, "You wicked, lazy servant! The master is not agreeing with what the servant says. He is saying, in effect, "So that is your understanding of my character, is it? All right, then, out of your own mouth will I judge you."
>
> Of course, the real problem is that the unprofitable servant had no intention of being the servant he pretended to be. The master's argument is that no matter what his opinion of his master was, whether accurate or distorted, a true servant would

have acted in accord with his master's expectations. The unprofitable servant refused to do this. He ignored his master's wishes and went about his life as if he were not a servant at all.

That one talent is given to all who are drawn to follow Christ. They have the opportunity to risk themselves while yet relying upon God's Word. They can trust His redeeming grace, resting their hope for eternity upon Christ's work for them on the cross" (Ray C. Stedman, *What on Earth is Happening*: *What Jesus said About the End of the Age,* 2003 by Elaine Stedman, pp. 202-204).

Warren W. Wiersbe adds:

"Some feel that this unprofitable servant was not a true believer. But it seems that he was a true servant, even though he proved to be unprofitable. The "outer darkness" of Matthew 25:30 need not refer to hell, even though that is often the case in the Gospels (Matt. 8:12; 22:13). It is dangerous to build theology on parables, for parables illustrate truth in vivid ways. The man was dealt with by the Lord, he lost his opportunity for service, and he gained no praise or reward. To me, that is outer darkness. It is possible that the one-talent man thought that his one talent was not really very important. He did not have five talents, or even two. Why worry about one? *Because he was appointed as a steward by the Lord.* Were it not for the one-talent people in our world, very little would get accomplished. His one talent could have increased to two and brought glory to his master.

These three parables encourage us to love His appearing, look for His appearing, and labor faithfully until He comes. We should be watching, witnessing, and working. We may not be successful in the eyes of men, or even popular with others. But if we are faithful and profitable, we shall receive our reward" (The Bible Exposition Commentary: New Testament, Volume I, 1989, p. 92).

Dr. Louis A. Barbieri notes:

"Two of the servants were faithful in caring for the master's money (vv. 16-17) and were accordingly rewarded for their faithfulness with additional wealth, additional responsibilities, and sharing of the **master's** joy (v.v. 20-23). The third servant, having **received the one talent**, reasoned that his **master** might not be coming back at all. If he did return someday, the servant could simply return any poor investment (v. 25). But if he failed to return, the servant wanted to be able to keep the talent for himself. He did not want to deposit the talent in a bank where it would be recorded that the talent belonged to the master (v. 27)" (The Bible Knowledge Commentary: New Testament, 1983, p. 80, ed. John F. Walvoord, Roy B. Zuck).

John MacArthur remarks:

"The characterization by the third servant of the master maligns him as a cruel and ruthless opportunist, "reaping and gathering" what he had no right to claim as his own. This slothful servant does not represent a genuine believer, because it is obvious that this man does not know the master well. The man with five talents and the man with two received exactly the same reward, indicating that the reward is based on faithfulness, not results. The recipients of divine grace inherit immeasurable blessings in addition to eternal life and the favor of God (cf. Rom. 8:32). But those who despise the riches of God's goodness, forbearance, and long-suffering (Rom. 2:4), burying them in the ground and clinging instead to the paltry and transient goods of this world, will ultimately lose everything they have (cf. 6:19; John 12:25)" (The MacArthur Bible Commentary, 2005, p. 1175).

William Hendriksen observes:

"In light of the entire context and of other passages—such as 10:39; 16:26; Mark 8:34-38; Luke 9:23; 24; 17:32, 33; and

John 12:25, 26—one soon discovers the true meaning. It is this: the man who through diligent use of the opportunities for service given to him by God has by divine grace surrendered himself to the Lord, to love and to help others (Luke 10:29-37; Gal. 6:10; I Thess. 5:15), and who in so doing has enriched himself, shall by continuing in this course become more and more abundantly rich. On the other hand, from the person who has become poor, because he has never given himself, even whatever little he once had shall be taken away. For the rest, see 13:12.

There follows, in words strongly reminiscent of 8:12, and 22:13, **And fling the useless servant into the most distant darkness; there shall be weeping and grinding of teeth.** For the second part (weeping and grinding of teeth) see also 13:42; 24:51; and Luke 13:28. For the complete thought see on 8:12 (*but the sons of the kingdom shall be cast out into the outer darkness; in that place there shall be weeping and gnashing of teeth;* the "sons of the kingdom," that is, the Jews, called thus because of the many kingdom privileges they had enjoyed (Ps. 147:20; Isa. 63:8, 9; Amos 3:2; Rom. 9:4; Eph. 2:12, shall be cast into the *most distant* darkness, that is symbolically speaking, far away from the banqueting hall flooded with light)" (New Testament Commentary: Exposition of the Gospel according to Matthew, 2007, pp. 397; 884).

Dr. Herbert Lockyer states:

"As an unprofitable trader, the servant was cast out in darkness. The Bible does not reveal all that is implied by the term, "outer darkness," which seems to imply "darkness outside some region of light." Campbell Morgan speaks of it as "the darkness that is outside the kingdom of responsibility." This servant did not bury his talent because he only had one, but because he was a wicked and slothful servant. As those who claim to be the servants of the Lord, may be found serving Him to the limit of our ability and capacity, so that when He returns,

> His reward will be ours" (Lockyer, All the Parables of the Bible, 1963, p. 246).
>
> Lastly, Dr. Donald A Hagner concludes:
>
> "The disciple who fails to make productive use of what has been given faces the terrifying prospect of ultimate loss. The faithful will be further blessed; the unfaithful will lose all. The point cannot be missed: before the Son of Man comes and until that time whenever it may be, disciples are called to faithful and steady service of the kingdom" (Word Biblical Commentary, Volume 33B, 2000, p. 737, ed. Ralph P. Martin).

Finally, Jesus does communicate that there will be a day of reckoning for everyone. For believers, an accounting of the work that was done on behalf of the kingdom will be held. For those who do not have oil in their lamps, the judgment of eternal separation has already been pronounced, which has been unmistakably communicated in the messages found in the parables of the Wedding Feast (Matthew 22:1-14), the Wheat and the Tares (Matthew 13:24-43), the Dragnet (Matthew 13:47-50), and the Faithful and Wicked Servants (Matthew 24:45-51; Luke 12:42-48). For easy reference, following is an adapted table listing the three parables that were given to the Jewish religious leaders after Jesus had made His triumphal entry into Jerusalem, and the four prophecy parables that Jesus gave privately to His disciples while they were together on Mount Olivet.

> "*... I am He who searches the minds and hearts; and I will give to each one of you according to your deeds*" (Revelation 2:23).

Table II
Parables of the Kingdom

During Passover A.D. 30

PARABLE	PLACE	MATTHEW	MARK	LUKE
1. The Two Sons	Jerusalem	21:28-32		
2. The Wicked Tenant Farmers	Jerusalem	21:33-34	12:1-11	20:9-18
3. The Wedding Feast	Jerusalem	22:1-13		

Fifth Discourse—The Olivet Discourse Prophecy Parables

1. The Fig Tree	Mt. Olivet	24:32-44	13:28-32	21:29-36
2. The Faithful and Wicked Servants	Mt. Olivet	24:45-51		12:42-48
3. The Ten Virgins	Mt. Olivet	25:1-13		
4. The Ten Talents	Mt. Olivet	25:14-30		

(Adapted from Dr. Herbert Lockyer, "Table of Parables", *All the Teachings of Jesus*, 1991, p. 305; John MacArthur, "The Parables of Jesus", *The MacArthur Bible Commentary*, 2005, p. 1209; Louis A. Barbieri, Jr., "The Parables of Jesus", *The Bible Knowledge Commentary: New Testament*, 1983, p. 35, ed. John F. Walvoord, Roy B. Zuck).

The Parabolic Ministry of Jesus Recorded by Luke

The Good Samaritan—Luke 10:30-37

The telling of the parable of the Good Samaritan was instigated by a Jewish lawyer who tested Jesus by asking Him, "*what shall I do to inherit eternal life*?" Perceiving it was a test (Luke 10:25), Jesus responds by asking him, "*what is written in the Law*?" The lawyer then quotes the Law, *"You shall love the LORD your God with all your heart, and with all your soul, and with all your strength, and with all your mind* (Deuteronomy 6:5) *and your neighbor as yourself*" (Leviticus 19:18). When the lawyer replies to Jesus, he not only quotes the commandment under the Law set forth in Deuteronomy, but also quotes the Law from the Book of Leviticus. In response, Jesus quotes from the Law as well. *"DO THIS AND YOU SHALL LIVE"* (Leviticus 18:5). In an attempt to justify himself, the lawyer then asks Jesus, "*Who is my neighbor*?" (vv. 28-29). Perceiving the lawyer's motive, Jesus responds by paradoxically illustrating a Samaritan helping a Jew as opposed to a priest or a Levite helping a Samaritan in the parable.

The Good Samaritan – Luke 10:30-37: *"A certain man was going down from Jerusalem to Jericho; and he fell among robbers, and they stripped him and beat him, and went off leaving him half dead. And by chance a certain priest was going down was going down on that road, and when he saw him, he passed by on the other side. And likewise a Levite also, when he came to the place and saw him, passed by on the other side. But a certain Samaritan, who was on a journey, came upon him; and when he saw him, he felt compassion, and came to him, and bandaged up his wounds, pouring oil and wine on them; and he put him on his own beast, and brought him to an inn, and took care of him. And on the next day he took out two denarii and gave them to the* *innkeeper and said, 'Take care of him; and whatever more you spend, when I return, I will repay you.' Which of these three do you think proved to be a neighbor to the man who fell into the robbers' hands?"*

Historically, the deep-rooted animosity that existed between the Jewish people and the Samaritans went all the way back to the seventh century B.C., when after the final captivity of Israel, the king of Assyria brought idolaters from Babylon, Cuthah, Avva, Hamath, and Sepharvaim to colonize the city of Samaria (2 Kings 17:33). Centuries later, after the Hebrew people were freed they returned to the land of Judah, Nehemiah is put in charge of the rebuilding of the temple in Jerusalem, and the Samaritans, who by then had become open enemies, frustrated the building of the temple (Ezra 1:1—4:24). Thus in the time of Christ, the Samaritans were a racial mix of Assyrians who were considered to be heathen idolaters and carried a long history of hatred towards them by the Jewish people. Hence, the paradoxical illustration of a Samaritan helping a Jew may be seen as a deliberate feature of this parable.

The Good Samaritan tending the injured man
Image by Jan Wijnants (1670)
http://en.wikipedia.org/wiki/File:Jan_Wijnants_-_Parable_of_the_Good_Samaritan.jpg, 2012

In the illustration, Jesus highlights the attributes of both compassion and mercy that the Samaritan demonstrated. Whereas the Greek word for compassion, splagchnizomai, (pronounced *splangkh-nid'-zom-ahee*) means “to feel sympathy, to pity”, the Greek word for mercy, eleeō, (pronounced *el-eh-eh'-o*) means “to console the afflicted or to bring help to the one who is afflicted” (Thayer’s Greek Lexicon, 2009, G4697, G1653, pp. 584, 203). Thus, ‘feeling’ sympathy would not be enough, but ‘acting’ on that feeling is showing mercy. Jesus puts forth the question, “*Which of these three do you think proved to be a neighbor to the man who fell into the robbers’ hands?”* to which the lawyer replies, “*The one who showed mercy toward him,*” and Jesus then instructs him to “*Go and do the same”* (v. 37). Hence, the question remains, ‘who is our neighbor?’ to which Dr. John Nolland replies, “The Samaritan, through his compassionate action became a neighbor to the stranger on the road” (Word Biblical Commentary, Volume 35B, 2000, p. 597, ed. Ralph P. Martin).

Another interesting feature about the parable is that it is based on an actual location. In ancient times, the road from Jerusalem to Jericho was notoriously known to be extremely dangerous. Quoting from Jerome, William Barclay states that in the fifth century the road was still called “The Red, or Bloody Way” (William Barclay, The Gospel of Luke, 2001, p. 165). Dr. Lockyer notes, “The road between the two cities, a rocky and dangerous gorge filled with marauding robbers, who because of their violence, earned for this untenanted part of the wilderness, the name of Adummim (Joshua 15:7; 18:7)” (Lockyer, All the Parables of the Bible, 1963, p. 261). In a recent article published in Biblical Archaeology Review, Yitzhak Magen states, “by the Byzantine period, the site had become a place of Christian pilgrimage when a basilical church and a way station were built there.” He continues, “The place continued in use as a khan (a way station) for travelers for nearly 1,500 years, undergoing multiple rebuilding and expansions in the Crusader period and again in the Ottoman period (19th century)” (Biblical Archaeology Review, Volume. 38, No. 1, 2012, p. 53).

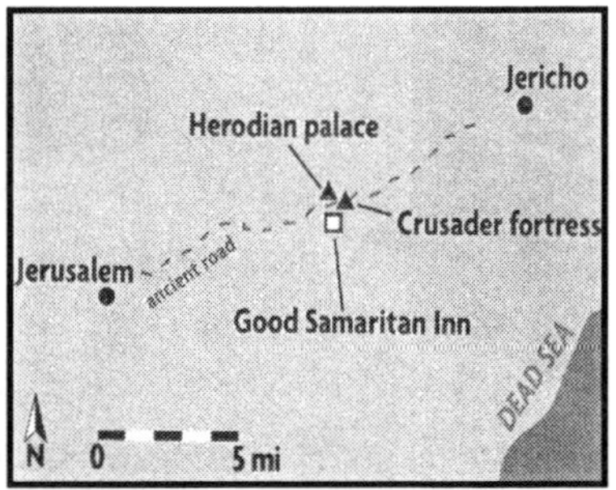

Old Road from Jerusalem to Jericho
Image provided by Yoni

Half-way between the two cities lies the site known as Ma'ale Adummin, "the Ascent of Blood"
Map provided by BAR, http://www.biblicalarchaeology.org, 2012.

http://commons.wikimedia.org/wiki/File:OldRoadFromJerusalemToJericho.jpg, 2007

Archeologists have recently excavated, and converted the site of the inn from the Good Samaritan parable in Luke's gospel into a unique museum featuring mosaics from Jewish, Samaritan, and Christian traditions" (Biblical Archaeology Review, Volume 38 No. 1, 2012, p. 48).

"*Go and do the same*" (Luke 10:37).

The Midnight Friend—Luke 11:5-13

Though the parable of the Midnight Friend introduces the new theme of persistence of prayer and faith, the underlying concept of 'a *fortiori'* in prayer is illustrated. This concept allows for an assumption of a greater fact to be true based on a conclusion that a lesser fact was already accepted to be true.

The Midnight Friend – Luke 11:5-13: "*And He said to them, "Suppose one of you shall have a friend, and shall go to him at midnight, and say to him, 'Friend, lend me three loaves; for a friend of mine has come to me from a journey, and I have nothing to set before him'; and from inside he shall answer and say, 'Do not bother me; the door has already been shut and my children and I are in bed; I cannot get up and give you anything.' I tell you, even though he will not get up and give him anything because he is his friend, yet because of his persistence he will get up and give him as much as he needs. And I say to you, ask, and it shall be given to you; seek and you shall find; knock, and it shall be opened to you. For everyone who asks, receives; and he who seeks, finds; and to him who knocks, it shall be opened. Now suppose one of you fathers is asked by his son for a fish; he will not give him a snake instead of a fish, will he? Or if he is asked for an egg, he will not give him a scorpion, will he? If you then, being evil, know how to give good gifts to your children, how much more shall your heavenly Father give the Holy Spirit to those who ask Him?"*

The example of the reluctant midnight friend, who because of his friend's persistent knock did eventually answer the door, contrasted with Jesus' forceful statement, "*And I say to you, ask, and it shall be given, seek and you shall find, knock and it shall be opened to you,"* the 'a *fortiori'* concept of prayer is illustrated. Jesus reinforces this concept by supposing if one of them had a son who asked for a fish he would certainly not give him a snake, or if he asked for an egg would not give him a scorpion. Therefore, it is reasonable to assume that if they as earthly fathers know how to give good gifts, how much more will the heavenly Father give what is good to His children. Warren W. Wiersbe notes:

> "Jesus did not say that God is like the grouchy neighbor. In fact, He said just the opposite .... The argument is clear. If persistence finally paid off as a man beat on the door of a reluctant friend, how much more would persistence bring blessing as we pray to a loving heavenly Father. After all, we are the children in the house with Him" (The Bible Exposition Commentary: New Testament, Volume I, 1989, pp. 214-215).

Dr. C. I. Scofield summarizes:

> "Christ's law of prayer may be thus summarized: (1) He grounds prayer upon relationship, and reveals God as freely charging Himself with all the responsibilities, as His heart glows with all the affections of a Father toward all who believe on Jesus Christ (Mt. 6. 25-32; 7. 9-11). Prayer, therefore, is a child's petition to an all-wise, all-loving, and all-powerful, Father-God. (2) In the Lord's Prayer Christ gives an incomparable model for all prayer. It teaches that right prayer begins with worship; puts the interest of the kingdom before merely personal interest; accepts beforehand the Father's will, whether to grant or withhold; and petitions for present need, leaving the future to the Father's care and love. (3) Prayer is to be definite (vs. 5, 6); and, (4) importunate, that is, undiscouraged by delayed answers" (Luke 11, pp. 1089-1090).

Finally, complimenting Dr. Scofield's summary, William Barclay concludes:

> "The lesson of this parable is not that we must persist in prayer; it is not that we must batter at God's door until we finally compel him for very weariness to give us what we want until we coerce an unwilling God to answer. What Jesus says is, 'If a

churlish and unwilling householder can in the end be coerced by a friend's shameless persistence into giving him what he needs, how much more will God who is a loving Father supply all his children's needs?' 'If you,' he says, 'who are evil, know that you are bound to supply your children's needs, how much more will God?' This does not absolve us from intensity in prayer. But it does mean this, that we are not wringing gifts from an unwilling God, but going to one who knows our needs better than we know them ourselves and whose heart towards us is the heart of generous love. If we do not receive what we pray for, it is not because God grudgingly refuses to give it but because he has some better thing for us. There is no such thing as unanswered prayer. The answer given may not be the answer we desired or expected, but even when it is a refusal it is the answer of the love and the wisdom of God" (William Barclay, The Gospel of Luke, 2001, pp. 173-174).

"And I say to you, ask, and it shall be given to you; seek and you shall find; knock, and it shall be opened to you. For everyone who asks, receives; and he who seeks, finds; and to him who knocks, it shall be opened" (Luke 11:9-10).

The Rich Fool—Luke 12:13-21

Chapter eleven of the Gospel of Luke concludes with six woes that were aimed directly at the Pharisees and the Scribes that denounce Pharisaism and Legalism (Luke 11:42-52). By this time, the Pharisees had become extremely hostile towards Jesus and were only following Him to see if they could hear Him say anything that went contrary to the Law. Chapter 12 begins with Luke's account of Jesus teaching on hypocrisy, covetousness, anxiety, and worry. The parable of the Rich Fool allegorizes the peril of greed and the folly of life, which was given in response to the statement, "*Teacher, tell my brother to divide the family inheritance with me*" that was made by someone in the crowd (v. 13).

The Rich Fool – Luke 12:13-21: *"But He said to him, 'Man, who appointed Me a judge or arbiter over you?' And He said to them, 'Beware, and be on your guard against every form of greed; for not even when one has abundance does his life consist of his possessions.' And He told them a parable, saying, 'The land of a certain rich man was very productive. And he began reasoning to himself, saying, 'What shall I do, since I have no place to store my crops?' And he said, 'This is what I will do: I will tear down my barns and build larger ones, and there I will store all my grain and my goods. And I will say to my soul, "Soul, you have many goods laid up for many years to come; take your ease, eat, drink and be merry." ' But God said to him, 'You fool! This very night your soul is required of you; and now who will own what you have prepared?' So is the man who lays up treasure for himself, and is not rich toward God."*

Consistent with Jesus' teachings, spiritual principles of the kingdom are always contrary to the principles by which the world operates. In lieu of using his life to prepare his soul for eternity, the rich man spent his life amassing possessions for his future security. The illustration of the rich man building larger storehouses to hold all of the goods that he had amassed, and the very words 'you fool, this very night your soul is required of you, now who will own what you have prepared', allegorizes the pitfalls of greed, and the folly of pursuing earthly security in lieu of eternal security. In the end, the rich man's earthly goods were all left behind. Dr. John Nolland poignantly summarizes by stating:

> "The foolishness of the farmer's narrow aims is highlighted by the contrast between his many years of supply and the few hours that remain to him of life. Did he think that in securing his economic future he had secured the future of his life as well?" (Word Biblical Commentary, Volume 35B, 2000, p. 688, ed. Ralph P. Martin).
>
> Warren W. Wiersbe sadly concludes:
>
> "The greatest tragedy is not what he man left behind but what lay *before* him: eternity without God" (The Bible Exposition Commentary: New Testament, Volume I, 1989, p. 221).

"For what will a man be profited, if he gains the whole world, and forfeits his soul?" (Matthew 16:26a).

The Watchful Servants—Luke 12:35-40

The example of the farmer risking the eternal security of his soul illustrates that the purpose of life is not preparing for how well we will spend the end of life, but for preparing where our souls will spend eternity the moment that they are required from us (v. 20). In connection with this purpose, the theme of 'readiness' illustrated in the prophecy parables of the Fig Tree, the Faithful and Wicked Servants, and the Ten Virgins (Matthew 24:32-44; Mark 13:28-32; Luke 21:29-36); (Matthew 24:45-51; Luke 12:42-48); and Matthew 25:1-13 respectively, is again emphasized.

The Watchful Servants – Luke 12:35-40: "B*e dressed in readiness, and keep your lamps alight. And be like men who are waiting for their master when he returns from the wedding feast, so that they may immediately open the door to him when he comes and knocks, Blessed are those slaves whom the master shall find on the alert when he comes; truly I say to you, that he will gird himself to serve, and have them recline at table, and will come up and wait on them. Whether he comes in the second watch, or even in the third, and finds them so, blessed are those slaves. And be sure of this, that if the head of the house had known at what hour the thief was coming, he would not have allowed his house to be broken into. You too, be ready, for the Son of Man is coming at an hour that you do not expect."*

The word 'blessed' used in the parable is translated from the Greek word makarios (pronounced *mak-ar'-ee-os*), meaning 'happy', is the same word that Jesus uses in the Beatitudes and in the of the Faithful and Wicked Servants (Thayer's Greek Lexicon, 2009, G3107, p. 386). Though the same theme of the importance of readiness found in the parable of the Wedding Feast is allegorized in this parable, the focus of the destiny of the soul is different. Whereas the parable of the Wedding Feast focuses on the tragedy of the man who was not dressed in readiness, and the parable of the Watchful Servants focuses on the rewards given to those who are dressed in readiness, Warren E. Wiersbe's keen observation focuses on the master's readiness to serve the servants. He writes:

> "The remarkable thing in this story is that the master serves the servants! In Jewish weddings, the bride was treated like a queen and the groom like a king, so you would not expect the "king" to minister to his staff. Our King will minister to His faithful servants when He greets us at His return, and He will reward us for your faithfulness" (The Bible Exposition Commentary: New Testament, Volume I, 1989, p. 222).

Finally, commenting on Jesus' exhortation to be ready, Dr. John Nolland concludes:

> "One should be equipped and alert at all times, ready to meet the master at the moment of his arrival" (Word Biblical Commentary, Volume 35B, 2000, p. 701, ed. Ralph P. Martin).

"You too, be ready, for the Son of Man is coming at an hour that you do not expect" (Luke 35:40).

The Barren Fig Tree—Luke 13:6-9

Preceding the telling of the parable of the Barren Fig Tree, while Jesus was speaking to the multitudes, someone in the crowd recounted the story of the eighteen Galileans who were killed when the tower of Siloam fell on them whose blood Pilate had mingled with that of their sacrifices (Luke 13:1). The name Siloam stems from the Old Testament word "Shiloah" (Nehemiah 3:15), which Dr. Payne believes most likely applied to an aqueduct that had been constructed on the east side of Jerusalem. The aqueduct led to one or more pools connected with Jerusalem's water supply, and finally to an area where the tower stood" (David F. Payne, Eerdman's *International Standard Bible Encyclopedia*, Volume Q-Z, 1988, p. 510, ed. Geoffrey W. Bromiley). The tower was evidently used as a watchtower in connection with the construction of an aqueduct going into Jerusalem by Pilate, which the Jews had violently opposed, and the Romans had avenged (The New Unger's Bible Dictionary, 1988, p. 1196, ed. R. K. Harrison).

Location of Siloam *Stone Tower
Image provided by David Q. Hall, January 2006, http://dqhall59.com/tower_of_Siloam.htm
Image provided by http://www.flw.org/landmarks.html#stone_tower,*not actual tower of Siloam, 2012.

Thus, the hearers would have all understood what was meant by the report. Jesus responds by asking them if the eighteen Galileans who were killed were greater sinners than other Galileans, or if they were worse sinners than all the men who live in Jerusalem. An answer to that question was not given; instead, Jesus likens those who perished in the fall of the tower of Siloam with all of those who, if they did not repent, would meet with the same fate. "*I tell you, no, but unless you repent, you will all likewise perish*" (vv. 2-5), and then tells the following parable.

The Barren Fig Tree – Luke 13:6-9: *"And He began telling this parable: "A certain man had a fig tree which had been planted in his vineyard; and he came looking for fruit on it, and did not find any. And he said to the vineyard-keeper, 'Behold, for three years I have come looking for fruit on this fig tree without finding any. Cut it down! Why does it even use up the ground?' And he answered and said to him, 'Let it alone, sir, for this year too, until I dig around it and put in fertilizer; and if it bears fruit next year, fine; but if not, cut it down." ' "*

The need for repentance in the present moment is the urgent message that Jesus has been illustrating through His parables all along. In the parable of the Barren Fig Tree, the theme is repentance and judgment. The owner of the vineyard must have known that the fig tree typically took three years before it bore fruit. Thus, the analogy of the vineyard owner looking to see if the fig tree had bore fruit implies that the tree was a mature one, and the time for bearing fruit was at hand, which parallels with John's message of *"Repent, for the kingdom of heaven is at hand"* (Matthew 3:2). In the Old Testament, the fig tree typically symbolized Israel (Hosea 9:10; Jeremiah 24:5), and though the house of Israel depended on the Law to justify their righteousness, it remained nonetheless like 'the barren fig tree'. The fig tree also symbolized prosperity and security: *"and Judah and Israel dwelt safely, every man under his vine and under his fig tree"* (1 Kings 4:25).

Another feature to consider is the vineyard landowner. The Prophet Isaiah had already disclosed that the "*vineyard of the Lord of hosts is the house of Israel*" (Isaiah 5:7). Also present is the parallel drawn between the three years the vineyard owner had been watching the fig tree, and the three years of Jesus' ministry which was nearing its end. Moreover, consistent with Jesus' teaching, the need for repentance in the present is illustrated by those who perished when the tower of Siloam suddenly fell on them, and parallels the urgent message of '*no one knows the hour*' that Jesus had been communicating throughout His ministry. Finally, the intercession of the vine-dresser who was willing to fertilize the tree before it met its final fate, metaphorically illustrates that there is still a chance for repentance, albeit, like the tree, the final execution of judgment is only held back for a season.

> "*I tell you, no, but unless you repent, you will all likewise perish*" (v. 5).

The Chief Seats—Luke 14:7-11

The following parables of the Chief Seats and the Great Banquet are lovingly termed "the table talk parables" by Dr. Lockyer. In the concluding verses of the previous chapter, Luke states that Jesus is three days journey from Jerusalem and the Pharisees had warned him not to go because King Herod wanted to kill him. Jesus replies by saying, "*tell that fox that I will cast out demons, and perform cures for the next three days until I reach My goal for it cannot be that a prophet should perish outside of Jerusalem*" (Luke 13:31-33). It is now the Sabbath day and Jesus is invited to eat at the house of a Pharisee of high position, but ... the invitation is not given in the spirit of hospitality. On the contrary, Jesus had just healed a man right in front of them on the Sabbath and *"they were watching Him with critical eyes"* (v. 1). Jesus accepts the invitation, and as they are reclining at the table, Jesus is making His own observations of the guests and begins to tell this parable to those who were sitting around him.

The Chief Seats – Luke 14:7-11: *"And He began speaking a parable to the invited guests when He noticed how they had been picking out the places of honor at the table; saying to them, When you are invited by someone to a wedding feast, do not take the place of honor, lest someone more distinguished than you may have been invited by him, and he who invited you both shall come and say to you, 'Give place to this man', and then in disgrace you proceed to occupy the last place. But when you are invited, go and recline at the last place, so that when the one who has invited you comes, he may say to you, 'Friend, move up higher'; then you will have honor in the sight of all who are at the table with you. For everyone who exalts himself shall be humbled, and he who humbles himself shall be exalted."*

The parable of the Chief Seats carries the same theme of 'genuine humility' found in the message, '*the first shall be last and the last first*' that Jesus taught in the parables of the Two Sons and the Marriage Feast (Matthew 21:28-32; 22:1-14) respectively. Consistent with Jesus' style of teaching, the principles of the world are juxtaposed alongside the *spiritual* principles of the kingdom. Jesus concludes His parable by stating, *"Everyone who exalts himself shall be humbled, and he who humbles himself shall be exalted."* The word humble, metaphorically used in the statement, '*he who humbles himself shall be exalted'* is interesting in that the word itself carries a history of being thought of in terms of self-abasement. However, the word humble (as used in this context) is translated from the Greek word tapeinoō (pronounced *tap-i-no'-o*), which means "to bring down one's pride; to behave in an unassuming manner devoid of all haughtiness" (Thayer's Greek Lexicon, 2009, G5013, p. 614). Thus, Jesus is not referring to self-abasement, but to a genuine condition of the heart. The same meaning in applies to, "*Whosoever therefore shall humble himself as this little child, the same is greatest in the kingdom of heaven"* (Matthew 18:4). This is also true of the word 'exalt' as used in context of the message, *"for everyone who exalts himself shall be humbled."* The word exalt is translated from the Greek word upsoō (pronounced *hoop-so'-o*), which means 'to be raised to honor' (Thayer's Greek Lexicon, 2009, G5312, p. 647). Hence, the last phrase, "*For everyone who exalts himself shall be humbled, and he who humbles himself shall be exalted,"* is analogous to being raised to a high a place of honor in the heavenly places as opposed to those who exalt themselves to a place of honor at an earthly banquet table. Dr. Lockyer concludes, "Our highest place is lying low at our Redeemer's feet (Proverbs 25:6, 7)" (Lockyer, All the Parables of the Bible, 1963, p. 274).

"I tell you, this man went down to his house justified rather than the other; for everyone who exalts himself will be humbled, but he who humbles himself will be exalted" (Luke 18:14).

The Great Banquet—Luke 14:16-24

Following the telling of the parable of the Chief Seats, Jesus continues the conversation by giving a short lesson on the principle of heavenly reciprocity as opposed to earthly reciprocity (vv. 12-14) and was overheard by another, who, after listening to Jesus, remarks, *"Blessed is everyone who shall eat bread in the kingdom of God"* (v. 15). In response, Jesus then presents the parable of the Great Banquet. Although the parable of the Great Banquet seemingly parallels the parable of the Wedding Feast, which was also addressed directly to the Jewish religious leaders, some differences may be found between them.

The Great Banquet – Luke 14:16-24: *"A certain man was giving a big dinner, and he invited many; and at the dinner hour he sent his slave to say to those who had been invited, 'Come; for everything is ready now.' But they all alike began to make excuses. The first one said to him, 'I have bought a piece of land and I need to go out and look at it; please consider me excused.' And another one said, 'I have bought five yoke of oxen, and I am going to try them out; please consider me excused.' And another said, 'I have married a wife, and for that reason I cannot come.' And the slave came back and reported this to his master. Then the head of the household became angry and said to his slave, 'Go out at once into the streets and lanes of the city and bring in here the poor and crippled and blind and lame.' And the slave said, 'Master, what you commanded has been done, and still there is room.' And the master said to the slave, 'Go out into the highways and along the hedges, and compel them to come in, that my house may be filled. For I tell you, none of those men who were invited shall taste of my dinner.' "*

—Versus—

The Wedding Feast – Matthew 22:1-14: *"And Jesus spoke to them again in parables, saying, The kingdom of heaven may be compared to a king, who gave a wedding feast for his son. And he sent out his slaves to call those who had been invited to the wedding feast, and they were unwilling to come. Again he sent out other slaves saying, 'Tell those who have been invited, "Behold, I have prepared my dinner; my oxen and my fattened livestock are all butchered and everything is ready; come to the wedding feast." ' But they paid no attention and went their way, one to his own farm, another to his business, and the rest seized his slaves and mistreated them and killed them. But the king was enraged and sent his armies, and destroyed those murderers, and set their city on fire. Then he said to his slaves, 'The wedding is ready, but those who were invited were not worthy. Go therefore to the main highways, and as many as you find there, invite to the wedding feast.' And those slaves went out into the streets, and gathered together all they found, both evil and good; and the wedding hall was filled with dinner guests. But when the king came in to look over the dinner guests, he saw there a man not dressed in wedding clothes, and he said to him, 'Friend, how did you come in here without wedding clothes?' And he was speechless. Then the king said to the servants, 'Bind him hand and foot, and cast him into the outer darkness; in that place there shall be weeping and gnashing of teeth.' For many are called but few are chosen."*

Some of the similarities and differences that may be seen between the parables of the Great Banquet presented by Luke, and the Wedding Feast presented by Matthew begin with the difference in the setting for the telling of the two. In the former, Jesus is reclining at a table at the house of one of the Jewish leaders, while in the latter, Jesus had already made His triumphal entry into Jerusalem and was now facing confrontation from the Jewish leaders in the temple.

Both parables are symbolic of a 'great feast' to which those who were invited snubbed the master by refusing the invitation. The former was represented by passiveness while the latter snub was represented by violence. In the parable of the Great Banquet, the servants only received lame excuses while in the parable of the Wedding Feast, the servants who were sent out to invite the first group were violently mistreated and killed. In both parables, after the first invited guests refused the invitation, the servants were sent out to the highways and streets to extend the invitations to all others. In the parable of the Great Banquet, it is said, 'and still there is room,' so the master broadened the scope of the invitation while in the Wedding Feast, it is said that the 'wedding hall was filled'.

Other similarities and differences that may be found in both parables are the responses to the snubbed invitation by the master. In the two analogies, both the master of the household in the Great Banquet and the king in the Wedding Feast are said to be angry over the refusal; however, their responses are different. In the former, those who passively refused the invitation are said to be excluded from the dinner, while in the latter, those who violently refused were destroyed and their cities burned. While no excuses are given for the refusal of the invitation in the parable of the Wedding Feast, the illustration of the three excuses given by the uninterested guests in the Great Banquet is unique to the parable.

Finally, though the teachings on the principles of the kingdom of heaven connote that they apply to the future, the application of them for the present. Bringing the future into the present is the genius of Jesus' parables. In them, we find the walls that we build to separate the future from the present do not exist. Thus, as illustrated by the analogy of the three excuses given for not accepting the invitation to the Great Banquet in the present does, in fact, direly affect the future as illustrated by Jesus' last statement in the parable of the Wedding Feast. Whereas Dr. Lockyer's observations show how these present excuses affect our future state, William Barclay comments on how they affect our present state. Dr. Lockyer writes:

> "*Excuse Number One*: 'I have bought a piece of ground, and I must needs to and see it.' The probability is that this man saw the land before he bought it and was more concerned about his investment than an invitation to a supper. He, therefore, remains a type of those whose large possessions necessitate all their attention, robbing them, thereby, of spiritual wealth.

Excuse Number Two: 'I have bought five yoke of oxen, and I go to prove them.' Without any apology for refusing the invitation, this man announces his intention, "assuming there to be no doubt as to its validity and propriety." No explanation is forthcoming. He feels his oxen come first and assures himself that the host inviting him has no claim upon his time. Does he not represent those who are so absorbed in their occupations as to leave no leisure or opportunity for concerns of the soul? How tragic it is when affairs mercantile, agricultural, financial, clerical, or industrial leave us no time for God.

Excuse Number Three: 'I have married a wife, and there I cannot come.' The hollowness of this excuse is proved by the fact that it was no 'stag party' to which the man had been invited. The host would know of the man's recent marriage and therefore included his wife in the invitation" (Lockyer, All the Parables of the Bible, 1963, pp. 276-277).

William Barclay notes:

"(1) The first man said that he had bought a field and was going to see it. It is still possible to be so immersed in this world that we have no time to worship, and even no time to pray.

(2) The second men said that he had bought five yoke of oxen and that he was going to try them out. It often happens that when people enter into new possessions they become so taken up with them that the claims of worship and of God get crowded out.

(3) The third man said, with even more finality than the others, 'I have married a wife, and I cannot come.' One of the wonderful merciful laws of the Old Testament laid it down, 'when a man is newly married, he shall not go out with the army or be charged with any related duty. He shall be free at home one year, to be happy with his wife whom he has married' (Deuteronomy 24:5)" (William Barclay, The Gospel of Luke, 2001, p. 230).

Finally, William Hendriksen comments on the parable as it relates to the nation of Israel and the Church. He writes:

> "When Israel, as a whole, rejects Christ (vv. 1-20), God's plan is not abandoned. Even among the Jews in the old dispensation and during the period of Christ's earthly ministry there were genuine believers (v. 21). There was always that little remnant (I kings 19:18; Isa. 14:32; 29:19; Luke 6:20; Rom. 9:27; 11:5). But now something very wonderful happens, already predicted, to be sure in the Old Testament (Isa. 54:2, 3; 60:1-3); cf. Ps. 72:8f.; 8): the church, present even during the old dispensation, now begins to *expand* among the Gentiles. It now becomes universal, international, the body of Christ consisting of both Jew and Gentile. Cf. Eph. 2:14, 18. The old Israel, that is, those who rejected God's gracious invitation, extended first by the old dispensation prophets and afterward by Jesus Himself and his apostles (vv. 16,17), perishes. Not one of the rejecters is saved (v. 24). The new Israel, consisting of both Jew and Gentile (Gal. 6:16), lives on. "There can be neither Jew nor Greek; there can be neither slave nor freeman; there can be no male and female; for y o u are all one in Christ Jesus," says Paul (Gal. 3:28). In all this, the bountiful character of God's love is revealed" (New Testament Commentary: Exposition of the Gospel according to Luke, 2007, p. 733).

"For I tell you, none of those men who were invited shall taste of my dinner" (Luke 14:24).

The Rash Builder—Luke 14:26-30 The Rash King—14:31-33 The Salt—14:34-35

The parables of the Rash King, the Rash Builder, and the Salt, consecutively recorded by Luke, are presented as a single discourse in the Gospel. Each parable carries the theme of the necessity of pricing out the full cost of discipleship before making a commitment. Jesus begins His discourse with the parable of the Rash Builder, and concludes by metaphorically comparing failure to consider the full cost of making the commitment to discipleship with the parable of the Salt that is also recorded by Matthew (5:13) and Mark (9:50). After Jesus left the house of the Jewish leader, 'great multitudes' were following Him and Jesus turned to them and said,

---

The Rash Builder—The Rash King—The Salt – Luke 14:26-35: *"If anyone comes to Me, and does not hate his own father and mother and wife and children and brothers and sisters, yes, and even his own life, he cannot be My disciple. Whoever does not carry his own cross and come after Me cannot be My disciple. For which one of you, when he wants to build a tower, does not first sit down and calculate the cost, to see if he has enough to complete it? Otherwise, when he has laid a foundation, and is not able to finish, all who observe it begin to ridicule him, saying, 'This man began to build and was not able to finish' "* (vv. 26-30). "*Or what king, when he sets out to meet another king in battle, will not first sit down and take counsel whether he is strong enough with ten thousand men to encounter the one coming against him with twenty thousand? Or else, while the other is still far away, he sends a delegation and asks terms of peace"* (vv. 31-32). "*So therefore, no one of you can be My disciple who does not give up all his own possessions. Therefore, salt is good; but if even salt has become tasteless, with what will it be seasoned? It is useless either for the soil or the manure pile; it is thrown out. He who has ears to hear, let him hear"* (vv. 33-35).

The parables of the Rash Builder and the Rash King both give a clear picture of what a follower will need to do before he makes a commitment to discipleship, and what it will take to succeed. Jesus begins the parable by saying that *no one* can be His disciple unless he (1) hates his family and his own life, and (2) carries his own cross. On the surface, these strong words seem to communicate that it is an extremely high, if not an impossible price to pay for being one of His disciples. However, knowing that Jesus is the full embodiment of love, and His figurative teachings on the spiritual principles of kingdom of heaven allegorize the condition of our hearts while living in the present, close examination of the word hate, used in context of this phrase, does, in fact, reveal that the meaning is in relation *to love*. The word love is translated from the Greek word miseō (pronounced *mis-eh'-o*), which means "to love less" (Thayer's Greek Lexicon, 2009, G3404, p. 415), parallels the words of the greatest commandment. "*You shall love the LORD your God with all your heart, and with all your soul, and with all your strength, and with all your mind* (Deuteronomy 6:5) *and your neighbor as yourself*" (Leviticus 19:18). Thus, by illustration in the parable of the Rash Builder, the importance of pricing out the cost of making a true commitment to being a disciple is seen metaphorically as a condition of the heart that hinges on having built a solid foundation upon the commandment. Likewise, the analogy may also be seen in Jesus' closing statement of, "*no one of you can be My disciple who does not give up all his own possessions*" (v. 33).

Second, the phrase, "*Whoever does not carry his own cross and come after Me cannot be My disciple*" (v. 27), was often used by Jesus when addressing the followers (Matthew 10:38; 16:24; Mark 8:34; Luke 9:23). Close examination of the word 'cross' (as used in context of the parable) is also important in understanding the analogy. The word cross is translated from the Greek term stauros (pronounced *stow-ros'*), which means "used of those who on behalf of God's cause do not hesitate cheerfully and manfully to bear persecutions, troubles, distresses—thus recalling the fate of Christ and the spirit in which he encountered it" (Thayer's Greek Lexicon, 2009, G4716, p. 586).

William Hendriksen sheds light on the meaning of this phrase seen in context of the parable:

> "The underlying figure is that of a condemned man who is forced to take up and carry his own cross to the place of execution. However, what the convict does under duress, the disciple of Christ does willingly. He voluntarily and decisively accepts the pain, shame, and persecution that is going to be his particular—note: his, not someone else's—lot because of his loyalty to Christ and his cause" (New Testament Commentary: Exposition of the Gospel according to Luke, 2007, p. 498).

By comparing the requirements involved in making a commitment illustrated in the parable of the Rash Builder and the Rash King, distinguishing features between pricing out the cost *before* entering discipleship that is illustrated in former and pricing out the cost *after* the commitment involved in discipleship is notable. The illustration drawn in the parable of the Rash King tells that the king *already* had an army at his disposal ... the question is, will he consider whether he will be strong enough to face his enemy who has double the amount of resources, or will he throw in the towel and wave the white flag. Along this line, Dr. John Nolland concludes:

> "The parables in 14:28-32 (the builder) provide support for the challenge of vv. 26-27 (the king). It is all very well to want to be a disciple, but the demands of vv. 26-27 (the king) identify the necessary resources, without which there could be no successful implementation of discipleship. To rush into the project of discipleship without thought is like the person who begins to build a tower without the resources needed to complete it: he looks ridiculous. Or it is to be like the king who when challenged by another king rushes out to sure defeat, without considering that with half the troops of his opponent he can anticipate only disaster: far better if he had sued for terms of peace" (Word Biblical Commentary, Volume 35B, 2000, p. 766, ed. Ralph P. Martin).

Finally, the Rash Builder who would be ridiculed for not completing the tower, and the Rash King who does not take council to see if he is militarily strong enough to face his enemy are exemplified as an obvious means to a successful end. Jesus then concludes His discourse by metaphorically comparing failure to consider the full cost of making the commitment to discipleship to the loss of the usefulness of salt. A brief summary of the different qualities of salt and of how it was used in the Old Testament drives home the concluding message in the parable of the Salt.

Salt has the quality of being used to preserve or to purify, and carries a long history of symbolic uses with it. In Old Testament, salt was used in connection with sterilizing the earth of a conquered city (Judges 9:45), as a symbol of desolation and barrenness (Deuteronomy 29:23; Psalms 107:34; Jeremiah 17:6; Zephaniah 2:9), and as a procedure in the cleansing of a newborn (Ezekiel 16:4). Other symbolic uses of salt in the Old Testament, and symbolic comparisons in connection with discipleship in the New Testament are traced by Dr. Larry Herr and William Vine respectively.

> "Because salt was a necessary ingredient in any meal, it could symbolize the hospitality that cemented friendships. The Arab expression "There is salt between us"; and "eat the salt of the palace," (Ezr. 4:14). The phrase Covenant of Salt arose from the use of salt in covenantal sacrifices, and also from its use as a preservative; thus a covenant of salt was an enduring covenant (Nu. 18:19) … The Synoptics all record sayings in which Jesus compares His disciples to salt and refers to the uselessness of salt that has lost its salinity. Mt. 5:13 emphasizes that Jesus' disciples must be a blessing and preservative in the world; Mk. 9:50 emphasizes that they must be faithful to their covenant relationship with one another; and Lk. 14:34 emphasizes they must maintain their allegiance to Christ" (L. G. Herr, Eerdman's *International Standard Bible Encyclopedia*, Volume Q-Z, 1988, p. 286, ed. Geoffrey W. Bromiley).

> "In the Lord's teaching it is also symbolic of that spiritual health and vigor essential to Christian virtue and counteractive of the corruption that is in the world, e.g., Matt. 5:13" (William Vine, Vine's Complete Expository Dictionary of Old and New Testament Words, 1996, p. 544).

Accordingly, the connection made to discipleship with symbolic uses for salt is not only metaphorically analogized as being another factor to consider in pricing out the cost of making a full commitment to discipleship, but is also analogized as being the *substance* that is required for maintaining it. In his concluding summary on the effectiveness of salt as it relates to discipleship, Dr. John A. Martin states:

> "Jesus climaxed His teaching on discipleship by proclaiming that **salt is good** only as long as it contains the characteristics of saltiness. If **it loses its saltiness**, it has no value at all and **is thrown out**. The same is true of disciples. They must contain the characteristics of discipleship—planning and willing sacrifice—or they are of no value at all" (The Bible Knowledge Commentary: Old Testament, 1983, p. 244, ed. John F. Walvoord, Roy B. Zuck).

"Therefore, salt is good; but if even salt has become tasteless, with what will it be seasoned? It is useless either for the soil or the manure pile; it is thrown out" (Luke 14:34).

The Lost Sheep—Luke 15:4-7
The Lost Coin—15:8-10
The Lost Son—15:11-32

The parables of the Lost Sheep, the Lost Coin, and the Lost Son, consecutively recorded by Luke, are also presented as a single discourse. In the opening verses of Chapter 15, Luke reports that the Pharisees and Scribes are grumbling because Jesus is associating himself with 'tax-gatherers and sinners' (v. 1-2). William Barclay provides insight into the mindset of the Pharisees and religious leaders that sheds light on the reasons for their perception in viewing Jesus' association with the tax-gathers and sinners' as offensive. He states: "It was an offence to the scribes and Pharisees that Jesus associated with men and women who, by the orthodox, were labeled as sinners. Consequently, the Pharisees gave to people who did not keep the law a general classification. They called them *the People of the Land*; and there was a complete barrier between the Pharisees and the "People of the Land". Barclay further states that "if a man was one of 'these people' they were not to be trusted with any money, or take their testimony, or be appointed a guardian of an orphan or custodian of any charitable funds, or to have any business dealings with him whatsoever. The religious leaders were forbidden to be a guest of any such man, much less have any one of them as a guest." In fact, William Barclay boldly states that in lieu of "the joy that is in the presence of the angels of God when one sinner repents" (vv. 7, 10), the Pharisee's mantra was "there will be joy in the presence of the angels of God when one sinner is *obliterated*" (William Barclay, The Gospel of Luke, 2001, pp. 236-237). Thus, in their mind's eye, by Jesus associating Himself with 'the People of the Land', He had crossed the line.

In the preceding parables of the Rash King, the Rash Builder, and the Salt, different aspects of the same truth were illustrated in one discourse. In the parables of the Lost Sheep, the Lost Coin and the Lost Son, a blend of the underlying themes of mercy, repentance, compassion, love, and forgiveness reflective of the free gift of salvation are highlighted. All three parables illustrate that something dear had been lost, and all three tell about the 'great rejoicing' that follows the successful recovery. Whereas the owners actively go in search for that which was lost illustrated in the parables of the Lost Sheep and the Lost Coin, the parable of the Lost Son reveals that the lost son is the one who actively searches for his father, and the father is the one who actively *receives* that which had been lost to him. The lengthy discourse begins with, *"And He told them 'this' parable"* (v. 3).

The Lost Sheep – The Lost Coin – Luke 15:4-10: *"What man among you, if he has a hundred sheep and has lost one of them, does not leave the ninety-nine in the open pasture, and go after the one which is lost, until he finds it? And when he has found it, he lays it on his shoulders rejoicing. And when he comes home, he calls together his friends and his neighbors, saying to them, 'Rejoice with me, for I have found my sheep which was lost!' I tell you that in the same way, there will be more joy in heaven over one sinner who repents, than over ninety-nine righteous persons who need no repentance* (vv. 4-7; Matthew 18:12-14). *Or what woman, if she has ten silver coins and loses one coin, does not light a lamp and sweep the house and search carefully until she finds it? And when she has found it, she calls together her friends and neighbors, saying, 'Rejoice with me, for I have found the coin which I had lost!' In the same way, I tell you there is joy in the presence of the angels of God over one sinner who repents"* (vv. 8-10).

In the parables of the Lost Sheep and the Lost Coin, we find the underlying theme of the purpose of Jesus' ministry. A brief biblical overview on the value of sheep, what they meant to the owners, and the purpose of the shepherd that are presented by Dr. Paul L. Garber highlights the truth that is illustrated in the parable of the Lost Sheep. He writes:

> "*Sheep* were so valuable that the wealthy man was described as the owner of "thousands" or "ten thousands" of sheep (cf. Ps. 144:13). Although sheep were also used for food, they were

raised principally for wool. Sheepskins were also used as clothing (cf. He. 11:37). For the average family the slaughtering of a sheep for a guest was generous hospitality (cf. 2 S. 12:4), and a sheep was an expensive sacrifice. Sheep's horns served as containers for oil (1 S. 16:1) and as musical instruments. From the bones were made needles, scrapers, lances, and arrowheads; from the hides clothing, curtains, and leather.

God's People as Sheep. We are the people of his [God's] pasture and the sheep of his hand" (Ps. 95:7); 100:3; cf. also Ps. 74:1; Ezk. 34:31). These familiar words use a common biblical metaphor that emphasizes the utter dependence of human beings upon God for their existence, survival, and welfare....Conversely, people – like sheep – can go "astray" (Isa. 53:6. Mt. 18:12 par.); thus separated from the Shepherd (1 Pet. 2:25) they can become "lost sheep" (Ps. 119:176); Jer. 50:6), variously described as "a hunted sheep driven away by lions" (v. 17), "scattered over all the face of the earth" (Ezk. 34:6; cf. v. 12), and "the lost sheep of the house of Israel" (Mt. 10:6, 15:24).

Shepherds were responsible for the survival and welfare of their master's flocks, and depended on the shepherd to find pasture for them (cf. Ezk. 34:2, 9, 13f); they required "quiet" water (Ps. 23:3). Shepherds also had to provide shelter, medication, aid in lambing time, and provision for lameness and weariness. Without the shepherd the sheep wee helpless (Nu. 27:17; 1 K. 22:17; 2 Ch. 18:16; Zec. 10:2; Mt. 9:36 par. Mk. 6:34).

God as Shepherd. Among the very earliest names given to God is "the Shepherd, Rock of Israel" (Gen. 49:24). In Ps. 78:52f. the psalmist recounts how in the Exodus the Most High God "led forth his people like sheep, and guided them in the wilderness like a flock. He led them in safety, so that they were not afraid ...."

Jesus as Shepherd and as Lamb. The selfless, caring attitudes of the good shepherd are attributed to Jesus throughout the NT. The

Synoptic Gospels describe Jesus; compassion for people as that of a shepherd for "sheep without a shepherd" (Mt. 9:36 par.; cf. 26:31 par., quoting Zec. 13:7; cf. also 1 K. 22:17 par. 2 Ch. 18:16; Isa. 13:14; Zec. 10:2; 11:4, 6) .... The application to Jesus of this familiar OT image for God establishes an identity of moral character and mission between the God of the OT and Jesus. A unique element is added in the description of Jesus as "the good shepherd [who] lays down his life for the sheep" (Jn. 10:11)" (Eerdman's *International Standard Bible Encyclopedia*, Volume Q-Z, 1988, pp. 463-464, ed. Geoffrey W. Bromiley).

William Hendriksen cites an observation made in K. E. Bailey's writings of *The Cross*, p. 23 on the Mid-Eastern customs of the shepherd:

> "Even though the search is time-consuming and physically exhausting, once having found his sheep, the shepherd, in typically Mid-Eastern fashion, places the sheep over his two shoulders, with its stomach against the back of his neck, and with its four feet tied together in front of his face. Loaded down thus heavily, he returns to his home in the village. The shepherd he loves that sheep. His shepherd's heart rejoices because the sheep was not devoured or did not perish in some other way. The shepherd even invites his male friends and neighbors to rejoice with him" (New Testament Commentary: Exposition of the Gospel according to Luke, 2007, p. 745).

Likewise, a parallel is drawn on the high value placed upon the lost item by the owner in the parable of the Lost Coin, and a brief overview of the significance of the coin is insightful. While John A. Martin comments on the financial value of the coin, Dr. Lockycr's view is on the 'romantic' value of it:

> "A *drachma*, a Greek silver coin referred to only here in the New Testament, equaled about a day's wages. The point would have been clear to Jesus' listeners: the sinners with whom He was associating were extremely valuable to God. (cf. similar

> wording is vv. 6, 9)" (The Bible Knowledge Commentary: Old Testament, 1983, p. 244, ed. John F. Walvoord, Roy B. Zuck).

Quoting from Campbell Morgan's comments on the 'romantic' value of the coin, Dr. Lockyer writes:

> "The women of that time often wore upon their brow a frontlet that was called *semedi.* It was made up of coins, in themselves largely valueless … But it was a coin that had stamped upon it the image of authority. The frontlet signified betrothal or the marriage relationship. Whether it was of little monetary value or not, it was of priceless value to the woman who wore it. This is evidenced by the fact that she sought it diligently, sweeping the house until she found it. Becausc thc coin had sentimental value, and was an article of charm, and adornment, the woman's search for it was earnest and thorough. She was anxious to recover that which perfected the symbolism of her frontlet" (Lockyer, All the Parables of the Bible, 1963, p. 285).

Finally, by concluding, "*I tell you there is joy in the presence of the angels of God over one sinner who repents"* (vv. 7, 10), Jesus leaves no room for doubt that the illustration in the Lost Sheep and the Lost Coin analogizes a lost sinner, and that the owner in both represents Jesus and the purpose of His ministry.

> *"For the Son of Man has come to seek and to save that which was lost"* (Luke 19:10).

The Lost Son—15:11-32

Though the parable of the Lost Son is a continuation of the preceding discourse, and equally illustrates the great rejoicing in heaven that occurs when a lost sinner repents, a blend of the themes of compassion, love, and forgiveness reflected in the father are more pronounced. Reminiscent of the sentiments between two brothers contrasted in the stories of Cain and Abel, Ishmael and Isaac, and Esau and Jacob, the story begins when the younger of the two sons asks his father to give him his share of the estate. The son takes his portion of the estate, goes away to a 'far country', squanders it all away, and grows hungry and has to work for food. A severe famine strikes the land, and as he lay dying of hunger, he begins to remember all of the good food that his father provides his servants, comes to his senses, and returns home in repentance (vv. 12-19).

The Lost Son – Luke 15:11-32: *"A certain man had two sons; and a younger of them said to his father, 'Father, give me the share of the estate that falls to me.' And he divided his wealth between them. And not many days later, the younger son gathered everything together and went on a journey into a distant country, and there he squandered his estate with loose living. Now when he had spent everything, a severe famine occurred in that country, and he began to be in need. And he went and attached himself to one of the citizens of that country, and he sent him into his fields to feed swine. And he was longing to fill his stomach with the pods that the swine were eating, and no one was giving anything to him. But when he came to his senses, he said 'How many of my father's hired men have more than enough bread, but I am dying here with hunger! I will get up and go to my father, and will say to him, "Father, I have sinned against heaven, and in your sight; I am no longer worthy to be called your son; make me as one of your hired men." ' And he got up and came to his father. But while he was still a long way off, his father saw him, and felt compassion for him, and ran and embraced him, and kissed him. And the son said to him, 'Father, I* *have sinned against heaven and in your sight; I am no longer worthy to be called your son.' But the father said to his slaves, 'Quickly bring out the best robe and put it on him, and put a ring on his hand and sandals on his feet; and bring the fattened calf, kill it, and let us eat and be merry; for this son of mine was dead, and has come to life again; he was lost, and has been found.' And they began to be merry. Now his older son was in the field, and when he came and approached the house, he heard music and dancing. And he summoned one of the servants and began inquiring what these things might be. And he said to him, 'Your brother has come, and your father has killed the fattened calf, because he has received him back safe and sound.' But he became angry, and was not willing to go in; and his father came out and began entreating him. But he answered and said to his father, 'Look! For so many years I have been serving you, and I have never neglected a command of yours; and yet you have never given me a kid, that I might be merry with my friends; but when this son of yours came, who has devoured your wealth with harlots, you killed the fattened calf for him.' And he said to him, 'My child, you have always been with me, and all that is mine is yours. But we had to be merry and rejoice, for this brother of yours was dead and has begun to live, and was lost and has been found' "* (vv. 11-32).

In contrast to the illustration of the shepherd in the Lost Sheep and the woman in the Lost Coin parables who actively search for that which was lost, in the parable of the Lost Son, it is the younger son who actively returns home in repentance. The parallel of the shepherd and the woman who both greatly rejoice after finding their lost treasure, which illustrates the same concluding theme of the 'great rejoicing' in heaven that occurs when a lost sinner repents, is exemplified by the father telling his servants to prepare a fattened calf for a feast of celebration (vv. 20-24). Similarly, by paralleling the illustration of the lost son with the tax-gatherers, and contrasting it with the grumbling older son who had been obedient to all of his father's commands, exemplifies the attitude of the Pharisees and Scribes who were the recipients and guardians of the covenantal Law and opposed Jesus for associating Himself with the tax-gatherers and the sinners. Likewise, in the concluding paragraph of the parable, the illustration of the father leaving the reception to entreat his older son to come and join them, and his son's refusal, exemplifies the Pharisees and the Scribes refusal to enter into the New Covenant of grace. Jesus concludes the parable with the same message of the great rejoicing in heaven that occurs when one sinner repents by saying, " *'But we had to be merry and rejoice, for this brother of yours was dead and has begun to live, and was lost and has been found'* " (v. 32). In his concluding summary, Dr. Lockyer makes this poignant statement:

> "In this chapter in which we have considered the word *lost* in each parable, it is not so much related to the condition of what is lost, as to the agony upon the heart of the one who has lost. The shepherd suffered more than the straying sheep; the woman suffered more than her silver which was destitute of life and feeling; the father had a depth of agony either of his sons could not share. It is thus with God, whose loving heart is moved with deep compassion over those who are lost in sin, and who fail to understand the anguish of His heart" (Lockyer, All the Parables of the Bible, 1963, p. 289).

A perspective on the two opposing philosophies of life illustrated by the two sons is observed by Warren W. Wiersbe. He notes:

> "In His portrait of the prodigal and the elder brother, Jesus described two opposite philosophies of life. Prior to his repentance, the prodigal wasted his life, but his elder brother only spent his life as a faithful drudge. Both attitudes are wrong, for the Christian approach to life is that we should invest our lives for the good of others and the glory of God" (The Bible Exposition Commentary: New Testament, Volume I, 1989, p. 238).

"I tell you, there will be there will be more joy in heaven over one sinner who repents, than over ninety-nine righteous persons who need no repentance" (v. 7).

The Unrighteous Steward—Luke 16:1-13

In conjunction with the previous setting, Jesus began telling the parable of the Unrighteous Steward to His disciples. All the while, the Pharisees, who were official stewards of the covenantal Law, were listening and mocking what Jesus was saying (v. 14). Like the preceding parable of the Lost Son, this story also has three characters—the rich man, the unrighteous steward, and the debtors, and is presented in two parts. The story in the first part of the parable (vv. 1-8) lays the foundation for the spiritual principles that are illustrated by the conclusion (9-13).

The Unrighteous Steward – Luke 16:1-13: *"There was a certain rich man who had a steward, and this steward was reported to him as squandering his possession. And he called him and said to him, 'What is this I hear about you? Give an account of your stewardship, for you can no longer be steward.' And the steward said to himself, 'What shall I do, since my master is taking the stewardship away from me? I am not strong enough to dig; I am ashamed to beg. I know what I shall do, so that when I am removed from the stewardship, they will receive me into their homes.' And he summoned each one of his master's debtors, and he began saying to the first, 'How much do you owe my master?' And he said, 'A hundred measures of oil.' Then he said to another, 'And how much do you owe?' And he said, 'A hundred measures of wheat.' He said to him, 'Take your bill, and write eighty.' And his master praised the unrighteous steward because he had acted shrewdly; for the sons of this age are more shrewd in relation to their own kind than the sons of light"* (vv. 1-8).

This parable carries the theme of the kingdom principle of stewardship of the riches of His grace that God entrusts to His disciples along with a blend of the underlying themes of righteousness, faithfulness, and integrity. A connection is made between the Pharisees and the unrighteous steward whose actions are paralleled with those of the 'sons of the age'. The story begins when the rich man finds out that his steward had been misusing his position by squandering his possessions and calls on him to give a full account of his stewardship. Much like the 'power of attorney' that we are familiar with today, in Jewish custom, when a rich man entrusted his possessions to a steward, it included the authority to handle a variety of business transactions on his behalf (J. Nolland, Word Biblical Commentary, Volume 35B, 2000, p. 802, ed. Ralph P. Martin), which of course implies trust. In the story, after the stewardship of the unrighteous steward is questioned by the rich man, the steward quickly assesses the situation, summons each one of his master's debtors, reduces the amount of their debts, and by doing so, now indebts them to both himself and to his master. When the rich man finds out what his steward has done, he praises him for his shrewdness. Although the steward lacked the qualities of righteousness, faithfulness, and integrity that is expected of stewards, the idea that the rich man praised his steward for acting so shrewdly appears as though he is praising him for his unrighteous deeds. However, the term shrewd, as used in context of the parable, is translated from the Greek word phronimōs (pronounced *fron-im'-oce*), which means "to act prudently, wisely" (Thayer's Greek Lexicon, 2009, G5430, p. 658). Thus, the prudence and foresight that the steward showed in preparing for his future is what the rich man was praising. Dr. Nolland's comprehensive analysis on the Jewish customs from the viewpoint of the debtors sheds further light on the seeming praise of the steward's unrighteous behavior. He writes:

> "The steward had the authority to write and even rewrite contracts in the name of his master. For example, in times of natural calamity it was customary to reduce the amount due on the least of farmland. The debt amounts in these contracts would be written in the hand of the debtor (thus discouraging falsification). The debt amount in the contract of each of the debtors is reduced by a huge amount. (While the percentage reduction is quite different, the value of the reduction would be about the same). From the point of view of the debtors, the

> steward will have used his last moments in office (though they will only learn later that these are his last moments in office) to show generosity to them on a grand scale.
>
> The ancient world ran on the basis of a reciprocity ethic: good turns given and returned. The steward's move gave him claim upon his master's debtors that was much more secure than any contract. Public honor required that they make some appropriate return to their benefactor. The steward had secured his future!
>
> But what of the master's reaction to this? This last set of actions had not made him any more criminal than he was already, and the reaction to his former squandering was to be dismissal. Nothing more could be done from that angle. What about recovery? If the steward had sought to lay claim to more of his master's goods for himself at this point, the master, now alerted and present, would have made all legal moves necessary for their recovery. The stroke of brilliance was the transfer to a series of third parties. Here the wealth is out of the master's reach, but on the basis of the reciprocity ethic, it was effectively within the reach of the steward. The master can do nothing more than he had already done. However, grudgingly, the master can only acknowledge the cleverness of the now dismissed steward" (Word Biblical Commentary, Volume 35B, 2000, pp. 802-803, ed. Ralph P. Martin).

Jesus ends this section of the parable by comparing the steward with the 'sons of this age' and says to His disciples, "*For the sons of this age are more shrewd in relation to their own kind than the sons of light"* (v. 8). The short phrase, the 'sons of this age', is translated to mean "those who are controlled by the thoughts and pursuits of this present time" (Thayer's Greek Lexicon, 2009, G165, p. 19).

Part two of the story begins with Jesus telling His disciples to *apply* the prudence and foresight exercised by the 'sons of the age' to the stewardship of the riches of the kingdom with which He was entrusting to them.

"And I say to you, make friends for yourselves by means of the mammon of unrighteousness; that when it fails, they may receive you into the eternal dwellings. He who is faithful in a very little thing is faithful also in much; and he who is unrighteous in a very little thing is unrighteous also in much. If therefore you have not been faithful in the use of unrighteous mammon, who will entrust the true riches to you? And if you have not been faithful in the use of that which is another's, who will give you that which is your own? No one can serve two masters; for either he will hate the one, and love the other, or else he will hold to one and despise the other. You cannot serve God and mammon" (vv. 16:9-13).

A collection of individual proverbs is used to illustrate the principals of righteousness and faithfulness of stewardship. Jesus begins by saying, *"make friends by means of the mammon of unrighteousness that when it fails, they may receive you into the eternal dwellings"* (v. 9). In context, the term mammon is translated to mean riches (Thayer's Greek Lexicon, 2009, G3126, p. 215). Thus, with the same kind of prudence and foresight exemplified by the unrighteous steward's use of his master's riches in preparing for his future, the principle of using earthly wealth in preparing for the future of the kingdom is illustrated. John A. Martin notes:

> "Jesus plainly taught that the "the people of the light" should use worldly wealth; wise use of wealth would help lead others to believe the message of the kingdom and bring them to accept that message" (The Bible Knowledge Commentary: Old Testament, 1983, p. 246, ed. John F. Walvoord, Roy B. Zuck).

William Barclay adds:

> "The Rabbis had a saying, "The rich help the poor in this world, but the poor help the rich in the world to come" " (William Barclay, The Gospel of Luke, 2001, p. 247).

Characteristic of Jesus' parabolic style of teaching, the comparisons and contrasts made between the principles and standards by which the world operates, and the spiritual principles of the kingdom, illustrate a condition of the heart. The illustration of steward's ulterior motive in reducing the debts of the debtors and of squandering his master's riches exemplifies a lack of integrity and a lack of faithfulness. With emphasis on faithfulness and righteousness, Jesus parallels the rich man's wealth with the riches of the kingdom and paradoxically uses the unrighteous steward's unfaithfulness in managing someone else's riches to illustrate the importance of faithfulness in managing the riches of the kingdom.

In concluding, Jesus illustrates that a righteous steward is not double-minded and there are no double standards in the kingdom. If a steward can be trusted with the righteous use of the temporal riches of the world, then it stands to reason that he can also be trusted with the true riches of the kingdom and vice versa. Finally, Jesus cautions His disciples on the danger of double-mindedness—He reminds His disciples that it is impossible to be a servant of God and a servant of wealth at the same time. Dr. Lockyer concludes:

> "Our choice is between two motives—love of possessions for their own sake, which is love of self and results in the forgetfulness of others; or the use of possessions as a trust from God for the benefit of others, and for the glory of the Giver of all good gifts. Too many fail to enjoy their Mammon because their service of it is spoiled by the scruples and rebukes of conscience. These people also fail to enjoy God because their visible service for Him is spoiled by their indulgence of alien desire.
>
> Our Lord's final lesson is that the manifestation of common-sense or prudence is the test of faithfulness. If what we have, whether much or little, is faithfully used as a servant,

and as a discipline of fidelity, then it is capable of providing us with resources of eternal value. Faithfulness is to be the basis of reward in eternity (Revelation 2:10). Gifts and graces used as unto God bring a present satisfaction, and go to build a memorial in the ages to come" (Lockyer, All the Parables of the Bible, 1963, pp. 291-292).

"*No one can serve two masters; for either he will hate the one, and love the other, or else he will hold to one and despise the other*" (v .13).

The Rich Man and Lazarus—Luke 16:19-31

Continuity in the theme of 'a condition of the heart' seen in the preceding parable of the Unfaithful Steward may also be seen in the parable of the Rich Man and Lazarus. In verse 14, Luke boldly states that the "Pharisees were lovers of money" and were mocking what Jesus was teaching His disciples. In response, Jesus exposes the Pharisees saying, *"You are those who justify yourselves in the sight of men, but God knows your heart. What is highly esteemed among men is detestable in the sight of God"* (v. 15). William Hendriksen puts it this way. "Y o u are those people who pass yourselves off before men as if you were living in harmony with God's holy law. But y o u r righteousness is only a façade. On the inside y o u are the very opposite of what you want people to believe you are. However, God has y o u r number. He knows that y o u r religion is sham. For, what men *see* of y o u and admire is an abomination in *God's* sight" (New Testament Commentary: Exposition of the Gospel according to Luke, 2007, p. 774). Before Jesus relates the powerful parable of the Rich Man and Lazarus, He reminds them that before John the Baptist came to proclaim the Gospel of the kingdom of God publicly, the whole revelation had been given to them in the Law and the Prophets (v. 16).

The Rich Man and Lazarus – Luke 16:19-31: *"Now there was a certain rich man, and he habitually dressed in purple and fine linen, gaily living in splendor every day. And a certain poor man named Lazarus was laid at his gate, covered with sores, and longing to be fed with the crumbs which were falling from the rich man's table; besides, even the dogs were coming and licking his sores. Now it came about that the poor man died and he was carried away by the angels to Abraham's bosom; and the rich man also died and was buried. And in Hades he lifted up his eyes, being in torment, and saw Abraham far away, and Lazarus in his bosom. And he cried out and said, 'Father Abraham, have mercy on me, and send Lazarus, that he may dip the tip* *of his finger in water and cool off my tongue; for I am in agony in this flame.' But Abraham said, 'Child, remember that during your life you received your good things, and likewise Lazarus bad things; but now he is being comforted here, and you are in agony. And besides all this, between us and you there is a great chasm fixed, in order that those who wish to come over from here to you may not be able, and that none may cross over from there to us.' And he said, 'Then I beg you, Father, that you send him to my father's house — for I have five brothers — that he may warn them, lest they also come to this place of torment.' But Abraham said, 'They have Moses and the Prophets; let them hear them.' But he said, 'No, Father Abraham, but if someone goes to them from the dead, they will repent!' But he said to him, 'If they do not listen to Moses and the Prophets, neither will they be persuaded if someone rises from the dead.' "*

The parallel drawn between the Pharisees and the rich man is sharply contrasted with a poor beggar named Lazarus. It most likely is not a coincidence that Jesus names the character in the parable Lazarus. The name Lazarus means, "Whom God helps, or without help" (Thayer's Greek Lexicon, 2009, G2976, p. 367). Although the name is fictitiously used in the story, there was a real person named Lazarus whom Jesus dearly loved, and who was raised from the dead by Him (John 11:43-44). It is also most likely not a coincidence that Jesus chooses to say that the rich man was *habitually* dressed in purple and fine linen cloth. In Biblical times purple was an extremely expensive dye, and the dyed linen cloths were used almost exclusively by kings or for other devotional purposes. The spiritual symbology of purple can be seen in the Book of Exodus where Moses states that the tabernacle curtains, veil, and screen were made of purple and linen material (Exodus 26:1, 31, 36). Aaron's priestly vestments were made of purple and fine linen (Exodus 28:5, 8, 15). In other passages of the Old Testament we are told that purple is the clothing that was used by idols who were doomed to perish (Jeremiah 10:9), and of Assyrian governors and high officials who were eventually conquered by the Babylonians (Ezekiel 23:5). (D. Irvin, Eerdman's *International*

Standard Bible Encyclopedia, Volume K-P, 1986, p. 1057, ed. Geoffrey W. Bromiley). Finally, the woman upon whose forehead is written *"BABYLON THE GREAT, THE MOTHER OF HARLOTS AND OF THE ABOMINATIONS OF THE EARTH"* is dressed in purple (Revelation 17:4-5).

The symbology of the great wealth and power seen in the rich man's clothing is sharply contrasted to the hungry beggar, full of sores, who was lying at his gate longing to be fed with just a few crumbs that were falling from his table. Although the beggar outwardly appears destitute, the phrase, 'even the dogs were licking his sores', signifies that even the dogs had more mercy on the beggar than the rich man did, thus illustrating the poverty-stricken heart of the rich man.

Symbolic of spiritual reality, the story goes on to say that both men die, one is carried away by the angels to Abraham's bosom, the other sees Abraham and Lazarus from Hades and ironically cries out to Abraham to send Lazarus with just a drop of water so that his tongue may be cooled. Abraham then reminds the rich man that during his life he was comforted with great wealth while Lazarus was not, and now Lazarus (true to his name) is comforted while he is not. The spiritual reality of the deep gap that exists between paradise and Hades is illustrated by the conversation that is held between Abraham and the rich man wherein Abraham tells the rich man that he cannot send Lazarus because no one is able to cross over to either side of the gap (v. 26). The rich man then begs Abraham to send someone to 'his father's house' to warn them of their doom, and Abraham reminds him that like he, his brothers have the testimony that was given to them by Moses and the Prophets. Jesus concludes the parable by saying, *"If they do not listen to Moses and the Prophets, neither will they be persuaded if someone rises from the dead"* (v. 31). Dr. Lockyer solemnly concludes:

> "If the parables of Luke 15 speak of mercy and compassion of God toward the penitent, the parable just considered presents in the clearest light the righteousness and righteous indignation

toward those who died impenitent (Romans 1:18). The solemn lessons we are left with should be seriously considered by all:

(1) Man cannot serve two masters. If he gains the world, and loses his soul, his loss will be eternal.
(2) The choice made on earth determines the life to come, and such a choice is final. The grave can work no miracle
(3) In the future, personality continues—feeling, knowing, seeing, reasoning and remembering. Are these faculties to aid our bliss, or add to our torment?
(4) Heaven and hell are realities, and our eternal destiny depends, not upon wealth or poverty, but upon our relationship to Jesus Christ, who came as prophesied by Moses and the prophets as the Savior of the world" (Lockyer, All the Parables of the Bible, 1963, p. 295).

In today's world, both affluent believers and non-believers, and poor believers and non-believers exist together, and whether affluent or poor, neither one are considerations used in determining the outcome of eternal destiny. Warren Wiersbe quotes an excerpt by C.S. Lewis who was told about a gravestone inscription that read, "Here lies an atheist—all dressed up and no place to go." Lewis quietly replied, "I bet he wishes that were so!" (The Bible Exposition Commentary: New Testament, Volume I, 1989, p. 241).

> *"For what will a man be profited, if he gains the whole world, and forfeits his soul? Or what will a man give in exchange for his soul?"* (Matthew 16:26).

The Servant's Reward—Luke 17:7-10

In the parable of the Servant's Reward, the continuity of the spiritual principles involved in discipleship that Jesus had been teaching His disciples prior to the telling of the Rich Man and Lazarus is continued. In the introductory verses, Jesus is speaking to His disciples saying: 1) it is impossible to live in a world without facing temptations that may cause them and others to stumble in their faith, 2) restates the principles of forgiveness and faith that He had already taught them (vv. 1-6), and 3) reminds them to exercise these principles. In previous parables, Jesus had already illustrated the spiritual principles of pricing the full cost of making a commitment to discipleship and on stewardship. The theme of the parable in the Servant's Reward is the spiritual position and disposition of servitude. By comparing the disciples to the slave-owner, Jesus begins telling the parable by saying, "*But which of you*" ....

The Servant's Reward – Luke 17:7-10: *"But which of you, having a slave plowing or tending sheep, will say to him when he has come in from the field, 'Come immediately and sit down to eat'? But will he not say to him, 'Prepare something for me to eat, and properly clothe yourself and serve me until I have eaten and drunk; and afterward you will eat and drink'? He does not thank the slave because he did the things which were commanded, does he? So you too, when you do all the things which are commanded you, say, 'We are unworthy slaves; we have done only that which we ought to have done.' "*

On the surface, the parable seems to illustrate a thankless tyrannical master who will not allow his tired and hungry slave to eat and rest before continuing with his duties. However, closer examination of the word *slave* sheds light on the kind of relationship the slave has with his owner in context of the parable. Though the words slave and servant are sometimes used interchangeably in the

New Testament, the term slave (as used in context of the parable) is translated from the Greek word doulos (pronounced *doo'-los*) to mean "slave; man of servile condition; serving, subject to" (Thayer's Greek Lexicon, 2009, G1401, p. 158). In viewing slavery from within the framework of the relationship of a slave to his master in the Jewish community in the first century A.D., Dr. Scott Bartchy writes:

> "The lower position in a relationship of dominance-dependency was regulated in the case of slaves by various and extensive legal traditions in all Mediterranean cultures in the NT period....The extent of the owner's control over the life, the family, the production, and potential freedom of the enslaved person varied greatly. In contrast to the practice of the AV, doulos should be translated "slave" instead of "servant" in order to point to the legal subordination of the "slave" as property of the owner.
>
> Furthermore, the significant differences among the three traditions relevant to NT texts (Jewish, Greek and Romans) require examination each to determine which of the legal-philosophical frameworks was presupposed.....In the Roman tradition slaves on the one hand were rigorously regarded in much legislation as things and property, yet as fully human beings who were usually granted Roman citizenship when set free, as happened regularly. However, Jewish traditions saw the slave as one who had already become exclusively a "slave of God" by means of the liberation of his or her ancestors from Egyptian bondage and therefore inappropriately living as a slave of any human being (Lev. 25:25)" (Eerdman's *International Standard Bible Encyclopedia*, Volume Q-Z, 1988, p. 420, ed. Geoffrey W. Bromiley).

William Hendriksen observes:

> "It is clear that we are dealing with the owner of a small farm. This farmer has only one servant. Some insist that the word used in the original—namely *doulos*—a word which

> sometimes means slave, sometimes servant, must here be rendered *slave.* We should remember, however, that Jesus is addressing his message primarily to "his disciples" (v. 1). He is saying, "Who among y o u …?" Further we should understand that what the parable is picturing is that which does ***not*** happen in the realm in which God is consistently recognized as King. In fact the very opposite takes place here.
>
> The servant pictured in this parable does only what he has been ordered to do, and the *spirit* of a *slave* has taken possession of him. All day long he has been plowing or tending sheep. When he comes in from the field, his boss orders him to wait on him while he, the master, is eating and drinking. The servant is told, "When I'm finished, you can eat." The servant pictured in this parable does exactly what he has been ordered to do—no less, no more" (New Testament Commentary: Exposition of the Gospel according to Luke, 2007, p. 796).

Finally, to further illustrate the difference between having a spiritual attitude of servitude as opposed to the worldly one exemplified by the slave, Jesus then says to his disciples, "*So you too, when you do all the things which are commanded you, say, 'We are unworthy slaves; we have done only that which we ought to have done.' "* On this point, William Hendriksen states:

> "We believe that Robertson, Word Pictures, Vol. II, p. 227, has interpreted the parable correctly when he states, "The slavish spirit gains no promotion in business life or in the kingdom of God." In the kingdom of God—the realm in which God's sovereignty is gladly recognized—matters are entirely different. To be sure, here, too, God's children aim to do is will, but they do it with *gladness of heart, in the spirit of love and gratitude"* (Ibid., pp. 796-797).

Thus, a disciple, like the slave, is not only positionally in subjection to his master, but is also dependent upon him. And, as opposed to serving with a 'slavish spirit', his service is given out of gratitude and obedience in the 'spirit of love' without expecting or obliging his master to reward him in return, which is consistent with Jesus' parabolic spiritual teachings that *genuine* servitude is an attitude of the heart that stems from faith bonded in love. As Matthew Henry commented in the parable of Ten Talents, "the faithful servants of Christ shall not be put off with bare commendation; no all their work and labour of love shall be rewarded" (Matthew Henry's Commentary on the Whole Bible, 1991, Volume 5, p. 303).

> *"Therefore, my beloved brethren, be steadfast, immovable, always abounding in the work of the Lord, knowing that your toil is not in vain in the Lord"* (1 Corinthians 15:58).

The Unjust Judge—Luke 18:1-8

The introductory verses of Chapter 17 begins with Jesus telling His disciples that it is impossible to live in a world without facing temptations that may cause them and others to stumble in their faith—the introductory verses of this chapter begins with Jesus telling his disciples not lose heart but to pray at all times (v. 1). To illustrate the importance of persevering in faith and in prayer, Jesus began illustrating the principle.

The Unjust Judge – Luke 18:1-8: *"There was in a certain city a judge who did not fear God, and did not respect man. And there was a widow in that city, and she kept coming to him, saying, 'Give me legal protection from my opponent.' And for a while he was unwilling; but afterward he said to himself, 'Even though I do not fear God nor respect man, yet because this widow bothers me, I will give her legal protection, lest by continually coming she wear me out.' "*

Reminiscent of the theme found in the Midnight Friend, the parable of the Unjust Judge likewise emphasizes the importance of perseverance in faith and prayer. In both parables, there are two distinct characters and two distinct circumstances. In the former, the two characters are the midnight friend and his friend—in this parable, the two characters are the unjust judge and the widow. The former parable illustrates the friend who needs food for his guest, while the latter illustrates a widow who needs legal protection from her adversary. Both the midnight friend and the widow persevered, and though both the friend and unjust judge did eventually respond to their petitions out of weariness, neither the midnight friend nor the widow ever lost heart.

Unlike the circumstance of the midnight friend, the circumstance that the widow finds herself in is quite precarious. In Israelite society, it was commonplace for the widow to be neglected or even exploited.

If a widow had no adult male relative who would claim her for his wife or could not return to her father's house, she was left abandoned and unprotected (Deuteronomy 25:5-10). In David Holwerda's study of widowhood in Israelite society, he says that though a widow could be wealthy, more often than not, she was very poor and disadvantaged. Moreover, though the Old Testament law forbade the exploitation of the widow (Exodus 22:22), they were nonetheless victimized. Part of the reason for their abandonment and harsh treatment, David E. Holwerda writes, "is that widowhood was seen as a reproach from God Himself, and their cause was seldom heard in court" (Eerdman's *International Standard Bible Encyclopedia*, Volume Q-Z, 1988, p. 1060, ed. Geoffrey W. Bromiley).

Similarly, the perseverance illustrated by both the midnight friend and the widow exemplifies the importance of perseverance in faith and prayer. By sharp contrast, the illustration given of the attitude that the unjust judge held towards God and the widow both, illustrates that if the persistent petition of a widow is answered by an unjust judge, how much more will not God vindicate His own who seek His face daily in prayer. Jesus concludes the parable by stating, "*shall not God bring about justice for His elect, who cry to Him day and night, and will He delay long over them? I tell you that He will bring about justice for them speedily. When the Son of Man comes, will He find faith on the earth?*" (vv. 7-8). William Hendriksen concludes: "Jesus was not referring to faith in general, but to the kind of faith exercised by the widow" (New Testament Commentary: Exposition of the Gospel according to Luke, 2007, p. 823). To which Dr. Lockyer adds:

> "God has assured us that He hears and answers prayer, and this should induce us to continue asking. The links of the chain reaching from earth to heaven, and which draws heaven down to earth, are links resulting in effectual prayer:
>
> A sense of continual, personal need
> An unfailing desire to receive what God sees I need
> An unshaken faith that He has what I need in store

A consciousness that though He withholds awhile, He loves to be asked, and asked again
A firm belief that if I ask, believing, I shall receive" (Lockyer, All the Parables of the Bible, 1963, p. 301).

> *"Pray at all times and do not lose heart"* (v. 1).

The Pharisee and the Publican—Luke 18:9-14

The theme of prayer and faith is continued by sharply contrasting the prayer spoken by the Pharisee with that of the prayer of the Publican. In the preceding parable, the focus of prayer is on both perseverance of faith and prayer. However, in the parable of the Pharisee and the Publican, by contrasting the prayer of the Pharisee with the prayer of the tax-collector, Jesus illustrates that prayer is an attitude of the heart.

The Pharisee and the Publican – Luke 18:9-14: *"Two men went up into the temple to pray, one a Pharisee stood and was praying thus to himself, 'God, I thank Thee that I am not like other people; swindlers, unjust, adulterers, or even like this tax-gatherer. I fast twice a week; I pay tithes of all that I get.' But the tax-gatherer, standing some distance away, was unwilling to lift up his eyes to heaven, but was beating his breast, saying, 'God, be merciful to me, the sinner!' I tell you, this man went down to his house justified rather than the other; for every one who exalts himself shall be humbled, but he who humbles himself shall be exalted."*

Both men go into the temple and stand before God to pray. Though the parable places the two men on equal ground, they are not on equal footing. One is a law-keeper, the other a law-breaker; one exalts himself before God, while the other humbles himself before God. One does not acknowledge his inward need for mercy and justifies himself by his outward deeds, while the other acknowledges his condition and prays for mercy. One relies on obedience to the Law for justification, while the other asks God to be propitious. After making the sharp contrast between the two prayers, Jesus concludes that the tax-collector went home justified, while the other did not, and by using the same concluding words that He used in the parable of the Chief Seats (Luke 16:15), explains why the Pharisee did not. William Hendriksen observes:

"To be genuine, faith must not only persevere; it must also be the expression of a humble heart. If the heart is humble, so will be the prayer as Jesus sets forth in the gripping parable of the Pharisee and The Tax Collector, climaxed by the memorable epigram, "For everyone who exalts himself will be humbled, but he who humbles himself will be exalted" " (New Testament Commentary: Exposition of the Gospel according to Luke, 2007, p. 541).

On a different note, John MacArthur's writes:

"The parable is addressed to Pharisees who trusted their own righteousness (vv. 10, 11). Such confidence in one's inherent rightcousness is a damning hope (cf. Rom. 10:3; Phil. 3:9), because human righteousness—even the righteousness of the most fastidious Pharisee—falls short of the divine standard (Matt. 5:48). Scripture consistently teaches that sinners are justified when God's perfect righteousness is imputed to their account (cf. Gen. 15:6; Rom. 4:4, 5:2 Cor. 5:21; Phil. 3:4-9)—and it was only on that basis that this tax collector (or anyone else) could be saved" (The MacArthur Bible Commentary, 2005, p. 1316).

"For everyone who exalts himself shall be humbled, and he who humbles himself shall be exalted" (v. 14).

The Pounds—Luke 19:11-27

Aside from the parables of the Wicked Tenant Farmers and the Fig Tree recorded in Luke 20:9-18 and 21:29-31 that are covered under Matthew's parables (see Table II), the parable of the Pound is the last of the unique parables recorded in the Gospel of Luke. In the opening verses, Luke states that as Jesus is passing through Jericho (just northeast of the city of Jerusalem), the crowd is so large that a head tax-gatherer named Zaccheus climbs up into a tree to watch Jesus pass by. Jesus sees Zaccheus, and calls him down from the tree to tell him that He will be staying at his house. Meanwhile, the Pharisees are carefully watching Jesus and began to grumble among themselves because He went to stay at the house of a tax-gatherer. Zaccheus receives Jesus gladly, repents, and Jesus says to him, "*Today salvation has come to this house, because he, too, is a son of Abraham. For the Son of Man has come to seek and to save that which was lost.*" Before the telling of the parable, Luke mentions that there were those among the crowd who thought that the kingdom of God was going to appear immediately (vv. 1-10), which intimates two things: One that the parable was told to clarify that misconception, and secondly, to foretell of His upcoming death, resurrection, and ascension. "*He was near Jerusalem and while they were listening to these things, He said*",

---

The Pounds – Luke 19:11-27: *"A certain nobleman went to a distant country to receive a kingdom for himself, and then return. And he called ten of his slaves, and gave them ten minas, and said to them, 'Do business with this until I come back.' But his citizens hated him, and sent a delegation after him, saying, 'We do not want this man to reign over us.' And it came about that when he returned, after receiving the kingdom, he ordered that these slaves, to whom he had given the money, be called to him in order that he might know what business they had done. And the first appeared, saying, 'Master, your mina has made ten minas more.' And he said to him, 'Well done, good slave, because you have been faithful in a very little thing, be in* *authority over ten cities.' And the second came, saying, 'Your mina, master, has made five minas.' And he said to him also, 'And you are to be over five cities.' And another came, saying, 'Master, behold your mina, which I kept put away in a handkerchief; for I was afraid of you, because you are an exacting man; you take up what you did not lay down, and reap what you did not sow?' He said to him, 'By your own words I will judge you, you worthless slave. Did you know that I am an exacting man, taking up what I did not lay down, and reaping what I did not sow? Then why did you not put the money in the bank, and having come, I would have collected it with interest?' And he said to the bystanders, 'Take the mina away from him, and give it to the one who has the ten minas.' And they said to him, 'Master, he has ten minas already.' I tell you, that to everyone who has shall more be given but from the one who does not have, even what he does have shall be taken away. But these enemies of mine, who did not want me to reign over them, bring them here, and slay them in my presence."*

Similar to the parable of the Ten Talents, the same characteristics of faithfulness and unfaithfulness are also found in the parable of the Pounds. Likewise, both parables tell of rewards given to the servants by the master upon his return, both contain the same closing statement, "*I tell you, that to everyone who has shall more be given but from the one who does not have, even what he does have shall be taken away,*" and both conclude with judgment. Similarly, no specifics are given for the length of time that passes between the master leaving on his journey, and his return. However, three unique differences are found in the parable of the Pounds that distinguishes it from the Ten Talents. 1) In the former parable, though the distribution of the talents is *unequal*, the reward for faithfulness is *equal*. In the latter, the reverse is true; the distribution of the pounds is equal, and the rewards are given according to each of the servant's results. 2) While the theme found in the Ten Talents is on faithful stewardship, the theme found in the Pounds is on responsibility and diligence in caring for the master's interests while he is away. 3) A striking difference is notable in the illustration between the two main characters of the two parables. In the parable of the Ten Talents, the main character is a 'man' who entrusts his servants with his possessions while he is away. In the latter, the main character is a 'nobleman' who entrusts his servants with the responsibility of caring for his interests while he is away. The term nobleman (as used in context of the parable) is translated from the Greek word eugenēs (pronounced *yoog-en'-ace*) to mean "Well born of noble race of a prince" (Thayer's Greek Lexicon, 2009, G2104, p. 257). However, to define the characteristics of the nobleman in the parable, Nola J. Opperwall applies the Hebrew translation of nâdîyb (pronounced *naw-deeb')* as "one who gives himself voluntarily in the service of God or who—because of his exalted economic and social position—had a responsibility to do so. Thus, a true nâdîyb is generous and uses his resources wisely for the good of his community (cf. Nu. 21:18; Prov. 7:26; Isa. 32:5, 8)." Nola J. Opperwall further explains that, "Although the Greek term eugenēs originally denoted nobility of birth (Lk. 19:12; 1 Cor. 1:6), it also came to denote that the '*qualities'* of generosity and broad-mindedness were expected from nobility" (Eerdman's *International Standard Bible Encyclopedia*, Volume K-P, 1986, p. 546, ed. Geoffrey W. Bromiley).

A unique feature of the parable of the Pounds, however, is that it is based on an actual story. Dr. Harold Hoehner gives a brief recount of the history of the king Archelaus, the son of king Herod the Great. He states, "Before Herod the Great died in 4 B.C., he divided his kingdom between his sons Herod Antipas, Herod Philip, and Archelaus. Archelaus, whose inheritance was Judaea, was notoriously known for his brutality and tyranny of his citizens. Because the division had not yet been ratified by the emperor, Archelaus and Antipas journey to Rome to persuade Caesar Augustus to allow them to enter into their inheritance. Meanwhile, a Jewish revolt breaks out at the feast of Pentecost and a delegation of Jewish citizens are sent to Rome to plead autonomy for the nation" (Harold W. Hoehner, Eerdman's *International Standard Bible Encyclopedia,* Volume E-J, 1982, p. 694, ed. Geoffrey W. Bromiley). Thus, there would have been many 'citizens' in the crowd with similar sentiments towards Jesus who would have understood the parable. Warren W. Wiersbe comments:

> "The "citizens" or "enemies" are mentioned at the beginning and the ending and are an important part of the story, for most of the people in the crowd that day were in that category. Jesus was near Jerusalem, and in a few days He would hear the mob shout, "We have no king but Caesar" (John 19:15). In other words, "We will not have this Man to reign over us!" (The Bible Exposition Commentary: New Testament, Volume I, 1989, p. 253).

Secondly, the idea of the nobleman going away to 'a distant country' to receive a kingdom for himself and then returning, paints a picture of Jesus' anticipated death, resurrection, and ascension. On this point, Dr. Lockyer writes:

> "As a Nobleman, Jesus went into the far country to receive a kingdom. On His ascension, He sat at the right hand of the Majesty on high (Hebrews 1:3), and from there He exercises power (Philippians 2:9-11); Ephesians 1:17, 20-22). Presently, His kingdom is an invisible one and consists in the execution of the great plan of redemption, translating those in bondage into His kingdom of light and liberty (Colossians 1:13). In the far country, heaven, all power in heaven and on earth was granted to Jesus, and He received an investiture of a present spiritual kingdom, and the right to rule as the supreme King in His coming visible kingdom (Daniel 7:18, 22, 27; Hebrews 12:28)" (Lockyer, All the Parables of the Bible, 1963, p. 307).

However, according to the story the rewards are not given to the bond-servants until *after* the nobleman receives the kingdom. Dr. Lockyer continues.

> "What a pleasant transition it is from rebels to good and faithful servants! Here our Lord emphasized the fact of His return. "When he was returned, having received the kingdom." All regal rights have been granted Christ by the Father, and when He returns to earth, having already virtually received the kingdom, He will establish it among men. In the rule of such a

kingdom, the King must have trusted servants to assist Him in the government and control of all things" (Ibid., p. 308).

Concluding the parable, two important points on judgments are made. First, when the servant who did nothing with his pound gives his reasons why he did not, the nobleman does two things. First, using the same standard by which he was judged, the nobleman passes judgment on the servant saying, "*By your own words I will judge you, you worthless slave"* (v. 22). Secondly, the nobleman takes the servant's pound away from him and gives it to the one who had been awarded authority over ten cities, saying, "*I tell you, that to everyone who has shall more be given but from the one who does not have, even what he does have shall be taken away*" (v. 26). Dr. Lockyer notes:

> "The nobleman called his servants to appear before him to give an account of what they gained through trading with the deposit during his absence. There is a suggestive thought in the phrase, "that he might know". Our returning, heavenly Nobleman as the Omniscient One, knows all things. The lesson here is that our conduct as servants and citizens alike must be made known before others when He comes to reward and judge" (Ibid., p. 309).

Warren Wiersbe quotes the cherished words of Charles Spurgeon: "The gracious and faithful man obtains more grace and more means of usefulness, while the unfaithful sink lower and lower." Of his own observations, Wiersbe writes:

> "The servant was unfaithful because his heart was not right toward his master. He saw him as a hard man who was demanding and unfair. The servant had no love for his master; in fact he feared him and dreaded to displease him. Rather than lose the pound and incur his master's anger, he guarded it so that he would at least have something to give him if he returned and asked for a reckoning. It is sad when a Christian is motivated by slavish fear instead of loving faith" (The Bible Exposition Commentary: New Testament, Volume I, 1989, p. 253).

Finally, like the harsh judgment that was passed upon the wicked slave in the parable of the Ten Talents, a harsh and final judgment is passed upon those 'citizens who hated him', *But these enemies of mine, who did not want me to reign over them, bring them here, and slay them in my presence"* (v. 27). However, John MacArthur points out that Jesus' enemies had already concluded that He was not the Messiah therefore did not believe the message (The MacArthur Bible Commentary, 2005, p. 1315). To which Warren Wiersbe adds:

> "God was gracious to Israel and gave the nation nearly forty years of grace before judgment fell (Luke 19:41-44). But we must be careful to see in this a warning to all who reject Jesus Christ—Jew or Gentile—for during this time while He is away in heaven, Jesus Christ is calling men everywhere to repent and submit to Him. The faithful servants obeyed because they trusted their master and wanted to please him. The unfaithful servant disobeyed because he feared his master. But these citizens rebelled because they hated their king (Luke 19:14). Jesus quoted Psalm 69:4 and told His disciples, "They hated me without a cause" (John 15:25). We are living today in the period between Luke 19:14 and 15 when our Master is absent but will return according to His promise" (The Bible Exposition Commentary: New Testament, Volume I, 1989, pp. 253).

Concerning the judgment illustrated in the parable, Matthew Henry observes:

(1) "It is to be remembered that the Jews had particularly disclaimed and protested against Jesus' kingly office, when they said, '*We have no king but Caesar'*, nor would own him for their king. They appealed to Caesar, and to Caesar they shall go; Caesar shall be their ruin. They were brought forth and slain before him. Never was so much slaughter made in any war as in the wars of the Jews. That nation lived to see Christianity victorious in the Gentile world, in spite of their enmity and opposition to it, and then it was

taken away from them. The wrath of Christ came upon them to the uttermost (1 Thess. 2:15, 16), and their destruction redounded very much to the honour of Christ and the peace of the church.

(2) In the sentence passed upon them at his return: "*Those mine enemies bring hither"* (v. 27). When his faithful subjects are preferred and rewarded, then he will take vengeance on his enemies" (Matthew Henry's *Commentary on the Whole Bible*, 1991, Volume 5, p. 636).

Dr. John Gill adds:

" "But those mine enemies" though it is true of all natural men, that they are enemies to Christ, though particularly the Jews, who were enemies to the person of Christ, and hated and rejected him, as the King Messiah; and rebelled against him, and would not submit to his government; and were enemies to His people, and were exceeding mad against them, and persecuted them; and to His Gospel, and the distinguishing truths of it, and to his ordinances, which they rejected against themselves: *which would not that I should reign over them*; *bring hither, and slay them before me;* which had its accomplishment in the destruction of Jerusalem, when multitudes of them were slain with the sword, both with their own, and with their enemies; and to this the parable has a special respect, and of which Christ more largely discourses in this chapter" (Gills Expositor, Exposition of The New Testament, Volume VII, 1976, p. 691).

Dr. Lockyer concludes:

"During the Great Tribulation multitudes of Jews and Gentiles alike will be the rebellious citizens casting off all divine restraints (II Thessalonians 2:1-10; Revelation 13: 5-6; Psalm 2:2). The final manifestation of rebellion to His claims will be after His millennial reign with terrible results to the rebels. This final judgment will be executed on all His enemies (Proverbs

20:8; Revelation 20:11). All adversaries are to be punished" (Lockyer, All the Parables of the Bible, 1963, p 308).

To which Warren B. Wiersbe comments:

"We have been given a task to perform, and we must be faithful until He comes. What will the King say to us when He returns? Will His words mean reward, rebuke, or possibly retribution?" (The Bible Exposition Commentary: New Testament, Volume I, 1989, p. 254).

But when the Son of Man comes in His Glory, and all the angels with Him, then He will sit on His glorious throne. And all the nations will be gathered before Him; and He will separate them from one another, as the shepherd separates the sheep from the goats; and He will put the sheep on His right, and the goats on the left" (Mathew 25:31).

The Seed Growing—Mark 4:26-29

Inasmuch as the concluding words of the preceding parable, "*But these enemies of mine, who did not want me to reign over them, bring them here, and slay them in my presence,*" refers to a final judgment upon His return, it seems appropriate to conclude this section of Jesus' parabolic ministry with the unique parable of the Seed Growing recorded by Mark.

***The Seed Growing – Mark 4:26-29:** "*And He was saying, "The kingdom of God is like a man who casts seed upon the ground; and goes to bed at night and gets up by day, and the seed sprouts up and grows — how, he himself does not know. The earth produces crops by itself; first the blade, then the head, then the mature grain in the head. But when the crop permits, he immediately puts in the sickle, because the harvest has come."* "

*Only unique parable found in Mark.

Through Jesus' parabolic teaching of the mystery of the kingdom, God unveils spiritual concepts that had never before been revealed to humanity. Through those parables, Jesus reveals that He is the Sower and the seed is the Gospel. He also illustrates the way in which the Gospel is sown in the world, exemplifies the different conditions that affect the growth of the Word, and explains the conditions that contribute to the success or failure of the seed. Moreover, through the parable of the Tares, He teaches that the field is the world, the good seed are the sons of the kingdom, the bad seed are the sons of the evil one, the enemy is the devil, the harvest is the end of the age, and the reapers are His angels. Notable is the consistent omission of the length of time that passes between seedtime and harvest.

The timeless parable of the Seed Growing contains characteristics of all of the seven mysteries of the kingdom parables, which may be seen in three parts. 1) The seed is the Word, 2) the growth of the kingdom, and 3) the harvest is the end of the age. The unique feature of the parable of the Seed Growing is the illustration of the three stages of growth of the seed. Jesus explains that the seed first produces the blade, then the head, then the full crop. The seed symbolizes the Gospel, and the germination of the seed parallels the mystery of the leaven. The blade symbolizes the first stage of the growth of the kingdom, the head symbolizes Christ as head of the Church, the earth symbolizes the world, the crop symbolizes the presence of the kingdom on earth, the harvest symbolizes the end of the age, and judgment is analogized by the sickle. Dr. Robert A. Guelich's perspective on the parable of the Seed is on the timeless application of the growth of the kingdom in its present state and in the future. He writes:

> "Two features stand out in the story and both are related to the seed—the growth of the seed and the harvest. First, the seed grows on its own apart from any visible, external causes. Applied to the kingdom, the kingdom germinates, grows and matures of its own accord without any enhancement from visible, external forces. This may have originally addressed the question about the kingdom's presence despite the absence of the expected, visible enhancements either from Jesus' ministry or from those who heard and followed him. So understood, the parable would assure those who were finding it difficult to comprehend how the kingdom might be present and at work in a manner contrary to their expectations. The parable may have addressed any false assumptions that certain actions by Jesus' followers or by those who sought to usher in the kingdom for Israel by force could enhance the work of the kingdom.
>
> It may also indicate that the presence and work of the kingdom despite the disciples' lack of understanding and the absence of visible enhancements. It this is true for the disciples during Jesus' ministry, the need of assurance only increased for those after Passover who found the enigma of the kingdom all the more puzzling in view of the response from "outsiders" and especially in view of the failure of "insiders" who had "heard the word" (e.g., 4:14-19). The parable, therefore, assured the

reader that God's kingdom, like the seed, had a life of its own" (Word Biblical Commentary, Volume 34A, 2000, p. 245, ed. Ralph P. Martin).

Concerning the secret germination of the seed, the head of the blade, and the full crop Dr. Lockyer observes:

> "The *Blade*, or the kingdom in mystery, the Church Age during which the Holy Spirit is active completing "the mystery hid from ages," namely, the Church of the living God.
>
> The *Ear*, or the kingdom in manifestation, which will be experienced during the Millennial Reign of Christ, which was the main theme of Old Testament Prophets ..."Thy kingdom come."
>
> The *Full Corn,* suggests the kingdom in all its majestic perfection, the New Heavens and New Earth when God will be all in all. This will be the "kingdom Ultimate," The Eternal Ages: the "Dispensation of the fullness of times" about which Paul wrote (Ephesians 1:10)" (Lockyer, All the Parables of the Bible, 1963, p. 252).

Viewed from the presence of the kingdom of God in its present stage of growth, Henry Matthew writes:

> "The good seed of the Gospel sown in the world, and sown in the heart, does by degrees produce wonderful effects, but without noise (v. 26); *So is the kingdom of God;* so is the gospel, when it is sown, and received, as seed in the ground.
>
> 1) It will *come up*; though it seems lost and buried under the clods, it will find or make its way through them. The seed *cast into the ground will spring.* Let but the word of Christ have the place it ought to have in a soul, and it will show itself as the *wisdom from above does in good conversation.* After a field is sown with corn, how soon is the surface of it altered.
>
> 2) The husbandman cannot describe how it comes up; He sees it has grown, but he cannot tell in what manner it

grew, or what was the cause and method of its growth. Thus we know not how the Spirit by the word makes a change in the heart, any more than we can account for the blowing of the wind, which we hear the sound of, but cannot tell from where it comes or where it goes.

3) The husbandman, when he has sown the seed does nothing toward the springing of it up; Thus, the *word of grace*, when it is received in faith, is in the heart a work of the Spirit of God.

4) It comes to perfection at last (v 29). When the *fruit is brought forth*, that is, when it is *ripe*, and *ready* to be delivered into the owner's hand; then *he put in the sickle*. This intimates (1) That Christ now accepts the services which are done to Him by an honest heart from a good principle; from the fruit of the gospel taking place and working in the soul, Christ gathers in a harvest of honor to Himself. (2) That he will reward them in eternal life. When those that receive the gospel aright, have finished their course, the harvest comes, when they shall be gathered as wheat into God's barn (Matt. 13:30), as a shock of corn in his season" (Matthew Henry's *Commentary on the Whole Bible*, 1991, Volume 5, p. 383).

Finally, viewed from a two-dimensional perspective, Dr. Guelich concludes, "Though the kingdom is presently growing with a power of its own (4:27-28), its consummation, the harvest, is still future" (Word Biblical Commentary, Volume 34A, 2000, p. 246, ed. Ralph P. Martin). For easy reference, with the exception of the unique parable of the Seed Growing recorded by Mark, and the Unmerciful Servant, the Salt, the Lost Sheep, and the Laborers in the Vineyard recorded by Matthew, the following table contains all of the parables of Jesus that are *uniquely* recorded in the Gospel of Luke.

Table III
Principles of the Kingdom

(From Early Summer A.D. 28 to Passover A.D. 29)

PARABLE	PLACE	MATTHEW	MARK	LUKE
1. The Seed Growing	Galilee		4:26-29	

(From Passover A.D. 29 to Autumn A.D. 30)

PARABLE	PLACE	MATTHEW	MARK	LUKE
2. The Unmerciful Servant	Capernaum	18:23-35		

(From Autumn A.D. 29 to Spring A.D. 30)

PARABLE	PLACE	MATTHEW	MARK	LUKE
3. The Good Samaritan	Judea			10:30-37
4. The Midnight Friend	Judea			11:5-13
5. The Rich Fool	Judea			12:13-21
6. The Watchful Servants	Judea			12:35-40
7. The Barren Fig Tree	Judea			13:6-9

Table III **(Continued)**
Principles of the Kingdom

(From Autumn A.D. 29 to Spring A.D. 30)

PARABLE	PLACE	MATTHEW	MARK	LUKE
8. The Chief Seats	Perea			14:7-11
9. The Great Banquet	Perea			14:16-24
10. The Rash Builder	Perea			14:25-30
11. The Rash King	Perea			14:31:35
12. The Salt		5:13	9:50	14:34-35
13. The Lost Sheep	Perea	18:12-14		15:3-7
14. The Laborers in the Vine-yard	Perea	20:1-16		
15. The Lost Coin	Perea			15:8-10
16. The Lost Son	Perea			15:11-32
17. The Unrighteous Steward	Perea			16:1-13
18. The Rich Man and Lazarus	Perea			16:19-31

Table III **(Continued)**
Principles of the Kingdom

(From Autumn A.D. 29 to Spring A.D. 30)

	PARABLE	PLACE	MATTHEW	MARK	LUKE
19.	The Servants Reward	Perea			17:7-10
20.	The Unjust Judge	Samaria/Gali lee			18:1-8
21.	The Pharisee and the Publican	Samaria/Gali lee			18:9-14
22.	The Pounds	Jericho			19:11-27

(Adapted from Dr. Herbert Lockyer, "Table of Parables", *All the Teachings of Jesus*, 1991, p. 305; John MacArthur, "The Parables of Jesus", *The MacArthur Bible Commentary*, 2005, p. 1209; Louis A. Barbieri, Jr., "The Parables of Jesus", *The Bible Knowledge Commentary: New Testament*, 1983, p. 35, ed. John F. Walvoord, Roy B. Zuck).

Other Figurative Teachings of Christ

The Light of the World—Matthew 5:14a
A City on a Hill—5:14b
The Lamp—5:15-16

The metaphors of the Light of the World, the City on a Hill, and the Lamp were all spoken directly to the disciples during Jesus' first great discourse of the Sermon on the Mount. The metaphor of the Salt is considered under the parables of pricing out the cost of making a full commitment to discipleship (Luke 14:26-35), but is worth mentioning in connection with the impact the disciples would be making in the world. Jesus said to them, *"Y o u are the salt of the earth; but if the salt has become tasteless, how will it be made salty again? It is good for nothing any more, except to be thrown out and trampled underfoot by men"* (v. 13).

The Light of the World—City on a Hill—The Lamp – Matthew 5:14-16: *"You are the light of the world. A city set on a hill cannot be hidden. Nor do men light a lamp, and put it under the peck-measure, but on the lampstand; and it gives light to all who are in the house"* (Mark 4:21; Luke 8:16; 11:33).

The opening verses of Chapter 5 state that Jesus went up the mountain (v. 1) and began teaching His disciples. Following the beatitudes, the metaphors and similitudes recorded are given directly to the disciples. After Jesus compares His disciples to salt, He then says to them, "*y o u* are the light of the world", and immediately began to illustrate it by saying, "*a city set on a hill cannot be hidden*". Dr. Donald A. Hagner makes a spiritual observation on the term "light" as used in Scripture. He writes, "Light is a very important metaphor in the Bible; "God is light" (1 John 1:5), and Christ is described in the Fourth Gospel as "the light of the world" (John 8:12; 9:5; 12:46; cf. 1:7-8). Moreover, God has come in Christ to bring light into the darkness (John 1:4-5), 9; 12:46; cf. Ps. 27:1" (Word Biblical Commentary, Volume 33A, 2000, pp. 99-100, ed. Ralph P. Martin). However, Dr. Lockyer's observation on light is three-fold in nature. He notes:

> "Light is natural, artificial, and spiritual. The light of the sun is natural; that of a lamp, artificial; that of the Word and of those who believe it, is spiritual. The "light" of the glorious gospel (II Corinthians 4:4, 6; Psalm 119:105). The word Christ used to describe His own is not "lights" as the A.V. has it, but luminaries (Philippians 2:15). How wonderful it is of the Master to give us the distinctive title He appropriates to Himself. "I am the Light of the World" (John 1:4, 9; 3:19; 8:12; 9:5; 12:35, 36)" (Lockyer, All the Parables of the Bible, 1963, p. 147).

William Hendriksen's beautiful observation also focuses on the spiritual nature of light:

> "*You* are the light of the world" probably means that the citizens of the kingdom not only have been blessed with these endowments but are also the means used by God to transmit them to the men who surround them. The light-possessors become light-transmitter. Collectively believers are the "the light." Individually they are "lights" (luminaries, stars, Phil. 2:15). Both ideas may well have been included in the words as spoken by Jesus, though the emphasis is on the collective" (New Testament Commentary: Exposition of the Gospel according to Matthew, 2007, p. 284).

The second part of the phrase, *"A city on a hill cannot be hidden, nor do men light a lamp and put it under a peck-measure, but on a lampstand",* illustrates the purpose of the light. Hendriksen continues with his analysis stating:

> "Two ideas are combined with the symbol of light. The followers of Christ must be both *visible* and *radiant*. They must be "in the light" and must also send out rays of light. The first idea is conveyed by the city situated on a hill. Such a city, with its walls and fortresses, "cannot be hidden." It is clearly visible to everybody.
>
> The second idea is set forth by the figure of the lamp set on the lampstand (not "a candle put on a candlestick," A.V.). Such a lamp "gives light"; it "shines." The lamps of that day can be seen today in any large museum and in many private collections. What Jesus is saying, then, is this, that no one would be foolish enough to light such a lamp—evidently for the purpose of illumining the surroundings—and then immediately place it under the peck-measure. Any sensible person would of course set the lit lamp on the lampstand" (Ibid., p. 285).

Finally, Jesus ends with an exhortation to, "*Let your light shine before men in such a way that they may see your good works, and glorify your Father who is in heaven*" (V. 16), to which Lockyer concludes:

> "A lamp or candle is a dark body and can give no light until it is lighted. Likewise we can give no light until we have received divine grace and enlightenment from the Spirit of God. Once lighted, we are to shine and not hide our light under a bushel or a bed .... Thus our Lord ends with the exhortation to let our line shine, a light reflected in good works and resulting in the glory of God" (Lockyer, All the Parables of the Bible, 1963, p. 147).

Image provided by NASA
http://visibleearth.nasa.gov/view.php?id=56512, 2001.

"You are the light of the world" (Matthew 5:14).

Two Gates—Matthew 7:13
Two Ways—Matthew 7:14
Two Foundations—Matthew 7:24-27

The Sermon on the Mount (Matthew Chapters 5-7) now culminates with the allegories of the Two Gates, Two Ways, and Two Foundations. Following the metaphoric comparison of the disciples to being like the Salt and the Light of the World (Matthew 5:13-16), Jesus states, "*do not think that I came to abolish the Law, but to fulfill it*" (Matthew 5:17), and then continues His discourse by presenting a new set of kingdom laws. By prefacing them with, *"you have heard—but I say"* (Matthew 5:21-38), Jesus contrasts the commandments given under the Law to the kingdom way to righteousness, and the kingdom's new law of grace that fulfills the Law and the writings of the prophets (Matthew 5—7). Jesus then metaphorically illustrates the new spiritual way to righteousness and salvation by comparing the two ways in life with two gates, and concludes by comparing the destiny of those who choose the small gate and narrow way to a wise man, and those who choose the wide gate and broad way to a foolish man in the allegory of Two Foundations.

Two Gates—Two Ways—Two Foundations – Matthew 7:13-27: "*Enter by the narrow gate; for the gate is wide, and the way is broad that leads to destruction and many are those who enter by it. For the gate is small, and the way is narrow that leads to life, and few are those who find it"* (7:13-14). "*Therefore every one who hears these words of Mine, and acts upon them, may be compared to a wise man, who built his house upon the rock. And the rain descended, and the floods came, and the winds blew, and burst against that house; and yet it did not fall, for it had been founded upon the rock. And every one who hears these words of Mine, and does not act upon them, will be like a foolish man, who built his house upon the sand. And the rain descended, and the floods came, and the winds blew, and burst against that house; and it fell, and great was its fall"* (Matthew 7:24-27; Luke 6:47-49).

A parallel of the small gate and the narrow way leading to life contrasted with the wide gate and broad way leading to destruction symbolizes the two ways in life—one leads to salvation by grace, the other to eternal separation from God. Dr. Lockyer asserts:

> "The solemn truth unfolded before us is that there are only two ways for humanity to choose: the way of the righteous or the way of the ungodly. The world may think there are three kinds of people; good, bad, neutral, but Scripture knows of only two kinds; sinners and saved sinners. We are either black or white. There is no grey. There is no debatable, or no man's land. We are either "in Christ" or "without Christ," travelers to heaven or hell. And the blessed truth of Scripture is that "the Lord knoweth them that are His" " (Lockyer, All the Parables of the Bible, 1963, p. 243).

The culminating allegory of the Two Foundations begins by Jesus comparing the wise man that builds his house upon the rock to those who hear His words and *does* them as opposed to the foolish ones who hear His words but *ignores* them. Whereas the house on the rock metaphorically symbolizes a life built upon the foundation of Christ, the house built upon sand symbolizes a life without Christ and parallels the analogy of the wide gate and the broad road leading to a final state of destruction. Dr. Louis A. Barbieri concludes.

> "Hearing and heeding Jesus' words is wise; one who does not is foolish. Only two courses of action are possible—two kinds of roads and gates possible—two kinds of trees with fruit (vv. 15-20), two kinds of foundations and two kinds of builders" (The Bible Knowledge Commentary: New Testament, 1983, p. 36, ed. John F. Walvoord, Roy B. Zuck).

"Therefore every one who hears these words of Mine, and acts upon them, may be compared to a wise man who built his house upon the rock " (Matthew 7:24).

New Cloth/New Wineskins—Matthew 9:16-17

In the introductory verses of Chapter 9, Matthew states that Jesus has now returned to His city of Galilee, and while He is reclining at a table (probably in Peter's house, Matthew 13:36) many tax-gathers, sinners, and disciples of John the Baptist joined him (vv. 1-10). Then one of John's disciples asks Jesus, "*Why is it that we and the Pharisees fast often, but your disciples do not fast?*" (v. 14). With the ushering in of the new era of grace on the horizon, Jesus responds to that question by presenting the metaphors of the New Cloth and the New Wineskins.

New Cloth/New Wineskins – Matthew 9:16-17: *"But no one puts a patch of unshrunk cloth on an old garment; for the patch pulls away from the garment, and a worse tear results. Nor do men put new wine into old wineskins; otherwise the wineskins burst, and the wine pours out, and the wineskins are ruined; but they put new wine into fresh wineskins, and both are preserved"* (Matthew 9:16-17; Mark 2:21-22; Luke 5:36-37).

By using the cloth and the wineskin to illustrate His metaphor, those listening would have understood the comparison that Jesus was making quite well. In biblical times, fabrics such as cotton, linen, and wool were used for making garments, and among the several uses for animal skins, sheep and goat skins were especially used for making outer garments. Once the skin was processed, it would shrink and then be used for making tunics and coats. (Stephen Westerholm, Eerdman's *International Standard Bible Encyclopedia*, Volume Q-Z, 1988, p. 536, ed. Geoffrey W. Bromiley). Thus, the concept of using a fresh piece of unshrunk fabric or unprocessed skin to cover a tear on an old garment would mean that the fresh piece would eventually shrink, worsen the tear, and ruin the garment. Hence, by illustrating that it's not possible to superimpose something new over something old analogizes that the ushering in of the new age of grace cannot be used as a patch to repair the old institution of the Law.

Likewise, the same analogy is seen in the concept of using old wineskins to store new wine. In particular, Stephen Westerholm states, "goatskins were used for making containers to store liquids, and were especially used for fermenting new wine. The early stages of new wine required that the wineskin be pliable enough to withstand the pressure of the fermenting process. Eventually, the skins would lose all of their elasticity, and in order to prevent the wineskins from bursting while new wine was fermenting, they would have to replace them with new ones (Mat. 9:17 par. Mk 2:22; Lk. 5:37f)" (Ibid., p. 536).

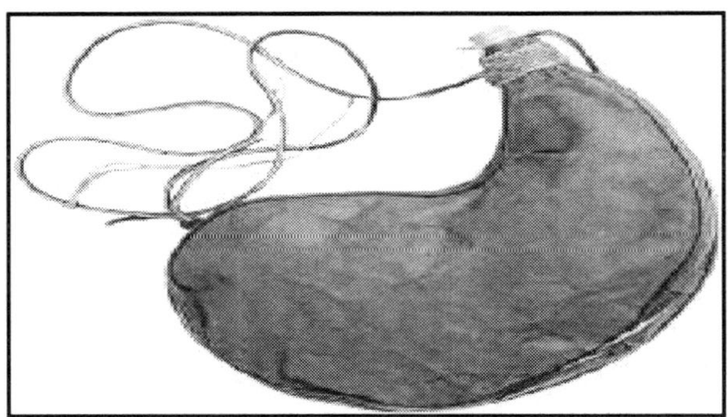

Wineskin
Image provided by Seth Barnes
http://www.sethbarnes.com, 2010.

Thus, by paralleling the analogy of the new cloth and the new wine with the new era of grace and a new kind of righteousness on the one hand, and the analogy of the old cloth and the old wineskins with the old kind of righteousness based on the Law on the other, Jesus illustrates the incompatibility of the two. Dr. Lockyer concludes:

> "Jesus used the figures of mended garments and wine skins in order to make plain His teaching of the nature of the kingdom. Would it be enough to sew on a patch of new cloth where the old was wearing into holes? Not so He answers here .... Christ virtually abrogates the old Levitical Law and offers a charter of

a new freedom. To force His new teachings into the old formulae would bring decomposition and ruin. To take His truth and try to press it into some other form other than His, would be to make it deteriorate, as unfermented wine. The new energies and gifts of the Spirit, given on the Day of Pentecost are likened unto a new wine (Acts 2:13)" (Lockyer, All the Parables of the Bible, 1963, p. 162).

"Therefore, if any man is in Christ, he is a new creature; the old things passed away; behold, new things have come"
(2 Corinthians 5:17).

The Return of the Unclean Spirit—Matthew 12:43-45

Preceding the telling of the allegory of the Unclean Spirit, Matthew records that while Jesus was on His way to the synagogue on the Sabbath day, He was performing miracles along the way and the trailing Pharisee's are complaining about it. The first complaint to Jesus is against the disciples for picking and eating heads of grain from the wheat fields. Jesus responds by reminding them that when David was hungry he ate the consecrated bread that was reserved only for the priests and that when the priests profaned the Sabbath in the temple with their sacrifices they were proclaimed innocent. He then tells them, "*I desire COMPASSION, not SACRIFICE; For the Son of Man is Lord of the Sabbath*" (vv. 1-8).

The second complaint by the Pharisees is against Jesus for healing a man's hand, and Jesus responds by asking who among them would not save one of their own sheep who had fallen into a pit on the Sabbath. Meanwhile, Jesus is healing everyone who comes to Him along the way (vv. 10-21), and seeing all that Jesus is doing, the Pharisee's huddle together to devise a plan to destroy Him. However, when the demon-possessed man is brought to Jesus for deliverance, the Pharisee's did not complain, instead, they attributed His powers to Satan (v. 22). Knowing their thoughts, Jesus strongly rebukes them (vv. 26-34), and concludes his lengthy rebuke by saying that every careless word that originates from the heart of a man will be accounted for in the Day of Judgment, "*by your words you shall be justified, and by your words you shall be condemned*" (vv. 36-37). With this in mind, Jesus presents the allegory of the Unclean Spirit.

The Return of the Unclean Spirit – Matthew 12:43-45: *"Now when the unclean spirit goes out of a man, it passes through waterless places, seeking rest, and does not find it. Then it says, 'I will return to my house from which I came'; and when it comes, it finds it unoccupied, swept, and put in order. Then it goes, and takes along with it seven other spirits more wicked than itself, and they go in and live there; and the last state of that man becomes worse than the first. That is the way it will also be with this evil generation"* (Matthew 12:43-45; Luke 11:24-26).

As illustrated in the allegories of the New Cloth and the New Wineskins, the ushering in of the kingdom of God through Christ fulfills the Law and the writings of the prophets—the old has passed away. It is probably not a coincidence that Jesus metaphorically uses the number seven in the allegory. The unclean spirit leaving the man is symbolic of a state of natural man who was justified under the Law, and with justification by the Law no longer in effect, the house is left empty. The seven spirits symbolizes complete dominion, and by rejecting the new Gospel of salvation by grace, it leaves man in a state of total condemnation. Knowing that the 'first born' nation would completely reject Him as the Messiah and the Gospel of salvation, Jesus concludes by saying, *"That is the way it will also be with this evil generation"* (v. 45). On a personal note, Warren Wiersbe writes:

> "It is not enough to clean house; we must also invite in the right tenant. The Pharisees were proud of their "clean houses," but their hearts were empty. Mere religion, or reformation, will not save. There must be regeneration, the receiving of Christ into the heart (see Rev. 3:20). We cannot be neutral about Jesus Christ" The Bible Exposition Commentary: New Testament, Volume I, 1989, p. 44).
>
> To which Dr. Hagner concludes:
>
> "Those who respond to the Gospel in faith and commitment need not worry about the return of demons, nor need they quaver at future ...." (Word Biblical Commentary, Volume 33A, 2000, pp. 357-358, ed. Ralph P. Martin).

"Any kingdom divided against itself is laid waste; and any city or house divided against itself shall not stand" (Matthew 12:25).

The Doorkeeper—Mark 13:34

The short allegory of the Doorkeeper, recorded exclusively by Mark, is in relation to the prophecy parables found in Matthew 24—25, which are part of Jesus' fifth discourse known as the Olivet Discourse. In the first three prophecy parables of the Fig Tree, the Faithful and Wicked Servants, and the Ten Virgins, Jesus concludes each parable with an exhortation to keep on the alert. In the parable of the Fig Tree, Jesus concludes by stating that we do not know which ***day*** He is coming (Matthew 24:42). In the parable of the Faithful and Wicked Servants He states that we do not know which ***hour*** He is coming (Matthew 24:44), and in the Ten Virgins He tells us that we do not know which ***day*** nor ***hour*** He is coming (Matthew 25:13). However, in the unique allegory of the Doorkeeper, Jesus reminds us to learn from the parable of the Fig Tree, and tells us to stay on the alert because no one knows the ***appointed time*** of His coming (Mark 13:28-37).

The Doorkeeper – Mark 13:34: *"It is like a man, away on a journey, who upon leaving his house and putting his slaves in charge, assigning to each one his task, also commanded the doorkeeper to stay on the alert."*

The short but powerful allegory of the Doorkeeper carries the same theme of 'readiness' that is found in the parables of the Faithful and Wicked Servants (Matthew 24:45-51; Luke 12:42-48), the Ten Virgins (Matthew 25:1-13), and the Watchful Servants (Luke 12:35-40). Dr. Craig A. Evans succinctly concludes:

> "The principal lesson here is that Christians are to be watchful and prepared, not caught up in attempts to calculate the time of the Parousia. It is enough to know that day will eventually and finally come, but it cannot be predicted. Christians are to be about their Master's work, faithfully observing His word, alert

and watchful" (Word Biblical Commentary, Volume 34B, 2000, p. 342, ed. Ralph P. Martin).

> *"Therefore, be on the alert — for you do not know when the master of the house is coming, whether in the evening, at midnight, at cockcrowing, or in the morning— "* (Mark 13:35).

The Rude Children—Luke 7:31-32

Preceding the telling of the similitude of the Rude Children, Luke gives the account of Jesus healing the centurion's servant, raising the widow's son (vv. 1-15), and curing so many people of their diseases, illnesses, evil spirits, deafness, and blindness that the reports flooded the land of Judea and all of its surrounding district (vv. 11-21). Luke then states that as Jesus was preaching to the multitudes, He was proclaiming that John the Baptist was the one who was sent by God to prepare the way for His coming as prophesied by Malachi (3:1; 4:5). In spite of all of the astonishing miraculous healings, deliverances, and prophetic teachings that Jesus was doing throughout the land, the religious leaders continued to refuse to believe or to accept the messages of either John or Jesus (vv. 22-30). Jesus illustrates their position by comparing them to the discontented children in the Rude Children similitude.

The Rude Children – Luke 7:31-32: *"To what then shall I compare the men of this generation, and what are they like? They are like children who sit in the market place and call to one another; and they say, 'We played the flute for you and you did not dance; we sang a dirge, and you did not weep.' "* (Matthew 11:16-17; Luke 7:31-32)

The term market place is translated from the Greek word agora (pronounced *ag-or-ah'*), which means "a public square that functioned as the center of public life in New Testament times" (Thayer's Greek Lexicon, 2009, G58, p. 8). Dr. Marvin W. Meyer explains that the market place was a broad open plaza near the city gates of Jerusalem where children danced and played, celebrations and meetings were held, proclamations were made, and speeches were given. It was where sick ones were brought to Jesus for healing, and where the religious leaders meandered throughout the day (Eerdman's *International Standard Bible Encyclopedia*, Volume K-P, 1986, p. 260, ed. Geoffrey W. Bromiley).

Market Place
Photo provided by Bruce Satterfield
http://emp.byui.edu/SATTERFIELDB/Jerusalem/JerusalemPhoto Display.htm, 2012.

There is an inherent sadness in the illustration Jesus presents to the religious leaders. Throughout His teaching ministry, Jesus often used parables, metaphors, and allegories that presents two choices that are offered in life—accept the free gift of salvation or reject it—one leads to eternal life while the other to destruction. Although the religious leaders knew what was written in Scripture (Matthew 11:13), they nonetheless rejected the Messiah and the message of the imminent coming of the kingdom of God that was proclaimed by both John the Baptist, and particularly by Jesus, not only because of the way they carried the message, but also because of their outer appearance. John the Baptist's call to baptism of repentance was given from out of the wilderness, Jesus' message of salvation was given from 'outside' of the religious establishment. John's clothing was made of camel hair, and his diet was that of locust and wild honey (Mark 1:6), Jesus' clothing was that of a carpenter's son, and he broke bread with 'tax-gatherers and sinners'. Both were thought to be the reincarnation of the Prophet Elijah (John 1:21; Mark 6:14), yet both were declared to have demons (Luke 7:33;

Matthew 12:24). Thus, all of the teachings of both John and of Jesus should have been reminders to the religious leaders of the prophecies of old. Moreover, with all of Jesus' astounding prophetic teachings, miraculous healings, deliverances, and miracles, there should have been no question about the fulfillment of the prophecies of the coming of the kingdom of God, of the Messiah, of divine forgiveness, salvation, and of the establishment of the 'New Temple' of God. More importantly, there should have been no question about the ultimate destiny of those who refuse to believe as illustrated by the four prophecy parables spoken by Christ in the Olivet Discourse (Matthew 24—25), and the prophecy parables of the Wheat and the Tares, the Dragnet, and the Wedding Feast (Matthew 13:24-30; 47-50; 22:1-13). William Barclay closes with these sorrowful words:

> "This passage tells of the perils of free will. The scribes and the Pharisees had succeeded in frustrating God's purpose for themselves. The tremendous truth of Christianity is that the coercion of God is not of force but of love. It is precisely there that we can glimpse the sorrow of God. It is always love's greatest tragedy to look upon some loved one who has taken the wrong way and to see what might have been what could have been and what was meant to have been. That is life's greatest heartbreak" (The Gospel of Luke, 2001, p. 109).

In spite of the rejection of Jesus as the Messiah, the establishment of the kingdom of heaven, of the new plan for redemption, and of His great love for His 'first born' and for all of humanity, Jesus ends on a positive note by saying, *"Yet wisdom is vindicated by all her children"* (v. 35).

> *"For the LORD of hosts has planned, and who can frustrate it? And as for His stretched-out hand, who can turn it back?"* (Isaiah 14:27).

The Two Debtors—Luke 7:41-43

Following the account of the allegory of the Rude Children, Luke tells the touching story about a certain woman who heard that Jesus had been invited to the house of a Pharisee named Simon. The unnamed woman takes a vial of alabaster perfume and sets out to Simon's house to find Jesus. When she enters the room, she approaches Jesus from behind, and falls on her knees weeping. As she is weeping, she is wetting His feet with her tears, wiping them with her hair, kissing them, and anointing them with perfume. Meanwhile, Simon the Pharisee is watching and thinking to himself that *if* Jesus were truly a prophet, He would know what a sinner the woman was and would not allow her so much as to even touch Him. Perceiving Simon's thoughts, Jesus then looks at him and says, *"Simon, I must tell you something"* (vv. 36-40).

The Two Debtors – Luke 7:41-43: *"A certain moneylender had two debtors: one owed five hundred denarii, and the other fifty. When they were unable to repay, he graciously forgave them both. Which of them therefore will love him more?"*

Reminiscent of the principal Jesus taught on forgiveness in the parable of the Unmerciful Servant (Matthew 18:23-35), this short but powerful allegory also carries the themes of repentance, faith, love, and salvation. The situation at hand as perceived and judged by Simon is allegorically represented by the three characters: the money-lender representing Jesus, the debtor who owed five hundred denarii representing the repentant woman, and the debtor who owed only fifty representing the unrepentant Pharisee. Though the debt owed by one was much greater than the other, by Jesus using the example of the money-lender forgiving them both equally, illustrates that anyone who repents will be forgiven equally. Jesus then asks Simon the real question—"*Which of them will love him more?*" To which Simon replies, *"The one whom he forgave more"* (vv. 42-43). Jesus answers by telling Simon that he had judged correctly, and then goes on to explain the metaphor by saying, *"For this reason I say to you, her sins which are many have been forgiven, for she loved much; but he who is forgiven little, loves little"* (v. 47). Jesus concludes by saying to the woman, *"your faith has saved you; go in peace"* (v. 50). Dr. Lockyer acutely points out the obvious lesson. He states:

> "The lessons of the parable for our hearts are obvious. We are all bankrupts, debtors, in the sight of our heavenly Creditor. "All have sinned." Then the best of and the best of us, like the worst of us, have nothing wherewith to discharge our debt. But through His willingness to take our debt and make it His own, Christ can now forgive all who truly repent of their sin and turn to Him in faith. If forgiven, then love and devotion to the One who forgave us should now be ours to give" (Lockyer, All the Parables of the Bible, 1963, p. 259).

The metaphor of the Two Debtors closes the section on Jesus' parabolic teachings. Though there are many figurative teachings of Christ recorded in Scripture, Table IV reflects only those figurative tcachings that arc oftimcs included under 'all the parables of Jesus'. Inasmuch as many of Jesus' parabolic teachings are considered in five of the six great discourses of Christ, a brief topical outline of each of those discourses is listed in Table V.

> *"Your faith has saved you; go in peace"* (v. 50).

Table IV
Other Figurative Teachings of Christ

	MATTHEW	MARK	LUKE
1-3. The Light—The City on a Hill— The Lamp	5:14-16	4:21-22	8:16-17; 11:33-36
4-5. Two Gates—Two Ways—Two Foundations	7:13-14; 24-27		6:47-49
6-7. New Cloth—New Wineskins	9:16-17	2:21-22	5:36-38
8. The Return of the Unclean Spirit	12:43-45		11:24-26
9. The Doorkeeper		13:34-37	
10. The Rude Children	11:16-17		7:31-35
11. The Two Debtors			7:41-43

(Adapted from Dr. Herbert Lockyer, "Table of Parables", *All the Teachings of Jesus*, 1991, p. 305; John MacArthur, "The Parables of Jesus", *The MacArthur Bible Commentary*, 2005, p. 1209; Louis A. Barbieri, Jr., "The Parables of Jesus", *The Bible Knowledge Commentary: New Testament*, 1983, p. 35, ed. John F. Walvoord, Roy B. Zuck).

Table V
The Five Great Discourses of Christ in Matthew

Along with the titles of each of the six discourses of Christ recorded in Scripture, Table V provides a short reference outline of the major topics covered under each discourse.

The First Discourse—The Sermon on the Mount
Matthew 5:1—7:29

The Sermon on the Mount is the first and lengthiest of the five discourses found in the Gospel of Matthew. The new divine law of righteousness in the kingdom of God is introduced for the first time in the history of humanity. Jesus compares and contrasts the new way to righteousness with the Mosaic Law. The discourse includes the establishment of the foundation of a *new way* of righteous living, the Beatitudes, the Lord's Prayer, the essence of discipleship, and the figurative teachings of the Salt, the Light, the Lamp, and the Two Foundations (Word Biblical Commentary, Volume 33A, 2000, pp. 83-84, ed. Ralph P. Martin).

The Second Discourse—The Missionary Discourse
Matthew 10:1—11:1

The second discourse, commonly known as the Missionary Discourse, is Jesus' discourse on the commissioning of the disciples. It includes empowering the Twelve Apostles, their mission instructions, cautions of persecution and rejection of the message of the kingdom, encouraging words on persecution, and on division and discipleship in the new Church (Ibid., pp. 262-263).

The Third Discourse—The New Kingdom Parables
Matthew 13:1–58

The third discourse is a lengthy discourse on the Seven Mysteries of the Kingdom. It includes the seven parables of the Sower, the Wheat and the Tares, the Mustard Seed, the Leaven, the Hidden Treasure, and the Dragnet that are listed in Table I.

The Fourth Discourse—Life in the Kingdom Community
Matthew 18:1–35

The fourth discourse is devoted to spiritual principles of the new life in the kingdom community of the Church. It includes the subjects of the greatness of the kingdom, warnings against causing others to stumble, and handling disciplinary matters concerning the Church. The discourse concludes with the importance of forgiveness as illustrated in the parables of the Lost Sheep (vv. 12-14) and the Unmerciful Servant (vv. 23-35) that are listed in Table III (Word Biblical Commentary, Volume 33B, 2000, p. 515, ed. Ralph P. Martin).

The Fifth Discourse—The Olivet Discourse Prophecy Parables
Matthew 24:1—25:46

Jesus' fifth and final 'public' discourse, commonly called the Olivet Discourse, is recorded exclusively by Matthew. The discourse covers the four prophecy parables on the destruction of the temple, the end of the age, and judgment that Christ foretold in the parables of the Fig Tree, the Unfaithful Servants, the Ten Virgins, and the Ten Talents that are listed in Table II.

The Sixth Discourse—The Farewell Discourse or The Upper Room Discourse John 13:1—17:26

Jesus' final discourse, commonly called the Upper Room Discourse, is recorded exclusively by John. The farewell discourse covers the subjects of the meaning of the washing of the disciples' feet, the Last Supper, the announcement of the betrayal, and the prediction of Peter's denial. In the discourse, Jesus reveals to His disciples the truth concerning His departure and return, the power of the disciples' mission, and the promise of the Holy Spirit. He presents the metaphor of the Vine and the Branches, and speaks on the awareness of the world's hatred of Him and of His disciples, on the joy that overcomes the tribulation, and then concludes with the prayer of consecration known as the Great Priestly Prayer. Finally, Jesus' final discourse outlines the new standard of living in the kingdom for the new Creation that can be seen in seven different ways.

1) A new way of praying.
2) A new relationship with the Godhead.
3) A new relationship with believers.
4) A new relationship to the Holy Spirit.
5) A new abiding with Christ for fruit bearing.
6) A new way of cleansing to continue in fellowship with God.
7) Finally, a new hope in the promise of His return.

In his summary of the Farewell Discourse, George R. Beasley-Murray writes:

> "The farewell discourse, unlike the discourses that have preceded it, is addressed to disciples of Jesus. Some elements of it relate uniquely to them, e.g., 13:33, 36-38 (addressed to Peter), 7-9 (to Philip), 18-20 (to those who were to witness

resurrection appearances of Jesus), 27-31. The bulk of the discourse, however, is addressed to the disciples as representatives of the Church that is to be, and most of the passages just named have obvious relevance to the Church. While some elements admittedly can be incorporated into the Church's proclamation of the good news to the world (e.g., 14:1-3), 6, 8-11, 18-24, 27) the discourse is fundamentally *The Testament of Jesus to His Church*" (Word Biblical Commentary, Volume 36, Second Edition, 2000, p. 263, ed. Ralph P. Martin).

Part III—The Miraculous Healing Ministry of the Great *I AM* through Jesus

The Virgin Birth—Matthew 1:18-25

"In the beginning was the Word, and the Word was with God, and the Word was God. He was in the beginning with God" (John 1-2). *"And the Word became flesh, and dwelt among us, and we beheld His glory, glory as of the only begotten from the Father, full of grace and truth"* (v. 14).

Beginning with the miraculous way in which Jesus came into the world, and ending in the miraculous way in which He conquered death and ascended to the bosom of the Father, there are over *fifty* supernatural miracles that God executed through the hands of Jesus that are found recorded in Scripture by the four Gospel writers. However limited this knowledge is, it nevertheless does give us an overwhelming sense of God's omniscient and omnipotent power, and of His deep compassion, grace, mercy, and love, which He demonstrated by sending His only begotten Son to be the ultimate blood sacrifice for the sin of the world. Before we begin our journey of tracing the footprints of the healing miracles that were manifested through Jesus, we must first begin with the stupendous act of the miraculous nature of Jesus' conception recorded in the Gospels of Matthew and Luke.

MATTHEW	LUKE
"Now the birth of Jesus Christ was as follows. When His mother Mary had been betrothed to Joseph, before they came together she was found to be with child by the Holy Spirit. And Joseph her husband, being a righteous man, and not wanting to disgrace her, desired to put her away secretly. But when he had considered this behold, an angel of the Lord appeared to him in a dream, saying, "Joseph, son of David, do not be afraid to take Mary as your wife; for that which has been conceived in her is of the Holy Spirit. And she will bear a Son; and you shall call His name Jesus, for it is He who will save His people from their sins." Now all this took place that what was spoken by the Lord through the prophet might be fulfilled, saying, "BEHOLD, THE VIRGIN SHALL BE WITH CHILD AND SHALL BEAR A SON, AND THEY SHALL CALL HIS NAME IMMANUEL," which translated means "GOD WITH US." And Joseph arose from his sleep and did as the angel of the Lord commanded him, and took her as his wife, and kept her a virgin until she gave birth to a Son; and he called His name Jesus. Now after Jesus was born in Bethlehem of Judea in the days of Herod the king, behold, magi from the east arrived in Jerusalem saying	*"Now in the sixth month the angel Gabriel was sent from God to a city in Galilee, called Nazareth, to a virgin engaged to a man whose name was Joseph, of the descendants of David: and the virgins name was Mary. And coming in, he said to her, "Hail, favored one! The Lord is with you." But she was greatly troubled at this statement, and kept pondering what kind of salutation this might be. And the angel said to her, "Do not be afraid, Mary; for you have found favor with God. And behold, you will conceive in your womb, and bear a son, and you shall name Him Jesus. He will be great, and will be called the Son of the Most High; and the Lord God will give Him the throne of His father David; and He will reign over the house of Jacob forever; and His kingdom will have no end." And Mary said to the angel, "How can this be, since I am a virgin?" And the angel answered and said to her, "The Holy Spirit will come upon you, and the Most High will overshadow you; and for that reason the holy offspring shall be called the Son of God." Now it came about in those days that a decree went out from Caesar Augustus, that a census be taken of all the inhabited earth. This was the first census taken while Quirinius was governor of Syria. And all were proceeding to register for the census,*

"where is He who has been born King of the Jews? For we say His star in the east, and have come to worship Him" " (Matthew 1:18-25; 2:1-2).

everyone to his own city. A And Joseph also went up from Galilee, from the city of Nazareth, to Judea, to the city of David, which is called Bethlehem, because he was of the house and family of David in order to register, along with Mary, who was engaged to him, and was with child. And it came about that while they were there the days were completed for her to give birth. And she gave birth to her first-born son; and she wrapped Him in cloths, and laid Him in a manger, because there was no room for them in the inn" (Luke 1:26-35; 2:1-7).

The miraculous way in which our invisible God manifested Himself visible through the veil of His flesh defies all human understanding. The first Adam became a living soul, the last Adam a living spirit; the first Adam came from the earth, the last Adam came from heaven. The first Adam breathed in life, and the last Adam breathed out life (1 Corinthians 15:45-47). In his unique way of expressing words, Dr. Herbert Lockyer writes:

> "God was able to bring a clean Babe out of a woman tainted with inherited sin. We cannot account for the sinlessness of Jesus if we reject His birth through a virgin by the Holy Spirit. As Mary was truly His mother, an additional miracle must have been necessary to prevent the transmission of the taint through her, and this subsidiary miracle took place within her womb. In the moment of conception, the Holy Spirit laid hold of that part of the Virgin's flesh out of which the body of Jesus was to be formed and purified it, as the alchemist purifies his metal, making possible the fulfillment of Gabriel's reference to "that Holy thing that shall be born of thee" (Luke 1:35).

> Another aspect of the supernatural in our Lord's birth was that in the moment of conception, the Holy Spirit took deity and humanity and, fusing them together, made possible the Lord Jesus, who came as the God-Man. The Spirit was the love-know between our Lord's two natures. In such a miracle there was no violation of the laws of nature but the introduction of a new Agent. The Holy Spirit supplied the seed which Joseph would have if Mary and he had been man and wife" (All of the Miracles of the Bible, 1961, pp. 156-157).

And in Dr. Lewis Sperry Chafer's concise way of expressing words, he writes:

> "These are written, the Gospel testifies, 'that ye may believe that Jesus is the Christ, the Son of God' (20:31); that Jesus who came as a man (1:30) was thoroughly known in His human origin (7:27), confessed Himself man (8:40), and died as a man dies (19:5), was, nevertheless, not only the Messiah, the Sent of God, the fulfiller of all the Divine promises of redemption, but also the very Son of God, that God only begotten, who, abiding in the bosom of the Father, is His sole adequate interpreter" (*Systematic Theology,* 1978, Volume V, p. 41).

"And He is the image of the invisible God, the first-born of all creation" (Colossians 1:15).

The Healing Ministry of Jesus Recorded by Matthew

The Wedding in Cana—John 2:1-11

Before we begin the Healing Ministry of Jesus as recorded by Matthew, it is prudent to begin with the *first* miracle Jesus accomplished while attending a wedding in Cana that is uniquely recorded by John. Prior to arriving at the wedding in Cana, Matthew and Mark record that after Jesus was baptized by John (Matthew 3:13, Mark 1:9), He is led by the Spirit into the wilderness for forty days where He is tempted by Satan, overcomes him, and begins His ministry (Matthew 4:1-11; Mark 1:11-13). In John's prelude, he states that as Jesus is on His way to Cana, He calls his first four disciples, Andrew, Peter, Philip, and Nathanael (John 1:37-51), and on the third day He attends the wedding with His disciples in Cana, where John reveals, is the inauguration of Jesus' miracle ministry.

The Wedding in Cana – John 2:1-11: *"And on the third day there was a wedding in Cana of Galilee; and the mother of Jesus was there; and Jesus also was invited, and His disciples, to the wedding. And when the wine gave out, the mother of Jesus said to Him, "They have no wine." And Jesus said to her, "Woman, what do I have to do with you? My hour has not yet come." His mother said to the servants, "Whatever He says to you, do it." Now there were six stone waterpots set there for the Jewish custom of purification, containing twenty or thirty gallons each. Jesus said to them, "Fill the waterpots with water." And they filled them up to the brim. And He said to them, "Draw some out now, and take it to the headwaiter." And they took it to him. And when the headwaiter tasted the water which had become wine, and did not know where it came from (but the servants who had drawn the water knew), the headwaiter called the bridegroom, and said to him, "Every man serves the good wine first, and when men have drunk freely, then that which is poorer; you have kept the good* *wine until now." This beginning of His signs Jesus did in Cana of Galilee, and manifested His glory, and His disciples believed in Him."*

John's narrative reveals that the miracle of the transformation from water into wine at the wedding feast accomplished three things. First, it inaugurated Jesus' miracle ministry. Secondly, it was the first manifestation of Jesus' glorious Deity, and lastly, John notes, *"His disciples believed in Him"* (2:11). Noteworthy is John's detailed description of the water jars. He states that there were six jars, each containing twenty or thirty gallons of water (vv. 6-8). Furthermore, John comments on Jesus giving specific instruction to have them all filled to the brim (v. 7). To give us an idea of what these water jars may have looked like, David Q. Hall and David Couchman have graciously provided the following photos.

Photo provided by David Q. Hall

"Two stone water jars used to prevent ritual contamination of water in the Burnt House Museum, Old City, Jerusalem. This museum contains Roman era artifacts found in the basement of the home of a high priest destroyed c. 70 A.D." http://dqhall59.com/artifacts.htm, 2011.

David Couchman goes on further to say that archaeologists have uncovered several water jars that were believed to be used in the first-century. He states:

> "Archaeologists have found several stone jars in the ruined houses of first-century Jerusalem. At least six of them stood in the basement kitchen of the 'Burnt house'. They are 65-80 cm (2-2.5 feet) tall, each cut from a block of stone that could weigh as much as half a ton. They were shaped and finished on a very big lathe, given a pedestal foot and simple decoration. Such stone jars would hold large quantities of water for washing and kitchen needs - up to 17 gallons. Flat discs of stone served as lids. The jars at Cana may have been similar to these" (Facing the Challenge, by David Couchman, http://www.facingthechallenge.org/stonejars.php, 2011).

Stone Water Jars
Photos provided by *David Couchman*
http://www.facingthechallenge.org/stonejars.php,
http://www.facingthechallenge.org/burnt.php, 2011.

Moreover, John states that when the headwaiter tasted the wine, he was astonished, calls the bridegroom over, and says, *"Every man serves the good wine first, and when men have drunk freely, then that which is poorer; you have kept the good wine until now"* (v. 10), which implies that all six of the stone jars were filled to the brim with wine of excellent quality. Dr. Barry L. Bandstra highlights the spiritual symbology of this miraculous event. He states:

> "Wine was viewed as a blessing from God "that gladdens the heart of man" (Ps. 104:15; cf. also Eccl. 2:3; 9:7; 10:19; Zec. 10:7). It is mentioned along with grain and oil as a gift of God and a sign of His blessing (Gen. 27:28; t. 7:13; Ps. 104:15)" (Barry L. Bandstra, Eerdman's *International Standard Bible Encyclopedia*, Volume Q-Z, 1988, p. 1070, ed. Geoffrey W. Bromiley).

Whereas Dr. Bandstra's focus is on the spiritual symbology of the wine, Dr. Edwin A. Blum highlights the joyous side of Jesus' nature, and David Couchman observes the event from a cultural perspective. Edwin Blum states:

> "Jesus brings joy. His first miracle was a gracious indication of the joy which He provides by the Spirit. The sign points to Jesus as the Word in the flesh, who is the mighty Creator. Each year He turns water to wine in the agricultural and fermentation processes. Here, He simply did the process immediately. The 120 gallons of fine wine were His gift to the young couple" (The Bible Knowledge Commentary: New Testament, 1983, p. 278, ed. John F. Walvoord, Roy B. Zuck).

Finally, David Couchman comments:

> "At that time rural weddings were major social events that went on for days. Everyone was invited. This particular account in John's Gospel records how the wedding ran out of wine - a social catastrophe of unimaginable proportions. Jesus solved the host's embarrassment by changing the water in six large jars into wine" (Facing the Challenge, by David Couchman, http://www.facingthechallenge.org/stonejars.php, 2011).

The Healing Ministry of God through Jesus

A Portrait of the Invisible God made Visible through Christ

Jesus' public ministry included teaching, preaching the good news of the kingdom, healing, miracles, and so many other things which He did that, *"if written in detail, not even the world itself could contain the books that would be written about them*" (John 21:25). However, by following the footprints of Jesus' healing ministry recorded in Scripture by the four Gospel writers, God gives us a taste of His sovereignty through the merciful healing power that was accomplished through the loving hands of Jesus. The first account of Jesus healing the multitudes begins in Chapter 4 of the Gospel of Matthew.

Healing the Multitudes – Matthew 4:23-24: *"And Jesus was going about in all Galilee, teaching in their synagogues, and proclaiming the gospel of the kingdom, and healing every kind of disease and every kind of sickness among the people. And the news about Him went out into all Syria; and they brought to Him all who were ill, taken with various diseases and pains, demoniacs, epileptics, paralytics; and He healed them"* (Matthew 4:23-24; Mark 1:39).

After the news about Jesus' healing power spread throughout all of Syria, *great* multitudes from Galilee, the Decapolis, Jerusalem, Judea, and from beyond the Jordan followed Him (v. 25). A visual perspective of the area covered by Jesus during His ministry shows the surrounding areas of where these *great* multitudes travelled from to see Jesus.

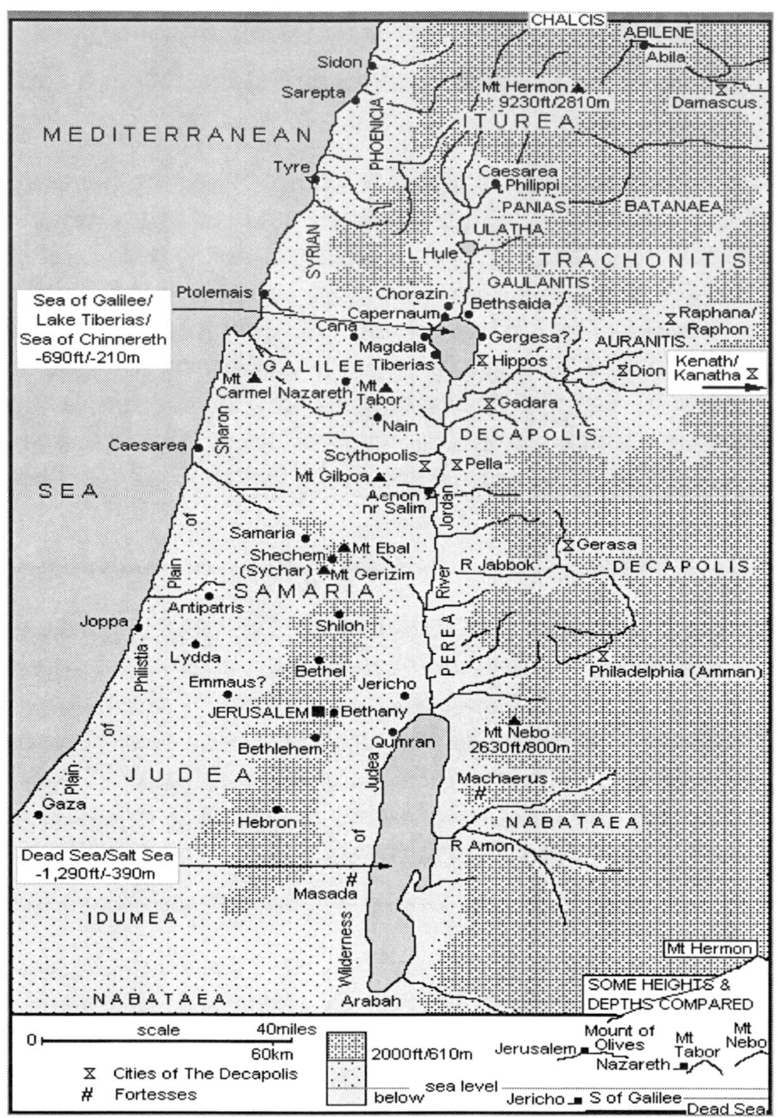

The Land of Palestine at the time of Jesus
Image provided by J. B. Phillips
http://www.ccel.org/bible/phillips/CP051GOSPELMAPS.htm, 2003.

William Hendriksen writes a short description on the cities included in the region northeast of Samaria up to the area east of the Jordan.

> "From Decapolis, that is, from the region of the *ten cities*, a federation extending, for the most part, northeast of Samaria, and to some extent even northeast of Galilee, and consisting of the cities: Damascus, Kanata, Dion, Hippos, Gadara, Abila, Scythopolis, Pella, Geresa, and Philadelphia. Jerusalem, too, and in fact all of Judea, heart what was happing in the north. So, also from the south people came to swell the crowds that followed Jesus. They heard his words and saw—and in many cases were benefitted by—his miracles. Even Perea, the region east of the Jordan and, mostly, south of Decapolis sent its representatives. The multitude must have been immense!" (New Testament Commentary: Exposition of the Gospel according to Matthew, 2007, pp. 252-252)

> *"And great multitudes followed Him from Galilee and Decapolis and Jerusalem and Judea and from beyond the Jordan"* (Matthew 4:25).

The Leper—Matthew 8:1-4

After Jesus concluded His first great discourse of the Sermon on the Mount, He came down from the mountain, and a man with leprosy goes to Jesus, bows down before Him, and says,

---

The Leper – Matthew 8:2-4: *"Lord, if You are willing, You can make me clean. And stretching out His hand, He touched him, saying "I am willing; be cleansed." And immediately his leprosy was cleansed. And Jesus said to him, "see that you tell no one; but go, SHOW YOURSELF TO THE PRIEST, and present the offering that Moses prescribed, for a testimony to them"* (Matthew 8:2-4; Mark 1:40-42; Luke 5:12-13).

Though the leper's conviction that Jesus *could* cure him is impressive, Dr. Hagner points out that he was not sure whether Jesus *would* be willing to do so, which indicates that he was one of the multitudes who had already seen His supernatural power to heal, but does not necessarily mean that he believed that He was truly the Messiah. Moreover, by Jesus making the point to tell the leper that he yet had to present himself before the priest to make the offering that Moses had prescribed for a testimony to them indicates that he was fully under the Law (Word Biblical Commentary, Volume 33A, 2000, p. 198, ed. Ralph P. Martin). Dr. Roland Harrison explains why this would have acted as a testimony to the religious leaders. In his study on leprosy during the time of Christ, Dr. Roland Harrison states that leprosy in Palestine still prevailed, and as such, the Israelite Priests were still using the regulations given to them under the Levitical Law (Leviticus 14). However, it was only by divine healing that a leper could get a medical discharge. He further comments that once the lepers were deemed cleansed by the priest, then the appropriate ceremony for the offering of thanksgiving had to be presented before God (vv. 3-7) (Eerdman's *International Standard Bible Encyclopedia,*

Volume K-P, 1986, pp. 103-104, ed. Geoffrey W. Bromiley). Thus, the man's instantaneous cure of his leprosy proved that it was indeed a divine healing, which further acted as a testimony of the Deity of Christ to the religious leaders. William Hendriksen comments that in addition to the healing of the leper acting as a testimony of the Deity of Christ, it also acted as a testimony for His respect to the Mosaic Law, and of His love and power (New Testament Commentary: Exposition of the Gospel according to Matthew, 2007, p. 393).

Finally, Dr. Hagner concludes:

> "The leper was cured immediately by only a word from Jesus. This same Jesus cures his people, the Church, from a whole host of maladies stemming from the fall, both spiritual and physical" (Word Biblical Commentary, Volume 33A, 2000, p. 200, ed. Ralph P. Martin).

"I am willing—be cleansed" (v. 3).

The Centurion's Servant—Matthew 8:5-13

Immediately following the healing of the leper, Matthew records that when Jesus entered Capernaum, a centurion came to him earnestly saying,

---

The Centurion's Servant – Matthew 8:5-13: *"Sir my servant is lying paralyzed at home, suffering great pain. And He said to him, "I will come and heal him." But the centurion answered and said, "Lord, I am not qualified for You to come under my roof, but just say the word, and my servant will be healed. For I, too, am a man under authority, with soldiers under me; and I say to this one, 'Go!' and he goes, and to another, 'Come!' and he comes, and to my slave, 'Do this!' and he does it." Now when Jesus heard this, He marveled, and said to those who were following, "Truly I say to you, I have not found such great faith with anyone in Israel. And I say to you, that many shall come from east and west, and recline at table with Abraham, and Isaac, and Jacob, in the kingdom of heaven; but the sons of the kingdom shall be cast out into the outer darkness; in that place there shall be weeping and gnashing of teeth." And Jesus said to the centurion, "Go your way; let it be done to you as you have believed." And the servant was healed that very hour"* (Matthew 8:5-13; Luke 7:2-10).

A sharp contrast between the faith of the leper and the faith of the Roman officer can easily be seen. Whereas the leper was convinced of the supernatural power of Jesus to heal, he was not sure whether Jesus would be willing to do so. Furthermore, by viewing the instructions that Jesus gave the leper to present himself before the priest to make the offering of thanksgiving according to the Mosaic Law, implies that the leper was a Jew. On the other hand, the Roman gentile who *recognized* and honored Jesus' authority *knew* that by Jesus merely speaking a word of command, his servant would be healed. William

Barclay points out the significance of the kind of faith that the centurion showed. He writes:

> "Not only was this centurion quite extraordinary in his attitude to his servant; he was also a man of most extraordinary faith. He wished for Jesus' power to help and to heal his servant, but there was one problem. He was a Gentile and Jesus was a Jew; and, according to the Jewish law, a Jew could not enter the house of a Gentile, for all Gentile dwelling places were unclean. The *Mishnah* lays it down: 'The dwelling places of Gentiles are unclean' " (William Barclay, The Gospel of Matthew, Volume I, 2001, p. 349).

Knowing that it was not possible for Jesus to enter his home to heal his servant, the centurion nonetheless had complete faith that it would be done. The unparalleled, profound faith that the centurion manifested, and his unwavering belief that by Jesus merely speaking a word would heal his servant moves Jesus so much that He not only publically commends the centurion's faith, but publically contrasts it to the faith of the 'sons of kingdom' (vv. 10-12). Jesus then tells the centurion, *"Go your way; let it be done to you as you have believed"* (v. 13a), and 'in that very hour' the servant was healed (v. 13b).

In conclusion, in stating that, "the faith the centurion exhibited is worthy of a paragraph", Dr. Lockyer writes:

> "That Christ should marvel at the magnitude of his faith is an evidence of His human consciousness. The act of faith which Jesus called "great" was so because the man asked for no sign but believed in Christ's conscious, supernatural ability and asked for nothing more. There are two instances of faith which were called "great faith" by Jesus, and both of those manifesting such faith were Gentiles—namely, the Roman centurion and the Syrophoenician woman (Matthew 15:28; Luke 4:26). The first begged for his servant—the second for her daughter. Both cases show how the principle of faith is

supreme over all privileges of race and birth" (All of the Miracles of the Bible, 1961, p. 179).

"Let it be done to you as you have believed" (v. 13a).

Peter's Mother-in-Law—Matthew 8:14-15

"And when Jesus had come to Peter's home, He saw his mother-in-law lying sick in bed with a fever. And He touched her hand, and the fever left her; and she arose, and began to wait on Him" (Matthew 8:14-15; Mark 1:30-31; Luke 4:38-39).

On the surface, the healing of Peter's mother-in-law may appear to be a simple healing in passing. However, the few sentences written by Matthew carry a profound message in them. In the preceding healing accounts of the leper and the centurion, Matthew records that Jesus first touched the leper, and then healed him by a word. In the second account of healing the centurion's servant, without seeing or touching the servant, Jesus heals him from a distance. In the third account of Peter's mother-in-law, Jesus *sees* Peter's mother-in-law lying sick in bed, goes to her side, gently touches her hand, and she was healed immediately. The illustration of the three distinct healings of the leper, the gentile centurion, and 'a woman' not only demonstrates that Jesus shows no partiality, but also typifies those who were rejected by the nation of Israel in general. Moreover, when Jesus entered Peter's house, He did not wait for someone to ask Him to heal his mother-in-law; He *saw* that Peter's mother-in-law was sick and healed her immediately. He came—He saw—He healed.

Healing the Multitudes—8:16-17

"And when evening had come, they brought to Him many who were demon-possessed; and He cast out the spirits with a word, and healed all who were ill in order that what was spoken through Isaiah the prophet might be fulfilled saying, "HE HIMSELF TOOK OUR INFIRMITIES, AND CARRIED AWAY OUR DISEASES" (Matthew 8:16-17; Mark 1:32-34; Luke 4:40-41).

William Hendriksen comments that the word spread so quickly that when the Sabbath was over, the whole city was gathered at the door of Peter's house (Mark 1:33) fervently hoping that they or their loved ones might be healed (New Testament Commentary: Exposition of the Gospel according to Luke, 2007, p. 269).

The Demon Possessed Gerasene—Matthew 8:28-33

To appreciate the dramatic, powerful healing of the demon possessed man more fully, it is important to note the narratives of the three Gospel writers together. By comparing the accounts of Matthew, Mark, and Luke, we will know: 1) where the healing took place, 2) where the demon possessed man lived, 3) his physical condition, 4) his state of mind, and 5) the countless number of demons that had possessed the man's body.

MATTHEW	MARK	LUKE
"And when He had come to the other side into the country of Gadarenes, two men who were demon-possessed met Him as they were coming out of the tombs; they were so exceedingly violent that no one could pass by that road. And behold, they cried out, saying, "What do we have to do with You, Son of God? Have You come here to torment us before the time?" Now there was at a distance from them a herd of many swine feeding. And the demons began to entreat Him, saying, "If You are going to cast us out, send us into the herd of swine." And He said to them, "Begone!" And they came out, and went into the swine, and behold, the whole herd rushed down	*"And they came to the other side of the sea, into the country of the Gerasenes. And when He had come out of the boat, immediately a Man from the tombs with an unclean spirit met Him, and he had his dwelling among the tombs. And no one was able to bind him any more, even with a chain; because he had often been bound with shackles and chains, and the chains had been torn apart by him, and shackles broken in pieces, and no one was strong enough to subdue him. And constantly night and day, among the tombs and in the mountains, he was crying out and gashing himself with stones. And seeing Jesus from a*	*"And they sailed to the land of the Gerasenes, which the is opposite Galilee. And when He had come out onto the land, a certain man from the city met Him who was possessed with demons, and who had not put on any clothing for a long time, and was not living in a house, but in the tombs. And seeing Jesus, he cried out and fell before Him, and said in a loud voice, "What do I have to do with You, Jesus Son of the Most High God? I beg You, do not torment me." For He had been commanding the unclean spirit to come out of the man. For it had seized him many times; and he was bound with chains and shackles and kept under guard;*

the steep bank into the sea and perished in the waters" (8:28-33).

distance, he ran up and bowed down before Him; and crying out with a loud voice, he said, "What do I have to do with You, Jesus, Son of the Most High God? I implore You by God, do not torment me"! For he had been saying to him, "Come out of the man, you unclean spirit!" And He was asking him, "What is your name?" And he said to Him, "My name is Legion; for we are many." And he began to entreat Him Permission not to send them out of the country. Now there was a big herd of swine feeding there on the mountain side. And they entreated Him, saying, "Send us into the swine so that we may enter them." And He gave them permission. And coming out, the unclean spirits entered the swine; and the herd rushed down the steep bank into the sea, about two thousand of them; and they were drowned in the sea" (5:1-13).

and yet yet he would burst his fetters and be driven by the demons into the desert. And Jesus asked him, "What is your name?" And he said, "Legion"; for many demons had entered him. And they were entreating Him not to command them to depart into the abyss. Now where was a herd of many swine feeding there on the mountain; and the demons entreated Him to permit them to enter the swine. And He gave them permission. And the demons came out from the man and entered the swine; and the herd rushed down the steep bank into the lake, and were drowned" (8:26-33).

In the preceding account of the healing of Peter's mother-in-law, we know that Jesus was in Capernaum. *Matthew* previously stated that when evening had come, the people throughout the city came to

Peter's house to be healed by Jesus. *Luke* continues the narrative by saying, "when day came, Jesus left Peter's house and kept on preaching in the synagogues of Judea" (vv. 4:42-44). Though Matthew does not reveal the length of time Jesus spent preaching in Judea before they sailed to the country of the Gerasenes (v. 26), he does state that Jesus got into a boat and went to the other side into the country of the Gadarenes. However, Mark and Luke record that Jesus came to the other side of the sea into the land of the Gerasenes. Though the differences in the accounts between the locations may appear to be inconsistent, Dr. Howard F. Vos' study of the land along with an ancient map indicating where the land was located explains the differences between the accounts.

In the first century AD, the location of *Gadara* was situated inland southeast of the Sea of Galilee, east of the Jordan River. On the other hand, *Gergesa*, the land of the Gerasenes, was situated on the northeastern shore of the Sea of Galilee, which was considered the countryside of the city of Gerasa that was part of the federation of the region of the 'ten cities' of Decapolis (Eerdman's *International Standard Bible Encyclopedia,* Volume E-J, 1979, p. 448, ed. Geoffrey W. Bromiley).

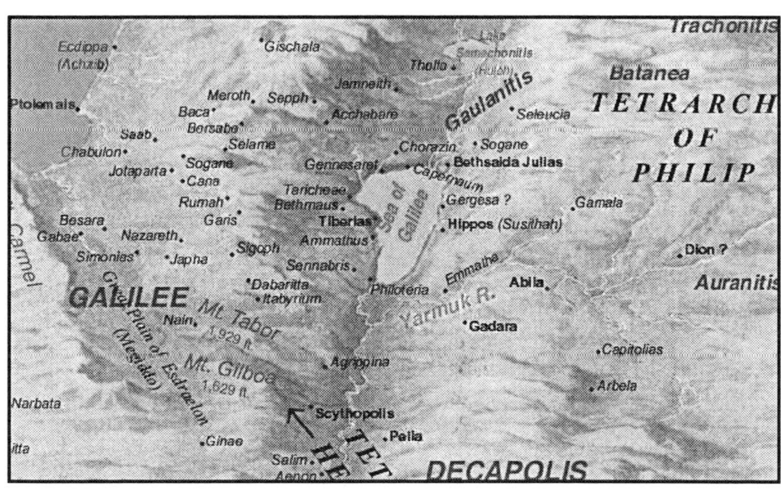

Territory of Gadara/Gergesa
http://www.bible-history.com/geography/ancient-israel/israel-first-century.html, 2012.

Dr. Howard F. Vos' further states that ruins of a cliff town that have been found near a modern village located on the eastern shore of the Sea of Galilee have been identified as the locale of the healing of a demoniac, and of the subsequent drowning of a herd of swine in the sea. However, he writes, "the Greek and Arabic names are not exact equivalents, leaving the identification of the actual name uncertain" (Ibid., p. 448). Though Dr. Vos states that the identification of the actual name is uncertain, the Jerusalem Institute for Biblical Exploration has discovered the ruins of a Byzantine Christian monastery currently located in a national park in the Israel occupied Golan Heights. These ruins are believed to be the site of the location of ancient Kursi (Gergesa), which include the findings of an ancient hillside chapel that may have been the location of the 'tomb' Luke mentions in (v. 27). However, Dr. Paul E. McCracken of the Jerusalem Institute for Biblical Exploration states, "the cave was covered by the Byzantines (as was their custom) and a chapel built over it" (Dr. Paul E. McCracken, Jerusalem Institute for Biblical Exploration).

Hillside Chapel
Photo provided by Dr. Paul E. McCracken, 2012. Jerusalem Institute for Biblical Exploration

Additionally, Dr. Charles R. Page, II of the Jerusalem Institute for Biblical Exploration states:

> "The ruins of Kursi, a Byzantine Monastery memorializing two of Jesus' miracles, are located approximately 3 ½ miles (6 km) north of Kibbutz En Gev, on the eastern shore of the Kinneret. The monastery dates to the 5th century CE. During the Persian invasions in the 7th century CE, the monastery was destroyed. Although Kursi, with its Byzantine church and monastery on the northeastern shore of the Sea of Galilee, has been identified as Gadara or Gergesa and the site of the exorcism and drowning of the swine, no remains dating from the first century C.E. were found there, which makes the site a most improbable location. However, the discovery of a tower and chapel 200 meters (656 feet) south of the Byzantine church may support the identification of the site with the location of the miracle of the Gadarine swine"
> http://www.bibleinterp.com/excavations/kursi.htm, 2001.

Kursi/Gergesa Excavation

Finally, Dr. Unger concludes:

> "Kersa, apparently formerly Gergesa, on the eastern shore of the Galilean Sea across from Magdale seems to be the most likely location. It has the topography fitting the details of the narrative (Luke 8:33)" (The New Unger's Bible Dictionary, 1988, p. 846, ed. R. K. Harrison).

Having a better idea of the location of the demon-possessed man, the Gospel writers then give a vivid description of the kind of torment the man suffered. Mark and Luke record that he was naked, unclean, and that he possessed such supernatural strength that he would break the chains and shackles that were used to try to subdue him. So tormented was he, Mark writes, that he roamed the mountains day and night crying out and mutilating himself with stones (v. 5), so when the demon possessed man sees Jesus, he literally runs and falls down before Him. When the spirits possessing the man recognize who Jesus was and what He was about to do, they implore Him not to cast them into the abyss. Dr. Lockyer keenly observes that Jesus first asked the spirits for their names, to which they replied, "My name is Legion for we are many" (Mark 5:9; Luke 8:30). Secondly, Dr. Lockyer observes that because of the *divine permission* that Jesus gave to the spirits when they asked to be sent into the swine, when Jesus commanded them to "Begone!" the demons immediately *obeyed.* Quoting from the works of Aquinas, Dr. Lockyer writes:

> "That the swine were driven into the sea was no work of the divine miracle, but was the work of the demons by divine permission. The swine, panic-stricken as they became demon-possessed, lost control of themselves on the steep incline of the hillside, and once on the move, they could not stop. The swine preferred suicide to demon possession. Without doubt, there is the element of judgment here upon the owners of the swine as an article of food. Though the Jews did not eat pork, Roman soldiers did, and the Jews had no compunction of conscience in providing forbidden meat for others. Thus the destruction of

the swine was deserved punishment for the violation of God's law. Christ, therefore, had every right to deal with such illicit trading" (All of the Miracles of the Bible, 1961, pp. 189-190).

The Paralytic—Matthew 9:1-8

Unlike most of those who believed in Jesus *after* they were divinely healed, in the case of the paralytic, Jesus heals the paralytic spiritually *before* He heals him physically. Phase 1 of the three narratives give an account of the paralytic's divine spiritual healing followed by his dramatic *physical* healing in phase 2. To gain a fuller picture of the scene in which the paralytic's divine healings took place, it is once again worthy to note the narratives of the three Gospel writers together. Whereas Matthew's account is brief, Mark and Luke both describe the dramatic effort, and the tremendous faith that it took the paralytic's friends to get him to Jesus to be healed.

MATTHEW	MARK	LUKE
"*And getting into a boat, He crossed over, and came to His own city. And behold, they were bringing to Him a paralytic, seeing their faith said to the paralytic, "Take courage, My son, your sins are forgiven" "* (9:1-2).	"*And when He had come back to Capernaum several days afterward, it was heard that He was at home. And many were gathered together, so that there was no longer, room, even near the door; and He was speaking the word to them. And they came, bringing to Him a paralytic, carried by four men. And being unable to get to Him on account of the crowd, they removed the roof above Him; and when they had dug an, opening they let down the pallet on which the paralytic was lying. And Jesus seeing their faith said to the paralytic, "My son, your sins are forgiven" "* (2:1-5).	"*And behold, some men were carrying on a bed a man who who was paralyzed; and they were trying to bring him in, and to set him down in front of Him. And not finding any way to bring him in because of the crowd, they went up on the roof and let him down, through the tiles with his stretcher, right in the center, in front of Jesus. And seeing their faith, He said, "Friend, your sins are forgiven you" "* (5:17-20).

In Mark's account of the paralytic's divine spiritual healing, he states that the news of Jesus returning home had spread, and the crowd that had gathered to hear Him preach was so large that it was impossible to get to the door that led in or out of the house where Jesus was staying. William Barclay describes the life in Palestine at the time of Jesus as one of being public, and when people opened their doors, it was an invitation for anyone to come and go freely (William Barclay, The Gospel of Luke, 2001, pp. 52-53). Thus, the door to the house where Jesus was staying was open, and the house so crowded that it was impossible to get to the doorway. Mark records that because the crowd blocking the way was so immense, the four men carrying the paralytic on a stretcher climbed up to the rooftop, removed a section of the roof, dug an opening for the stretcher, lowered the paralytic down into the house, and as Luke states, they placed the stretcher directly at the feet of Jesus.

Typical Galilean village during first century A.D.
Photos provided by David Q. Hall
http://dqhall59.com/paralytic_healed.htm, 2005.

When Jesus sees the kind of faith that it took for them to get the paralytic to Him, he looks at the man and says, *"My son, your sins are forgiven"* (Matthew 9:2; Mark 2:5; Luke 5:20). William Hendriksen makes this profound observation:

> "The confidence of the five touched the very heart of Jesus, who now, in accents tender yet firm, said to the paralytic, "your

> sins are forgiven you." It was the faith of the five that caused these words to flow from the Savior's lips. For corroborating passages showing how very important Jesus regarded faith to be, see Luke 7:9; 8:48, 50; 17:19; 18:42; Heb. 11:32 .... And by saying "Forgiven are your sins" (thus literally), Jesus had not only lifted a burden from the soul of this sin-burdened sufferer, but had also proclaimed that the cleansing of the soul was even more important than the healing of the body. He had done one more thing: he had claimed for himself the divine prerogative of pronouncing and actually bringing about freedom from guilt" (New Testament Commentary: Exposition of the Gospel according to Luke, 2007, p. 296).

However, this is not the end of the story. Unlike the healing of the Gerasene whereby the spirits recognize Jesus as "*The Son of the Most High God*", on this specific occasion, Jesus announces His name as "*The Son of Man*". William Hendriksen states that this is the first time that the title of the "Son of Man" is introduced.

> "This is Christ's self-designation, *revealing* something with reference to him, *concealing* even more, especially to those not thoroughly acquainted with the Old Testament. The use of the term is what led to the question, "Who, then, is this Son of man?" (John 12:34). The term characterizes Jesus as the Sufferer, the One who is going to be betrayed and killed (9:12; 14:21, 41), all of this in accordance with the divine decree, voluntarily, and vicariously (10:45) .... The glory of the Son of man is clearly evident .... The man believed that the One who ordered him to get up, take up his pallet and go home would also enable him to obey the order. So "in full view of"—all the onlookers he at one obeyed the threefold command and went home" (New Testament Commentary: Exposition of the Gospel according to Mark, 2007, p. 91).

Thus, when Jesus forgives the paralytic's sin, the unbelieving scribes think that He had blasphemed. Perceiving their hearts, Jesus explains why he chose to heal the paralytic spiritually *before* healing him physically (Matthew 9:3-5; Mark 2:7; Luke 9:21). He says,

MATTHEW	MARK	LUKE
"But in order that you may know that the Son of Man has authority on earth to forgive sins"—then He said to the paralytic, "Rise, take up your bed, and go home." And he rose, and went to his home. But when the multitudes saw this, they were filled with awe, and glorified God, who had given such authority to men" (9:6-8).	*"But that you may know that the Son of Man has authority on earth to forgive sins, He said to the paralytic, "I say to you, rise, take up your pallet and go home." And he rose and immediately took up the pallet and went out in the sight of all; so that they were all amazed and were glorifying God, saying, "We have never seen anything like this"* (2:10-12).	*"But in order that you may know that the Son of Man has authority on earth to forgive sins, He said to the paralytic, "I say to you, rise, and take up your stretcher and go go home."" And at once he rose before them, and took up what he had been lying on, and went home, glorifying God. God. And they were all seized with astonishment and began glorifying God; and they were filled with fear, saying, "We have seen remarkable things today" "* (5:24-26).

In conclusion, when Jesus gave His one all-powerful word of command—"Rise", the saved paralytic immediately rose, took up his pallet, and went home.

The Ruler's Daughter Raised from the Dead —Matthew 9:18-19; 23-25 The Hemorrhaging Woman—Matthew 9:20-22

A Healing on the Road to a Healing—the following two accounts of the resurrection of Jarius' daughter, and healing the hemorrhaging women are recorded by the three Gospel writers in two parts. Whereas Matthew's narrative of the resurrection of Jarius' daughter is brief, Mark and Luke add more detail to the stupendous miracles, and of the extraordinary amount of faith that Jarius demonstrated in Jesus' unlimited power to heal. In part two, the combination of the narratives of the three Gospel writers together illustrates the dramatic effort and profound faith the hemorrhaging woman had in Jesus' unlimited power to heal. In the opening verses of Chapter 9, Matthew records that the daughter of an official of the synagogue had died, and the distraught official goes to find Jesus. When he finds Him, the official pleads for his daughter's life to be restored to him.

The Ruler's Daughter – Matthew 9:18-19: *"While He was saying these things to them, behold, there came a synagogue official, and bowed down before Him, saying, "My daughter has just died; but come and lay Your hand on her, and she will live" "* (Mark 5:22-24; Luke 8:41-42).

Reminiscent of the kind of profound, unwavering faith that the centurion demonstrated, the unfaltering, extraordinary faith that Jarius exhibits in believing that solely by Jesus' divine touch, his daughter would be restored to him, also illustrates his remarkable faith in believing in Jesus' unlimited power to heal. Meanwhile, as Jesus is on his way to Jarius' house, a woman who had been hemorrhaging for twelve years manages to get through the crowd and get close enough to touch the outer edge of His garment, and by doing so, she was immediately healed.

MATTHEW	MARK	LUKE
"And behold, a woman who had been suffering from a hemorrhage for twelve years, came up behind Him and touched the fringe of His cloak; for she was saying to herself, "If I only touch His garment, I shall get well." But Jesus turning and seeing her said, "Daughter, take courage; your *faith has made you well." And at once the woman was made well"* (9:20-22).	*"And a woman who had had a hemorrhage for twelve years, and had endured much at the hands of many physicians, and had spent all that she had and was not helped at all, but rather had grown worse, after hearing about Jesus, came up in the crowd behind Him, and touched His cloak. For she thought, "If I just touch His garments, I shall get well." And immediately the flow of her blood was dried up; and she felt in her body that she was healed of her affliction. And immediately Jesus, perceiving in Himself that the power proceeding from Him had gone forth, turned around in the crowd and said, "Who touched My garments?" And His disciples said to Him, "You see the multitude pressing in on You, and You say, 'Who touched Me?' " And He looked around to see the woman who had done this. But the woman fearing and trembling, aware of what had happened to her, came and fell down before Him, and told Him the whole truth. And He said to her, "Daughter, your faith has made you well; go in peace, and be healed of your affliction" "* (5:25-34).	*"And a woman who had a hemorrhage for twelve years, and could not be healed by anyone, came up behind Him, and touched the fringe of His cloak; and immediately her hemorrhage stopped. And Jesus said, "Who is the one who touched Me?" And while they were all denying it, Peter said, "Master, the multitudes are crowding and pressing upon You." But Jesus said, "Someone did touch Me, for I was aware that power had gone out of Me." And when the woman saw that she had not escape notice, she came trembling and fell down before Him, and declared in the presence of all the people the reason why she had touched Him, and how she had been immediately healed. And He said to her, "Daughter, your faith has made you well; go in peace" "* (8:43-48).

The faith that the woman exhibited is also quite extraordinary. Much like the centurion, she *knew* that if she could only touch Jesus' outer garment she would be healed. Filled with this strong conviction, the moment she did touch Jesus' garment, her hemorrhaging stopped instantly. Of great significance, like the healing of the paralytic, the woman of faith is not only physically healed immediately, but Jesus completes her faith by healing her spiritually as well. William Hendriksen writes:

> "The greatness of this woman's faith consisted in this, that she believed that the power of Christ to heal was so amazing that even the mere touch of his clothes would result in an instant and complete cure. That this faith was, nevertheless, by no means perfect appears from the fact that she thought that such an actual touch was necessary and that Jesus would never notice it. But imperfect through her faith was, the Lord rewarded it. The recovery, moreover, was instant—in one brief moment the hemorrhage stopped completely. The reward affected not only her body, also her soul. Not only was her faith *rewarded*, it was also *improved*, brought to a higher stage of development, so that *faith concealed* became: *faith revealed* .... Lovingly, Jesus calls her "Daughter," even though she may not have been any younger than he was. But he speaks as a father to his child. Moreover, he praises her for her faith, even though that faith, as has been indicated, was by no means perfect .... Finally, probably even more encouraging is the command, "Go in peace." In view of the fact that in all probability Jesus spoke these words in the then current language of the Jews (Aramaic), have we not a right to conclude that nothing less than the full measure of the Hebrew *Shalom*, well-being for both body and soul, is here implied?" (New Testament Commentary: Exposition of the Gospel according to Luke, 2007, pp. 457-460).

On this same point, Dr. Robert A Guelich adds:

> "Go in peace" expresses a common Semitic farewell. But it represents more than simply a dismissal formula here. Together with the following imperative, it sets forth the full meaning of the previous declaration, "Your faith has made you well!" Going in peace means to go as one "restored to a proper relationship with God" (Schweizer, 118). Her healing, though certainly including her physical illness as the next statement indicates, involved more than simply the physical dimension of her existence (cf. 2:5-11)" (Word Biblical Commentary, Volume 34A, 2000, p. 245, ed. Ralph P. Martin).

Finally, Dr. Louis A. Barbieri shares his profound insight into the affectionate new title of 'Daughter' that Jesus uses in His farewell blessing of the healed woman. He states:

> "The affectionate title, **Daughter** (its only recorded use by Jesus) signified her new relationship with Him (cf. 3:33-35). Jesus attributed her cure to her **faith** rather than the touch of His clothing. Her faith **healed** her (lit., "has saved or delivered you"; cf. 5:28; 10:52) in that it caused her to seek healing *from Jesus*. Faith, confident trust, derives its value not from the one who expresses it, but from the object in which it rests (cf. 10:52); 11:22)" (The Bible Knowledge Commentary: New Testament, 1983, p. 125, ed. John F. Walvoord, Roy B. Zuck).

The Ruler's Daughter Raised from the Dead **(Continued)** —Matthew 23-25

The combination of narratives by the three Gospel writers together gives us a richer picture of the divine healing that is accomplished by a sole touch of the omnipotent hand of God through Jesus, and illustrates that even death is subject to His sovereign word of command.

MATTHEW	MARK	LUKE
"And when Jesus came into the official's house, and saw the flute-players, and the crowd crowd in noisy disorder, He began to say, "Depart; for the girl is not dead, but is asleep." And they were laughing at Him. But when the crowd had been put out, He entered and took her by the hand; and the girl arose" (9:23-25).	*"While He was still speaking, they came from the house of the synagogue official, saying, "Your daughter has died; why trouble the Teacher any more?" But Jesus, overhearing what was being spoken, said to the synagogue official, "Do not be afraid any longer, only believe." And He allowed no one to follow with Him, except Peter and James and John the brother of James. And they came to the house of the synagogue official; and He beheld a commotion, and people loudly weeping and wailing. And entering in, He said to them, "Why make a commotion and weep? The child has not died, but is asleep." And they were laughing at Him. But putting them all out, He took along the child's father and mother and His own companions, and child was. And taking the*	*"While He was still speaking, someone came from the house of the synagogue official, saying, "Your daughter has died; do not trouble the Teacher any more." But when Jesus heard this, He answered him, "Do not be afraid any longer; only believe, and she shall be made well." And when He had come to the house, He did not allow anyone to enter with Him, except Peter, John and James, and the girl's father and mother. Now they were all weeping and lamenting for her; but He said, "Stop weeping, for she has not died, but is asleep." And they began laughing at Him, knowing that she had died. He, however, took her by the hand and*

child by the hand, He said to her, "Talitha kum!" (which translated, means "Little girl, I say to you, arise!") And immediately the girl got up and began to walk; for she was twelve years old. And immediately they were completely astounded. And He gave them strict orders that no one should know about this; and He said that something should be given her to eat" (5:35-43).

called, saying "Child, arise!" And her spirit returned, and she rose up immediately; entered the room where the and He gave orders for something to be given her to eat. And her parents were amazed; but He instructed them to tell no one what had happened" (8:49-56).

The preceding two accounts speak of two individual women: one who was inflicted by death at the age of twelve, and the other who had been afflicted with an incurable bleeding disorder for twelve years. Both cases illustrate that there was no natural cure for either one of them. The one commonality that leads to their saving grace is the one in which Jesus consistently rewards, and that is simply—***believe***, which is demonstrated by the woman who *knew* that if she could only touch the fringe of Jesus' outer garment she would be healed, and the leper who was convinced that Jesus could heal him and was healed. Much like the unshakable faith the centurion had in believing in the divine power of Jesus to heal solely by command, Matthew states that when Jarius found Jesus, his unparalleled faith in believing that Jesus' divine power was limitless is demonstrated by him simply saying, "*but come and lay Your hand on her, and she will live"* (v. 18). William Hendriksen remarks:

> "**.....** That Jesus may lay His hand upon the dead girl, adding, "*and she will live*." This conviction on the part of the ruler is all the more remarkable in view of the fact that the Gospels do not report a restoration-to-life miracle performed by Jesus previous to this time" (p. 430) .... "Repeatedly the Gospels

> speak about the healing touch of Christ's hand (8:3, 15; 9:18, 25, 29; 17:7; 20:24; Luke 7:14; 22:51). Sometimes the sick would themselves touch Jesus (Matt. 9:20-22; 14:36). Either way the afflicted ones were healed. Evidently in connection with such physical contact healing power issued from the Savior and was transmitted to the person in need (Mark 5:30; Luke 8:46). This, however, was no magic! The healing power did not originate in the fingers or his garment. It came straight from the divine and human Jesus, from His almighty will and infinitely sympathetic heart. There was healing power in the touch because He was, and is, "touched with the feeling of our infirmities" (Heb. 4:15)" (New Testament Commentary: Exposition of the Gospel according to Matthew, 2007, pp. 392, 430).

Between the narratives of Mark and Luke, we read that Jesus then took three of His disciples and the parents into the child's room, affectionately placed the child's hand in His own, and by one sovereign word of command—"Arise!" death immediately obeyed. Luke writes, "Her spirit returned and she rose up immediately" (v. 55). On this point, Dr. Lockyer comments:

> "Luke, with his medical precision, says that, "her spirit, or breath" returned, proving that this was a resurrection, and no recovery from a death swoon. The spirit of the girl returned from the unseen world and became reunited with her body. The Jews have an ancient legend that after death the soul of the departed hovers near the body for several days before it takes its final farewell. Paul, however, instructs us to believe that the moment we are freed from the body we are present with the Lord. How the miracle took place is a mystery. This we know, that no power but Christ's can raise the dead, and He knew not only the when of miracles but also the why and the how. It is thus with every spiritual resurrection—a divine act" (All of the Miracles of the Bible, 1961, p. 193).

Finally, the one outstanding characteristic consistently found in the three divine healings of the paralytic, the centurion's servant, and Jarius' daughter, is the unshakable faith that the paralytic's friends, the centurion, and Jarius all had in the divine power of Jesus to heal, which illustrates that it not only applied to them, but was also extended to their loved ones. The confidence that was demonstrated by the paralytic's friends in believing that if they could only get their friend to Jesus is what led Jesus to heal the paralytic both spiritually and physically. The centurion's unshakeable faith that Jesus need only to say the word and his servant would be healed touches Jesus in such a way that He not only commends it publicly, but by the time the centurion arrived home, his servant had already been healed. Lastly, by Jarius' unparalleled faith in Jesus' sovereign power to restore his daughter to him, Jesus rewards his faith by resurrecting her from the dead.

"And without faith it is impossible to please Him, for he who comes to God must believe that He is, and that He is a rewarder of those who seek Him" Hebrews 11:6).

The Two Blind Men—Matthew 9:27-31

Matthew continues to guide us through Jesus' journey by stating that when Jesus leaves Jarius' house, He is followed by two blind men who are constantly yelling, "*Son of David*" have mercy on us. William Hendriksen states that during the time of Jesus' ministry on earth, the title of "the Son of David" had become synonymous with His title of the Messiah. This strongly suggests that the blind men had no doubt that Jesus was the Messiah, and did have the divine power to restore their eyesight (New Testament Commentary: Exposition of the Gospel according to Matthew, 2007, p. 435).

The Two Blind Men Healed – Matthew 9:27-31: *"And as Jesus passed on from there, two blind men followed Him, crying out, and saying, "Have mercy on us, Son of David!" And after He had come into the house, the blind men came up to Him, and Jesus said to them, "Do you believe that I am able to do this?" They said to Him, "Yes, Lord." Then He touched their eyes, saying, "Be it done to you according to your faith." And their eyes were opened."*

Consistent with Jesus' teaching, the one and only requirement of believing in Him is what He responds to has consistently been demonstrated by His divine healings, which illustrates that the act always corresponds to each of the believer's faith. Thus, when Jesus asks the blind men, *"Do you believe that I am able to do this?"* (v. 28), and they reply by saying, *"Yes, Lord"*, then by one sovereign touch of His hand, Jesus confirms it, and their eyesight was restored immediately.

> *"Be it done to you according to your faith"* (v. 29).

The Demon Possessed Mute—Matthew 9:32-33

"And as they were going out, behold, a dumb man, demon-possessed, was brought to Him. And after the demon was cast out; the dumb man spoke; and the multitudes marveled, saying 'Nothing like this was ever seen in Israel'."

Immediately following the restoration of the two blind men's eyesight, as Jesus is leaving the house where He was staying, a demon-possessed mute is brought to Him. Matthew's narrative is short and simply states that after the demon was cast out of the man, he immediately spoke. However, Dr. Hagner sees it as a Messianic sign that points to Jesus' sovereign power and authority over all which is above and beneath the earth. He writes:

> "This reaction points to the newness of what Jesus represents. The direct, unmediated healing of the man's inability to speak symbolizes the fulfillment and joy of the kingdom announce by Jesus. The image of the mute being given the gift of speech is itself again suggestive of the gospel. The readers of Matthew know that they participate in the good experienced by the mute demoniac. And those who have been healed in the most fundamental sense of the word—who have experienced salvation—are now themselves liberated to speak the good news of the kingdom. The response to what proclamation will be mixed, as it was to the ministry and message of Jesus. While some will respond positively, others like the Pharisees will be all to ready to find only evil in Jesus and His disciples (cf. 10:25)" (Word Biblical Commentary, Volume 33A, 2000, p. 258, ed. Ralph P. Martin).

Healing the Multitudes—Matthew 9:35

"And Jesus was going about all the cities and the villages, teaching in their synagogues, and proclaiming the gospel of the kingdom, and healing every kind of disease and every kind of sickness."

This single verse (solely found in Matthew) demonstrates the full essence of Jesus' ministry—teaching—preaching the good news of the kingdom—and healing every kind of disease and sickness. To further influence our understanding, Matthew describes the full extent of His ministry by using only one small three-letter word, namely—"*all*". "He went throughout ***all*** of the cities and villages teaching, preaching the good news, and healing every kind of disease and sickness throughout ***all*** the land. Below is an indexed map taken from Bible History that is believed to be all of the areas where Jesus taught, preached, and healed during the course of His earthly ministry.

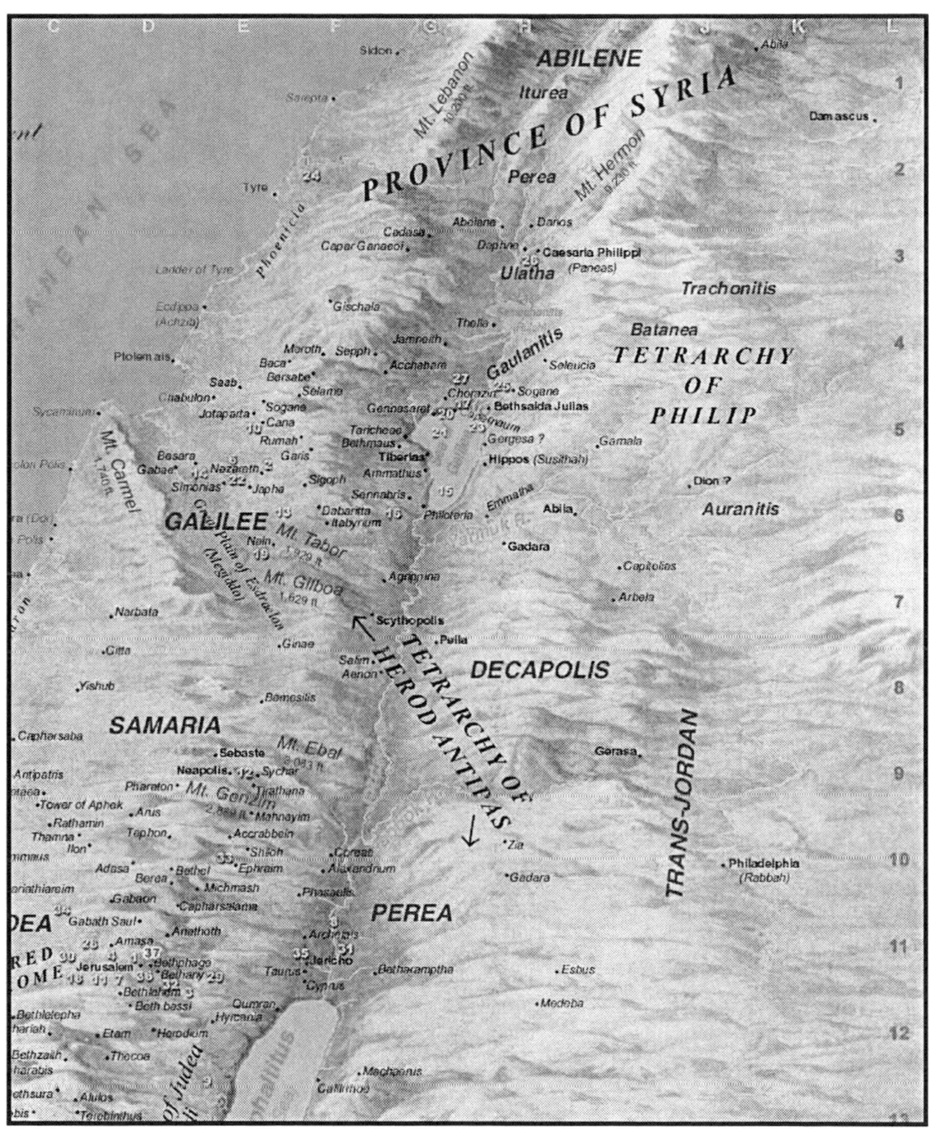

The Ministry of Jesus
Image provided by Bible History, http://www.bible-history.com/map_jesus/, 2012.

Table VI – The Ministry of Jesus
Index

The Man with A Withered Hand—Matthew 12:9-14

Matthew records that it is the Sabbath and while Jesus and His disciples are on their way to the synagogue, the hungry disciples begin to pick and eat some heads of grain from a wheat field. Although the Law had made provision for doing so (Deuteronomy 23:25), the trailing Pharisees nonetheless begin to complain to Jesus about it. Jesus responds by reminding them that when David was hungry, he ate the consecrated bread reserved only for the priests, and when the priests profaned the Sabbath in the temple with their sacrifices, they were proclaimed innocent. It is at this point that Jesus establishes His sovereign title as "*Lord of the Sabbath*" when He says, "*I desire COMPASSION, not SACRIFICE; For the Son of Man is Lord of the Sabbath*" (vv. 1-8). Departing from there, Jesus goes into the synagogue where He meets a man suffering from a withered hand.

The Healing of the Man with a Withered Hand – Matthew 12:9-14: *"And departing from there, He went into their synagogue. And behold, there was a man with a withered hand. And they questioned Him, saying, "Is it lawful to heal on the Sabbath?" —in order that they might accuse Him. And He said to them, "What man shall there be among you, who shall have one sheep, and if it falls into a pit on the Sabbath, will he not take hold of it, and lift it out? Of how much more value then is a man than a sheep! So, then, it is lawful to do good on the Sabbath." Then He said to the man, "Stretch out your hand!" And he stretched it out, and it was restored to normal, like the other"* (Matthew 12:9-14; Mark 3:1-6; Luke 6:6-11).

In all three Gospel accounts of the healing, Matthew, Mark, and Luke state that when Jesus told the man to stretch out his hand, he immediately obeyed and his hand was restored to normal. This is the first healing recorded in the Gospels whereby the man who is healed is not asked *if* he believed that he could be healed—When Jesus told the man to stretch out his hand, he immediately obeyed, and his obedience was rewarded. William Barclay comments:

1. "He gave him back his *health.* Jesus is vitally interested in people's physical well-being.
2. Because Jesus gave this man back his health, he also gave him back his *work.*
3. Because Jesus gave this man back his health and his work, he gave him back his *self-respect.* We might well add a new beatitude: blessed are those who give us back our self-respect. We discover our own worth again when, on our two feet and with our own two hands, we can face life and, with independence, provide for your own needs for the needs of those dependent on us" (William Barclay, The Gospel of Matthew, Volume II, 2001, pp. 36-37).

> "*I desire COMPASSION, not SACRIFICE; For the Son of Man is Lord of the Sabbath"* (v. 8).

Healing the Multitude—Matthew 12:15

The combined narratives of the Matthew and Mark state that after Jesus healed the man with the withered hand, the Pharisee's huddle together to devise a plan to destroy Him (Matthew 12:14; Mark 3:6; Luke 6:11). Perceiving their thoughts, Jesus withdraws from the synagogue and goes to the seashore. Meanwhile, a great multitude is following Him. Whereas Matthew briefly states that those in the multitude who needed healing were being healed, Mark adds, *"He had healed many, with the result that all those who had afflictions pressed about Him in order to touch Him,"* which communicates the sense of the desperation of those who were tormented and afflicted. Mark's addition also illustrates that in acknowledgment of Jesus' almighty power and authority over all that is above and beneath the earth, even unclean spirits fall before Him in obeyance.

MATTHEW	MARK
"But Jesus, aware of this, withdrew from there. And many followed Him, and He healed them all" (Matthew 12:15).	*"And Jesus withdrew to the sea with His disciples; and a great multitude from Galilee followed; and also from Judea, and from Jerusalem, and from Idumea, and beyond the Jordan, and the vicinity of Tyre and Sidon, a great multitude heard of all that He was doing and came to Him. And He told His disciples that a boat should stand ready for Him because of the multitude, in order that they might not crowd Him; for He had healed many, with the result that al those who had afflictions pressed about Him in order to touch Him. And whenever the unclean spirits beheld Him, they would fall down before Him and cry out, saying, "You are the Son of God!" "* (Mark 3:7-11).

Dr. John Gill's conclusion draws a vivid picture of the desperation of those in the crowd. He observes:

> "The Arabic version of Scripture renders it as they *rushed upon Him*, so *that they fell*: they pushed on, and pressed so hard to get to Him, they fell upon one another, and on Him" (Gills Expositor, Exposition of The New Testament, Volume VII, 1976, p. 394).

The Demon Possessed Blind Mute – Matthew 12:22-23

Meanwhile, as Jesus is healing everyone who comes to Him, a demon-possessed man who could neither see nor speak is brought to Him for deliverance.

"Then there was brought to Him a demon-possessed man, who was blind and dumb, and He healed him, so that the dumb man spoke and saw. And all the multitudes were amazed, and began to say, "This man cannot be the Son of David, can he?" " (Matthew 12:22-23; Luke 11:14).

In Luke's account of the mute's divine encounter with Jesus, he states that the moment that Jesus cast the demon out of the man, he was immediately healed.

Healing the Multitude—Matthew 14:14

"*And when He came out, He saw a great multitude, and felt compassion for them, and healed their sick*" (Matthew 14:14; Luke 9:10-11; John 6:1-3).

From the time that Jesus healed the demon possessed blind mute in Galilee, William Hendriksen traces Jesus' journey from the Capernaum synagogue (12:9) to His temporary departure (12:15), His implied return (12:47), teaching from a boat near the Galilean seashore (13:1, 2), and back to Capernaum (13:36). From Capernaum, Jesus returns to Nazareth (13:54), then retreats from Nazareth and goes back to the seashore (New Testament Commentary: Exposition of the Gospel according to Matthew, 2007, p. 581). Matthew then writes that after Jesus hears about the death of John the Baptist, He gets into a small boat and goes to a lonely place by Himself (14:13). However, it does not end there—Matthew continues the trail by telling us that when the multitudes heard that Jesus had left by boat, they followed Him on foot (14:13). In Luke's narrative (9:11), he says that Jesus withdrew privately to Bethsaida on the northeastern shore of the sea, which is confirmed by John (6:2).

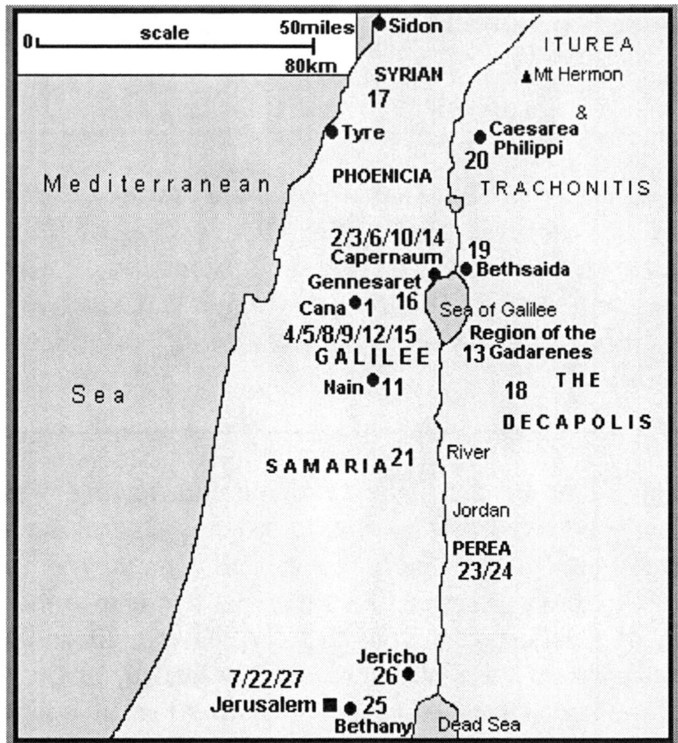

Image provided by J. B. Phillips
http://www.ccel.org/bible/phillips/JBPhillips.htm, 2003.

William Barclay's comment on this solitary verse reveals the deep compassion Jesus felt for the multitude. He states, "When He saw the crowds, He was moved with compassion to the depths of his being, and He healed them" (William Barclay, The Gospel of Matthew, Volume II, 2001, p. 116).

Healing the Sick in Gennesaret—Matthew 14:34-36

"And when they had crossed over, they came to the land of Gennesaret, and when the men of that place recognized Him, they sent into all that surrounding district and brought to Him all who were ill; and they began to entreat Him that they might just touch the fringe of His cloak; and as many as touched it were cured" (Matthew 14:34-36; Mark 6:53-56).

Reminiscent of the faith of the hemorrhaging woman who firmly believed that by simply touching Jesus' outer garment she would immediately be healed, Matthew's account of healing the sick in Gennesaret illustrates that this is also the case with the people of Gennesaret All of those who were ill and did touch Jesus' outer garment were also immediately healed. In Dr. Lockyer's analysis of the account, he carefully points out that though the people may have felt that their healing depended upon contact with Jesus' garment, but the sovereign power to heal was in Christ alone (All of the Miracles of the Bible, 1961, p. 195). Hendriksen concurs. He concludes, "it is all in the power and love of Christ", not His garments (New Testament Commentary: Exposition of the Gospel according to Matthew, 2007, p. 604).

The Syrophoenician's Daughter—Matthew 15:21-28

"And Jesus went away from there, and withdrew into the district of Tyre and Sidon. And behold, a Canaanite woman came out from that region, and began to cry out, saying, "Have mercy on me, O Lord, Son of David; my daughter is cruelly demon-possessed." But He did not answer her a word. And His disciples came to Him and kept asking Him, saying, "Send her away, for she is shouting out after us." But He answered and said, "I was sent only to the lost sheep of the house of Israel." But she came and began to bow down before Him, saying, "Lord, help me!" And He answered and said, "It is not good to take the children's bread and throw it to the dogs." But she said, Yes, Lord; but even the dogs feed on the crumbs which fall from their master's table. Then Jesus answered and said to her, "O woman, your faith is great; let it be done for you as you wish." And her daughter was healed at once" (Matthew 15:21-28; Mark 7:24-30).

What a perfect example of the spiritual principle of the 'importance of perseverance in faith and prayer' that Jesus had formerly taught in the parables of the Midnight Friend and the Unjust Judge. Through them Jesus illustrated that though neither the midnight friend nor the judge immediately responded to the petitions of either the friend or the widow, neither did either one of them ever lose heart. Consistent with His nature, Jesus not only rewards the Syrophoenician woman's remarkable perseverance in faith, but like that of the centurion, Jesus also commends it. On this point William Hendriksen notes:

> "Divine love is so infinite and marvelous that it even praises a human being for exercising a gift—in this case faith—with which this very divine love has endowed her, and which apart from the divine activity could not have gone into action at all.

> The praise which this woman receives cannot fail to remind us of the eulogy with which Jesus lauded the centurion (8:10)" (New Testament Commentary: Exposition of the Gospel according to Matthew, 2007, p. 625).

Moreover, like the centurion's servant, without physically seeing or touching the Syrophoenician's daughter, Jesus healed her from afar. Dr. Lockyer observes:

> "This much is clearly evident, that the woman believed that nearness or distance made no difference to His power to heal her daughter, and so went home in perfect confidence, there to find her loved one healed and at rest after the tumult that had so long raged within her" (All of the Miracles of the Bible, 1961, pp. 206-207).

"O woman, your faith is great; let it be done for you as you wish" (v. 28).

Healing the Multitudes on the Mountain —Matthew 15:29-31

"Departing from there, Jesus went along by the Sea of Galilee, and having gone up to the mountain, He was sitting there. And great multitudes came to Him, bringing with them those who were lame, crippled, blind, dumb, and many others, and they laid them down at His feet; and He healed them, so that the multitude marveled as they saw the dumb speaking, the crippled restored, and the lame walking, and the blind seeing; and they glorified the God of Israel" (Matthew 15:29-31).

After healing the Syrophoenician woman's daughter, Matthew records that Jesus travels along by the sea and goes up to a mountain. However, Mark adds more detail to the narrative. Mark says that Jesus left the region of Tyre for Galilee via Sidon and travelled through the region of the ten cities (7:31) before arriving to the mountain. As Jesus is sitting there, great multitudes are bringing Him all of those who have physical disabilities, and as Jesus is healing them, they are glorifying the God of Israel. William Barclay stresses the compassionate nature, love, graciousness, and mercy of Jesus. He writes:

> "We see Him curing physical disabilities. The maimed, the blind and the dumb are laid at His feet and cured. Jesus is infinitely concerned with the bodily pain of the world; and those who bring men and women health and healing are still doing the work of Jesus Christ. We see him concerned for the tired. He wants to strengthen their feet for a long, hard road. Jesus is infinitely concerned for the world's travelers, for the world's toilers, for those whose eyes are weary and whose hands are tired. And still He comes to us offering us also the

bread which will satisfy the immortal hunger of the human soul, and in the strength of which we shall be able to go all the days of our lives" (William Barclay, The Gospel of Matthew, Volume II, 2001, p. 148).

The Demonic Epileptic Boy—Matthew 17:14-21

After healing the multitudes, Jesus travels by boat to the region of Magadan, believed to be located on the west side of the sea south of Gennesaret (Matthew 15:39; Mark 8:10). Six days later, Jesus takes Peter, James, and John and together they go up to a high mountain (17:2). Matthew then says that after they came down from the summit, they meet up with a multitude, and a man runs to Jesus, falls on his knees, and beseeches Him to heal his only son, who since childhood, had been possessed by a malicious spirit. Between the narratives of the three Gospel writers, we are not only given the intimate details of the grievous suffering that both the father and his only beloved son had long endured, but we also get a sense of the father's desperation and of Jesus' exasperation by the weakness of his faith.

MATTHEW	MARK	LUKE
"And when they came to the multitude, a man came up to Him, falling on his knees before Him, and saying, "Lord, have mercy on my son, for he is an epileptic, and is very ill; for he often falls into the fire, and often into the water. And I brought him to Your disciples, and they could not cure him." And Jesus answered and said, "O unbelieving and perverted generation, how long shall I be with you? How long	*"And one of the crowd answered Him, "Teacher, I brought You my son, possessed with a spirit which makes him mute; and whenever it seizes him, it dashes him to the ground and he foams at the mouth, and grinds his teeth, and stiffens out. And I told Your disciples to cast it out, and they could not do it." And He answered them and said, "O unbelieving generation how long shall I be with you? How long shall I put up with you? Bring him to Me!" And they brought the boy to Him. And when he saw him, immediately the spirit threw*	*"And it came about on the next day, that when they had come down from the mountain, a great multitude met Him. And behold, a man from the multitude shouted out, saying, Teacher I beg You to look at my son, for he is my only boy, and behold, a spirit seizes him, and he suddenly screams, and it throws him into a convulsion with foaming at the at the mouth, and as it mauls him, it scarcely leaves him. And I begged Your disciples to cast it out, and they could not." And*

shall I put up with you? Bring him here to Me." And Jesus rebuked him, and the demon came out of him, and the boy was cured at once" (Matthew 17:14-21).

him into a convulsion, and falling to the ground, he began rolling about and foaming at the mouth. And He asked his father, "How long, has this been happening to him?" And he said "From childhood. And it has often thrown him both into the fire and into the water to destroy him. But if you can do anything, take pity on us and help us!" And Jesus said to him, " 'If you can!' All things are possible to him who believes." Immediately the boy's father cried out and began saying "I do believe; help me in my unbelief." And when Jesus saw that a crowd was rapidly gathering, He rebuked the unclean spirit, saying to it, "You deaf and dumb spirit, I command you, come out of him and do not enter him again." And after crying out and throwing him into terrible convulsions, it came out; and the boy became so much like a corpse that most of them said, "He is dead!" But Jesus took him by the hand and raised him; and he got up" (Mark 9:17-29).

Jesus answered, and said, "O unbelieving and perverted generation, how long shall I be with you, and put up with you? Bring your son here." And while he was still approaching, the demon dashed him to the ground, and threw him into a violent convulsion. But Jesus rebuked the unclean spirit, and healed the boy, and gave him back to his father" (Luke 9:37-43).

Taking all of Jesus' miraculous healings into consideration, the one consistent feature that stands out is—Jesus rewards *faith*. Despite all of the astonishing miraculous healings and deliverances that had already taken place in His ministry, as opposed to Jesus marveling or being impressed by the father's faith, Jesus is amazed at the weakness of faith that the despairing father exhibits. However, in spite of the father's weak faith, *after* Jesus reprimands the faithless and perverse generation, He (1) reprimands the demon, (2) commands it to leave the boy, (3) forbids it to return, and (4) in subjection to His command, the spirit departs and the boy was immediately cured (Matthew 17:21). Dr. Lockyer comments, "No case, however depraved or demon-ridden, is too hard for Christ to whom all power was given" (All of the Miracles of the Bible, 1961, p. 217).

Healing the Multitudes—Matthew 19:2

From the time that Jesus heals the epileptic boy, Matthew writes that He and His disciples go back to Capernaum (17:24), and after a time of teaching and preaching the good news of the kingdom throughout Galilee, Jesus departs and travels to the region of Judea beyond the Jordan River (19:1). However, Mark and Luke add more detail. Whereas Mark writes that after Jesus and His disciples leave Capernaum, they go through the region of Judea beyond the Jordan (Mark 9:33; 10:1), Luke writes that after Jesus and His disciples leave Capernaum, He sets His sights on Jerusalem, and as He is going through the villages in Samaria, He is not being received very well (Luke 9:51-57). Dr. Louis A. Barbieri adds, "As Jesus was making His way back to the city of Jerusalem through the region of Judea to the east side of the Jordan River. That area was known as Perea. There, as often before, Jesus was followed by large crowds of needy people, and He healed them all" (The Bible Knowledge Commentary: New Testament, 1983, p. 63, ed. John F. Walvoord, Roy B. Zuck).

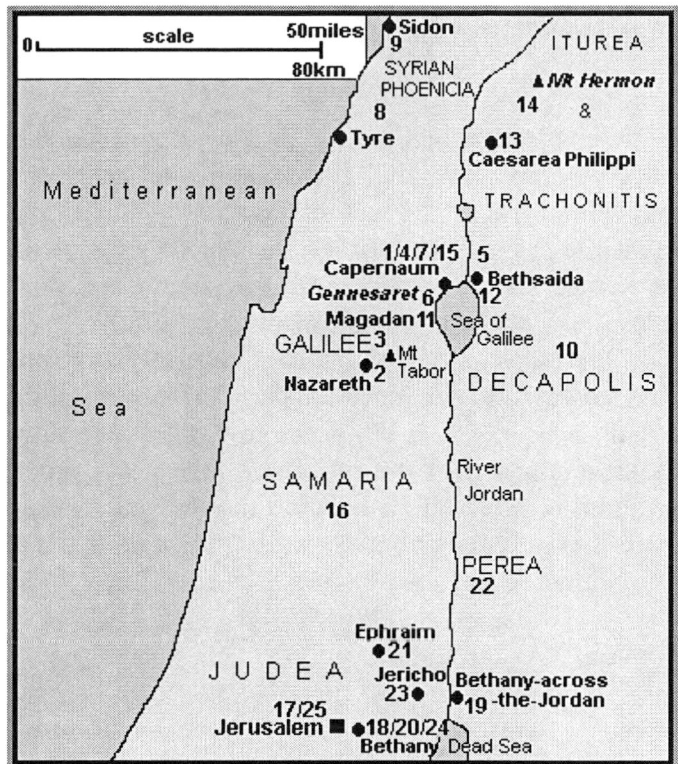

Image provided by J. B. Phillips
http://www.ccel.org/bible/phillips/JBPhillips.htm, 2012.

This single verse, uniquely found in Matthew, illustrates the nature of the profound compassion and mercy of Jesus in caring not only about people's spiritual well-being, but of their physical well-being as well.

Healing the Multitude – Matthew 19:12: *"And it came about that when Jesus had finished these words, He departed from Galilee, and came into the region of Judea beyond the Jordan; and great multitudes followed Him, and He healed them there"* (Matthew 19:2).

The Two Blind Beggars—Matthew 20:29-34

The opening verses of Chapter 19 give a few more details that lead up to the healing of Bartimaeus and his friend. Prior to Jesus telling the parable of the Pounds (Luke 19:11-27), Luke records that while Jesus is in Jericho, the crowd grew so large that a tax-gatherer named Zaccheus climbs up a sycamore tree to watch Him pass by. Jesus sees Zaccheus and calls him over to tell him that He will be staying at his house. (Luke 19:1-10). Matthew then picks up the narrative by saying that as Jesus is on His way to Jerusalem via Jericho, on His way out, two blind beggars who were sitting by the road hear the commotion of the multitude that were following Jesus and inquire about it. Mark and Luke continue by writing that when the beggars heard it was Jesus who was passing by, one of the two, called Bartimaeus, begins to cry out saying, *"Jesus, Son of David, have mercy on me!"*.

MATTHEW	MARK	LUKE
"And as they were going out from Jericho, a great multitude followed Him. And behold, two blind men sitting by the road, hearing that Jesus was passing by, cried out, saying, "Lord, have mercy on us, Son of David!" And the multitude sternly told them to be quiet; but they cried out all the more, saying, "Lord, have mercy on us, Son of David!" And Jesus stopped and called them, and said, "What do you wish Me to do for you?" They said to Him, "Lord, we want our eyes to be opened." And	*"And they came to Jericho. And as He was going out from Jericho with His disciples and a great, multitude a blind beggar named Bartimaeus, the son of Timaeus, was sitting by the road. And when he heard that it was Jesus the Nazarene, he began to cry out and say, "Jesus, Son of David, have mercy on me!" And many were sternly telling him to be, quiet but he began crying out all the more, "Son of David, have mercy on me!" And Jesus stopped and said, "Call*	*"And it came about that as He was approaching Jericho, a certain blind man was sitting by the road, begging. Now hearing a multitude going by, he began to inquire what this might be. And they told him that Jesus of Nazareth was passing by. And he called out, saying, "Jesus, Son of David, have mercy on me!" And those who led the way were sternly telling him to be quiet; but he kept crying out all the more, "Son of David, have*

moved with compassion, Jesus touched their eyes; and immediately they received their sight, and followed Him" (Matthew 20:29-34).

him here." And they called the blind man, saying to him, "Take courage, arise! He is calling for you." And casting aside his cloak, he jumped up, and came to Jesus. And answering him, Jesus, said "What do you want Me to do for you?" And the blind man said to Him, "Rabboni, I want to regain my sight!" And Jesus said to him, "Go your way way; your faith has made you well." And immediately he received his sight and began following Him on the road" (Mark 10:46-52).

mercy on me!" And Jesus stopped and commanded that he be brought to Him; and when he had come near, He questioned him, "What do you want Me to do for you?" And he said, "Lord, I want to receive my sight!" And Jesus Jesus said to him, "Receive your sight; your faith has made you well." And immediiately he received his sight, and began following Him, glorifying God; and when all, the people saw it, they gave praise to God" (Luke 18:35-43).

The account in the three narratives once again illustrate the nature of the deep compassion, love, graciousness, and mercy of Jesus in caring about people's spiritual and physical well-being, and of His respect and response to faith in believing that He is the rewarder of those who seek Him. In determinedly crying out, "*Lord, have mercy on us, Son of David*" (v. 30), the vocal blind beggar, whom Mark calls Bartimaeus, recognizes and acknowledges Jesus as being the Messiah intimates that he fully believed in Jesus' sovereign power to heal. Jesus is moved with compassion, calls them to come before Him, and by His loving, compassionate and merciful touch, the blind men were instantly healed. However, William Hendriksen, John Calvin, and Dr. John Gill all conclude that the blind men were not only healed physically, but were healed spiritually as well. Hendriksen notes:

> "It would appear that when Jesus makes him well by promptly restoring to him his vision, he blesses him not only physically but also spiritually" (New Testament Commentary: Exposition of the Gospel according to Luke, 2007, p. 844).

John Calvin writes:

"By the word *faith* is meant not only a confident hope of recovering sight, but a loftier conviction, which was, that this blind man had acknowledged Jesus to be the Messiah whom God had promised. For the *blind man* did not at random bestow on Christ the name of *Son of David*, but embraced him as that person whose coming he had been taught by the divine predictions to expect .... And therefore, when Christ says, *thy faith hath saved thee*, the word *saved* is not limited to an outward *cure*, but includes also the *health* and *safety* of the soul; as if Christ had said, that by *faith* the blind man obtained that God was gracious to him, and granted his wish. And if it was in regard to *faith* that God bestowed his favor on the blind man, it follows that he was justified by *faith*" (John Calvin, *Harmony of the Evangelists*, 2009, Volume I, p. 432).

Dr. John Gill concludes:

"*And they followed Him*....for at the same time he restored their bodily sight, he gave them a spiritual one to look to Him, and follow Him, the light of the world, that they might enjoy the light of life in another world" (Gills Expositor, Exposition of The New Testament, Volume VII, 1976, p. 231).

> *"Your faith has made you well"* (Mark 10:52a).

The Blind and the Lame in the Temple—Matthew 21:12-14

"And Jesus entered the temple and cast out all those who were buying and selling in the temple, and overturned the tables of the moneychangers and the seats of those who were selling doves. And He said to them, "It is written, 'MY HOUSE SHALL BE CALLED A HOUSE OF PRAYER'; but you are making it a robber's den." And the blind and the lame came to Him in the temple, and He healed them."

The solitary verse, "*And the blind and the lame came to Him in the temple, and He healed them*" (v. 14), recorded exclusively by Matthew, is his final account of the healing ministry of God through Jesus. From the preceding accounts of Jesus' journey, we know that Jesus is on His way to Jerusalem via Jericho (21:1). Before He arrives, Jesus stops at Bethphage, near Mount Olives, and sends His disciples into the village to acquire the donkey that He used to make His triumphal entry into Jerusalem (vv. 1-13). After overturning the tables of the moneychangers, Matthew states that while Jesus is in the temple, the blind and the lame came to Him, and Jesus healed them all.

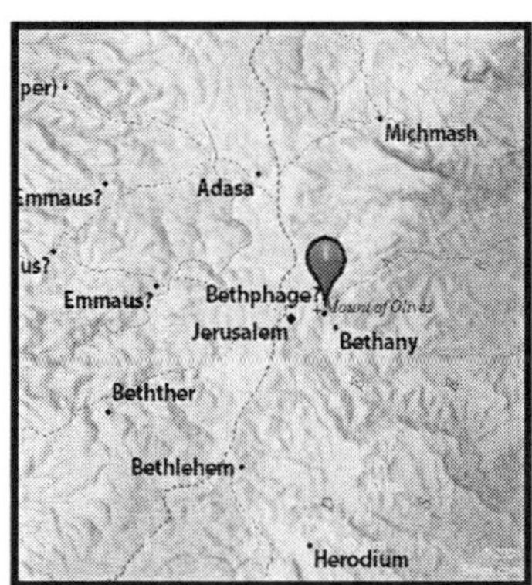

Bethphage and surrounding area
Image provided by Bible Atlas
http://bibleatlas.org/bethphage.htm, 2012.

Associated with Bethany, Dr. Ralph Earle describes Bethphage as a small village believed to be located on the lower slopes of the Mount of Olives near the Jericho road. It is mentioned three different times in Scripture (Matthew 21:1; Mark 11:1 and Luke 19:29), and all three are in association with Jesus' triumphal entry into Jerusalem (Eerdman's *International Standard Bible Encyclopedia,* Volume A-D, 1979, p. 474, ed. Geoffrey W. Bromiley).

Finally, before continuing with Mark's unique accounts of the healing ministry of God manifested through Jesus, for easy reference, the following table contains a list of twenty-five of God's miraculous healings that were accomplished through the sovereign hands of Jesus that are recorded in the Gospel of Matthew. Included in the listing is the miraculous birth of Jesus, as well as the first nature miracle of transforming water into wine at the wedding in Cana that inaugurated Jesus' miracle ministry that is recorded exclusively by John.

"*And the blind and the lame came to Him in the temple, and He healed them*" (Matthew 21:14).

Table VII
The Healing Ministry of God through Jesus Recorded in Matthew

	MIRACLES	PLACE	MATTHEW	LUKE	JOHN
1.	The Virgin Birth	Bethlehem	1:18-25	1:26-35	
2.	Transforming Water into Wine	Cana			2:1-11

	HEALING	PLACE	MATTHEW	MARK	LUKE
3.	The Multitudes	Throughout Galilee	4:23-24	1:39	
4.	The Leper	Galilee	8:1-4	1:40-42	5:12-14
5.	The Centurion's Servant	Capernaum	8:5-13		7:2-10
6.	Peter's Mother-in-Law	Capernaum	8:14-15	1:30-31	4:38-39
7.	The Multitudes	Capernaum	8:16-17	1:32-34	4:40-41
8.	The Demon Possessed Gerasene	Gergesa	8:28-34	5:1-20	8:26-39
9.	The Paralytic Cured	Capernaum	9:1-8	2:1-12	5:17-26
10.	The Daughter of Jarius Raised from the Dead	Galilee	9:18-19; 23-25	5:22-24; 35-42	8:40-42; 49-55
11.	The Hemorrhaging Woman	Galilee	9:20-22	5:25-34	8:43-48
12.	The Two Blind Men	Galilee	9:27-31		
13.	The Demon Possessed Mute	Galilee	9:32-34		
14.	The Multitudes	Throughout The Land	9:35		
15.	The Man with a Withered Hand	The Synagogue	12:9-14	3:1-6	6:6-11
16.	The Multitudes	Throughout The Land	12:15-21	3:7-12	

Table VII **(Continued)** The Healing Ministry of God through Jesus Recorded in Matthew

	HEALING	PLACE	MATTHEW	MARK	LUKE
17.	The Demon Possessed Blind Mute	Galilee	12:22-23		11:14
18.	The Multitudes	Bethsaida/Galilee	14:13-14		9:10-11; John 6:1-3
19.	Healing the Sick	Gennesaret	14:34-36	6:53-56	
20.	The Syrophoenici an's Daughter	Tyre/Sidon	15:21-28	7:24-30	
21.	The Multitudes	Galilee	15:29-31		
22.	The Demonic Epileptic Boy	Galilee	17:14-21	9:17-29	9:37-43
23.	The Multitudes	Judea	19:2		
24.	Two Blind Men	Jericho	20:29-34	10:46-52	18:35-43
25.	The Blind and The Lame In the Temple	Jerusalem	21:14		

(Adapted from John MacArthur, "The Healing Ministry of God through Jesus", *The MacArthur Bible Commentary* , 2005, pp. 1152, 1293; Edwin A. Blum, "The Miracles of Jesus", *The Bible Knowledge Commentary: New Testament*, 1983, p. 277, ed. John F. Walvoord, Roy B. Zuck; Colin Brown, "Miracles", Volume K-P, 1986, p. 374, Eerdman's *International Standard Bible Encyclopedia*).

The Healing Ministry of Jesus Recorded by Mark

Casting Out the Unclean Spirit—Mark 1:21-27

With the exception of the recording of the Unclean Spirit found in Luke's Gospel, the account of Casting out the Unclean Spirit is the first of three *unique* divine healings recorded in the Gospel of Mark. The account of the deliverance is preceded by a short narrative written by the three Gospel writers of Jesus healing the multitudes who had crowded around Peter's house in Capernaum (Matthew 8:16-17; Mark 1:32-34; Luke 4:40-41). However, prior to the arrival at Peter's house, it is the Sabbath and while Jesus is teaching in the synagogue, a man with an unclean spirit cries out to Him saying,

---

Casting Out the Unclean Spirit – Mark 1:21-27: *"What do we have to do with You, Jesus of Nazareth? Have You come to destroy us? I know who You are—the Holy One of God!" And Jesus rebuked him, saying "Be quiet, and come out of him!" And throwing him into convulsions, the unclean spirit cried out with a loud voice, and came out of him"* (Mark 1:21-27; Luke 4:31-37).

Like the demonic spirits that possessed the man of Gerasene, this unclean spirit recognizes and acknowledges Jesus as being the '*Holy One of God.*' Though Scripture is silent with regards to whether or not this demonic spirit tortured the man in the synagogue, solely by Jesus' divine power and authority over evil, the moment that Jesus rebukes the evil spirit and commands it to leave the man, the unclean spirit, albeit unwillingly, throws the man into convulsions and immediately departs.

Healing a Deaf-Mute—Mark 7:31-35

Following the miraculous healing of the Syrophoenician woman's daughter (Matthew 15:29-31; Mark 7:24-30), Matthew states that Jesus leaves the region following the Sea of Galilee and goes up to a mountain. While He is sitting up on a mountain, great multitudes are bringing Him all of those who have physical disabilities, and Jesus heals them all (Matthew 15:29-31). Mark, however, adds more detail to the narrative. He says that *after* Jesus healed the Syrophoenician's daughter, He leaves the region of Tyre for Galilee via Sidon, and as He is travelling within the region of the 'ten cities' (7:31), a deaf-mute man was brought to Him and Jesus takes him aside to heal him privately (v. 33).

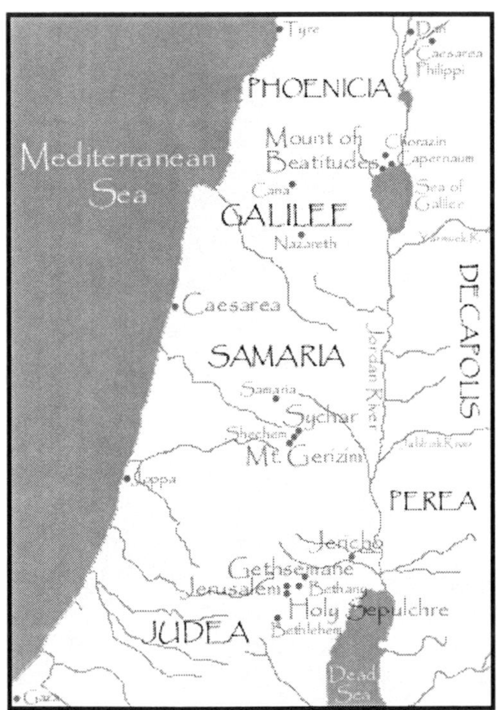

Image provided by Edward Fudge
http://www.edwardfudge.com/beatitudes.html, 2012.

Healing a Deaf-Mute – Mark 7:31-35: *"And again He went out from the region of Tyre, and came through Sidon to the Sea of Galilee, within the region of Decapolis. And they brought to Him one who was deaf and spoke with difficulty, and they entreated Him to lay His hand upon him. And He took him aside from the multitude by himself, and put His fingers into his ears, and after spitting, He touched his tongue with the saliva; and looking up to heaven with a deep sigh, He said to him, "Ephphata!" that is, "Be opened!" And his ears were opened, and the impediment of his tongue was removed, and he began speaking plainly."*

Much has been written about why Jesus used His own saliva to heal certain blind men and to loosen the bonds of the deaf-mute's tongue. In both Dr. Guelich and Dr A. Dorsey's summaries, they state that in both the Greco-Roman and Jewish worlds, spittle was thought to contain therapeutic qualities. During the course of Jesus' healing ministry, He applied this special method on three different occasions (Mark 7:33; 8:23; John 9:6) (Word Biblical Commentary, Volume 34A, 2000, p. 395, ed. Ralph P. Martin; Eerdman's *International Standard Bible Encyclopedia,* Volume Q-Z, 1988, p. 604, ed. Geoffrey W. Bromiley). Whatever the special case may have been, what we can know is that by solely touching the deaf man's ears and tongue with His own personal saliva, after Jesus gives His loving and compassionate sovereign word of command—"*Ephphatha!*" (*ef-fath-ah')*, meaning "Be opened!" the deaf-mute's ears were immediately opened, and he began to speak plainly (Thayer's Greek Lexicon, 2009, G2188, p. 265). William Barclay is touched by the special tender consideration that Jesus gave the deaf-mute when healing him. He writes:

> "The whole story shows us most vividly that Jesus did not consider the man merely *a case*; he considered him as *an individual*. The man had a special need and a special problem,

and with the most tender considerateness Jesus dealt with him in a way that spared his feelings and in a way that he could understand" (William Barclay, The Gospel of Luke, 2001, p. 210).

Healing the Blind Man in Bethsaida—Mark 8:22-26

The account of healing the Blind Man in Bethsaida, found exclusively in the Gospel of Mark, is similar in nature to the healing of the deaf-mute. Matthew, Luke, and John have previously written that after Jesus hears about the death of John the Baptist, He gets into a small boat and retreats to a lonely place in Bethsaida. The people hear about His arrival and begin to bring all of their sick loved ones to Him for healing (Matthew 14:14; Luke 9:10-11; John 6:1-3). Mark picks up the narrative by adding that *while* Jesus is in Bethsaida, a blind man is brought to Him, and Jesus takes him by the hand and leads him out of the village.

Healing the Blind Man in Bethsaida – Mark 8:22-26: *"And they came to Bethsaida. And they brought a blind man to Him, and entreated Him to touch him. And taking the blind man by the hand, He brought him out of the village; and after spitting on his eyes, and laying His hands upon him, He asked him, "Do you see anything?" And he looked up and said, "I see men, for I am seeing them like trees, walking about." Then again He laid His hands upon his eyes; and he looked intently and was restored, and began to see everything clearly."*

A few similarities and differences between the healing of the deaf-mute and the healing of the blind man are notable. In the both accounts, Jesus takes them aside privately and uses His personal saliva to heal them. However, in the case of healing the deaf mute, Jesus puts His saliva on His fingers, touches the deaf mute's ears and tongue, and commands the deaf mute's ears to be opened whereas in healing the blind man, Jesus puts His saliva directly on the blind man's eyes and then lays hands on him. As opposed to the immediate healing of the deaf-mute, when Jesus heals the blind man, He does so twice (v. 26). Dr. Lockyer sees this double healing as a double blessing. He observes:

> “The double benediction of the hands of Jesus was effective, for the man saw clearly. If, in His spittle, Jesus gave the man a part of Himself, did virtue also stream from His person through His hands as He touched the man twice? Spurgeon, in his unique, suggestive way, supposes that after the divine touch and the man’s eyes were fully opened, “the first person he saw was Jesus” ” (All of the Miracles of the Bible, 1961, p. 212).

Thus, in both cases, Jesus 1) intimately involves Himself with the individual men, 2) uses His personal saliva, 3) tenderly touches them, and 4) heals them privately. For easy reference, with the exception of the Unclean Spirit that is also recorded by Luke, the following table contains a listing of two unique accounts whereby God ministers His divine healing through the compassionate and merciful hand of Jesus that are found recorded exclusively in the Gospel of Mark.

Table VIII
The Healing Ministry of God through Jesus Recorded in Mark

HEALING	PLACE	MARK	LUKE
1. The Unclean Spirit	Capernaum	1:21-28	4:31-37
2. The Deaf-Mute Man	Decapolis	7:31-35	
3. The Blind Man	Bethsaida	8:22-26	

(Adapted from John MacArthur, "The Healing Ministry of God through Jesus", *The MacArthur Bible Commentary* , 2005, pp. 1152, 1293; Edwin A. Blum, "The Miracles of Jesus", *The Bible Knowledge Commentary: New Testament*, 1983, p. 277, ed. John F. Walvoord, Roy B. Zuck; Colin Brown, "Miracles", Volume K-P, 1986, p. 374, Eerdman's *International Standard Bible Encyclopedia*).

The Healing Ministry of Jesus Recorded by Luke

Healing the Multitudes—Luke 5:15

Beginning with Chapter 5, the following recorded miraculous healings are found exclusively in the Gospel of Luke. In the preceding verses, Luke writes about the Leper who was healed by Jesus while He was in Galilee (Matthew 8:1-4; Mark 1:40-42; Luke 5:12-14). In Matthew's narrative, he records that after Jesus concluded His first great discourse, He came down from the mountain, and a man with leprosy goes to Jesus, bows down before Him, and asks to be cured. After Jesus cures the leper, Matthew takes us to Capernaum where Jesus heals the centurion's servant, Peter's mother-in-law, and the multitudes at Peter's house. Matthew then takes us to Gergesa where Jesus cures the demon possessed man of all of his malicious spirits and then brings us back to Capernaum where the paralytic is lowered down from a rooftop and placed at the feet of Jesus. Somewhere between Jesus travelling between Gergesa and Capernaum (v. 12), Luke records the solitary verse of, *"and great multitudes were gathering to hear Him and to be healed of their sicknesses"* (Luke 5:15).

Refreshingly, this is the first recorded healing of the multitudes wherein we are told that in addition to Jesus healing the multitudes, the multitudes also came to '*hear*' Jesus teach and preach the good news of the kingdom, thus illustrating a unification of Jesus' entire ministry in one solitary verse.

Healing the Multitudes—Luke 5:15: *"and great multitudes were gathering to hear Him and to be healed of their sicknesses."*

Healing the Multitudes—Luke 6:17-19

Returning to Matthew's narratives in Chapter 4, Matthew writes about Jesus travelling throughout all of Galilee preaching the good news of the kingdom and healing every kind of sickness and disease among the people (4:23). Matthew, Mark, and Luke then record that after Jesus selects His twelve disciples (Matthew 10:1-4; Mark 3:13-20; Luke 6:12-16), He goes up on a mountain and begins His first discourse (Sermon on the Mount, Matthew 5:1—7:31). However, before delivering the Sermon on the Mount, Luke guides us through the events that lead up to Jesus' healing of the great multitude. Luke states that Jesus spent the night up on the mountain praying to God, and on the second day, He gathers His disciples and selects twelve whom He names His apostles (vv. 12-16). Then, on His way down from the mountain, Jesus stands at 'a level place' where a great 'throng' of people had gathered to hear Him and to be healed. Similar to Mark's account of the great multitude crowding Jesus in order to touch Him (3:7-11), Luke states that the power emanating from Jesus was so great that the *throng* of people were trying to get close enough to touch Him.

Healing the Multitudes—Luke 6:17-19: *"And He descended with them, and stood on a level place; and there was a great multitude of His disciples, and a great throng of people from all Judea and Jerusalem and the coastal region of Tyre and Sidon, who had come to hear Him, and to be healed of their diseases; and those who were troubled with unclean spirits were being cured. And all the multitude were trying to touch Him, for power was coming from Him and healing them all."*

In similar manner to the multitude Jesus encountered and healed in Mark's narrative of Jesus healing the multitude (3:7-11), Luke uses the word 'throng' to describe the multitude that was waiting for Jesus when

He came down from the mountain. By using the word 'throng', Luke gives us a visual perspective on how the multitude was reacting to Jesus' power. The Oxford Dictionary of English Etymology describes a 'throng' as a large crowd of people who are closely crushed together in a manner that result in pushing and pulling within the crowd (The Concise Oxford Dictionary of English Etymology, 1996, http://www.encyclopedia.com/doc/1O27-throng.html, 2012).

The Mount of the Beatitudes
Image provided by Edward Fudge
http://www.edwardfudge.com/beatitudes.html, 2012.

With very few words, Luke says that purely by the tremendous amount of power radiating from within Jesus, those who were touching Him were being healed instantly (v. 19). Dr. John Gill makes a fastidious point of stating that by virtue of releasing His divine compassionate and merciful healing power from within Himself, all of the believing sick or possessed ones who touched Jesus were immediately healed.

"*There went virtue out of Him*; in great abundance, as water from a fountain; without speaking a word or using any gesture, such as laying his hands on them; *and they were healed*; in this secret and private way, of whatsoever disease they were afflicted with" (Gills Expositor, Exposition of The New Testament, Volume VII, 1976, p. 561).

Dr. John Nolland concludes:

"The healing capacity of the power that went forth from Jesus was complete and it reached them all" (Word Biblical Commentary, Volume 35A, 2000, p. 277, ed. Ralph P. Martin).

The Widow of Nain—Luke 7:11-17

The unique recording of the Widow of Nain by Luke is the second of the three recorded resurrections in Scripture that demonstrate God's omnipotence in restoring the life of loved ones through the almighty powerful and loving hands of Jesus. Luke states that after Jesus healed the centurion's servant in Capernaum (Matthew 8:5-13; Luke 7:2-10), He and His disciples travel south to the city of Nain. As Jesus approaches the gate to the city, by special Providence, He encounters a grief-stricken crowd who are carrying the coffin of a widow's only son to burial.

The Widow of Nain – Luke 7:11-17: *"And it came about soon afterwards, that He went to a city called Nain; and His disciples were going along with Him, accompanied by a large multitude. Now as He approached the gate of the city, behold a dead man was being carried out, the only son of his mother, and she was a widow; and a sizeable crowd from the city was with her"* (vv. 11-12).

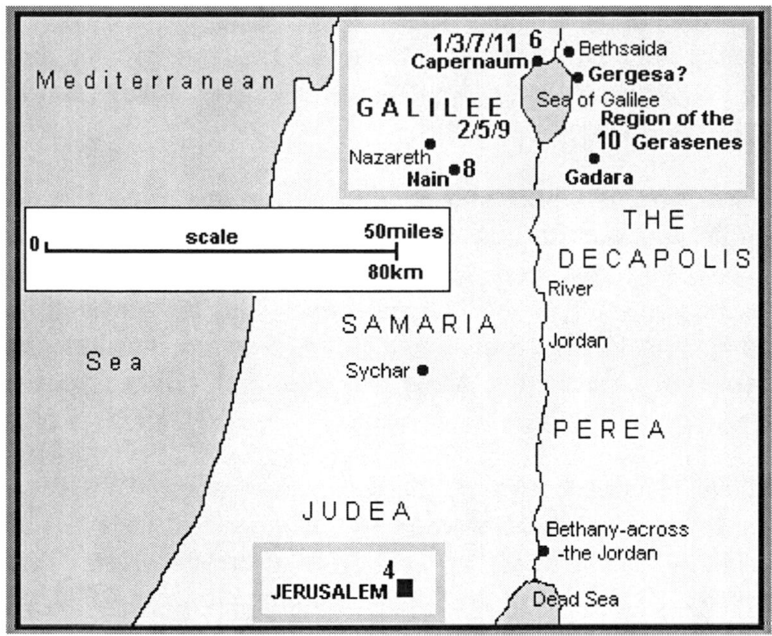

Image provided by J. B. Phillips

http://www.ccel.org/bible/phillips/JBPhillips.htm, 2012.

When Jesus sees the weeping widow, Luke writes, "He felt compassion for her," and said to her,

---

The Widow of Nain – Luke 7:13-15: *" "do not weep." And He came up and touched the coffin; and the bearers came to a halt. And He said, "Young man, I say to you, arise!" And the dead man sat up, and began to speak. And Jesus gave him back to his mother."*

Jesus *saw* her sorrow and *felt* her broken heart so deeply, and without anyone asking, He immediately comforted her by saying, "do not weep." Like the raising of Jarius' daughter, by one sovereign word of His command—'arise', even death obeyed. Though Scripture is silent about the number of days that the widow's son had been dead, we nevertheless see that when Jesus touched the coffin and commanded the boy to arise, death obeyed Him directly. Dr. John Gill offers a touching comment about Jesus' sensitive, loving, tender, and compassionate nature by writing:

> "Wherefore, as Christ showed his power in raising the dead man, he discovered great humanity, kindness, and tenderness, in delivering him alive to his mother; which might be done after he came off of the bier, by taking him by the hand, and leading him to his mother, and giving him up into her arms: think what an affecting scene this must be" (Gills Expositor, Exposition of The New Testament, Volume VII, 1976, p. 568).

William Hendriksen makes the same observation. "What was very clear, however, was this comforting fact, namely, that the *heart* of Jesus went out to this widow in her deep distress" (New Testament Commentary: Exposition of the Gospel according to Luke, 2007, p. 385).

Mary Magdalene and Other Women—Luke 8:1-2

"And it came about soon afterwards, that He began going about from one city and village to another, proclaiming and preaching the kingdom of God; and the twelve were with Him, and also some women who had been healed of evil spirits and sicknesses: Mary who was called Magdalene, from whom seven demons had gone out, and Joanna the wife of Chuza, Herod's steward, and Suzanna, and many others who were contributing to their support out of their private means."

Luke is the only one of the Gospel writers who distinguishes Mary, Joanna, and Suzanna from all of the women whom Jesus healed. Though there is no specific record of their healings, what we can know about Mary, Joanna, and Suzanna is what Luke specifically recorded—they were all touched by the almighty healing hand of Jesus. Of significance, in Luke's account of Mary Magdalene, he specifically states that she was possessed by 'seven' demons, which, as illustrated in the parable of the Return of the Unclean Spirit, metaphorically symbolizes complete dominion (Matthew 12:43-45; Luke 11:24-26). In writing about Mary Magdalene, Dr. Edwin H. Palmer states that after Jesus had cast the demons out of her, she became a devoted follower of Him (Eerdman's *International Standard Bible Encyclopedia*, Volume K-P, 1986, p. 268, ed. Geoffrey W. Bromiley).

The Crippled Woman—Luke 13:10-13

"And He was teaching in one of the synagogues on the Sabbath. And behold, there was a woman who for eighteen years had had a sickness caused by a spirit; and she was bent double, and could not straighten up at all. And when Jesus saw her, He called her over and said to her, "Woman, you are freed from your sickness." And He laid His hands upon her; and immediately she was made erect again, and began glorifying God."

Consistent with Jesus' compassionate and caring nature, while Jesus is teaching in the synagogue, He sees the suffering woman, calls her over to Him, and *before* touching her, Jesus says, "*Woman, you are freed from your sickness.*" Though Luke does not give us any details about the woman's faith, from the narrative, we can easily surmise that when Jesus told her that she was freed, she believed Him. Then with one gentle touch of His loving hand, she is divinely healed, and immediately begins to glorify God. Exactly what Jesus perceived in the suffering woman that had kept her in bondage for so long is not known, but He surely saw through more than just her debilitating disease. Luke says that after Jesus healed her, He is confronted by the synagogue official for healing on the Sabbath, and Jesus refers to her as being 'the daughter of Abraham' whom Satan had kept in bondage for eighteen years (v. 16). Quoting from the ancient writings of John Chrysostom, Dr. Lockyer writes:

> "Chrysostom says, "He lays also His hands on her, that we may learn that the holy body possessed the power and energy of the Word of God." " Thou are loosed"—this is the only passage in the New Testament where this word is used of disease. "Medical writers use it of releasing from disease, relaxing tendons, and taking off bandages." Accompanying the Master's

word of power was a current of new life entering the woman, so that her bonds, spiritual and physical, were loosened. "She was made straight." The word use here to describe her immediate erectness after eighteen years is *setting up* of the tabernacle of David, and of *lifting up* the hands with hang down (Acts 15:16; Hebrews 12:12). And for this immediate, unasked-for act of divine power, there was immediate gratitude, for the woman "glorified God" " (All of the Miracles of the Bible, 1961, p. 224).

Finally, like the healing of Peter's mother-in-law and the widow of Nain, Jesus *saw* the need and healed each of them without being asked.

> *"It will also come to pass that before they call, I will answer"* (Isaiah 65:24a).

The Man with Dropsy—Luke 14:1-4

The setting for the healing of the Man with Dropsy was considered under the section of all of the parables recorded in the Gospel of Luke that can be found under the 'table talk parables' of the Chief Seats and the Great Banquet (Luke 14:7-24). After Jesus heals the crippled woman at the synagogue, Luke states that He is three days journey from Jerusalem, and the Pharisees warn Him not to go because King Herod wanted to kill him. Jesus responds by saying, *"I will cast out demons and perform cures until I reach My goal"* (Luke 13:31-33). Subsequently, Jesus is invited to eat at the house of one of the Pharisee's where He is met by a man suffering from the condition of dropsy.

The Man with Dropsy – Luke 14:1-4: *"And it came about when He went into the house of one of the leaders of the Pharisees on the Sabbath to eat bread, that they were watching Him closely And there, in front of Him was a certain man suffering from dropsy. And Jesus answered and spoke to the lawyers and Pharisees, saying, "Is it lawful to heal on the Sabbath, or not?" But they kept silent. And he took hold of him, and healed him, and sent him away."*

Though Luke is not specific about the severity of the disease that the man was suffering, Dr. Roland Harrison states that the word (hudrōpikos) used by Luke is a medical term widely used by Greek physicians for dropsy. He notes, "It is not a disease in itself, but is the symptom of a disease of the heart, kidneys, or liver that causes water to collect in the limbs, on the surface of the body, or in the abdomen, which indicated the disease was in an advanced stage. Dr. Harrison further states that the symptoms could only be cured if the disease itself was curable" (Eerdman's *International Standard Bible Encyclopedia,* Volume A-D, 1979, p. 994, ed. Geoffrey W. Bromiley). Thus, in accordance with the bountiful character of God in showing

His loving kindness, mercy, and love that is completely unmerited, Jesus did not heal the symptoms of the man's disease, He 'took hold of him', and with a single touch of His power filled hands, He healed his disease completely.

Noteworthy, and with the exception of Jesus divinely healing the man at the pool of Bethesda and the man born blind recorded by *John*, this is the last of the *seven* recorded healings Jesus divinely effected on the Sabbath day that are recorded by the four Gospel writers:

1) The healing of the man with a withered hand (Matthew 12:9-14; Mark 3:1-6; Luke 6:6-11).
2) Casting out the unclean spirit (Mark 1:21-27; Luke 4:31-37).
3) Healing the crippled woman (Luke 13:10-13).
4) Healing the man with dropsy (Luke 14:1-4).
5) Healing Peter's mother-in-law (Matthew 8:14-15; Mark 1:30-31; Luke 4:38-39).
6) Healing the lame man at the pool of Bethesda (John 5:1-9).
7) Healing the man born blind in Jerusalem (John 9:1-14).

The Ten Lepers—Luke 17:11-21

"And it came about while He was on the way to Jerusalem, that He was passing between Samaria and Galilee. And as He entered a certain village, there met Him ten leprous men, who stood at a distance; and they raised their voices, saying, "Jesus, Master, have mercy on us!" And when He saw them, He said to them, "Go and show yourselves to the priests." And it came about that as they were going, they were cleansed."

Like the miraculous healing of the centurion's servant, the power of Jesus to heal from afar is demonstrated by the Ten Lepers, who, from a distance cry out to Jesus for mercy. As a testimony to the full power of His Deity, without a commanding word or touch, Jesus responds by simply saying,—*"Go and show yourselves to the priests"*, and before they arrived, they were all healed. Moreover, of the ten lepers who were healed, Luke states that one of lepers was a Samaritan, who, when he saw that he had already been healed, turned back glorifying God, and with deep gratitude, fell on his face at the feet of Jesus, and thanked Him. In response to his heartfelt gratitude, Jesus blesses him a second time by granting him the miraculous free gift of salvation (v. 19). Quoting from Charles J. Ellicott's comments on this deeply touching act by the Samaritan, Dr. Lockyer states:

> "His cure was confirmed by Jesus and to it was added the moral cure—a pronounced salvation. "The nine had health of their body," says Ellicott; "his had gone further, and had given a new and purer life to his soul" " (All of the Miracles of the Bible, 1961, p. 232).

"Your faith has made you whole" (v. 19a).

Malchus' Ear—Luke 22:50-51

The essence of the compassionate heart of Jesus is demonstrated by the extraordinary divine restoration of a bodily member to the very man who is ironically the one who was sent to lead Jesus to His death, fully illustrates the very essence of Jesus' new kingdom principle of love your enemies and pray for those who persecute you (Matthew 5:43). Moreover, though we have not yet covered the healing ministry of God through Jesus as recorded by *John*, the restoration of Malchus' ear is the last divine healing of Jesus' earthly ministry recorded in the Gospel of Luke.

MATTHEW	MARK	LUKE	JOHN
"And behold, one of those who were with Jesus reached and drew out his sword, and struck the slave of the high priest, and cut off his ear. Then Jesus said to him, "Put your sword back into its place; for all those who take up the sword shall perish by the sword" " (26:51-52).	*"But a certain one of those who stood by drew his sword, and struck the slave of the high priest, and cut his ear. And Jesus answered and said to them, "Have you come out with swords and clubs to arrest Me, as though I were a Robber?" "* (14:47-48).	*"And a certain one of them struck the slave of the high priest and cut off his right ear But Jesus answered and said, "Stop! No more of this." And He touched his ear and healed him"* (22:50-51).	*"Simon Peter therefore having a sword, drew it, and struck the high priest's slave, and cut off his right ear; and the slave's name was Malchus. Jesus therefore said to Peter, "Put the sword into sheath; the cup which the Father has given Me, shall I not drink it?" "* (18:10-11).

While this incident is recorded by all four Gospel writers, typical of Luke's meticulous attention to detail, he is the only one to record that Jesus *healed* Malchus' ear, while John is the only one to give us his name. In one last touching demonstration of His deep compassion for humanity, Jesus witnessing the violent destruction of Malchus' ear, calmly reached out and with a loving touch of His healing grace, Malchus' ear was miraculously restored to him.

For easy reference, with the exception of the restoration of Malchus' ear that is recorded by all four Gospel writers, the following table contains a list of the unique divine healings of God manifested through the compassionate hand of Jesus that are solely recorded in the Gospel of Luke.

Table IX
The Healing Ministry of God through Jesus Recorded in Luke

HEALING	PLACE	LUKE
1. The Multitudes	Galilee	5:15
2. The Multitudes	Galilee	6:17-19
3. The Widow of Nain	Nain	7:11-17
4. Mary Magdalene and Other Woman		8:2
5. The Crippled Woman	Perea	13:10-13
6. The Man with Dropsy	Perea	14:1-4
7. Ten Lepers	Samaria/Galilee	17:11-21
8. *Malchus' Ear	Jerusalem	22:50-51

*(Matthew 26:51-52; Mark 14:47-48; Luke 22:50-51 John 18:10-11).

(Adapted from John MacArthur, "The Healing Ministry of God through Jesus", *The MacArthur Bible Commentary* , 2005, pp. 1152, 1293; Edwin A. Blum, "The Miracles of Jesus"*, The Bible Knowledge Commentary: New Testament*, 1983, p. 277, ed. John F. Walvoord, Roy B. Zuck; Colin Brown, "Miracles", Volume K-P, 1986, p. 374, Eerdman's *International Standard Bible Encyclopedia*).

The Healing Ministry of Jesus Recorded by John

The Nobleman's Son—John 4:46-54

Whereas Matthew highlights the ministry of Jesus from the viewpoint of His Kingship as Son of David, Mark highlights Jesus' ministry from the viewpoint of His servitude as the Son of God, and Luke highlights the ministry of Jesus from the viewpoint of His Humanity as Savior. John on the other hand highlights Jesus' ministry from the viewpoint of His Deity as the eternal Son of God. Beginning in Chapter 4 of the Gospel of John, commonly known as 'the love book', the following miraculous healings are recorded exclusively by John.

From preceding accounts recorded by Matthew, we know that Jesus is on His way to Jerusalem from Jericho. Before He arrives, Matthew notes that Jesus stops at Bethphage before making His triumphal entry into Jerusalem. However, John fills in the narrative by adding that while Jesus is on His way to Cana, He calls his first four disciples who were Andrew, Peter, Philip, and Nathanael (John 1:37-51). While in Cana, Jesus goes to a wedding (where He miraculously changes water to wine (John 2:1-11), then travels to Capernaum where He stays a few days before going on to Jerusalem (2:12-13). When Jesus arrives at Jerusalem, he goes to the temple, finds the moneychangers and overthrows their tables, rebukes them, and cleanses the temple (vv. 14-16). After overturning the tables of the moneychangers at the temple, the blind and the lame went to Jesus, and He healed them all (Matthew 21:1-14). In John's narrative, after Jesus leaves Jerusalem, before He journeys through Samaria (where He meets the Samaritan woman at the well (4:3-24), He returns to Judea for a few days before going back to Cana in Galilee (3:22). Arriving in Cana, John now introduces us to the royal official from Capernaum whose son is gravely ill.

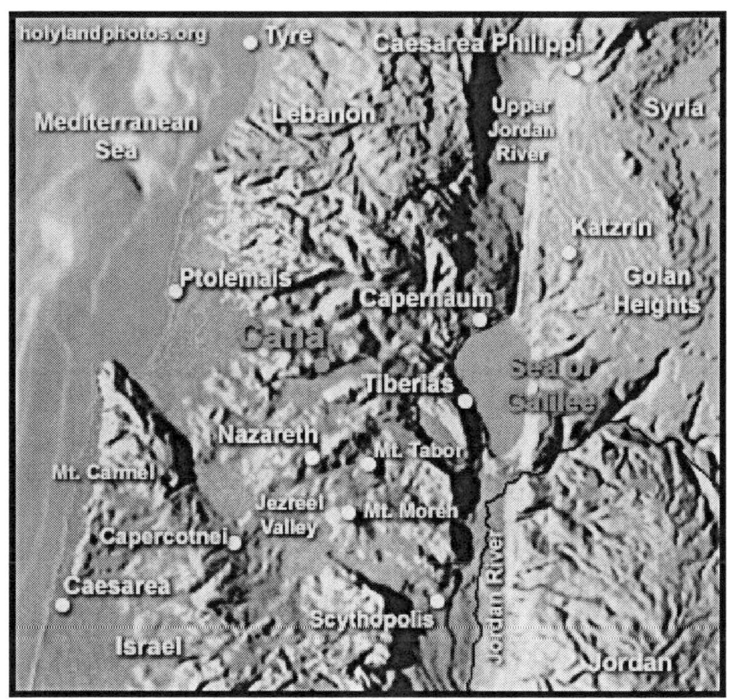

Cana in Galilee between Capernaum and Nazareth
Image provided by Bible Atlas
http://www.gods-word-first.org/bible-maps/cana-bible-map.html, 2010.

John inconspicuously reveals that in addition to Cana being the place where Jesus first manifested His glory at the wedding, the healing of the nobleman's son is the only recorded miraculous *healing* in Cana.

The Nobleman's Son – John 4:46-53: *"He came therefore again to Cana of Galilee where He had made the water wine. And there was a certain royal official whose son was sick at Capernaum. When he heard that Jesus had come out of Judea into Galilee, he went to Him, and was requesting Him to come down and heal his son; for he was at the point of death. Jesus therefore said to him, "Unless you people see* *signs and wonders, you simply will not believe." The royal official said to Him, "Sir, come down before my child dies." Jesus said to him, "Go your way; your son lives." The man believed the word that Jesus spoke to him, and he started off. And as he was now going down, his slaves met him, saying that his son was living. So he inquired of them the hour when he began to get better. They said therefore to him, "Yesterday at the seventh hour the fever left him." So the father knew that it was at that hour in which Jesus said to him, "Your son lives"; and he himself believed, and his whole household."*

Reminiscent of Matthew's accounts of the healing of the centurion's servant whom Jesus healed from afar (8:5-13), and of the resurrection of Jarius' daughter (9:18-19), like the centurion, when the nobleman 'heard' that Jesus was in Cana, he immediately leaves Capernaum to seek Him. However, unlike the centurion whose faith Jesus publicly commended, or that of Jarius' who believed that Jesus' divine power was limitless, the nobleman entreats Jesus to "come *before* she dies," illustrating that his faith in Jesus' almighty power to heal was *not* absolute. Nevertheless, being the full embodiment of the omniscient, omnipotent, and omnipresent God, by Jesus merely speaking the words, *"go, your son lives"*, the nobleman believed, and his son was healed instantly. On the road home, when the nobleman meets up with his slaves and they give him the news that his son was well, the nobleman's feeble faith goes from a flickering ray of hope to a burning flame of fire, and he and his entire household were saved (4:54). Quoting from the works of John Laidlaw, Dr. Herbert Lockyer writes:

> "In all these healing miracles Jesus takes the utmost pains to call out faith on the part of those to be healed, or (as in this case at Cana) those who sought healing for their dear ones. Notice the instructive variety which these narratives give us, of kinds and actions of faith. Sometimes Jesus is tenderly directing a weak faith. Again, by apparent refusal, he is drawing into view the strength of a strong faith. Another time,

> He is teaching that miracle is not the cause of faith so much as it's a reward; that bodily cures are chiefly of use to bring spiritual help; that belief in Him as a Healer is meant to lead men to faith in Him as a Saviour" (All of the Miracles of the Bible, 1961, p. 164).

Finally, concurring with Laidlaw's exposition quoted by Dr. Lockyer, George R. Beasley-Murray writes:

> "The clue to the Evangelist's purpose in the narrative, its "sign" value lies in the threefold reference to the statement of Jesus to the officer: "Your son lives" (vv 50, 51, 53). The healing of the boy is a sign of the power of Jesus to give life, which in the discourse that follows will be defined as "eternal life" (5:24), and even life from the dead, resurrection life. Its appropriateness to the latter aspect is clear in the light of 4:47—the boy was at the point of death. Along with the emphasis on the word of Jesus, the narrative reveals a corresponding progression in the officer's faith (vv 48, 50, 53). These two features, the authoritative word of the Lord and the faith of the officer, provide "the form by which the final truth is made known" " (Word Biblical Commentary, Volume 36, Second Edition, 2000, p. 263, ed. Ralph P. Martin).

The Lame Man at Bethesda—John 5:1-9

John's exclusive account of Jesus healing the lame man at Bethesda begins with John's opening statement, *"After these things"*, meaning the account of the miracle at Cana, the cleansing of the temple, healing the royal official's son, Jesus' journey through Samaria, His stay in Judea, His return to Cana, and His return to Jerusalem for Passover. After these things, John writes, Jesus arrives at Jerusalem, and as He is passing by the pool of Bethesda, He *sees* the lame man lying by the pool and stops to heal him.

The Lame Man – John 5:1-9: *"After these things there was a feast of the Jews; and Jesus went up to Jerusalem. Now there is in Jerusalem by the sheep gate a pool, which is called in Hebrew Bethesda, having five porticoes. In these lay a multitude of those who were sick, blind, lame, withered, waiting for the moving of the waters; for an angel of the Lord went down at certain seasons into the pool, and stirred up the water; whoever then first, after the stirring up of the water, stepped in was made well from whatever disease with which he was afflicted. And a certain man was there, who had been thirty-eight years in his sickness. When Jesus saw him lying there, and knew that he had already been a long time in that condition, He said to him, "Do you wish to get well?" The sick man answered Him, "Sir, I have no man to put me into the pool when the water is stirred up, but while I am coming, another steps down before me." Jesus said to him, "Arise, take up your pallet, and walk." And immediately the man became well, and took up his pallet and began to walk."*

The Pool of Bethesda has been identified at the north side of the city, (Dr. Dorothea W. Harvey, Eerdman's *International Standard Bible Encyclopedia,* Volume K-P, 1986, p. 905, ed. Geoffrey W. Bromiley). Images provided by http://commons.wikimediaorg/wiki/Pool_of_Bethesda; http://www.bible-study-lessons.com/Jesus-on-the-cross-2.html, 2010.

The title "Pool of Bethesda" is translated from the Greek word *Bethzatha*, meaning "house of mercy, or flowing water", and is only mentioned once in the New Testament (Thayer's Greek Lexicon, 2009, G964, p. 101). William Hendriksen comments, "In those days, the waters of the pool were believed to receive supernatural power to heal only when it was intermittently stirred by an angel of the Lord." John also comments on those who would lay in wait until the waters were stirred (v. 7). Hendriksen furthers states that when the waters would be supernaturally stirred, the first ones to enter the pool were the ones who would be healed (New Testament Commentary: Exposition of the Gospel according to John, 2007, p. 190). Consistent with the compassionate nature of Jesus, as He is passing by the pool, He *sees* the invalid man helplessly lying in wait and stops to ask him if he would like to be healed. However, in lieu of answering Jesus' question directly, the lame man gives Jesus the reason why he has not yet been healed (v. 7). Nevertheless, Jesus responds compassionately saying, "*Arise, take up your pallet, and walk*" (v. 8), and the lame man believed, immediately rose, took up his pallet, and for the first time in thirty-eight years, began to walk. But it doesn't end there—John continues by adding that they later meet in the temple and Jesus cautions him to sin no more or something worse would befall him (v. 14). In Dr. Beasley-Murray's summation, he quotes the wise words of E. Hoskins stating: "There is a more serious disease than lameness or paralysis; there is a more serious possibility of judgment, and there is a righteousness that sets men free" (Word Biblical Commentary, Volume 36, Second Edition, 2000, p. 263, ed. Ralph P. Martin). Hendriksen further observes, "Jesus is not referring to the man's past illness, but to the present condition of the man. Right now, he was in the state of being unreconciled with God. Jesus knew this and warns him not to continue in that condition" (Ibid., p. 195).

Finally, like the widow of Nain (Luke 7:11-17), the crippled woman whom Jesus healed in the synagogue (Luke 13:10-13), and Peter's mother-in-law (Matthew 8:14-15; Mark 1:30-31; Luke 4:38-39), by the omnipotent, compassionate, and merciful hand of Jesus, before they asked, He answered (Isaiah 65:24), and graciously healed them all.

> *"Behold, thou art made whole"* (John 5:14).

The Man Born Blind—John 9:1-7

The man born blind is the last of the *seven* recorded miraculous healings that Jesus accomplished on the Sabbath. Before concluding The healing ministry of God through Jesus as recorded by the four Gospel writers, it is noteworthy to outline Jesus' travels and divine healings accomplished *after* He healed the lame man at the pool of Bethesda. Prior to Jesus healing the man born blind, the combined narratives of Matthew, Mark, Luke, and John state that after Jesus met the lame man in the synagogue, He left Jerusalem and travelled north to Galilee. During the course of His journey, Jesus heals the man with the withered hand (Matthew 12:9; Mark 3:1; Luke 6:6), the multitudes throughout the land (Matthew 12:15; Mark 3:7), and then goes back to Capernaum (Matthew 8:5; Luke 7:1) where He heals the Roman centurion's servant (Matthew 8:5; Luke 7:2). Subsequently, as Jesus is travelling throughout Galilee, He resurrects the widow's son of Nain (Luke 7:11), heals the demon possessed man in Gergesa (Matthew 8:28; Mark 5:2; Luke 8:27), and goes back across the Sea of Galilee (Mark 5:21) to Capernaum (Matthew 9:1). Entering into Capernaum Jesus heals the woman who had been hemorrhaging for eighteen years and returns Jarius' daughter to him by raising her from the dead (Matthew 9:20; Mark 5:25; Luke 8:43). Jesus then travels from Capernaum through Nazareth (Mark 6:1), and continuing His journey through Galilee (Matthew 13:58; Mark 6:6), He returns to Capernaum once again (Mark 6:30, Luke 9:10).

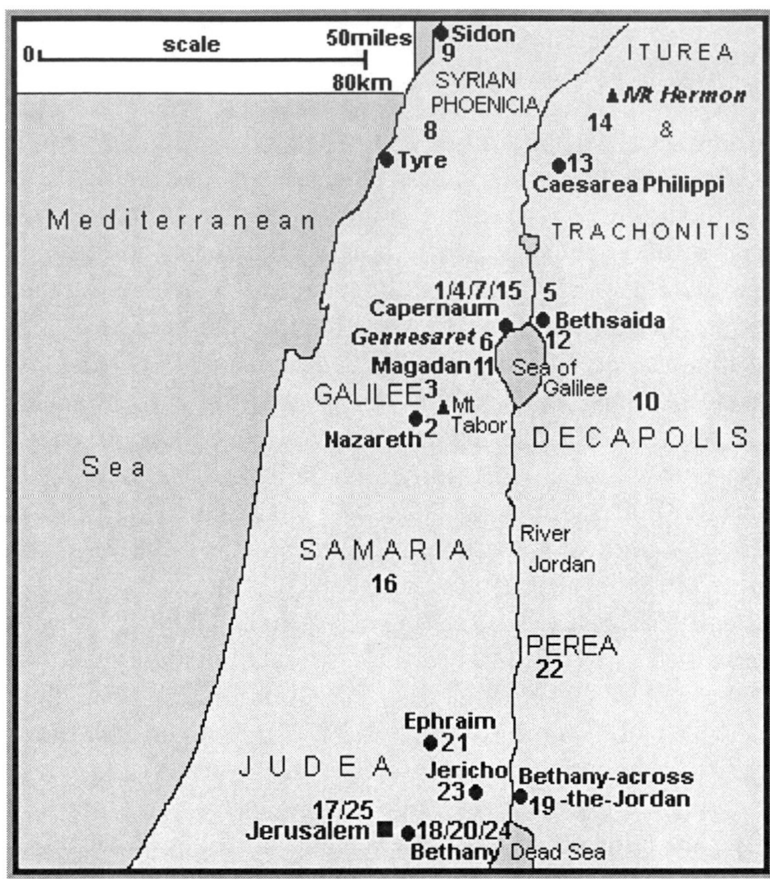

Image provided by J. B. Phillips
http://www.ccel.org/bible/phillips/JBPhillips.htm, 2012.

From Capernaum, Jesus and His disciples travel by boat to a quiet place (Mark 6:32) near Bethsaida where Jesus saw a great multitude, felt compassion, and healed all of their sick (Matthew 14:14; Luke 9:10; John 6:2). The disciples then cross the Sea of Galilee (Matthew 14:22; Mark 6:45), and land near the Plain of Gennesaret where a great many people from all the surrounding district came to Jesus to be healed, and as many of those who touched His outer garment were immediately healed (Matthew 14:34; Mark 6:53). From Gennesaret, Jesus and His disciples make their way back to Capernaum (John 6:24), and along the way Jesus heals the Syrophoenician's daughter

(Matthew 15:21; Mark 7:25). On His way back to Jerusalem (Luke 9:51; John 7:10), Jesus travels through the region of the 'ten cities', heals the deaf mute man (Mark 7:32), passes by Samaria and heals the ten lepers (Luke 17:11) before arriving at Jerusalem for the Feast of the Tabernacles (John 7:10). John now fills in the narrative by introducing us to the man born blind (John 9:1), who, after having his eyesight restored to him on the Sabbath, is interrogated by the Pharisees and thrown out of the synagogue. Subsequently, Jesus seeks him, finds him, and blesses him a second time by granting him the miraculous free gift of salvation (vv. 13-38)

The Man Born Blind – John 9:1-7: *"And as He passed by, He saw a man blind from birth. And His disciples asked Him, saying, "Rabbi, who sinned, this man or his parents, that he should be born blind?" Jesus answered, "It was neither that this man sinned, nor his parents, but it was in order that the works of God might be displayed in him." We must work the works of Him who sent Me, as long as it is day; night is coming, when no man can work. "While I am in the world, I am the light of the world." When He had said this, He spat on the ground, and made clay of the spittle, and applied the clay to his eyes, and said to him, "Go, wash in the pool of Siloam" (which is translated, Sent). And so he went away and washed, and came back seeing."*

Similarities between Jesus healing the deaf-mute (Mark 7:31), healing the blind man in Bethsaida (Mark 8:22), and this special account of the man born blind are notable. In all three special cases, Jesus used His personal saliva to heal them. Also worthy of mention are the similarities of the double blessing that the paralytic (Matthew 9:1-2; Mark 2:1-5; Luke 5:17-20), the blind man of Bethsaida (Mark 8:22-26), and the blind beggar receive. Using clay mixed with His personal saliva, Jesus first restores the blind beggar's sight, and then restores his soul. Moreover, the disciples assume that the man was born blind because of sin. However, Jesus makes it plainly known to them that his blindness could be traced back to God's omniscience in allowing the man to be born blind in this special place and time so that through the divine restoration of his blindness, His Deity may be made manifest to him personally, and to all others. After Jesus restores the blind man's sight, John notes that although the man now sees, he does not yet perceive, as illustrated by the interrogation of the Pharisees (v. 13-33). Part two of John's narrative reveals that it is *after* the man is thrown out of the synagogue that Jesus *seeks* him and finds him. Knowing that the man did not yet perceive, Jesus reveals Himself to him, and by this revelation, the man recognizes Jesus as being the Son of God, confesses his faith, and falls on his face in worship (vv. 34-38). As Divine Providence would have it, through the blind man's intimate experience with Jesus, his physical and spiritual healing became a testimony to all. In Dr. Lockyer final analysis, he perceptively notes the progress in which the man goes from gaining his physical sight to gaining his spiritual sight. He writes:

> "It is interesting to note the man's progress of knowledge respecting his Healer. He speaks of Him as a Man (v. 11), a Prophet (v. 17), from God (v. 33), Son of God (v. 38). Is ours an ever-deepening knowledge of Him? Is ours the confession, "Whereas I was blind, now I see?" This man believed, confessed and worshiped" (All of the Miracles of the Bible, 1961, p. 223).

"if you confess with your mouth Jesus as Lord, and believe in your heart that God raised Him from the dead, you shall be saved" (Romans 10:9).

The Resurrection of Lazarus—John 11:1-45

The crowning miracle that closes Jesus' earthly healing ministry is the stupendous miracle of the resurrection of Lazarus, which is recorded exclusively in the Gospel of John. Moreover, like the man who was divinely purposed to be blind from birth, Jesus reveals that God also allowed Lazarus to meet death so that through his resurrection, the full Deity of Christ may be manifested to the world one last time. John begins the lengthy narrative by taking us to Perea, where sometime after the Feast of the Tabernacles, he writes that Jesus leaves Jerusalem and travels to Bethabara located on the east bank of the Jordan River (1:28 KJV), which is where John the Baptist first began his ministry (10:40). While Jesus is working at Bethabara, He receives a message that His friend Lazarus is deathly ill. Instead of immediately travelling back to Judea, Jesus tells the messenger that *"his sickness was not unto death, but for the glory of God that the Son of God may be glorified by it"* (v. 4), and delays His journey for two additional days (v. 7).

The Resurrection of Lazarus – John 11:1-45: *"Now a certain man was sick, Lazarus of Bethany, of the village of Mary and her sister Martha. And it was the Mary who anointed the Lord with ointment, and wiped His feet with her hair, whose brother Lazarus was sick. The sisters therefore sent to Him, saying "Lord, behold, he whom You love is sick." But when Jesus heard it, He said, "This sickness is not unto death, but for the glory of God, that the Son of God may be glorified by it." Now Jesus loved Martha, and her sister, and Lazarus. When therefore He heard that he was sick, He stayed then two days longer in the place where He was. Then after this He said to the disciples, "Let us go to Judea again." The disciples said to Him, "Rabbi, the Jews were just now seeking to stone You; and are You going there again?" Jesus answered, "Are there not twelve hours in the day? If anyone walks in the day, he does not stumble, because he sees the light of this world. But if anyone walks in the night, he stumbles, because the light* *is not in him." This He said, and after that He said to them, "Our friend Lazarus has fallen asleep; but I go, that I may awake him out of sleep." The disciples therefore said to Him, "Lord, if he has fallen asleep, he will recover." Now Jesus had spoken of his death; but they thought that He was speaking of literal sleep. Then Jesus therefore said to them plainly, "Lazarus is dead, and I am glad for your sakes that I was not there, so that you may believe; but let us go to him." Thomas therefore, who is called Didymus, said to his fellow disciples, "Let us also go, that we may die with Him." So when Jesus came, He found that he had already been in the tomb four days. Now Bethany was near Jerusalem, about two miles off; and many of the Jews had come to Martha and Mary, to console them concerning their brother. Martha therefore, when she heard that Jesus was coming, went to meet Him; but Mary still sat in the house. Martha therefore said to Jesus, "Lord, if You had been here, my brother would not have died. Even now I know that whatever You ask of God, God will give You." Jesus said to her, "Your brother shall rise again." Martha said to Him, "I know that he will rise again in the resurrection on the last day." Jesus said to her, "I am the resurrection and the life; he who believes in Me shall live even if he dies, and everyone who lives and believes in Me shall never die. Do you believe this?" She said to Him, "Yes, Lord; I have believed that You are the Christ, the Son of God, even He who comes in the world." And when she had said this, she went away, and called Mary her sister, saying secretly, "The Teacher is here, and is calling for you." And when she heard it, she arose quickly, and was coming to Him. Now Jesus had not yet come into the village, but was still in the place where Martha met Him. The Jews then who were with her in the house, and consoling her, when they saw that Mary rose up quickly and went out, followed her, supposing that she was going to the tomb to weep there. Therefore, when Mary came where Jesus was, she saw Him, and fall at His feet, saying to Him, "Lord, if You had been here, my brother would not have died." When Jesus therefore saw her weeping, and the Jews who came with her, also weeping, He was deeply moved in spirit, and was troubled, and said, "Where have you laid him?" They said to Him, "Lord, come and see." Jesus wept. And so the Jews were saying, "Behold how He loved him!" But some of them said, "Could not this man, who opened the eyes of him who was blind, have kept this man also from dying?" Jesus therefore again being deeply moved within, came to the tomb. Now it was a cave, and a stone was lying against it. Jesus said, "Remove the stone." Martha, the sister of the deceased, said to Him, "Lord, by this time there will be a stench; for he has been dead four days." Jesus said to her, "Did I not say to you, if you believe, you will see the glory of God?" And so they removed the stone. And Jesus raised His eyes, and said, "Father, I thank Thee that Thou heardest Me. And I knew that Thou hearest Me always; but because of the people standing around I said it, that they may believe that Thou didst send Me." And when He had said these things, He cried out with a loud voice, "Lazarus, come forth." He who had died came forth, bound hand and foot with wrappings; and his face was wrapped around with a cloth. Jesus said to them, "Unbind him, and let him go." Many therefore of the Jews, who had come to Mary and beheld what He had done, believed in Him"* (John 11:1-45).

In John's beautifully written narrative of the miraculous resurrection of a dearly loved one, the expressions of differing depths of faith and human emotion by differing personalities are brought to light. The first illustration of *limited* faith is exemplified by the conversation between Jesus and His disciples. After Jesus hears about Lazarus' sickness, He delays His journey to Bethany for two days. Afterwards, Jesus tells His disciples that 'Lazarus has fallen asleep'; let us go back to Judea (vv. 6-11). John, in his loving way, writes that the disciples thought that Jesus meant it literally so did not understand why they would have to go back to Bethany (v. 13). In Jesus' own loving way, He rebukes His disciples by plainly telling them that Lazarus has died, and for the sake of their own faith, He was glad that He was not there when it happened (vv. 14-15).

Now we see the wavering of faith of two sisters—Martha, who was more practical than spiritual, and Mary, who was more spiritual than practical (Luke 10:38-42). John illustrates the strength of their faith by stating that the message they sent to Jesus simply stated, *"he whom You love is sick"* (v. 3), which implies that they either assumed that

Jesus would immediately come to heal Lazarus as He had done with so many others, or that Jesus would heal him from afar. In either case, it is through Martha that John describes the differences in the emotional state of mourning they each were experiencing. When Martha hears that Jesus was coming, she immediately goes to meet Him and reaffirms her faith by telling Jesus that ***if*** He had been with them Lazarus would not have died; then she says, "even now I know that whatever you ask God He will give it to you" (vv. 20-22). Yet, when Jesus tells Martha that Lazarus will rise again, she responds by saying, 'yes, I know he will rise again on the last day', illustrating as the disciples did, that she had not yet fully grasped the fullness of Jesus' Deity or of His omnipotence (vv. 23-27). Likewise, though Mary falls at Jesus' feet in worship, by expressing the same words, *"Lord,* ***if*** *You had been here, my brother would not have died",* like Martha did (v. 32), also illustrates that she did not fully grasp the full extent of His Deity either. John then poignantly writes—*"When Jesus saw her weeping, and the Jews who came with her, also weeping, He was deeply moved and troubled in spirit—and He wept"* (v. 33). Through this deeply moving scene, and by the short conversation that Jesus had with Martha that follows, John clearly illustrates that their faith in Him was still quite limited. After recording this deeply moving scene, John writes that when Jesus asked for the stone to be removed from the burial site, Martha reminds Him that Lazarus' body was already in the state of decomposition (vv. 38-40).

Of great significance, the recorded prayer illustrates that when Jesus thanks His Father for what He *knew* was already done, it was specifically meant for the people so that by the stupendous, omnipotent, divine transfer of Lazarus from a decomposing state of death back to life, they would ultimately come to believe in Him (vv. 41-42). Then, with one climatic shout, Jesus commands Lazarus to come forth from the grave. Through the dramatic, unforgettable, and omniscient fully efficacious resurrection of Lazarus, many of the Jews who beheld this stupendous miracle believed in Him (v. 45). Later, John writes that Mary, in worship of Jesus, manifested her deep faith in Jesus by anointing His feet with very expensive oil and wiping them with her own hair (12:1-3). In his closing remarks, Dr. George R. Beasley-Murray highlights these reflective words:

> "The name Bishop Gore gave to the community he founded is an excellent characterization of the Church: "The Community of the Resurrection." Insofar as we who bear the name of Christian fail to recognize who we are, we do well to ponder again the sign of Lazarus, and grasp afresh the present relationship of faith as well as the joy of hope for the future" (Word Biblical Commentary, Volume 36, Second Edition, 2000, p. 263, ed. Ralph P. Martin).

Finally, in a few short days, the most important eternal life giving, and fully efficacious resurrection miracle would take place—the resurrection of Jesus Christ our Lord (Matthew 28; Mark 16; Luke 24; John 20).

By tracing the footprints of God's miraculous healings through the eyes of the four Gospel writers, we discovered that there were no two individual healings alike. Each divine healing was accomplished by our omniscient, omnipotent, and omnipresent God through the loving, compassionate, and all-powerful hands of His Son, Jesus Christ, efficaciously affecting, strengthening, or engendering the heart of each man's faith. For easy reference, the following table contains a list of the four unique divine healings of God through the compassionate hand of Jesus that are recorded exclusively by John.

> *"I am the resurrection and the life; he who believes in Me shall live even if he dies,"* (John 11:25).

Table X
The Healing Ministry of God through Jesus Recorded in John

HEALING	PLACE	JOHN
1. The Nobleman's Son	Capernaum	4:46-54
2. The Lame Man	Jerusalem	5:1-9
3. The Man Born Blind	Jerusalem	9:1-7
4. The Resurrection of Lazarus	Bethany	11:1-45

(Adapted from John MacArthur, "The Healing Ministry of God through Jesus", *The MacArthur Bible Commentary* , 2005, pp. 1152, 1293; Edwin A. Blum, "The Miracles of Jesus", *The Bible Knowledge Commentary: New Testament*, 1983, p. 277, ed. John F. Walvoord, Roy B. Zuck; Colin Brown, "Miracles", Volume K-P, 1986, p. 374, Eerdman's *International Standard Bible Encyclopedia*).

The Nature Miracles of God Manifested through Jesus

The Pre-Resurrection Miraculous Catch of Fish —Luke 5:1-11

Luke and John are the only two Gospel writers who record the two nature miracles of the miraculous catch of fish. Whereas Luke's meticulous account of the miraculous catch of fish is on the pre-resurrection occurrence, John's account is on the post-resurrection occurrence. Luke's account is easily remembered as being attached to the commissioning of Simon Peter as Jesus' disciple, or as Jesus lovingly termed it, 'catcher of men' (5:10). Tracing the footprints of God through the Gospel of Luke, he writes that after Jesus was baptized by John, He was led by the Spirit into the wilderness for forty days (4:1-13), and returned to Galilee to inaugurate His ministry (14). Luke continues the trail by stating that Jesus went to Nazareth, was rejected by the Nazarenes (vv. 16-29), travels to Capernaum, cures the man with the unclean spirit in the synagogue (v. 31-35), leaves the synagogue, goes to Peter's house and heals his mother-in-law (vv. 38-39). As the sun was setting, all of those who were sick or diseased were brought to Jesus, and He healed them all (vv. 40-41). At daybreak, Jesus leaves Capernaum and continues His ministry preaching in the synagogues throughout Judea (v. 44). Luke then takes us to the shore of the Sea of Galilee where the multitudes who had gathered to see Jesus begin to crowd Him. Jesus sees Simon Peter's boat, gets into it, asks Peter to put the boat out away from the shore, and continues teaching the multitude from the boat (5:1-3). Luke now introduces us to the miracle.

The Pre-Resurrection Miraculous Catch of Fish – Luke 5:1-11: *"Now it came about that while the multitude were pressing Him and listening to the word of God, He was standing by the lake of Gennesaret; and He saw two boats lying at the edge of the lake; but the fishermen had gotten out of them, and were washing their nets. And He got into one of the boats, which was Simon's, and asked him to put out a little way from the land. And He sat down and began teaching the multitudes from the boat. And when He had finished speaking, He said to Simon, "Put out into the deep water and let down your nets for a catch." And Simon answered and said, "Master, we worked hard all night and caught nothing, but at Your bidding I will let down the nets." And when they had done this, they enclosed a great quantity of fish; and their nets began to break; and they signaled to their partners in the other boat, for them to come and help them. And they came, and filled both of the boats, so that they began to sink. But when Simon Peter saw that, he fell down at Jesus feet, saying, "Depart from me, for I am a sinful man, O Lord!" For amazement had seized him and all his companions because of the catch of fish which they had taken; and so also James and John, sons of Zebedee, who were partners with Simon. And Jesus said to Simon, "Do not fear, from now on you will be catching men." And when they had brought their boats to land, they left everything and followed Him."*

Luke states that when Jesus had finished speaking to the multitude, He tells Simon Peter to launch the boat out into deeper water and cast out his fish net. Simon Peter, having previously fished all night and caught absolutely nothing, tells Jesus that they worked all night and did not catch a single fish. Nevertheless, Simon Peter says, *"I will do as you say and let down the fish nets"* (vv. 4-5). The moment Simon Peter casts his net into the sea, the omnipotent words, "*let down your net for a catch,"* instantaneously caused all of that which is beneath the sea to supernaturally hear and obey the sovereign command of Jesus. Luke states that the miraculous catch was so great that their nets began to break, so they had to call another boat to come and help them else the weight of the abundant catch would sink the boat.

Sea of Galilee
Photo provided by Wikimedia Commons

Miraculous Draught of Fish
Art by Raffaello Sanzio (1515, Roma)
Photo provided by Gallery of Art

http://commons.wikimediaorg/wiki/Pool_of_Bethesda, http://www.wga.hu/frames-e.html?/html/r/raphael/6tapestr/2draught.html, 2012.

In his study of the Sea of Galilee, Dr. Roland K. Harrison describes the sea as being pear shaped with the narrow end pointing south, and the wider end at the northwest. The sea was also known by other names such as Lake Gennesaret, Sea of Tiberius, and 'the sea'. It was only about thirteen miles long and eight miles wide, and "is the place where much of Jesus' ministry took place" (Eerdman's *International Standard Bible Encyclopedia,* Volume E-J, 1979, p. 391, ed. Geoffrey W. Bromiley).

Satellite Photo provided by Wikimedia Commons
http://commons.wikimedia.org/wiki/Sea_of_Galilee, 2012.

Finally, in revelation of Jesus' sovereign power and authority over all of which is above and beneath the earth, Dr. John Nolland states that the event not only changed the life of Simon Peter, but of James and John as well. He writes:

> "The miraculous catch that follows acts out in prophetic symbolism Simon's call to catch people. The greatness of the miracle is multiply attested: 'a great multitude,' nets about to break, and two fishing boats at the point of sinking. As in the classic call of the prophet (Isa 6) this experience functions as a manifestation of the divine, provoking amazement, fear, and a

sense of sinfulness in the presence of the holy. Jesus dispels the fear and issues the call to Simon: from now on he is to catch people. James and John also experience the greatness of the event. Participating in Simon's call, along with Simon they leave everything and follow Jesus into a new life of apostolic ministry" (Word Biblical Commentary, Volume 35A, 2000, p. 224, ed. Ralph P. Martin).

The Nature Miracle Ministry of Jesus Recorded by Matthew

Calming the Storm—Matthew 8:23-27

Matthew's trail takes us back to the narrative where Jesus concludes His first great discourse, The Sermon on the Mount, comes down from the mountain, and heals a man with leprosy (Matthew 8:2-4; Mark 1:40-42; Luke 5:12-13). After Jesus enters Capernaum, He heals the centurion's servant and publically commends him for manifesting such profound and unwavering faith (Matthew 8:5-13; Luke 7:2-10). In his writings, Dr. Lockyer believes that this particular miracle took place on the same night that Jesus had finished teaching the parables of the Seven Mysteries of the Kingdom (Matthew 13) (All of the Miracles of the Bible, 1961, p. 182).

Calming the Storm – Matthew 8:23-27: *"And when He got into the boat, His disciples followed Him. And behold, there arose a great storm in the sea, so that the boat was covered with the waves; but He Himself was asleep. And they came to Him, and awoke Him, saying, "Save us, Lord; we are perishing!" And He said to them, "Why are you timid, you men of little faith?" Then He arose, and rebuked the winds and the sea; and it became perfectly calm. And the men marveled, saying, "What kind of a man is this, that even the winds and the sea obey Him?" "* (Matthew 8:23-27; Mark 4:35-41; Luke 8:22-25).

By exercising His sovereign power, Jesus rebukes the powerful forces of nature that had turned an otherwise peaceful and calm night into chaos and confusion. By His commanding word, the wind instantly abated, the sea immediately returned to calm, and the disciples' faith grew a little bit stronger. In Dr. Locker's unique way of expressing words he states, "Christ is the true Sea-Lord, as well as the Land-Lord. He is the Lord of heaven, earth and sea—the sovereign Ruler of all things" (Ibid. p. 168).

"Be still and know that I am God" (Psalm 46:10a KJV).

Feeding the 5,000—Matthew 14:13-21

After Jesus hears about the death of John the Baptist, He gets into a small boat and goes to a lonely place by Himself (14:13). Hearing that Jesus had left by boat, the multitude follow Him on foot from the cities (v. 13). Luke's account tells that Jesus withdrew privately to Bethsaida on the northeastern shore of the sea, which is confirmed by John (6:1). Upon returning, Jesus saw the great multitude, felt compassion for them, and healed their sick (Matthew 14:14; Luke 9:10-11; John 6:1-3). Matthew continues by stating that it was late in the evening and the disciples suggested to Jesus that they send the multitude away into the village to buy food. Jesus tells them that they do not need to leave, and further instructs them to feed the multitude, to which the disciples reply, "*We only have five loaves and two fish.*" Jesus then tells His disciples to bring Him what they have (vv. 16-19).

Feeding the 5,000 – Matthew 14:19-21: "*And ordering the multitudes to recline on the grass, He took the five loaves and the two fish, and looking up toward heaven, He blessed the food, and breaking the loaves He gave them to the disciples, and the disciples gave to the multitudes, and they all ate, and were satisfied. And they picked up what was left over of the broken pieces, twelve full baskets. And there were about five thousand men who ate, aside from women and children*" (Matthew 14:13-21; Mark 6:35-44; Luke 9:12-17; John 6:1-14).

All four Gospel writers attest to the same miraculous event. Jesus simply blesses the few pieces of bread and fish, miraculously multiplies it, and continuously supplied it to His disciples until all of the people were fully satisfied. Moreover, all four writers equally testify to the bounty being so great that there were twelve full baskets of leftovers. This dramatic supernatural act of creative power in supplying beyond sufficiency is outside the realm of finite comprehension, but not outside of the realm of the One who is able to supply it. Dr. Donald A. Hagner points out several significant and profound messages perceived in the occurrence of the miraculous event. He writes:

"There is no need to deny the historicity of the miracle simply because we have never witnessed a miraculous multiplication of food. At the same time, however, the literal, historical miracle of Jesus on this occasion is full of ongoing and important significance for us. Indeed, the miracle is a deed filled with symbolism at more than one level, which is why Matthew takes the trouble to tell the very similar story of the feeding of the four thousand. The primary symbolism is that of messianic provision, which both points to the reality of present fulfillment and foreshadows the blessings of the eschaton (the Fourth Gospel develops this idea, relating the feeding miracle also to the eucharist; John 6). This provision takes place in the wilderness, just as manna was provided in the wilderness. It is a kind of messianic banquet in which the people recline at table (cf. 8:11). Jesus is the messianic provider, the Christ—a point left implicit by Matthew in this passage. The hungry are filled now as they will also be filled in the future. The miracle typifies the full and complete blessing of humanity in the meeting of human need and the experience of ultimate well-being, universal shalom. The feeding of the multitude is thus the harbinger of good news for Matthew's church and for Christians of every era. At another level and in specific contrast to the feeding of the four thousand, the symbolism of the twelve baskets suggests the special significance of this miracle for Israel. And the feeding of the five thousand is an indication to the Jews that the Messiah is in their midst, offering to them—as in the miracle of manna in the wilderness—the reality of salvation, the fulfillment of the promises" (Word Biblical Commentary, Volume 33B, 2000, p. 419, ed. Ralph P. Martin).

"I am the bread of life; he who comes to Me shall not hunger, and he who believes in Me shall never thirst" (John 6:35).

The Three-Fold Miracle
Jesus Walks on Water—Matthew 14:22-33
Jesus Calms the Wind—Matthew 14:32
Jesus Instantaneously Transports a Boat to the other Side of the Sea—John 6:21

Following the miraculous feeding of the multitude of over five-thousand at Bethsaida, Jesus compels His disciples to get into the boat and go to the other side (Capernaum) ahead of Him. After He sends the multitudes away, Jesus went up to the mountain to pray. Matthew then reveals that because the wind was blowing contrary, the disciples had only rowed about three or four miles out to sea, and sometime between three and six in the morning (v. 25), the disciples see Jesus walking upon the waters of the sea coming toward them.

MATTHEW	MARK	JOHN
"And in the fourth watch of the night He came to them, walking walking upon the sea. And when the disciples saw Him walking on the sea, they were frightened, saying, "It is a ghost!" And they cried out for fear. But immediately Jesus spoke to them, saying, "Take courage, it is I; do not be afraid." And Peter answered Him and said, "Lord, if it is You, command me to come to You on the water." And He said, "Come!" And Peter got out of the boat, and	*"And immediately He made His disciples get into the boat and go ahead of Him to the other side to Bethsaida, while He Him self was sending the multitude away. And after bidding them farewell, He departed to the mountain to pray. And when it was evening, the boat was in the midst of the sea, and He was alone on the land. And seeing them straining at the oars, for the wind was against them, at about the fourth watch of the night, He came to them, walking*	*"Now when evening came, His disciples went down to the sea, and after getting into a boat, they started to cross the sea to Capernaum. And it had already become dark, and Jesus had not yet come to them. And the sea began to be stirred up because a strong wind was blowing. When therefore they had rowed about three or four miles, they beheld Jesus walking on the*

walked on the water and came toward Jesus. But seeing the wind, he became afraid, and beginning to sink, he cried out, saying "Lord, save me!" And immediately Jesus stretched out His hand and took hold of him, and said to him, "O you of little faith, why did you doubt?" And when they got into the boat, the wind stopped. And those who were in the boat worshiped Him, saying, "You are certainly God's Son!" " (Matthew 14:22-33).

on the sea; and He intended to pass by them. But when they saw Him walking on the sea, they supposed that it was a ghost, and cried out; for they all saw Him and were frightened. But immediately He spoke with them and said to them, "Take courage; it is I, do not be afraid." And He got into the boat with them, and the wind stopped; and they were greatly astonished" (Mark 6:45-51).

sea and drawing near to the boat; and they were frightened. But He said to them, "It is I; do not be afraid." They were willing therefore to receive Him into the boat; and immediately the boat was at the land to which they were going" (John 6:16-21).

Between the narratives of the three Gospel writers, we are told that even the powerful force of gravity obeys the sovereign wishes of God. First, the moment Jesus entered into the boat, the wind became instantly still, and the roaring waves of the sea were abated. Secondly, in exercising His sovereignty, recalling that the Sea of Galilee is only eight miles wide and the disciples had rowed only halfway out, *John* reports that upon Jesus entering the boat, it was *immediately* at the land to which they were headed. What a miraculous transport! The Greek word John uses is eutheōs (pronounced *yoo-theh'-oce*), which is translated to mean "at once, forthwith or immediately" (Thayer's Greek Lexicon, 2009, G2112, p. 258). Thus, in a blink of the eye, by exercising His sovereign power and authority over nature, the sea, and the land, the powerful forces of nature were held in abeyance, and by divine motion, the boat was instantaneously transported to land.

Image provided by: The Prophetic Explorer http://www.propheticobserver.com/walking_on_the_water.aspx#.T4So89WiaxN, 2012.

Finally, with respect to the revelation of the full Deity of Christ, Dr. Herbert Lockyer concludes:

> "At the heart of the miracle was that of Jesus walking on the sea, we must consider such a direct act of control over natural law. How are we to explain this seeming contradiction of the known law of gravity? Actually, there was no contradiction or suspension of the universal law of gravity, but the exercise of a stronger power. The law of gravity is not set aside when the magnet collects the iron filings; it is only that the superior force of magnetism has overcome gravitation. So what happened that stormy night was the exercise of Christ's omnipotence, as He, the Creator of seas and winds, revealed His authority over them, and they being His, He could use them as He desired. It

was His will which bore Him triumphant above those waters. Such a supernatural feat was a further evidence of His sovereignty, and also of foregleam of the time when, in His spiritual and glorified human body, He would be able to counteract ordinary natural laws, like that of passing through closed doors (John 20:19)" (All of the Miracles of the Bible, 1961, pp. 201-202).

Feeding the 4,000—Matthew 15:30-38

Unlike the miracle of Jesus divinely multiplying the bread and fish to feed a greater multitude of 5,000 reported by the four Gospel writers, the miracle of feeding a multitude of greater than 4,000 is only recorded by Matthew and Mark. In the preceding verses, after healing the Syrophoenician woman's daughter (Matthew 15:21-28; Mark 7:24-30), Matthew states that Jesus travels along the sea and goes up to a mountain. Mark fills in the narrative by stating that Jesus leaves the region of Tyre for Galilee via Sidon, but travels through the region of the ten cities (7:31) before arriving to the mountain. As Jesus is sitting there, great multitudes are bringing Him all of those who have physical disabilities, and Jesus heals them all. (Matthew 15:29-31).

Feeding the 4,000 – Matthew 15:30-38: "*And Jesus summoned to Himself His disciples, and said, "I feel compassion for the multitude, because they have remained with Me now for three days and have nothing to eat; and I do not wish to send them away hungry, lest they faint on the way." And the disciples said to Him, "Where would we get so many loaves in a desert place to satisfy such a great multitude?" And Jesus said to them, "How many loaves do you have?" And they said, "Seven and a few small fish." And He directed the multitude to sit down on the ground; and He took the seven loaves and the fish; and giving thanks, He broke them and started giving them to the disciples and the disciples in turn, to the multitudes. And they all ate, and were satisfied, and they picked up what was left over of the broken pieces, seven full baskets. And those who ate were four thousand men, besides women and children"* (Matthew 15:32-38; Mark 8:1-9).

Inasmuch as the divine healing of the multitude is covered under the section of the Divine Healing Ministry of God through Jesus, feeding the multitude of over 4,000 demonstrates a double miracle.

While Jesus is on the mountain, He is healing all of those who had physical disabilities (Matthew 15:29-31), three days pass, the people are hungry, and by exercising His omnipotent creative power, Jesus supernaturally provides their food. Characteristic of Jesus' nature of compassion, mercy, and love in caring not only about people's spiritual well-being, but of their physical well-being as well, as always, Jesus gives thanks to God the Father for what He is *about to do* and then began to miraculously multiply the few pieces of bread and fish. Moreover, consistent with His power to provide abundantly beyond all that we ask or think (Ephesians 3:20), Matthew reports that there were seven full baskets of leftovers. In his gifted way of perceiving spiritual reality, Dr. Lockyer writes this touching note:

> "The thoughtful kindness of Jesus in refusing to send the multitude away exhausted and hungry and miraculously supplying their need teaches us that He is our kind, considerate, ever-watchful Provider, able to undertake for us no matter what necessities or circumstances may arise" (All of the Miracles of the Bible, 1961, p. 211).

> *"Now to Him who is able to do exceeding abundantly beyond all that we ask or think, according to the power that works within us, to Him be the glory in the church and in Christ Jesus to all generations forever and ever. Amen"* (Ephesians 3:21-21).

The Transfiguration—Matthew 17:1-13

To witness the pre-resurrected Christ in all of His glory, and the powerful way in which Jesus supernaturally transcended time and space is in and of itself a miracle above all miracles. Three eyewitnesses testify to the dramatic, miraculous way in which Jesus made visible the glorified bodies of Elijah and Moses, the representatives of the dispensational ages of the Prophets and the Law, together with Himself representing the new creation of His Church and the future dispensational age of grace. Between the accounts of the three narratives of the occurrence of this stupendous event, Matthew begins the narrative by writing that after Jesus miraculously provided food for the multitude, He and His disciples cross the sea to the land of Magadan (15:39). Then, travelling north from Galilee to Caesarea (16:13), Peter is given the revelation of Jesus being the true Son of the living God (16:16), his name changes from Simon Peter to Peter, and Jesus gives him the keys of the kingdom of heaven (16:17-28). In the opening verses of Chapter 17, Matthew writes that six days later, Jesus takes Peter, James, and his brother John with Him up to a high mountain where they witness the timeless event of the miraculous unification of past, present, and future, and hear the audible voice of Almighty God. It is no great wonder that the Gospel writers say that the disciples were awed.

MATTHEW	MARK	LUKE
"And six days later Jesus took with Him Peter and James and John his brother, and brought them up to a high mountain by themselves. And He was transfigured before them; and His face shone like the sun, and His garments became as white as light. And behold, Moses and Elijah	*"And six days later, Jesus took with Him Peter and James and John, and brought them up to a high mountain by themselves. And He was transfigured before them; and His garments became radiant and exceedingly white, as no launderer on earth can*	*"And some eight days after these sayings, it came about that He took along Peter and John and James, and went up to the mountain to pray. And while He was praying, the appearance of His face became different, and His clothing became white and*

appeared to them, talking with Him. And Peter answered and said to Jesus, "Lord, it is good for us to be here; if You wish, I will make three tabernacles here, one for You, and one for Moses, and one for Elijah." While he was still speaking, behold, a bright cloud over-shadowed them; and behold, a voice out of the cloud, saying, "This is My beloved Son, with whom I am well-pleased; hear Him!" And when the disciples heard this, they fell on their faces and were much afraid. And Jesus came to them and touched them and said, "Arise, and do not be afraid." And lifting up their eyes, they saw no one, except Jesus Himself alone" (Matthew 17:1-13).

whiten them. And Elijah appeared to them along with Moses; and they were conversing with Jesus. And Peter answered and said to Jesus. "Rabbi, it is good for us to be here; and let us make three tabernacles, one for You, and one for Moses, and one for Elijah." For he did not know what to answer; for they became terrified. Then a cloud formed, over-shadowing them, and a voice came out of the cloud, "This is My beloved Son, listen to Him!" And all at once they looked around and saw no one with them any more, except Jesus only." (Mark 9:2-13).

gleaming. And behold, two men were talking with Him; and they were Moses and Elijah, who, appearing in glory, were speaking of His departure which he was about to accomplish at Jerusalem. Now Peter and his companions had been overcome with sleep; but when they were fully awake, they saw His glory and the two men standing with Him. And it came about, as these were parting from Him, Peter said to Jesus, "Master, it is good for us to be here; and let us make three tabernacles: one for You, and one for Moses, and one for Elijah"—not realizing what he was saying. And while he was saying this, a cloud formed and began to overshadow them; and they were afraid as they entered the cloud. And a voice came out of the cloud, saying, "This is My Son, My Chosen One; listen to Him!" And when the voice had spoken, Jesus was found alone. And they kept silent, and reported to no one in those days any of the things which they had see" (Luke 9:28-36).

Dr. C. I. Scofield states that the magnificent display of divine power that the three chosen representatives of the Church and of the New Covenant of grace were privileged to witness was the turning point of redemption in the history of humanity. It was a glimpse of the future resurrected Christ confirming His promise of our resurrection as represented by the glorified bodies of Moses and Elijah. Moses being the representative of those who are redeemed under the Law of the Old Covenant, and Elijah as representative of those, who, when born again, are translated from the darkness of the world into the light of the kingdom.

> "The miraculous transfiguration contains, in miniature, all the elements of the future kingdom in manifestation: (1) The Lord, not in humiliation, but in glory (v. 2). (2) Moses, glorified, representative of the redeemed who have passed through death into the kingdom (Mt. 13. 43; cf. Lk. 9. 30, 31). (3) Elijah, glorified, representative of the redeemed who have entered the kingdom by translation (1 Cor. 15, 50-53; 1 Thes. 4. 14-17). (4) Peter, James, and John, not glorified, representatives (for the moment) of Israel in the flesh in the future kingdom (Ezk. 37. 21-27). (5) The multitude at the foot of the mountain v. 14), representative of the nations who are to be brought into the kingdom after it is established over Israel (Isa. 11. 10-12, etc.)" (Matthew 17, pp. 1022-1023).

Dr. Lewis Sperry Chafer's analysis of this miraculous event opens with a short but powerful statement. He writes, "This was an event marvelously spectacular—yet more meaningful than spectacular .... The Old Testament saints—Moses and Elijah—are present with those disciples—Peter, James, and John—who afterward became the apostles of the Church", and closes by writing:

> "The miraculous transfiguration was not the final appearing of Christ in the glory of His Father and of the holy angels, but is a preview which presented it as a thing to be seen and to which "eyewitnesses" could bear testimony. It was a momentary

enactment of that which shall constitute both the kingdom and its glory when it is set up on the earth. The presence of the angels and the stupendous world-transforming events which accompany the actual coming of Christ are not included in the preview; but the elements as were required to accomplish the divine purpose in the transfiguration were present" (*Systematic Theology,* 1978, Volume V, p. 87).

The Temple Tax Coin in the Mouth of a Fish —Matthew 17:24-27

Subsequent to the magnificent, glorious, and historical miraculous transfiguration of Jesus, Matthew records that they came down from the summit and meet up with a multitude. A man comes to Jesus and beseeches Him to heal his only son who had been possessed by a malicious spirit of epilepsy since childhood (Matthew 17:14-21; Mark 9:14-29; Luke 9:37-43). After Jesus divinely heals the epileptic boy, upon reaching Capernaum, Matthew introduces us to the extraordinary miracle of the creative way in which Jesus provides Peter with the money to pay the Temple tax. Considering that Matthew was a tax collector, it is no wonder this miraculous event was not overlooked.

The Temple Tax Coin in the Mouth of a Fish – Matthew 17:25-27: *"And when they had come to Capernaum, those who collected the two-drachma tax came too Peter, and said, "Does your teacher not pay the two-drachma tax?" He said, "Yes." And when he came into the house, Jesus spoke to him first, saying, "What do you think, Simon? From whom do the kings of the earth collect customs or poll-tax, from their sons or from strangers?" And upon his saying, "From strangers," Jesus said to him, "Consequently the sons are exempt. But, lest we give them offense, go to the sea, and throw in a hook, and take the first fish that comes up; and when you open its mouth, you will find a stater. Take that and give it to them for you and Me." "*

Jesus calling one solitary fish out of multitudes directly to Peter's hook may be incomprehensible to the finite mind, but clearly manifests His divine authority as Lord of all that is above and below the sea in a magnificently creative way. Moreover, the fact that Jesus tells Peter to throw in a hook and take the *first* fish that comes up is not only a manifestation of His omnipotence, but of His omniscience as well. In particular, of knowing which particular fish in the multitude had the coin (stater) in its mouth.

> "This coin measures 24mm in diameter and weighs 13.8g. It shows a bust of the Phoenician god Melkart on the obverse and an eagle on the reverse. This coin type was both the type used to pay Judas and the type found by Peter in the fish's mouth" (Michael Swoveland, Biblical Artifacts and Coins, http://www.wncoins.com//0006.htm, 2012).

In Dr. Merrill F. Unger's findings, he states, "The standard silver currency used in Palestine was minted from the highest quality of Greek imperial silver and was the same weight as the Hebrew shekel." The image of the stater is believed to be the standard coin used during this period (The New Unger's Bible Dictionary, 1988, p. 847, ed. R. K. Harrison).

Finally, of the attributes of God manifested in Christ, Dr. John Gill writes:

> "This was a wonderful instance of the omniscience of Christ, who knew there was in such a fish, such a piece of money, as exactly answered the present exigence, and that would come first to Peter's hook; and of His Omnipotence, if not in forming this piece of money immediately in the fish's mouth, as is

thought by some, yet in causing this fish to come to Peter's hook first, and as soon as cast in; and of his power and dominion over all creatures, even over the fishes of the sea; and so proved Himself to be what He claimed to be—the son of the King of kings" (Gills Expositor, Exposition of The New Testament, Volume VII, 1976, p. 199).

To which Dr. Herbert Lockyer adds:

"The miracle before us did not consist only in our Lord's foreknowledge—a second sight He possessed to an eminent degree—that the fish would yield the necessary money, but also in the fact that the first fish that came to Peter's hook contained the precise sum that had been indicated. It was the purpose of Christ's wil—a will to which all creation was obedient—that guided that single fish out of the myriads in the lake, to the hook of Peter. The psalmist reminds us that the Lord controls all things, even "the fish of the sea." Further, because "the silver and the gold are his," He was able that day to bring the fish and the coin together. So, He not only knows all things but can do all things. "All things were made by Him, and for Him." It was therefore through the exercise of His deity that Jesus made a fish produce sufficient money to pay the temple dues" (All of the Miracles of the Bible, 1961, p. 219).

The Withering Fig Tree—Matthew 21:18-22

The miracle of the Withering Fig Tree is the last nature miracle recorded in the Gospels prior to the crucifixion and death of Jesus. It can be viewed in three parts: 1) A miracle, 2) an illustrated spiritual principle, and 3) a prophecy. From Matthew and Mark's previous accounts of Jesus' healing ministry, Jesus has already made His triumphal entry into Jerusalem, has gone to the temple and overturned the tables of the moneychangers, has healed the multitudes at the temple (21:12-17; Mark 11:11-12), and leaves for Bethany. It is now early morning and Jesus and His disciples leave Bethany and are on their way back to Jerusalem (v. 18).

MATTHEW	MARK
"Now in the morning, when He returned to the city, He became hungry. And seeing a lone fig tree by the road, He came to it, and found nothing on it except leaves only; and He said to it, "No longer shall there ever be any fruit from you." And at once the fig tree withered. And seeing this, the disciples marveled, saying, "How did the fig tree wither at once?" " (21:18-22).	*"And on the next day, when they had departed from Bethany, He became hungry. And seeing at a distance a fig tree in leaf in He went to see if perhaps He would find anything on it; and when He came to it, He found nothing but leaves, for it was not the season for figs. And He answered and said to it, "May no one ever eat fruit from you again!" And His disciples were listening"* (Mark 11:12-14). *"And whenever evening came, they would go out of the city. And as they were passing by in the morning, they saw the fig tree withered from the roots up. And being reminded, Peter said to Him, "Rabbi, behold the fig tree which You cursed has withered" "* (Mark 11:19-21).

Between Matthew and Mark's account of the withering fig tree, Mark adds a few more interesting details. Whereas Matthew briefly states that after Jesus rebukes the tree it withered at once, Mark adds the detail of the lapse of time between Jesus rebuking the tree, and His disciples noticing the shriveled tree. Mark notes that 'as they pass by the fig tree the next morning', the disciples take notice that it had shriveled from the roots up. Secondly, in recalling the words spoken in the parable of the Fig Tree (Matthew 24:32-44; Mark 13:28-37; Luke 21:29-36), Jesus illustrated the signs of the end of the age by comparing them with the seasons in which the figs ripen. Likewise, by Jesus supernaturally drying up the fig tree at the root level, symbolized the end of the Old Covenant whereby righteousness had been established under the Law. Throughout His ministry, Jesus' divine attributes and sovereign power were manifested by His miraculous healings, deliverances, and miracles that were witnessed to, and experienced by the multitudes. Furthermore, the illustrations given in His parabolic teachings on divine forgiveness, salvation, and of the establishment of the 'New Temple' of God, should have left no question about the coming fulfillment of prophecy in the minds of those who knew them. Since the fig tree symbolized fertility, peace, and prosperity to the Israelite nation under the Old Covenant (William Barclay, The Gospel of Matthew, Volume II, 2001, p 293), the supernatural act of withering the fig tree symbolically represented the end of the Old Covenant, and the dawning of a new standard of living for His 'new Creation'. His death, resurrection, and ascension would prove to be the ushering in of the New Covenant, the new kingdom law of salvation based on the sole merit of the stupendous work of the crucifixion, death, and resurrection of Christ, and the new Dispensation of Grace. Dr. John Gill somberly observes:

> "This tree was an emblem of the Jewish nation: Christ being hungry, and very desirous of the salvation of men, came first to them, from whom, on account of their large profession of religion, and great pretensions to holiness, and the many advantages they enjoyed, humanly speaking, much fruit of righteousness might have been expected; but alas, he found nothing but mere words, empty boasts, and outward show of religion, an external profession, and a bare performance of

trifling ceremonies, and oral traditions; wherefore Christ rejected them, and in a little time after, the kingdom of God, the Gospel, was taken away from them, and their temple, city, and nation entirely destroyed" (Gills Expositor, Exposition of The New Testament, Volume VII, 1976, p. 394).

Dr. Herbert Lockyer concludes:

"The tree represented Israel under the old covenant, soon to be utterly rejected as hopelessly unfruitful to God. When God does gather fruit for His ancient people, it will be a new generation under the covenant of grace in the Millennial Kingdom" (All of the Miracles of the Bible, 1961, pp. 237-238).

> *"Behold, I will do a new thing; now it shall spring forth; shall ye not know it?"* (Isaiah 43:19).

The Resurrection of Jesus

The ultimate manifestation of God's supreme power over all that is in heaven and earth and beneath the earth was evidenced by the glorious miracle of the resurrected glorified body of Jesus Christ. Unlike those who witnessed the miraculous resurrection of Lazarus, heaven and earth *alone* were allowed to witness the ultimate and most celebrated miracle in the history of humanity.

MATTHEW	MARK	LUKE	JOHN
"Now late on the Sabbath, as it began to dawn toward the first day of the week, Mary Magdalene and the other Mary came to look at the grave. And behold, a severe earthquake had occurred, for an angel of the Lord descended from heaven and came and rolled away the stone and sat upon it. And his appearance was like lightning, and his garment as white as snow; and the guards shook for fear of him, and became like dead men. And the angel answered and said to the women, "Do not be afraid; for I	*"And when the Sabbath was over, Mary Magdalene, and Mary the mother of James, and Salome, brought spices, that they might come and anoint Him. And very early on the first day of the week, they came to the tomb when the sun had risen. And they were saying to one another, "Who will roll away the stone for us from the entrance of the tomb?" And looking up, they saw that the stone had been rolled away, although it was extremely large. And entering the tomb, they saw a young man sitting*	*"But on the first day of the week, at early dawn, they came to the tomb, bringing the spices which they had prepared. And they found the stone rolled away from the tomb, but when they entered, they did not find the body of the Lord Jesus. And it happened that while they were perplexed about this, behold, two men suddenly stood near them in dazzling apparel; and as the women were terrified and bowed their faces to the ground, the men*	*"Now on the first of the week Mary Magdalene came early to the tomb, while it was still dark, and saw the stone already taken away from the tomb. And so she ran and came to Simon Peter, and to the other disciple whom Jesus loved, and said to them, "They have taken away the Lord out of the tomb, and we do not know where they have laid Him." Peter therefore went forth, and the other disciple, and they were*

know that you are looking for Jesus who has been crucified. He is not here, for He has risen, just as He said. Come see the place where He was lying. And go quickly and tell His disciples that He has risen from the dead; and behold, He is going before you into Galilee, there you will see Him; behold, I have told you." And they departed quickly from the tomb with fear and great joy and ran to report it to His disciples. And behold, Jesus met them and greeted them. And they came up and took hold of His feet and worshiped Him. Then Jesus said to them, "Do not be afraid; go and take word to My brethren to leave for Galilee, and there they shall see Me" " (Matthew 28:1-10).

at the right, wearing a white robe; and they were amazed. And he said to them, "Do not be amazed; you are looking for Jesus the Nazarene, who has been crucified. He has risen; He is not here; behold, here is the place where they laid Him. But go, tell His disciples and Peter, He is going before you into Galilee; there you will see Him, just as He said to you." And they went out and fled from the tomb, for trembling and astonishment had gripped them; and they said nothing to anyone, for they were afraid. Now after He had risen early on the first day of the week, He first appeared to Mary Magdalene, from whom He had cast out seven demons. She went and reported to those who had been with Him, while they were mourning and weeping. And when they heard that was

said to them, "Why do you seek the living One among the dead? He is not here, but He has risen. Remember how He spoke to you while He was still in Galilee, saying that the Son of Man must be delivered into the hands of sinful men and be crucified, and the third day rise again." And they remembered His words, and returned from the tomb and reported all these things to the eleven and to all the rest. Now they were Mary Magdalene and Joanna and Mary the mother of James; also the other women with them were telling these things to the apostles. And these words appeared to them as nonsense, they would not believe them. But Peter arose and ran to the tomb; stoop-

going to the tomb. And the two were running together and the other disciple ran ahead faster than Peter, and came to the tomb first; and stooping and looking in, he saw the linen wrappings lying there; but he did not go in. Simon Peter therefore also came, following him, and entered the tomb; and he beheld the linen wrappings lying there, and the facecloth, which had been on His head, not lying with the linen wrappings, but rolled up in a place by itself. Then entered in therefore the other disciple also, who had first come to the tomb he saw, and believed. For as yet they did not understand the Scripture, that He must rise again alive, and had been seen by her, they refused to believe it" (Mark 16:1-11).

ing and looking in, he saw the linen wrappings only; and he went away to his home, marveling at that which had happened" (Luke 24:1-12).

from the dead. So the disciples went away again to their own homes. But Mary was standing outside the tomb weeping; and so, as she wept, she stooped and looked into the tomb; and she beheld two angels in white sitting, one at the head where the body of Jesus had been lying. And they said to her, "Woman, why are you weeping?" She said to them, "Because they have taken away my Lord, and I do not know where they have laid Him." When she had said this, she turned around, and beheld Jesus standing there, and did not know that it was Jesus. Jesus said to her, "Woman, why are you weeping? Whom are you seeking?" Supposing Him to be the gardener, she said to Him, "Sir, if you have carried Him away, tell me where you have laid Him, and I will take Him away." Jesus said to her, "Mary!" She turned and said to Him in Hebrew, "Rabboni!" (which means, Teacher). Jesus said to her, "Stop clinging to Me; for I have not yet ascended to the Father, but go to My brethren, and say to them, 'I ascend to My Father and your Father, and My God and Your God' " (John 20:1-18).

The account of the angels who testified to Mary Magdalene, Mary, the mother of James, and Salome that Christ had risen from the grave, is recorded by all four Gospels writers. However, each one contributes important details. Whereas Luke, Mark, and John are silent about how the stone was rolled away, Matthew explains that a severe earthquake had occurred and an angel of the Lord descended from heaven, rolled away the stone, and sat upon it (28:2). Though Mark comments that Jesus first appeared to Mary Magdalene, John, known for his particular focus on the Deity of Christ, adds the important detail of Jesus speaking directly to Mary, and remarks that when Jesus calls out her name, she immediately recognizes Him, and exclaims, *"Rabboni"!* (20:16). Moreover, the accounts of the many eyewitnesses to His post-resurrection appearances bear witness to the risen Christ. Quoting C. S. Lewis, J. N. D. Anderson, and John Warwick Montgomery, Josh D. McDowell writes about the importance of Christ's post-resurrection appearances. Quoting C. S. Lewis, he writes:

> "C. S. Lewis, in speaking of the importance of Christ's post-resurrection appearances writes: "The first fact in the history of Christendom is a number of people who say they have seen the Resurrection. If they had died without making anyone else believe this 'gospel' no gospels would ever have been written" (Lewis, M, 149)" (*The New Evidence that Demands a Verdict,* 1999, pp. 248-249).

> "J. N. D. Anderson writes of the testimony of the appearances: The most drastic way of dismissing the evidence would be to say that these stories were mere fabrications, that they were pure lies. But, so far as I know, not a single critic today would take such an attitude. In fact it would really be an impossible position. Think of the number of witnesses, over 500. Think of the character of the witnesses, men and women who gave the world the highest ethical teaching it has ever known, and who even on the testimony of their enemies lived it out in their lives. Think of the psychological absurdity of picturing a little band of defeated cowards cowering in an upper room one day and a few days later transformed into a company that no persecution could silence—and then attempting to attribute this dramatic change to nothing more convincing than a miserable fabrication they were trying to foist upon the world. That simply would not make sense (Anderson, RJC, 5-6)" (Ibid., 249).

> "John Warwick Montgomery comments: Note that when the disciples of Jesus proclaimed the resurrection, they did so as

eyewitnesses and they did so while people were still alive who had had contact with the events they spoke of. In 56 A.D. Paul wrote that over 500 people had seen the risen Jesus and that most of them were still alive (1 Corinthians 15:6ff.). It passes the bounds of credibility that the early Christians could have manufactured such a tale and then preached it among those who might easily have refuted it simply by producing the body of Jesus (Montgomery, HC, 78)" (Ibid., 249).

Below is a condensed listing of the eyewitness accounts to Jesus' post-resurrection appearances during His forty day presence on earth that are recorded by the four Gospel writers, the account of Jesus supernaturally transcending time and space by walking through closed doors, and of Jesus making Himself visible and invisible to those whom He chose. It also includes the last nature miracle of the post-resurrection miraculous catch of fish, followed by a short listing of eyewitness accounts to His post-resurrection appearances recorded outside of the Gospels.

1. Mary Magdalene at the empty tomb (Mark 16:9-11; John 20:11-18).

2. Mary Magdalene and Mary, the mother of James. After both women had been told by the angel that Jesus had risen, Jesus appears to them on the road back home (Matthew 28:9-10).

3. The two men on the road to Emmaus. Luke reveals that after a lengthy discussion with Jesus, two men on their way home to Emmaus invite Jesus to come to their home. While they are reclining at the table, Jesus takes the bread and blesses it, and after breaking it into pieces and giving it to them, their spiritual eyes were opened, and they immediately recognized Jesus. Luke then records that Jesus

vanishes from their sight, and the men immediately leave for Jerusalem to report it to the disciples (Mark 16:12-13; Luke 24:13-33). Moreover, of great import, by Luke using the Greek word aphantos (pronounced *af'-an-tos*), which means "vanished or made *invisible*", he is revealing that the resurrected Christ is no longer bound by the constraints of His mortal body (Thayer's Greek Lexicon, 2009, G855, p. 88).

4. The disciples without Thomas present. Luke records that after the men from Emmaus witnessed Jesus, they went to Jerusalem to tell the apostles, and while they were reporting the incident to them, Jesus manifests Himself in their midst, and spoke with them and ate with them (Mark 16:14-18; Luke 24:36-50; John 20:19-24). In John's narrative, however, he adds even more detail. John states that it was on the first day of the week and the apostles were inside together; the door was shut and without opening the door, Jesus supernaturally manifests Himself to them saying, *"Peace be with you"* (20:21). John further reveals that it was then that Jesus breathed on them, and said, *"Receive the Holy Spirit"* (John 20:22).

5. The disciples with Thomas present. John then continues by saying that eight days pass, and once again, without opening the door to where they were staying, Jesus transcends the natural law of time and space and supernaturally manifests Himself to them, only this time, Thomas is present. Knowing that Thomas needed proof of His resurrection, Jesus shows him the wounds on His hands and His side (John 20:26-29).

6. The third manifestation of Jesus to seven disciples by the Sea of Galilee: Peter, Thomas, Nathanael, John, James, and two others. (John 21:1-23).

7. The Ascension (Mark 16:19; Luke 24:50-52; Acts 1:3-12).

Eyewitnesses to the post-resurrection recorded outside of the Gospels

8. A multitude of 500 believers on a Galilean mountain (1 Corinthians 15:6).
9. James (1 Corinthians 15:7).
10. Paul (Acts 9:3-9; 17; 1 Corinthians 9:1; 15:8).
11. Stephen (Acts 7:55).
12. Paul in the temple (Acts 22:17-21; 23:11).
13. John on the island of Patmos (Revelation 1:10-19).

(Adapted from Josh D. McDowell's "The Appearance of Christ in the Lives of Individuals", *The New Evidence that Demands a Verdict,* 1999, p. 250; Herbert Lockyer, "All of the Miracles of the Bible", 1961, pp. 251-253).

The Post-Resurrection Miraculous Catch of Fish —John 21:1-23

Of the four Gospel writers, John is the only one to record the last nature miracle of the post-resurrection miraculous catch of fish that Jesus accomplished especially for His disciples during His third manifestation to them. John's narrative opens with the touching story of Peter, Thomas, Nathanael, John, James, and two others, all of whom had been fishing together the entire night and had caught nothing. Before the break of dawn, they head back to shore and Jesus (whom they do not yet recognize) asks them if they had caught any fish. Already knowing they had not, Jesus directs them to cast their net back out from the right-hand side of the boat (21:6). In the moment that the net was in the water, by His words, 'cast your net to the right and there you will find a catch', instantaneously caused all of that which is beneath the sea to hear and obey His sovereign word of command, and their net was miraculously filled to the brim.

The Post-Resurrection Miraculous Catch of Fish – John 21:1-14: *"After these things Jesus manifested Himself again to the disciples at the Sea of Tiberias; and He manifested Himself in this way. There were together Simon Peter, and Thomas called Didymus, and Nathanael of Cana in Galilee, and the sons of Zebedee, and two others of His disciples. Simon Peter said to them, "I am going fishing." They said to him, "We will also come with you." They went out, and got into the boat; and that night they caught nothing. But when the day was not breaking, Jesus stood on the beach; yet the disciples did not know that it was Jesus. Jesus therefore said to them, "Children, you do not have any fish, do you?" they answered Him, "No." And He said to them, "Cast the net on the right-hand side of the boat, and you will find a catch." They cast therefore, and then they were not able to haul it in because of the great number of fish. That disciple therefore whom Jesus loved said to Peter, "It is the Lord." And so when Simon Peter heard that it was the Lord, he put his outer garment on (for he was* *stripped for work), and threw himself into the sea. But the other disciples came in the little boat, for they were not far from the land, but about one hundred yards away dragging the net full of fish. And so when they got out upon the land, they saw a charcoal fire already laid, and fish placed on it, and bread. Jesus said to them, "Bring some of the fish which you have now caught." Simon Peter went up, and drew the net to land, full of large fish, a hundred and fifty-three; and although there were so many, the net was not torn. Jesus said to them, "Come and have breakfast." None of the disciples ventured to question Him, "Who are You?" knowing that it was the Lord. Jesus came and took the bread, and gave them, and the fish likewise. This is now the third time that Jesus was manifested to the disciples, after He was raised from the dead"* (John 21:1-14).

Of this last recorded miraculous catch of fish, Dr. Herbert Lockyer reverently notes,

> "The Almighty One knew where the fish were located, and could direct them into the net. Since He is the Creator of the fish, they obeyed His call (Psalm 8). Such a display of omniscience and power revealed to John, whom Jesus loved, the identity of the One who made the great haul of fish possible" (All of the Miracles of the Bible, 1961, p. 249).

Epilogue—The Ascension

Photo provided by Dapper Bantam
http://media.photobucket.com/image/ascension/DapperBantam/Ascension.jpg?o=72, 2012.

Luke closes his Gospel by including details of Mark's account of Jesus' Ascension that concluded His earthly stay. He writes:

"And He said to them, "These are My words which I spoke to you while I was still with you, that all things which are written about Me in the Law of Moses and the Prophets and the Psalms must be fulfilled." Then He opened their minds to understand the Scriptures, and he said to them, "Thus it is written, that the Christ should suffer and rise

again from the dead the third day; and that repentance for forgiveness of sins should be proclaimed in His name to all the nations, beginning from Jerusalem. You are witnesses of these things, and Behold, I am sending forth the promise of My Father upon you; but you are to stay in the city until you are clothed with power from on high." And He led them out as far as Bethany, and He lifted up His hands and blessed them. And it came about that while He was blessing them, He parted from them" (Mark 16:19; Luke 24:50-52; Acts 1:4-11).

The sovereign power over the universal laws of nature miraculously joining the fully efficacious resurrection, and glorious ascension of Jesus with His life and death on earth now concludes Christ's redemptive work on behalf of humanity. The Lamb of God, the Son of David, the Son of Man, and the Son of God, ***is*** the great I AM that I AM of the New Covenant of grace that was ratified solely by the shed blood of Jesus Christ. All of the chosen disciples who had walked with Jesus, talked with Him, ate with Him, were taught by Him, bore witness to His miracles, and to His resurrection are now led by Jesus to bear witness to the stupendous miracle of His divine transport from earth to heaven (Acts 2:33; Hebrews 1:3; 1 Peter 3:22). After Jesus instructs His disciples to return to Jerusalem to wait for the day of Pentecost, He blesses His disciples and departs from earth. However, in the writings of the Book of Acts, Luke adds an important detail of the two angels who appeared to the disciples after Jesus ascended, *"After He said these things, He was lifted up while they were looking on, and a cloud received Him out of their sight. And as they are gazing intently into the sky, behold, two men in white clothing stood beside them; and they also said, "Men of Galilee, why do stand there looking into the sky? This Jesus, who has been taken up from you into heaven, will come in just the same way as you have watched Him go into heaven" "* (Acts 1:9-11). In his summary of "the miracle above all miracles", Dr. David E. Holwerda shares his profound insight into what the Ascension meant to the world. He writes:

"The Ascension declares Christ's enthronement as cosmic ruler. Using the language of Psalms 68 and 110, the apostle Paul announces Christ's victory over all the principalities and powers that had been vying for world domination .... The Ascension is Christ's accession to power .... The Ascension was the essential prerequisite for the outpouring of the Holy Spirit (Jn. 7:39; 16:7; Acts 1). Thus, the Ascension inaugurates the coming into being of the new people of God, because the gift of the Spirit fulfills the promises made through the Old Testament prophets" (Eerdman's *International Standard Bible Encyclopedia,* Volume A-D, 1979, p. 312, ed. Geoffrey W. Bromiley).

For easy reference, Tables XI and XII contain the listing of thirteen of the nature miracles accomplished by the sovereign hands of Jesus, and fifty-two of the miracles that are recorded by the four individual Gospel writers. However limited our knowledge is of these great historical, miraculous events, none would have occurred without Jesus, who "is Himself the greatest miracle of them all" (Benjamin B.Warfield, *The Person and Work of Christ*, 1950, p. 19).

> *"And there are also many other things which Jesus did, which if they were written in detail, I suppose that even the world itself would not contain the books which were written"* (John 21:25).

Table XI
Nature Miracles of God Manifested through Jesus
Matthew – Mark – Luke – John

NATURE OF MIRACLE	PLACE	MATTHEW	MARK	LUKE	JOHN
1. Pre-Resurrection Catch of Fish	Sea of Galilee			5:1-11	
2. Calming the Storm	Sea of Galilee	8:23-27	4:35-41	8:22-25	
3. Feeding the 5000	Near Bethsaida	14:13-21	6:35-44	9:12-17	6:1-14
4. The Three-Fold Miracle Walking on Water Calming the Wind Transporting a Boat	Sea of Galilee	14:22-33	6:45-51		6:16-21
7. Feeding the 4000	Decapolis	15:32-38	8:1-9		
8. The Transfiguration	Mount Transfiguration	17:1-13	9:1-13	9:28-36	
9. Temple Tax in Coin in the Mouth of a Fish	Capernaum	17:24-27			
10. The Withering Fig Tree	On the Road from Bethany To Jerusalem	21:18-22	11:12-14; 19-21		
11. The Resurrection	Calvary	28:1-10	16:1-11	24:1-12	20:1-18
12. Post-Resurrection Catch of Fish	Sea of Galilee				21:1-13
13. The Ascension	Bethany		16:19-20	24:50-52	

(Adapted from John MacArthur, "The Healing Ministry of God through Jesus", *The MacArthur Bible Commentary* , 2005, pp. 1152, 1293; Edwin A. Blum, "The Miracles of Jesus", *The Bible Knowledge Commentary: New Testament*, 1983, p. 277, ed. John F. Walvoord, Roy B. Zuck; Colin Brown, "Miracles", Volume K-P, 1986, p. 374, Eerdman's *International Standard Bible Encyclopedia*).

Table XII
The Miracle Ministry of God Manifested through Jesus

NATURE OF MIRACLE	PLACE	MATTHEW	MARK	LUKE	JOHN
1. The Virgin Birth	Bethlehem	1:18-25; 2:1-2		1:26-35; 2:1-7	
2. The Wedding in Cana	Cana				2:1-11
3. The Multitude	Throughout Galilee	4:23-24	1:39		
4. The Leper	Galilee	8:1-4	1:40-42	5:12-14	
5. The Centurion's Servant	Capernaum	8:5-13		7:2-10	
6. Peter's Mother-in-Law	Capernaum	8:14-15	1:30-31	4:38-39	
7. The Multitude	Capernaum	8:16-17	1:32-34	4:40-41	
8. The Demon Possessed Gerasene	Gergesa	8:28-34	5:1-20	8:26-39	
9. The Paralytic Cured	Capernaum	9:1-8	2:1-12	5:17-26	
10. The Daughter of Jarius Raised from the Dead	Galilee	9:18-19; 23-25	5:22-24; 35-42	8:40-42; 49-55	
11. The Hemorrhaging Woman	Galilee	9:20-22	5:25-34	8:43-48	
12. The Two Blind Men	Galilee	9:27-31			
13. The Demon Possessed Deaf Man	Galilee	9:32-34			
14. The Multitude	Throughout The Land	9:35			
15. The Withered Hand	Synagogue	12:9-14	3:1-6	6:6-11	
16. The Multitude	Throughout The Land	12:15-21	3:7-12		
17. The Demon Possessed Blind Mute	Galilee	12:22-23		11:14	
18. The Multitude	Bethsaida/ Galilee	14:13-14		9:10-11	6:1-3
19. Healing the Sick	Gennesaret	14:34-36	6:53-56		

Table XII **(Continued)**
The Miracle Ministry of God Manifested through Jesus

NATURE OF MIRACLE	PLACE	MATTHEW	MARK	LUKE	JOHN
1. The Virgin Birth	Bethlehem	1:18-25; 2:1-2		1:26-35; 2:1-7	
2. The Wedding in Cana	Cana				2:1-11
3. The Multitude	Throughout Galilee	4:23-24	1:39		
4. The Leper	Galilee	8:1-4	1:40-42	5:12-14	
5. The Centurion's Servant	Capernaum	8:5-13		7:2-10	
6. Peter's Mother-in-Law	Capernaum	8:14-15	1:30-31	4:38-39	
7. The Multitude	Capernaum	8:16-17	1:32-34	4:40-41	
8. The Demon Possessed Gerasene	Gergesa	8:28-34	5:1-20	8:26-39	
9. The Paralytic Cured	Capernaum	9:1-8	2:1-12	5:17-26	
10. The Daughter of Jarius Raised from the Dead	Galilee	9:18-19; 23-25	5:22-24; 35-42	8:40-42; 49-55	
11. The Hemorrhaging Woman	Galilee	9:20-22	5:25-34	8:43-48	
12. The Two Blind Men	Galilee	9:27-31			
13. The Demon Possessed Deaf Man	Galilee	9:32-34			
14. The Multitude	Throughout The Land	9:35			
15. The Withered Hand	Synagogue	12:9-14	3:1-6	6:6-11	
16. The Multitude	Throughout The Land	12:15-21	3:7-12		
17. The Demon Possessed Blind Mute	Galilee	12:22-23		11:14	
18. The Multitude	Bethsaida/ Galilee	14:13-14		9:10-11	6:1-3
19. Healing the Sick	Gennesaret	14:34-36	6:53-56		

Table XII **(Continued)**
The Miracle Ministry of God Manifested through Jesus

NATURE OF MIRACLE	PLACE	MATTHEW	MARK	LUKE	JOHN
41. Pre-Resurrection Catch of Fish	Sea of Galilee			5:1-11	
42. Calming the Storm	Sea of Galilee	8:23-27	4:35-41	8:22-25	
43. Feeding the 5000	Near Bethsaida	14:13-21	6:35-44	9:12-17	6:1-14
44. The Three-Fold Miracle Walking on Water Calming the Wind Transporting a Boat	Sea of Galilee	14:22-33	6:45-5		6:16-21
47. Feeding the 4000	Decapolis	15:30-38	8:1-9		
48. Temple Tax in the Mouth of a Fish	Capernaum	17:24-27			
49. The Withering Fig Tree	On the Road from Bethany To Jerusalem	21:17-22	11:12-14; 19-21		
50. The Resurrection	Calvary	28:1-10	16:1-11	24:1-12	20:1-18
51. Post-Resurrection Catch of Fish	Sea of Galilee				21:1-13
52. The Ascension			16:19-20	24:50-52	

(Adapted from John MacArthur, "The Healing Ministry of God through Jesus", *The MacArthur Bible Commentary* , 2005, pp. 1152, 1293; Edwin A. Blum, "The Miracles of Jesus", *The Bible Knowledge Commentary: New Testament*, 1983, p. 277, ed. John F. Walvoord, Roy B. Zuck; Colin Brown, "Miracles", Volume K-P, 1986, p. 374, Eerdman's *International Standard Bible Encyclopedia*).

Part IV—Names and Titles of the Great I AM THAT I AM

Names and Titles of the Great I AM THAT I AM

Introduction

"I AM He, I AM the first, I AM also the last" (Isaiah 48:12b).

Under the section of "What's in a Name", we were introduced to the Old Testament Hebrew translation of Almighty God as *Elohiym* (Genesis 1:1) with the first two letters of El carrying the meaning of "the Strong One". Compounding EL with other names reflecting God's character, we were introduced to El *Shaddai*, God Almighty (Genesis 17:1), El *Elyon*, translated as the God Most High (Genesis 14:18), and El *Olam* as the everlasting or eternal God (Genesis 21:33) (Dr. C. I. Scofield, Genesis 1, pp. 3-6). When God spoke to Abraham about the covenant that He was entering into with him, He introduced Himself as El *Shaddai*, the Almighty, all-sufficient covenant name of God, "I am God Almighty" (Genesis 17:1). It was El *Shaddai* who changed Abraham's name from Abram to Abraham, the father of a multitude of nations, and Sarah's name from Sarai to Sarah, the mother of nations (Genesis 17:5, 15).

We have also been introduced to the supreme name of *Jehovah*, reflecting the spiritual personality and redemptive name of the great I AM, from which YHWH (Yahweh) is formed (Dr. C. I. Scofield, Genesis 2, p. 6). Compounding *Elohiym* we were given the combined divine name of *Jehovah-Elohiym*, LORD God (Genesis 2:4, 7), and LORD Jehovah, the self-existent One who reveals Himself (Exodus 3:14). When God spoke to Moses and to the Prophet Isaiah, He revealed His name to them as LORD (*Jehovah-Elohiym*, the covenant name of God and redemptive name of the Deity). To Moses He said, "I 'appeared' to Abraham, Isaac, and Jacob, as God Almighty (El *Shaddai*), but by *My* name, LORD (*Jehovah-Elohiym*), I did not make myself known to them" (Exodus 6:3; 20:3), and to the Prophet Isaiah, He said, "I am the LORD (*Jehovah-Elohiym*), that is *My* name" (42:8). *Jehovah-Elohiym* is who formed man of dust from the ground and breathed into his nostrils the breath of life (Genesis 2:7), which suggests that a plan of redemption was already in place. It was *Jehovah-Elohiym*, the supreme LORD Jehovah, who interceded on behalf of Abraham's sacrifice of Isaac by providing him with a sacrificial ram (Gen. 22:15-18), *Jehovah-Elohiym* is who redeemed the Hebrews from bondage by the hands of the Egyptians, and is He who entered into the covenant with Moses.

Compounding the supreme redemptive name of *Jehovah,* the majestic, omnipotent, omniscient, omnipresent, all-sufficient, self-existing Creator, and Master of the universe, Dr. Lewis Sperry Chafer introduced us to even more facets of God's character through Jehovah-*Adonai*, "Lord GOD", translated as Lord Master (Genesis 15:2); Jehovah-*Sabaoth*, translated as "LORD of hosts" (1 Samuel 1:3); Jehovah-*Jireh*, "the LORD will provide" (Genesis 22:14); Jehovah-*Rapha*, "The LORD that healeth" (Exodus 15:26); Jehovah-*Nissi*, "The LORD our banner" (Exodus 17:8-15); Jehovah-*Shalom*, "The LORD our peace" (Judges 6:23, 24); Jehovah-*Ra-ah*, "The LORD my shepherd" (Psalms 23:1); Jehovah-*Tsidkenu*, "The LORD our righteousness" (Jeremiah 23:6), and Jehovah-*Shammah*, "The LORD is there" (Ezekiel 48:35) (Systematic Theology, 1978, Volume I, p. 269). In the Book of Exodus, God introduces another facet of His character through His name Jehovah-*M'Kaddesh*, "the LORD who sanctifies" (Exodus 31:13). To our knowledge base, Dr. Hebert Lockyer adds "Jehovah-*Hoseenu*—The Lord Our Maker (Psalm 95:6); Jehovah-*Makkeh*—Jehovah that smites (Ezekiel 7:9), and lastly, Jehovah-*Gmolah*—The God of Recompense (Jeremiah 51:6)" (Lockyer, All the Divine Names and Titles in the Bible, 1975, pp. 20, 33, 56-57).

It is also through the Prophet Isaiah that God reveals the prophetic name of our Savior as `Immanuw'el, God with us. *"Therefore the Lord Himself will give you a sign: Behold, a virgin will be with child and bear a son, and she will call His name Immanuel"* (Isaiah 7:14; Matthew 1:23). God further reveals His name to be Wonderful

Counselor, Mighty God (El), Eternal Father (El *Olam*), and Prince of Peace (Jehovah-*Shalom*).

"For a child will be born to us, a son will be given to us; and the government will rest on His shoulders; and His name will be called Wonderful Counselor, Mighty God, Eternal Father, Prince of Peace. There will be no end to the increase of His government or of peace, on the throne of David and over his kingdom, to establish it and to uphold it with justice and righteousness from then on and forevermore. The zeal LORD of hosts will accomplish this" (Isaiah 9:6-7).

Names and Titles of the Great I AM THAT I AM

New Testament Gospels

The most staggering, supreme, redemptive name of the great I AM THAT I AM, the self-existent One who reveals Himself to humanity, is revealed in the New Testament as *Jesus Christ* (*Jehoshua-Elohiym*). To confirm the prophecy of Isaiah of the coming of Christ, God sent His angel Gabriel to Mary to make the final announcement that it was she whom God had chosen as the vessel of honor to bring forth the long awaited Messiah. Gabriel further revealed His name to be Jesus (*Jehoshua*), who would be given the throne of His father David, whose kingdom would have no end, who would be called the *Son of the Most High* (El Elyon) and the *Son of God* (El Olam) (Luke 1:32-33). At the birth of Jesus, an angel made the great announcement to the world of His name as *Savior*, who is *Christ the Lord* (Luke 2:11).

"*And she will bear a Son; and you shall call His name Jesus, for it is He who shall save His people from their sins*" (Matthew 1:21).

Many of Jesus' titles and names reflecting His nature, character, and purpose, both literal and metaphorical that paint a portrait of His divine and human nature in the four Gospels is by far not an exhaustive list. Dr. Herbert Lockyer states:

> "All the names and titles used of Christ represent the different *relationships* which are sustained by Him, and are most varied as we shall see. The solemn symbolism of these designations forges the Old and the New Testaments into one book, for no sooner do we open the New Testament than we read its first name *Jesus*, or *Jah, Hoshea – Jehovah*, my Saviour (Matthew

1:1, 21). He likewise comes to us as *Elohim* – His name shall be called "Emmanuel, *God-Elohim*, with us" (Lockyer, All the Divine Names and Titles in the Bible, 1975, p. 94).

MATTHEW

It is in the first Gospel of Matthew where we find the titles and names of Jesus as *Son of Abraham* and *Son of David* (Matthew 1:1). After the death of king Herod, an angel of the Lord appears to Joseph in a dream and calls Jesus the *Child* (2:20). He is called *King of the Jews* (2:2; Mark 15:2) and *Ruler and Shepherd* (2:6; Micah 5:2-4). Upon his departure from Egypt, Joseph took his family to live in Nazareth so that what was spoken through the prophets might be fulfilled. "Out of Egypt did I call *My Son*" (2:15; Hosea 11:1), and He shall be called a *Nazarene* (2:23), a *Rod* out of the *stem of Jesse* (Isaiah 11:1), the man whose name is the *BRANCH* (Zechariah 6:12). Matthew unveils the title of Jesus as *Son of God.* After Jesus was baptized, God loudly proclaimed Jesus to be *His beloved Son*, and confirmed it at the Mount of Transfiguration (3:17; 17:5). Jesus was called the *Teacher* (8:19), and while speaking to the scribe who declared that he would follow Jesus wherever He went, Jesus refers to Himself as the *Son of Man* (8:20). While responding to a question asked by the disciples of John the Baptist, the forerunner of Christ, why His disciples did not fast like they and the Pharisee's do, Jesus answered by explaining to them that one does not mourn while the *Bridegroom* is still with them (9:14-15). After healing the paralytic in Capernaum, Jesus announced that He, the *Son of Man,* has been given the authority on earth to forgive sins (9:6), to save that which was lost (18:11), to give His life as a *Ransom* (20:28; Mark 10:45), and sit on His glorious throne (19:28). Matthew also reveals the title of Jesus as the *Servant of God* as prophesied by Isaiah (12:18; Isaiah 42:1). More importantly, the first announcement of His own identity was when Jesus Himself unveiled His sovereign title of the *Lord of the Sabbath* (12:1-8; Luke 6:5). While explaining the parable of the Wheat and the Tares, Jesus declares Himself to be the *Good Seed* (13:37). In Nazareth, He was called the *carpenter's son*, the *son of Mary*, and the *son of Joseph* (13:55; Mark 6:3; Luke 4:22). After the disciples witnessed Jesus walking on water and calming the storm, they recognized Him to be *God's Son* (14:33), and it was Peter who was given the revelation that *Jesus Christ* is the *Son of the Living God* (16:16). Moreover, Jesus Himself avowed that He was the *Christ* (16:20). Matthew and Mark both record Jesus prophesying His own death and resurrection: "the *Son of Man* will be delivered up to the chief priests and the scribes; and they will condemn Him to death, and will deliver Him up to the Gentiles. And they will mock Him, spit on Him, scourge and kill Him, and three days later He will rise again" (20:18-19; Mark 10:33-34). Jesus was also called the *Prophet Jesus* from Nazareth in Galilee (21:10), and finally, when Jesus was speaking to the multitudes and to His disciples, He refers to Himself as your *Master,* even *Christ* (23:8).

MARK

Similar to the opening statements of Matthew's record of tracing Jesus' lineage by identifying Him as the *Son of Abraham* and the *Son of David*, the opening statement of the second Gospel of Mark opens by identifying Jesus as the *Son of God* (Mark 1:1). Mark's unique account of Jesus healing the man with an unclean spirit in the synagogue (1:21-27) carries an astounding revelation of even the spirits that rebelled against God *knew* Him be the *Holy One of God* (1:24). When Jesus was healing the multitudes at the Sea of Galilee (3:10), Mark states that the spirits fell down before Him and cried out, "*You* are the *Son of God!*" (3:11). While in the land of Gadara, when the spirits that possessed the Gerasene recognized Jesus they immediately cried out, "What do I have to do with you, *Jesus, Son of* (El *Elyon*) the *Most High God?*" (5:7). Lastly, when the high priest Caiaphas asked Jesus if He was the *Christ*, the *Son of the Blessed God*, Jesus declared, "*I AM*" (14:61-62).

LUKE

Likewise, Luke, the distinguished physician, historian, associate of Paul, and author of the third Gospel introduces us to other unique titles and names of Jesus. In Luke's account of the announcement of the birth of Jesus, Gabriel told Mary that Jesus would be called the *Son of the Highest* (1:32) and shall be called the *Son of God* (Elyon) (1:35). Mary, when visiting her Aunt Elizabeth, proclaimed the unborn *Child* as *God my Saviour* (1:47), who would be Israel's *Horn of Salvation* (1:69), and *Dayspring from on High* (1:78). At the birth of Jesus, an angel of the Lord made the announcement to the shepherds that a *Savior*, who is *Christ the Lord* (2:11) was born in the city of David. Luke records that the Prophet Simeon had been promised by God that he would not die until he saw the *Lord's Christ*, *His Consolation of Israel,* a *Light to the Gentiles*, and *His Salvation* (2:25-32). When Jesus was preaching in the synagogue at Nazareth, He prophesied to them that the day would come when they would say to Him, "*Physician*, heal thyself" (4:23). After Jesus resurrected the widow's son of Nain, He was called a G*reat Prophet* (7:16). Lastly, at Jesus' crucifixion, the rulers who sneered referred to Him as *Christ of God*, *His Chosen One* (23:35).

JOHN

Finally, it is in the account of John, nicknamed "Son of Thunder" (Mark 3:17), who was known to be one of the three inner circle disciples and intimate earthly friend of Jesus, that we find the historic record of Jesus' divine names identifying Him as the eternal living God, the great *I AM,* He that is who HE is, the self-existent One, the eternal living I AM, the *Jehovah-Elohiym* of the Old Covenant of redemption, *Wonderful Counselor*, *Mighty God* (El), *Eternal Father* (El *Olam*), and *Prince of Peace* (Jehovah-*Shalom*), *Jesus Christ*

(Jehoshua-Elohiym) ***is*** the same great I AM THAT I AM of the New Covenant of redemption in the New Testament.

"Truly, truly, I say unto you, before Abraham was, I AM" (John 8:58).

Recalling that the Hebrew word for *sworn* (shâba') is translated to mean "to swear, take an oath (of *Jehovah* by Himself)," Jesus unveils *seven* of His names that identify Him as being the eternal living God, the great I AM. Beginning in Chapter 6 and ending in Chapter 15, Jesus reveals His identity to the world, testifying:

1. *"I AM* the Living Bread of Life" (6:33, 35, 48, 51).
2. *"I AM* the Light of the world" (8:12).
3. *"I AM* the Door of the sheep" (10:7).
4. *"I AM* the Good Shepherd" (10:11, 14).
5. *"I AM* the Resurrection and the Life" (11:25).
6. *"I AM* the Way and the Truth and the Life" (14:6; Genesis 3:24).
7. *"I AM* the True Vine" (15:1-5).

It is also John who reveals the Deity of Christ through the divine title of Logos (the *Word*), who was with God since the beginning. In the beginning, the *Word* was with God, the *Word* was God, and the *Word* was made *Flesh* and dwelt among us. He is the *Life*, the *light* of men, and the *True Light* (John 1:1-14), the *Only Begotten Son,* which is in the Bosom of the Father (1:18; 3:16, 18), and *Son of God* (1:34). In Bethany, where John the Baptist was baptizing on the Jordon, when he saw Jesus coming towards him, he immediately recognized Him as the *Lamb of God* (1:29). After Jesus tells Nathanael of Cana that before Philip called him, He saw him from under the fig tree. Nathanael recognized Jesus, called Him "*Rabbi*", and professed, "You are the *Son of God,* and You are the *King of Israel"* (1:48-49). When Jesus met the Samaritan woman at Jacob's well, she told Him that she knew that the *Messiah* was coming, the One who is called

Christ, and Jesus declares—*I AM He* (4:25), and from that city, many Samaritans thereafter called Him the *Savior of the world* (4:42). While defending the woman caught in adultery, Jesus announced that He was the *Light* of the world. After hearing Jesus make His declaration, the Pharisees and scribes argued that the testimony of one witness was not valid. Jesus then validates it by saying to them, "*I AM He* who bears witness of *Myself* and *My Father* bears witness of *Me*. When you lift up the *Son of Man*, then you will know that *I AM HE*" (8:14, 28). At the Feast of Dedication in Jerusalem, many of the Jews kept insisting that Jesus plainly say, "I am the Christ", instead, Jesus plainly said, "*I and the Father are One*" (John 10:30), "*I am the Son of God*" (10:36), "I have come as *Light* into the world of darkness" (12:46). At Jesus' triumphal entry into Jerusalem, John records the prophecy of Zechariah (9:9) being fulfilled and states, "Behold your *King of the Daughter of Zion"* (12:15). At Jesus' crucifixion, the title that Pilate inscribed over His cross was "*JESUS THE NAZARENE, THE KING OF THE JEWS"* (19:19). Finally, after Jesus appeared to Mary Magdalene at the empty tomb, she ecstatically exclaimed, *"Rabboni"* (Lord, Master) (20:16). It was only after Jesus showed Thomas the wounds on His hands and on His side that Thomas perceives and cries out, "*My Lord and My God*" (20:28). Lastly, John ends his testimony by proclaiming, "*Jesus is the Christ, the Son of God,* that by believing you may have *Life* in His name" (20:31).

Moreover, apart from his Gospel, John also records other unique names and titles of Jesus that are found in his first two Epistles and in the Book of Revelation, which are believed to have been written after he wrote the Gospel. The first introductory words of John's first Epistle begins with the eyewitness testimony of what has been seen with their own eyes and handled with their own hands was the manifested *Word of Life* and the *Eternal Life* (1 John 1:1-2). He further testifies that Jesus Christ the *Righteous* is the *Advocate* (2:1), and records that *He* is the *Spirit* given to us, which abides in us testifies to the truth (3:24; 4:5, 13) that Jesus, *the Son,* was sent to be the *Savior of the world* (4:14). It is also in the first Epistle that John reveals love and God to be one essence —"for *God **is** Love"* (4:7-9). Lastly, a notable change takes place in John's second Epistle, he no longer calls Jesus Christ, the Son of God—but now refers to Him as Jesus Christ, the *Son of The Father* (2 John 3).

The most profound, majestic, and climatic names and titles of Jesus that were given to John to record, however, are recorded exclusively in the Book of Revelation, which were dictated to John by God Himself through Jesus by an Angel (Revelation 22:16) while he was on the island of Patmos (Halley's Bible Handbook, 1965, p. 683). In the first chapter, Jesus, the eternal living *I AM,* authoritatively affirms His absolute identity to John five times, and after writing all that John was instructed to write, the book closes with His signature.

1. "*I AM Alpha* and *Omega, the Lord God who is and who was and who is to come, the Almighty*" (Revelation 1:8).
2. "*I AM Alpha* and *Omega, the first and the last*" (Revelation 1:11).
3. "Fear not; *I AM the first* and *the last*" (Revelation 1:17).
4. "*I AM He that liveth, and was dead; and, behold, I am alive for evermore, Amen; and have the keys of hell and of death*" (Revelation 1:18).
5. "I *AM Alpha* and *Omega, the beginning and the end, the first and the last*" (Revelation 22:13).
6. "*I, Jesus, have sent my angel to testify to you. I AM the root and the offspring of David*, and the *Bright and Morning Star*" (Revelation 22:16).

The combined divine name of our majestic, omnipotent, omniscient, omnipresent, all-sufficient, self-existing Creator, Master, and King of the universe, *Jehoshua-Elohiym*, who is *Jehovah-Elohiym,* is explained with staggering revelation by Dr. Lockyer. He writes:

> "This absoluteness and the divine Being, who is independent self-existing is found in the declaration, "I am Alpha and

Omega, the beginning and the ending saith the LORD—Jehovah—which *is* and which *was*, and which is *to come*, the Almighty" (Revelation 1:8).

"Which is" – the ever-existing One – His relation to the present.
"Which was" – His relation to the past – the One who always was.
"Which is to come" – His relation to the future – who always will be" ".

"When Moses asked for God's name, He replies, I AM THAT I AM, or I AM WHAT I AM – A title expressive not only of self-existence, but of unchangeableness of character. He always was what He is, He is what He was; He will ever be what He was and is, with Him there is no variableness (James 1:17). No wonder "This name JEHOVAH, in all significance, is God's memorial, God's 'forget-me-not,' " (Lockyer, All the Divine Names and Titles in the Bible, 1975, p. 18).

Between the opening and closing pages of the Book of Revelation, John reveals other names and titles reflecting the fullness of the Godhead that are recorded exclusively by him. In his opening statement, John identifies Jesus Christ as the "*Faithful Witness*," the "*First Begotten of the dead,*" and "*Prince of the kings of earth*" (1:4). When writing to the seven churches, John records different names and titles given to him that identify Jesus.

In John's first letter to the church in Ephesus, however, it is Jesus who identifies Himself as "*the One who holds the 'seven stars'* in His right hand," and "*the One who walks among the seven lampstands*" (2:1) who gives the right to eat from "*tree* of *life*" (2:7; 22:2, 14; Genesis 3:23-24).

2) To the second church in Smyrna, Jesus reaffirms that He is "*the First and The Last, the One who was dead, and has come to Life*" (2:8).

3) However, to the third church in Pergamum, He states that He is "*the One who has the sharp, double-edged sword*" (2:12).
4) To the fourth church in Thyatira, Jesus describes Himself as "*the Son of God, whose eyes are like blazing fire and whose feet are like burnished bronze*"(2:18).
5) To the fifth church in Sardis, Jesus introduces Himself as *"the One who holds the Seven Spirits and the Seven Stars"* (3:1).
6) And to the sixth church in Philadelphia, the one known to be the faithful one, Jesus reaffirms that He is "*the One* who is *Holy and True* who holds the key of David" (3:7).
7) In addressing Himself to the seventh church in Laodicea, Jesus calls Himself "*the Amen,*" reaffirms that He is the "*Faithful and True Witness,*" and the *"the Beginning of the creation of God"* (3:14).

John further identifies Jesus as being "*the Lion of the tribe of Judah," "the Root of David,*" and "*the Lamb Slain*" (5:5-6; 13:8). Not only is the *Lamb* who was slain called "*the Lord God Almighty,"* but He is also called the "*King of the saints"* (15:3), "*Lord* above lords *and King* above kings" (17:14), "*Faithful and True*" (19:11), whose robe was dipped in blood whose name is called "*The Word of God*" (19:13). John ultimately describes Jesus wearing a robe on which is imprinted "*THE KING OF KINGS* and *LORD OF LORDS*" (19:16). Lastly, John identifies *God the Father* and the *Lamb of God* as "*the Temple*" that has no need to be lighted because the glory of God is the *light* and the *Lamb* is its lamp (21:22). Finally, in Dr. Herbert Lockyer's closing summary of all the divine names and titles of God, he poignantly writes:

> "As it takes many rays to make up the pure light of the sun, so it takes various descriptions to give us a true conception of the being and glory of God. No man is able to receive the whole revelation of His majesty at once. Only one part at a time can be comprehended yet such is sufficient to give great joy and

satisfaction. This is why it was the special purpose of the Great High God, who is One, to reveal Himself to saints of old in the development of their spiritual life in different names and titles of His nature and purpose" (Lockyer, All the Divine Names and Titles in the Bible, 1975, p. 19).

The Jehovah-Elohiym of the Old Covenant of redemption in the Old Testament *is* the same Great I AM THAT I AM, Jesus Christ—Jehoshua-Elohiym of the New Covenant of redemption in the New Testament.

"I AM He that liveth, and was dead; and, behold, I am alive for evermore, Amen; and have the keys of hell and of death" (Revelation 1:18).

Bibliography

American Bible Society. Samaritans, Then and Now, http://bibleresources.americanbible.org/bible-resources/bible-resource-center, (2012).

American Museum of Natural History. Pearls, http://www.amnh.org/exhibitions/pearls/history/index.html, (2012).

Bandstra, Barry L. "Wine." Eerdman's International Standard Bible Encyclopedia. Grand Rapids: William B. Eerdmans Publishing Company, 1988.

Barbieri, Louis A. Jr. "Matthew." The Bible Knowledge Commentary: New Testament Edition. Colorado Springs: David C Cook, 1983.

Barbieri, Louis A. Jr. "Mark." The Bible Knowledge Commentary: New Testament Edition. Colorado Springs: David C Cook, 1983.

Barclay, William. The Gospel of Matthew, Volume I, The New Daily Study Bible. Louisville, Westminster John Knox Press, 2001.

Barclay, William. The Gospel of Matthew, Volume II, The New Daily Study Bible. Louisville, Westminster John Knox Press, 2001.

Barclay, William. The Gospel of Mark, The New Daily Study Bible. Louisville, Westminster John Knox Press, 2001.

Barclay, William. The Gospel of Luke, The New Daily Study Bible. Louisville, Westminster John Knox Press, 2001.

Barrick, William D. The Mosaic Covenant, Master's Seminary Journal (Fall 1999). http://www.tms.edu/tmsj/tmsj10o.pdf, (2012).

Bartchy, Scott S. "Servant." Eerdman's International Standard Bible Encyclopedia. Grand Rapids: William B. Eerdmans Publishing Company, 1988.

Beasley-Murray, George R. "John." Word Biblical Commentary. Nashville: Thomas Nelson, Inc. Publishers, 2000.

Blank, Wayne. Children of Jacob, Church of God The Daily Bible Study. http://www.keyway.ca/htm2002/jacobch.htm, (2012).

Blum, Edwin A. "John." The Bible Knowledge Commentary: New Testament Edition. Colorado Springs: David C Cook, 1983.

Brown, Colin. “Miracles.” Eerdman’s International Standard Bible Encyclopedia. Grand Rapids: William B. Eerdmans Publishing Company, 1986.

Brown, Driver, Briggs and Gesenius, The NAS Old Testament Hebrew Lexicon. http://www.biblestudytools.com/lexicons/hebrew/nas/, 2010, (2012).

Bush, Fredrick W. “Plagues of Egypt.” Eerdman’s International Standard Bible Encyclopedia. Grand Rapids: William B. Eerdmans Publishing Company, 1986.

Calvin, John. Harmony of the Evangelists, Grand Rapids: Baker Books, Division of Baker Publishing Group, 2009.

Chafer, Lewis S. Systematic Theology, Dallas: Dallas Theological Seminary Press, 1948.

Couchman, David. “Stone Jars.” Facing the Challenge. http://www.facingthechallenge.org/stonejars.php, 2011, (2012).

Deere, Jack S. “Deuteronomy.” The Bible Knowledge Commentary: Old Testament Edition. Colorado Springs: David C Cook, 1983.

Dorsey, David A. “Spittle.” Eerdman’s International Standard Bible Encyclopedia. Grand Rapids: William B. Eerdmans Publishing Company, 1988.

Earle, Ralph, “Bethphage.” Eerdman’s International Standard Bible Encyclopedia. Grand Rapids: William B. Eerdmans Publishing Company, 1979.

Evans, Craig A. “Mark 1-8:27—16:20.” Word Biblical Commentary. Nashville: Thomas Nelson, Inc. Publishers, 2000.

Garber, Paul L. “Sheep.” Eerdman’s International Standard Bible Encyclopedia. Grand Rapids: William B. Eerdmans Publishing Company, 1988.

Geisler, Norman L. “Colossians.” The Bible Knowledge Commentary: New Testament Edition. Colorado Springs: David C Cook, 1983.

Gill, John. D.D. “Genesis.” Gills Expositor: Exposition of The Old Testament. Streamwood: Primitive Baptist Library Publisher, 1978.

Gill, John. D.D. “Matthew—John.” Gills Expositor: Exposition of The New Testament. Streamwood: Primitive Baptist Library Publisher, 1978.

Guelich, Robert A. “Mark 1—8:26.” Word Biblical Commentary. Nashville: Thomas Nelson, Inc. Publishers, 2000.

Hagner, Donald A. “Matthew 1—13.” Word Biblical Commentary. Nashville: Thomas Nelson, Inc. Publishers, 2000.

Hagner, Donald A. “Matthew 14—28.” Word Biblical Commentary. Nashville: Thomas Nelson, Inc. Publishers, 2000.

Hall, David Q. “Galilean village.” http://dqhall59.com/paralytic_healed.htm, 2005, (2012).

Hall, David Q. “Siloam.” http://dqhall59.com/tower_of_Siloam.htm, 2011 (2012).

Hall, David Q. “Stone Pots.” http://dqhall59.com/artifacts.htm, 2011, (2012).

Hannah, John D. “Exodus.” The Bible Knowledge Commentary: Old Testament Edition. Colorado Springs: David C Cook, 1983.

Harrison, Roland K. “Dropsy.” Eerdman’s International Standard Bible Encyclopedia. Grand Rapids: William B. Eerdmans Publishing Company, 1979.

Harrison, Roland K. “Eden.” Eerdman’s International Standard Bible Encyclopedia. Grand Rapids: William B. Eerdmans Publishing Company, 1979.

Harrison, Roland K. “Fig Tree.” Eerdman’s International Standard Bible Encyclopedia. Grand Rapids: William B. Eerdmans Publishing Company, 1982.

Harrison, Roland K. “First-Born.” Eerdman’s International Standard Bible Encyclopedia. Grand Rapids: William B. Eerdmans Publishing Company, 1982.

Harrison, Roland K. “Leprosy.” Eerdman’s International Standard Bible Encyclopedia. Grand Rapids: William B. Eerdmans Publishing Company, 1986.

Harrison, Roland K. “Sea of Galilee.” Eerdman’s International Standard Bible Encyclopedia. Grand Rapids: William B. Eerdmans Publishing Company, 1988.

Harvey, Dorothea Ward, “Pool.” Eerdman’s International Standard Bible Encyclopedia. Grand Rapids: William B. Eerdmans Publishing Company, 1988.

Halley, Henry H. "John." Halley's Bible Handbook: New Revised Edition. Grand Rapids: Zondervan Publishing House, 1965.
Hendriksen, William, "Matthew." New Testament Commentary: Exposition of the Gospel according to Matthew. Grand Rapids: Baker Academic, Division of Baker Publishing Group, 2007.
Hendriksen, William, "Mark." New Testament Commentary: Exposition of the Gospel according to Matthew. Grand Rapids: Baker Academic, Division of Baker Publishing Group, 2007.
Hendriksen, William, "Luke." New Testament Commentary: Exposition of the Gospel according to Luke. Grand Rapids: Baker Academic, Division of Baker Publishing Group, 2007.
Hendriksen, William, "John." New Testament Commentary: Exposition of the Gospel according to Luke. Grand Rapids: Baker Academic, Division of Baker Publishing Group, 2007.
Henry, Matthew. "Matthew—John." Matthew Henry's Commentary on the Whole Bible.
Hendrickson Publishers, Inc., 1991.
Herr, Larry G. "Salt." Eerdman's International Standard Bible Encyclopedia. Grand Rapids: William B. Eerdmans Publishing Company, 1988.
Hirsch, Frank E. "Inherit." Eerdman's International Standard Bible Encyclopedia. Grand Rapids: William B. Eerdmans Publishing Company, 1982.
Hoad, T. F. "Throng." The Concise Oxford Dictionary of English Etymology. 1996. Encyclopedia.com, (2012).
Hoehner, Harold W. "Herod." The Bible Knowledge Commentary: New Testament Edition. Colorado Springs: David C Cook, 1983.
Hoehner, Harold W. "Ephesians." The Bible Knowledge Commentary: New Testament Edition. Colorado Springs: David C Cook, 1983.
Holwerda, David E. "Ascension." Eerdman's International Standard Bible Encyclopedia. Grand Rapids: William B. Eerdmans Publishing Company, 1979.
Holwerda, David E. "Widow." Eerdman's International Standard Bible Encyclopedia. Grand Rapids: William B. Eerdmans Publishing Company, 1988.

Irvin, Dorothy. "Purple." Eerdman's International Standard Bible Encyclopedia. Grand Rapids: William B. Eerdmans Publishing Company, 1986.

Lockyer, Herbert D. "All the Divine Names and Titles of the Bible." Grand Rapids: Zondervan Publishing House, 1975.

Lockyer, Herbert D. "All the Miracles of the Bible." Grand Rapids: Zondervan Publishing House, 1961.

Lockyer, Herbert D. "All the Parables of the Bible." Grand Rapids: Zondervan Publishing House, 1964.

Lockyer, Herbert D. "All the Teachings of the Jesus." Peabody: Hendrickson Publishers, 1991.

Magen, Yitzhak. "Inn of the Good Samaritan becomes a Museum." Biblical Archaeology Review, Washington, 2012.

MacArthur, John F. The MacArthur Bible Commentary. Nashville: Thomas Nelson, Inc. Publishers, 2005.

Martin, John A. "Luke." The Bible Knowledge Commentary: Old Testament Edition. Colorado Springs: David C Cook, 1983.

Martin, Ralph P. "Peter." Eerdman's International Standard Bible Encyclopedia. Grand Rapids: William B. Eerdmans Publishing Company, 1986.

Masterman, Ernest W. G., Payne, D. F. "Siloam." Eerdman's International Standard Bible Encyclopedia. Grand Rapids: William B. Eerdmans Publishing Company, 1988.

McCracken, Paul E. "Hillside Chapel." Jerusalem Institute for Biblical Exploration, (2012).

McKim, Donald K. "Inherit." Eerdman's International Standard Bible Encyclopedia. Grand Rapids: William B. Eerdmans Publishing Company, 1982.

Meyer, Marvin W. "Market Place." Eerdman's International Standard Bible Encyclopedia. Grand Rapids: William B. Eerdmans Publishing Company, 1986.

McDowell, Josh D. The New Evidence that Demands a Verdict. Nashville: Thomas Nelson, Inc. Publishers, 1999.

Nolland, John. "Luke 1—9:20." Word Biblical Commentary. Nashville: Thomas Nelson, Inc. Publishers, 2000

Nolland, John. “Luke 9:21—18:34.” Word Biblical Commentary. Nashville: Thomas Nelson, Inc. Publishers, 2000.

Opperwall, Nola J. “Nobleman, Nobility.” Eerdman’s International Standard Bible Encyclopedia. Grand Rapids: William B. Eerdmans Publishing Company, 1988.

Padfield, David. Against All the Gods of Egypt, (2002). http://padfield.com/acrobat/history/gods_of_egypt.pdf, (2012).

Page, Charles R. II. “Kursi/Gergesa Excavation.” Jerusalem Institute for Biblical Exploration. http://www.bibleinterp.com/excavations/kursi.htm, (2012).

Palmer, Edwin H. “Mary Magdalene.” Eerdman’s International Standard Bible Encyclopedia. Grand Rapids: William B. Eerdmans Publishing Company, 1986.

Payne, David F. “Shiloah.” Eerdman’s International Standard Bible Encyclopedia. Grand Rapids: William B. Eerdmans Publishing Company, 1988.

Pettegrew, Larry D. The New Covenant, Master’s Seminary Journal, (Fall 1999). http://www.tms.edu/tmsj/tmsj10q.pdf, (2012).

Phillips, Tina. www.freeDigitalPhotos.net, (2012).

Ross, Allen P. “Genesis.” The Bible Knowledge Commentary: Old Testament Edition. Colorado Springs: David C Cook, 1983.

Saunders, Kevin. “The Book of Exodus” Logos Bible Teaching Ministry. Chandler, Arizona

Scofield, C. I. The Scofield Study Bible and Commentary. Oxford: New York. Oxford University Press, 1945.

Showers, Renald E. The Deuteronomic Covenant. http://www.ankerberg.com/Articles/_PDFArchives/biblical-prophecy/BP1W0502.pdf, (2012).

Stedman, Raymond C. Our Riches in Christ: Discovering the Believer’s Inheritance in Ephesians. http://www.raystedman.org/ephesians/richesinchrist.html#anchor18617, 2010, (2012).

Stedman, Raymond C. “What on Earth is Happening: What Jesus said About the End of the Age.” Grand Rapids: Discovery House Publishers, 2003 by Elaine Stedman.

Strong, James. Strong's Exhaustive Concordance of the Bible Concordance. Nashville: Crusade Bible Publishers, Inc.

Swoveland, Michael, "Shekels." Biblical Artifacts and Coins, http://www.wncoins.com//0006.htm, (2012).

Thayer, Joseph H. Thayer's Greek-English Lexicon of the New Testament. Peabody: Hendrickson Publishers, Inc., 2009.

Unger, Merrill Fredrick. Unger's Bible Dictionary. Chicago: Moody Press, 1967.

Unger, Merrill Fredrick. The New Unger's Bible Dictionary. Chicago: The Moody Bible Institute of Chicago, 2005.

Unger, Merrill Fredrick. Unger's Commentary on the Old Testament. Chattanooga: AMG Publishers, 2001.

Vine, William Edwy., Unger, Merrill Fredrick Vine's Complete Expository Dictionary of and New Testament Words. Nashville: Thomas Nelson, Inc. Publishers, 1996.

Vos, Howard F. "Gergesenes." Eerdman's International Standard Bible Encyclopedia. Grand Rapids: William B. Eerdmans Publishing Company, 1982.

Waltke, Bruce K. "Joshua." Eerdman's International Standard Bible Encyclopedia. Grand Rapids: William B. Eerdmans Publishing Company, 1982.

Walvoord, John F. Eschatological Problems VII: The Fulfillment of the Davidic Covenant. http://bible.org/seriespage/eschatological-problems-vii-fulfillment-davidic-covenant, 2009, (2012).

Ward, Fred. The History of Pearls, NOVA, 12.29.98, (2012). http://www.pbs.org/wgbh/nova/ancient/history-pearls.html, (2012).

Warfield, Benjamin B. "The Person and Work of Christ." Philadelphia: The Presbyterian and Reformed Publishing Company, 1950.

Westerholm, Steven. "Skins." Eerdman's International Standard Bible Encyclopedia. Grand Rapids: William B. Eerdmans Publishing Company, 1988.

Westerholm, Steven. "Tabernacle." Eerdman's International Standard Bible Encyclopedia. Grand Rapids: William B. Eerdmans Publishing Company, 1988.

Wiersbe, Warren W. "Matthew—Galatians." The Bible Exposition Commentary: New Testament Volume I. Colorado Springs: David C Cook, 1989.

Woods, Andy, The Prophetic Significance of the Davidic Line and Covenant, http://www.bibleprophecyblog.com/2011/06/prophetic-significance-of-davidic-line.html, 2011, (2012).

Photos provided by:

http://www.israel-a-history-of.com, (2012).
http://geography.about.com/library/cia/blciraq.htm, (2012).
http://www.bible-archaeology.info/abraham.htm, (2012).
http://www.israel-a-history-of.com/old-testament-map.html, (2012).
http://www.israel-a-history-of.com/old-testament-map.html#ground, (2012).
http://bibleatlas.org/mount_ebal.htm, (2012).
http://bibleatlas.org/bethel.htm, (2012).
http://www.israel-a-history-of.com/old-testament-map.html#The%20Negev%20-%20Home%20of%20Abraham, (2012).
http://www.israel-a-history-of.com/old-testament-map.html#ground, (2012).
http://www.israel-a-history-of.com/twelve-tribes-of-israel.html#Israelites%20Leave%20Egypt%20Under%20Moses, (2012).
http://commons.wikimedia.org/wiki/File:Tabernacle.png, 2009 (2012).
http://commons.wikimedia.org/wiki/File:Holman_The_Mercy_Seat.jpg, 2010, (2012).
http://en.wikipedia.org/wiki/Parable_of_the_Good_Samaritan#cite_note-4, (2012).
http://commons.wikimedia.org/wiki/File:OldRoadFromJerusalemToJericho.jpg, 2007, (2012)
http://www.biblicalarchaeology.org, 2012.
http://commons.wikimedia.org/wiki/File:SEC23B.gif, 1999.
http://encyclopedia.mitrasites.com/imgs/parable-of-the-budding-fig-tree.html, (2012).
http://www.publicdomainpictures.net/view-image.php?image=5443&picture=fig, (2012).

http://faithfulthoughtspot.wordpress.com, (2012).
http://dominicdemattos.blogspot.com/2011/07/sunday-reflection-wheat-and-tares.html, (2012).
Pearl Guide: http://www.yvel.com/Assets/PearlGuide.pdf, (2012).
http://www.flw.org/landmarks.html#stone_tower, (2012).
http://www.bible-history.com/maps/palestine_nt_times.html, (2012).
http://visibleearth.nasa.gov/view.php?id=56512, 2001, (2012).
http://www.sethbarnes.com/?filename=all-churches-need-wineskins, 2010, (2012).
http://emp.byui.edu/SATTERFIELDB/Jerusalem/JerusalemPhotoDisplay.htm, (2012).
http://www.bible-history.com/geography/ancient-israel/israel-first-century.html, (2012).
http://www.jibe-edu.org/templates/cusjibe/details.asp?id=28237&PID=171167, 2001, (2012).
http://www.bibleinterp.com/excavations/kursi.htm, 2001, (2012).
http://www.bible-history.com/map_jesus/, (2012).
http://www.bible-history.com/map_jesus/index.htm, (2012).
http://www.ccel.org/bible/phillips/JBPhillips.htm, 2003, (2012).
http://www.ccel.org/bible/phillips/CP051GOSPELMAPS.htm, 2003, (2012).
http://bibleatlas.org/bethphage.htm, (2012).
http://www.edwardfudge.com/beatitudes.html, (2012).
http://www.gods-word-first.org/bible-maps/cana-bible-map.html, 2010, (2012).
http://commons.wikimedia.org/wiki/Pool_of_Bethesda, 2012, (2012).
http://www.bible-study-lessons.com/Jesus-on-the-cross-2.html, 2010, (2012).
http://www.wga.hu/frames-e.html?/html/r/raphael/6tapestr/2draught.html, (2012).
http://commons.wikimedia.org/wiki/Sea_of_Galilee, 2012, (2012).
http://media.photobucket.com/image/ascension/DapperBantam/Ascension.jpg?o=72, (2012).
http://www.encyclopedia.com/doc/1O27-throng.html, 2012).

Used by Permission.

CPSIA information can be obtained at www.ICGtesting.com
Printed in the USA
LVOW080809261012

304535LV00003B/2/P

9 781936 746101